SPEAK it
LOUDER

SPEAK it LOUDER

Asian Americans Making Music

Deborah Wong

Routledge
Taylor & Francis Group

NEW YORK AND LONDON

Published in 2004 by
Routledge
29 W 35th Street
New York, NY 10001
www.routledge-ny.com

Published in Great Britain by
Routledge
11 New Fetter Lane
London EC4P 4EE
www.routledge.co.uk

Routledge is an imprint of the Taylor & Francis Group.
Printed in the United States of America on acid-free paper.

10 9 8 7 6 5 4 3 2 1

Library of Congress Cataloging-in-Publication Data

Wong, Deborah Anne.
   Speak it louder: Asian Americans making music / by Deborah Wong.
    p. cm.
   Includes bibliographical references and index.
    ISBN 0-415-97039-3 (hdb. : 0-415-970407 alk. paper) — ISBN 0-415-97040-7
(pbk. : alk.paper)
    1. Asian Americans--Music--History and criticism. 2. Music--Social
aspects--United States I. Title.
   ML3560.A85 W66 2004
   780'. 89'95073—dc22   2003024527

Dedication

For Asian American performers everywhere —
keep on doing it

Acknowledgments

Numerous colleagues have provided me with forums to air these materials as I worked on them. Papers first presented at the annual meetings of the Society for American Music, the Association for Asian Studies, the Society for Ethnomusicology and the Association for Asian American Studies appear here, much improved by suggestions from audience members and colleagues.

Time is everything for a scholar and I'm grateful to the University of Pennsylvania and its Department of Music for a sabbatical leave and a Faculty Research Fellowship during 1995–96 that allowed me to begin sustained work on this book. At Penn, Rosane Rocher was a friend and shining role model as she tirelessly, graciously, led the way toward an Asian American Studies Program. Colleagues in the Asian Pacific American Faculty and Staff Association (particularly Joe Sun and Alvin Alvarez) inspired me through their example as committed cultural workers. Numerous Asian American students at Penn humbled me with their commitment, organizational skills and zeal as they fought to bring Asian American Studies to Penn. Students have always been the lifeblood of Asian American activism and Penn's Asian American students have climbed a steep hill.

A small but dedicated group of scholars interested in Asian American music offered constant intellectual support during my research and writing. Our first get-together at Berkeley in 1995 was, I think, an important experience for all of us, and Oliver Wang's creation of an e-mail discussion group, AAIM (Asian Americans Interested in Music), sustained our sense of community for a time. Susan Asai, Jeff Chang, Joseph Lam, Adelaida Reyes, Amy Stillman, Oliver Wang, Cynthia Wong, Paul Yoon and Wei-hua Zhang have all been important touchstones, and their scholarship has left its mark on my thinking and on this book. Su Zheng's scholarship has consistently inspired me. The circle of Asian American Studies scholars who think and write about performance, including Dorinne Kondo, Josephine Lee, Rachel Lee and Karen Shimekawa, have offered both inspiration and response.

In Philadelphia, fellow members of the Asian Arts Initiative — René Marquez, Bing Mark, Lisa Yau, Ellen Somekawa, Huong Hoang, Roko Kawai and especially Gayle Isa — provided me with friendship and compelling examples for how art, performance and Asian American activism can pack a powerful punch.

In the greater Los Angeles area, my taiko pals and teachers are central to it all. I thank Rev. Shuichi Thomas Kurai, Audrey Nakasone and Elaine Fukumoto for hours of instruction and conversation about taiko and the taiko community, and my classmates in the Taiko Center of Los Angeles for their camaraderie; Carolyn Okazaki and Mary Baba generously entertained my questions about their experiences in our taiko classes. Kenny Endo was kind enough to grant me an extended interview after a rather demanding performance. Paul Yoon and Mark Tusler have been constant sources of information, always ready to share their insights as ethnomusicologists and as taiko players. Traise Yamamoto, Paul Simon and René T.A. Lysloff were brave enough to watch the taiko scene in *Rising Sun* with me several times and Traise offered detailed suggestions on a late draft of Chapter 9 that helped me see the forest through the trees. Members of the University of California Performance Studies Group and participants in *Audiences, Patrons and Performers in the Performing Arts of Asia,* in 2000 in Leiden, The Netherlands, also gave me some new ways to think about that scene in the film.

Teaching at the University of California, Riverside has given me the opportunity to interact with some of the liveliest, most unnatural thinkers on the performative. My colleagues in the Center for Asian Pacific America — Piya Chatterjee, Rodney Ogawa, Edward Chang, Hershini Bhana and Ruth Chao — provided intellectual support. Traise Yamamoto's keen critical eye pushed me in all the right ways and helped me tighten up my central arguments. Working in the Department of Music at UCR has allowed me to think and speak freely in ways that few scholar-educators get to experience; it has not been free of speed traps but has certainly helped me to move forward with this book. Its progressive environment is largely the work of Philip Brett, whose intellectual and practical support is really all over this book. Philip took to describing himself as "an aging radical" and I can only say that his example — as a scholar, mentor, teacher and activist — is an inspiration to many and now a specific role model for me. I am also grateful to UCR for several grants: a Regents Faculty Fellowship, a Faculty Research Incentive Grant and several Academic Senate Omnibus grants.

Colloquium presentations at various institutions were a great help. Tim Taylor organized the conference *Sounding the Difference: Musics and the Politics of Identity in America* at UC Berkeley, where I spent several exhilarating days talking identity politics with other scholars and students of performance. At UCLA, students in the Department of World Arts and Culture's Dance Program invited me to do a presentation on just the right kind of topic, helping me work through some tough points on race, identity and the body. Jim Moy and I had an important conversation at a critical juncture, just as I began serious work on this book. Presentations at UCLA, Rutgers University and SUNY-Stony Brook were also a great help.

Asian American performer-activists have, of course, been at the center of all. Tatsu Aoki, Anthony Brown, Peggy Choy, Pham Duy, Fred Ho, Glenn Horiuchi, Khamvong Insixiengmai, Mark Izu, Jon Jang, Miya Masaoka, Hafez Modirzadeh, The Mountain Brothers and Francis Wong all give new meaning to cultural work and cultural production. The dynamic line between the Asian American text and its performance has consistently moved and inspired me. Over the years, hearing the writers Frank Chin, Justin Chin, Alison De La Cruz, Jessica Hagedorn, Kimiko Hahn, Garrett Hongo, Maxine Hong Kingston, Emily Lawsin, Genny Lim, Sandra Tsing Loh, David Wong Louie, David Mura, Lois Ann Yamanaka and many others read their work has given me much food for thought about the performance of the Asian American word. Seeing performances by hereandnow, Club o'Noodles, Peeling the Banana, Charlie Chin, Ken Choy, Shishir Kurup, Dan Kwong, Nobuko Miyamoto, Jude Narita, Denise Uyehara, Yutian Wong and countless productions by the East West Players has provided me with rich ways for thinking about how Asian American texts for performances are generated and for whom they are intended.

I would like to recognize four recording labels that have consistently supported Asian American music making, often against the odds: Flavio Bonandrini and his father Giovanni Bonandrini of the Soul Note/Black Saint recording company, Fred Maroth of Music and Arts, Nelson Wong of AASRising and, of course, everyone who has helped shape and sustain Asian Improv over the years.

Several friends have been particularly important. Casey Man Kong Lum was endlessly enthusiastic, similarly fascinated by Asian American *karaoke,* always ready to respond to a question or idea. I'm grateful for his support and for his wildly punctuated e-mail notes. Marina Roseman gave new meaning to the word "colleague." Tim Taylor — friend, white male radical — took the time again and again to read, respond and help me think about the politics of ethnic studies. His keen mind and his insight into the promises and failings of cultural studies kept me on my toes. Gary Tomlinson — another white male radical — has left a profound mark on these pages. I'm grateful for his honesty in sharing his own struggles to find an appropriate voice and space from which to speak. George Lipsitz has been a major influence for years. I hope that the effects of his published work, his virtuosic spoken presentations and his feedback on this manuscript are apparent here in more ways than one.

René T.A. Lysloff, as always, has been my rock, my foundation, my closest colleague, my collaborator and a crucial source of intellectual agitation.

The following materials have been included with permission:

An earlier version of Chapter 4 was published as "I Want the Microphone: Mass Mediation and Agency in Asian American Popular Music" in *The Drama Review* [T143], 38 (2): 152–67. ©1994. Reprinted with permission of MIT Press.

An earlier version of Chapter 5 was published as "Pham Duy at Home: Vietnamese American Technoculture in Orange County," in *Music and Technoculture*, edited by René T.A. Lysloff and Leslie Gay. ©2003. Reprinted with permission of Wesleyan University Press.

An earlier version of Chapter 7 was published as "Listening to Local Practices: Performance and Identity Politics in Riverside, California," in *Decomposition: Post-Disciplinary Performance*, edited by Sue-Ellen Case, Susan Leigh Foster and Philip Brett, 18–36. ©2000. Reprinted with permission of Indiana University Press.

An earlier version of Chapter 8 was published as "The Asian American Body in Performance," in *Music and the Racial Imagination*, edited by Philip V. Bohlman and Ronald Radano, 57–94. ©2001. Reprinted with permission of The University of Chicago. All rights reserved.

Part of Chapter 9 was published as "Taiko and the Asian/American Body: Drums, *Rising Sun* and the Question of Gender," in *The World of Music*, special issue, Local Musical Traditions in the Globalization Process, 42 (3): 67–78. ©2000. Reprinted with permission of Dr. Max Peter Baumann, editor of *The World of Music and* the Universität Bamberg.

An earlier version of Chapter 10 was published as "Just Being There: Making Asian American Space in the Recording Industry," in *Musics of Multicultural America*, 1st edition by Kip Lornell and Anne Rasmussen. ©1997. Reprinted with permission of Wadsworth, a division of Thomson Learning.

An earlier version of Chapter 11 was published as "Finding an Asian American Audience: The Problem of Listening," in *American Music* 19 (4): 365–84, Special Issue on Asian American Music. ©2001. Reprinted with permission of the University of Illinois Press.

An earlier version of Chapter 13 was published as "Ethnography, Ethnomusicology, and Post-White Theory." In *Musicology and Sister Disciplines*, edited by David Greer, 439–454. ©2000. Reprinted with permission of Oxford University Press.

Table of Contents

I

Southeast Asian Immigrants Sounding Off

1
Asian American Performativities

This book brings together several lines of exploration. I look closely at Asian American musicians and their chosen means of performance and I problematize contemporary American discussions of power and representation focusing on race: I argue that music is performative and that it "speaks" with considerable power and subtlety as a discourse of difference. Indeed, the sounds I address are many things — loud, angry, anguished, joyful, defiant, nostalgic — and the Asian American musicians who make this noise have a lot to say about what they are doing. I trace their words, their music and how they are heard; I offer my own readings of their music and its stirring effects on me, but I place this within the broader political context(s) of American identity politics.

Speak It Louder emerged out of movement between southern California and Philadelphia over ten years' time. Two brief years in southern California, at Pomona College from 1991–93, were ground zero for this study; Asian American colleagues and students shaped my emergent ideas of how scholarship on Asian America must be an activist undertaking. Those two years on the eastern edge of Los Angeles County exposed me to a certain kind of racial politics and fundamentally redirected my intellectual energies. The beating of Rodney King and the Los Angeles uprising in 1992 were formative experiences; trying to teach while South Central and Koreatown burned was a turning point for me, and my personal desire to develop a critical pedagogy of multiculturalism emerged from those difficult days. Between 1993 and 1996, I lived in Philadelphia, a city whose racial politics are framed in terms of Black/White relations despite the presence of more than 20,000 Asians and Asian Americans. This left its mark on my political sensibilities and on my need for civic and cultural spaces defined by Asian Americans. My decision to return to southern California in 1996 was informed by an increasingly urgent sense that the West Coast — and California in particular — will be the site for the most important social and political struggles of the next few decades, and I remain convinced that these struggles will be defined around issues of race and ethnicity, and that they must include Asian Americans as well as other people of color.

My research centered around several convictions. I believe that music (and the arts generally) have the potential to compel social change by blurring the lines between political and intellectual response. Asian Americans are a problematic social category, apparently race-based, but actually one forged from a multiethnic activist response to institutionalized racism in the 1960s; the ethnic heterogeneity of the category begs the question of coalition politics, so I address not "Asian American music" but rather Asian Americans making music, often in environments of interethnic contact. Finally, I treat ethnographic work as a performative practice (particularly in Chapter 9), in this case as an Asian American ethnomusicologist (and sometime performer) talking with Asian American musicians. I believe that ethnography as a sustained, ground-level practice challenges some of the textualizing practices of cultural studies even as it is reinvigorated by questions of difference and differential power.

My title is taken from Peril-L, a member of the Asian American hip-hop crew called the Mountain Brothers, who raps:

Dumb nonsense I hate
The truth some contemplate
Ain't tryin to wait I possess the power
To speak it louder

— words that sum up the urgency of the sounds I address in my book. As an ethnomusicologist with a base in cultural studies and performance studies, I treat performance as constructive rather than reflective of social realities. If performance is a site of cultural production, then it is important to look closely at the realities created *through* performance and this is precisely what I try to do. When difference of any kind is explored through performance, the result is necessarily performative — that is, if "discourse produces the effect that it names" (Butler 1993: 2) then performing something means making or becoming something.

During the past ten years or so, a compelling body of criticism addressing the politics of race and representation in America has moved from the margins to the center of scholarly discourse. Much of this work suggests that race, as a cultural construct, is neither natural, innocent nor apolitical and is intimately linked to processes of commodification and control. I position Asian Americans within this larger conversation and enlarge on bell hooks' recuperation of an "oppositional gaze" (1992: 115–31) and Dorinne Kondo's construction of agency, wherein "performing alternative

visions of cultural possibility" is necessary because "without the refigura-
tion of the possible, there can be no social transformation" (Kondo 1997:
257). I shift my consideration of music away from interpretation and
toward activist commitment in a manner inspired by Robyn Wiegman's
argument for the "necessary disloyalties" (1995: 181–7) that constantly
reconfigure women's studies and ethnic studies by productively questioning their basic assumptions. Moving out from these compelling models
allows me to focus on those moments of looking — or, in this case, listening — back, when dominant patterns of production are ruptured and the
racialized Asian American subject becomes a noisy agent.

Hopefully, my book will occupy a special place, as very little work has
yet addressed Asian American performance or music. Most work in Asian
American studies has been focused on literature and history. I treat Asian
American expressive technologies as strategic responses to "historically
differentiated forms of disempowerment" (Lowe 1996: 96) that are often
directed toward social activism and community building. In this environment, popular culture of any kind becomes an arena for critique and social
transformation. I focus on music, but will point to certain ideological connections to Asian American literature, theater and cinema. I hope this
book prompts responses and further explorations.

Asian American Performance and the Performative

My work is fundamentally shaped by two approaches that bear some discussion. First, I am an ethnomusicologist and my commitment to ethnographic methods of doing research is profound — more on that below.
Second, I draw from a broad body of scholarship that addresses the work
of culture as performance and the mechanism for this as the performative.
This corpus links the fields of anthropology, performance studies and cultural studies and I would like to offer both a genealogy of the concept of
the performative ("this transformative becoming," as Peggy Phelan calls it)
as well as my own thoughts on its promise for work on race and ethnicity
(Phelan 1998: 11).

Put most simply, the performative is a consequence of performance:
performance constructs new critical realities and the operationalization of
the process of performance is key to this. Theories of the performative
emerged from and have been most deeply considered through the parameter of language, most particularly through J.L. Austin's speech act theory
(1962). More lately, the performativity of speech has been politicized and
given a new theoretical edginess through the work of Judith Butler (1997)
and Patricia Hill Collins (1998), which is focused on hate speech. Collins
argues that "fighting words," i.e., constructions of speech that compel
reactive response, have limited critical use. She submits that the "fighting
words" paradigm simply reaffirms powerful social binaries that construct
some discourses as elite and others as oppositional and that it does noth-

ing, ultimately, to encourage new kinds of oppositional social theory (1998: 87). Extending the idea of performative words into the realm of critical theory, Collins suggests that Afrocentrism constitutes a social theory of fighting words founded on essentialist and ahistorical treatments of class, gender and sexuality. She acknowledges that this powerful nationalist project has offered real hope to African Americans but concludes that, "Despite this essential contribution, the fighting words of Afrocentrism appear increasingly ineffective in both changing the academy and guiding Black political activism" (182), precisely because it silences unpopular speech without going to the roots of how difference is constructed and maintained (94). Her focus on the performativity of discourse thus goes far beyond an exclusive focus on the judicial and considers the operationalization of critical theory.

Theories of performativity drawn from speech act theory have proceeded along three separate (but not unrelated) paths, focused variably on ritual, gender and sexuality and everyday life. Victor Turner's work on ritual as performance opened up the now-established field of performance studies (1969, 1974, 1982, 1986); Richard Schechner joined anthropology and theater more explicitly (1985, 1990). Judith Butler applied the performativity of speech to the body and argued first that gender is a performative practice (1990) and then that gender *and* sexuality are discursively, performatively constructed (1993). The burgeoning field of performance studies extends the performative paradigm into every potential vector of difference, and a number of important edited collections have cogently explored this basic idea through any number of specific studies (Case, Brett and Foster 1995, 2000; Senelick 1992; Phelan and Lane 1998; Taylor and Villagas 1994).

I am not interested in asserting a simpleminded politics of empowerment in which performance is the magic wand of identity. Much writing on these matters has focused on what performance "does," creating a linear assumption of actualization. I will consider such moments but I also dwell on the all too real fissures that can be created through performance, when making and unmaking meet. Those interstices of assailability are just as worth knowing. Butler turns the idea of hate speech on its side, arguing that the language of trauma unwittingly opens up agency:

> Because I have been called something, I have been entered into linguistic life, refer to myself through the language given by the Other, but perhaps never quite in the same terms that my language mimes. The terms by which we are hailed are rarely the ones we choose (and even when we try to impose protocols on how we are to be named, they usually fail); but these terms we never really choose are the occasion for something we might still call agency, the repetition of an imaginary subordination for another purpose, one whose future is partly open (1998: 38).

This "linguistic vulnerability," as Butler calls it (1–41), puts agency and trauma into dynamic relation and I believe that performance — especially Asian American performance — walks a similar tightrope. The risk of reinscription, appropriation, or orientalist misreading is ever present in Asian American performance; the possibility of empowerment stands side by side with the susceptible audience that consumes with the greedy expectation of orientalist pleasure and is inevitably gratified. I want to balance this against the vulnerability of the researcher/fieldworker who runs yet another important risk. Anthropologist Ruth Behar argues for the importance of the vulnerable anthropological observer who writes to undercut the possibility of dispassionate reception, and she lays out the perils of positioning oneself in a text in this service (1996: 13–14):

> Writing vulnerably takes as much skill, nuance, and willingness to follow through on all the ramifications of a complicated idea as does writing invulnerably and distantly. I would say it takes yet greater skill. The worst that can happen in an invulnerable text is that it will be boring. But when an author has made herself or himself vulnerable, the stakes are higher: a boring self-revelation, one that fails to move the reader, is more than embarrassing; it is humiliating. ... Vulnerability doesn't mean that anything personal goes. The exposure of a self who is also a spectator has to take us somewhere we couldn't otherwise get to. ... It has to move us beyond that eclipse into inertia ... in which we find ourselves identifying so intensely with those whom we are observing that all possibility of reporting is arrested, made inconceivable. It has to persuade us of the wisdom of not leaving the writing pad blank.

This book is thus written from a particular point of view, at once ethnographic and postmodern, in an attempt to show how certain Asian Americans imbricate agency and rewriting through their engagement with music.

At the same time, I work against the cultural studies tendency to map postmodernist aesthetic concepts onto raced/gendered/sexualized bodies, keenly aware of the inherent dangers of postmodernist frameworks for thinking about difference. Virtuosic as those frameworks are, and as useful as they have been for making visible the play of polysemy and multiple positions, they potentially aestheticize the material realities and lived experience of difference. While undoing any modernist understanding of Asian American cultural production, I feel it all the more essential to name my own politics, as Rey Chow insists. Drawing on Baudrillard, she identifies the postmodernist trap, the "vicious circle," that reduces difference to the indifference of interchangeable positions and equivalent marginalities (1993: 59). The positioned observer and the located writer is thus no self-indulgence but rather a political necessity.

All this means, I think, that the performativity model is not yet exhausted. I focus on how performativity is the mechanism for critical newness, which may or may not be oppositional; I am not focused only on resistance, though I certainly scrutinize it where I believe it emerges. I argue here not only for the value of ethnographic research, but specifically for how it contributes to an understanding of these issues in Asian America. It opens up a useful window on the politics of placement and subject position. I need to lay out several matters here: I think that politically responsible ethnographic work is an essential critical inroad to the broader project of understanding people, music, power, etc. I am an Asian American scholar and musician who spends a lot of time with Asian American scholars and musicians — and I write about that interaction. I write not from the privileged stance of a cultural insider but as an activist mindful of difference and with a commitment to coalition politics. A shared sense of involvement with the Asian American movement sometimes created additional affective bonds between myself and the friends I write about. Some of the people I write about think of themselves as Vietnamese or Cambodian rather than as Asian American and our relative political and ethnic affiliations were sources of difference more than anything else. I am trying to make it clear that this is no voyeuristic insider's account, but rather a meeting ground between people with passionate investments in music and Asian America who rarely see things in the "same" way. I have had more than a few conversations with Philip Brett and Gary Tomlinson, both colleagues over the years, about the relative promises and pitfalls of ethnographic work and textual analysis. Both of these radical new musicologists have pushed the envelope of what's possible through textual analysis; both have fundamentally extended and problematized what it means to read or to interpret a text and how this inflects subject position. Both have suggested that ethnomusicologists tend to valorize ethnography. Philip has written that the "glorification of fieldwork often make[s] ethnomusicology as positivistic as historical musicology" (Brett 1994: 15). In turn, Ruth Behar has alluded to the "surprisingly ruthless criticism of the humanists" when it comes to ethnography (1996: 164). I take all these warnings to heart and will try, once more, to explain why my fascination with the ethnographic undertaking is both a political and an intellectual commitment.

I mean several things by "ethnographic research." Defining ethnographic research and "the" ethnographic method has been a contentious topic in anthropology since the 1980s, when its colonial genealogy was fully acknowledged and came under scrutiny. Ethnographic work means having direct, sustained contact with people and their activities — it means talking with them and spending time at it. It may mean doing historical research; one can certainly do historical research in an ethnographic way (Bohlman 1997). At some point, you transform the accumulation of particularities (personal histories, opinions, alliances etc.) into another medium — a book, a film — in which you probably try to make some larger points about broader matters implicitly or explicitly suggested by the particularities. This work of interpretation is the creative/ troubled/risky/difficult part — this is where the power play of research comes to the fore, where questions of location and investment are paramount. I place myself within specific traditions of ethnographic work that move out from poststructuralist and postmodern assumptions of difference, multiplicities, disjuncture and nonclosure. This is further complicated by my use of methods drawn from feminist ethnography and feminist pedagogy, in which subject position is constantly, deliberately questioned and resituated. In short, I am committed to ethnography because I think it is an ethically viable means through which to encounter and represent people if certain matters are reflexively addressed as part of the project. I like the messiness and the utopian qualities of ethnographic work, in which the subject never stays put and can never really be known. Yet one tries anyway, and the fact is, I had a whale of a good time while doing this research and have had moments of discovery and epiphany while listening, while writing, while learning, that are undeniable. I want this book to convey all that, and my base in ethnographic work is central to what you will come to know, through me, as you read.

Oral history work has long been a mainstay of American ethnic studies research — a way of asserting otherwise ignored or forgotten histories, "other" histories — but full-scale ethnographic work focused on Asian Americans is still relatively rare. Lane Hirabayashi's creative exploration of Japanese American fieldwork in the internment camps has extended across two books to date and raises challenging ethical issues. Hirabayashi has focused on two Japanese American researchers at Poston (the World War II relocation center in Arizona), one Issei and the other Nisei, whose work for Berkeley's Japanese American Evacuation and Resettlement Study (JERS) placed them in difficult circumstances. Tamie Tsuchiyama was hired by JERS while a doctoral student in anthropology at Berkeley, and Hirabayashi's study of her work is a consideration of the politics of fieldwork; Tsuchiyama could have returned to her parents in Hawaii to avoid incarceration but was encouraged by her professors at Berkeley to go to Poston as an inmate to study the camp as a hired fieldworker (Hirabayashi 1995: xliv). Tsuchiyama hired Richard Nishimoto, an Issei inmate, to act as her assistant. While the Poston authorities knew from the beginning about Tsuchiyama's research, Nishimoto's role was kept secret. Hirabayashi describes him as a "clandestine researcher" and notes that Nishimoto was at pains to conceal his role as a gatherer of information, as it would have not only affected his access to activities but would have implicated him as an *inu*, an informer (1995: xlv). Tsuchiyama's relationship with the JERS authorities eventually ended in "complete acrimony," fueled in part by the JERS director's "proprietary attitude toward her staff members' fieldnotes" (Hirabayashi 1995: iiv, fn. 47 and fn. 49). Tsuchiyama's resignation in protest from the project in 1944 marks a key moment in the cultural politics of Asian Americans studying Asian Americans (1999).

Martin F. Manalansan IV's edited collection *Cultural Compass: Ethnographic Explorations of Asian America* (2000a) is nearly unique in its close focus on how ethnographic methodologies can expand the scope of Asian American Studies. Manalansan notes the prevalence of textual analysis, historical and archival work, and demographic and community surveys in Asian American studies and describes the place of ethnography as "largely unacknowledged in Asian American studies despite some very impressive works" (2000b: 2). He lays out the challenges inherent to ethnographic work on Asian America: the proliferation of sites that must be considered (he argues for "multisited or multilocale ethnography"), issues of movement vs. immobility (especially for refugee populations), changes in immigration history and legislation and, of course, the broader complications of theoretical debates in the humanities and social sciences around ethnography (2000b: 5–6). Perhaps his most important observation (to my mind) is his hope that ethnographic work on Asian America will productively problematize the notion of "community," long a naturalized construction in Asian American studies that is too often uncritically juxtaposed against the academy, "mainstream" America, or some other site of imagined hegemony. As Manalansan puts it, "In many college courses and texts on Asian American issues, 'community' occupies a central and largely uninterrogated space. ... All the essays in this collection reclaim an idea of a contested community, intensely engaged with power dynamics both local and global" (2000b: 8–9). *Cultural Compass* thus offers an unprecedented look at postmodern/poststructural ethnography as refracted through the concerns of late twentieth-century Asian American studies.

Like Manalansan (2000: 4), I must refer to Kamala Visweswaran's notion of "homework" as a critical challenge to outdated constructions of "fieldwork" (Visweswaran 1994: 101–2). Relocating the field isn't new to anthropology — disturbing the elsewhere/here binary was at the heart of the critical turn in that discipline in the 1980s and 1990s. Ethnomusicologists too have struggled with the implications of bringing the field home (Barz and Cooley 1997 , Witzleben 1997, Reyes 1999b). Questioning relative location is deeply defamiliarizing; bringing the very construction of place under scrutiny jeopardizes the safety of the geographical. In other words, locale is shifting and multiple in much the same way that identity is. The construction of Asian American places/spaces/sites is doubly, triply complicated, as they are sometimes physically locatable but usually not; the boundedness of Asian American locales are continually open to redefinition, whether a Japantown or a student association meeting on a university campus. My own "homework" has brought these issues into sharp relief. It has taken place in concert halls, coffee houses, city streets, private homes, professors' offices, classrooms and over the telephone. Asian American space is where you find it.

I address these matters most explicitly in Chapter 9, when I write about my own engagement with taiko. I didn't start learning taiko in 1997 so I could write about it, i.e., I didn't go to it in search of a fieldsite. Rather, I wanted to learn taiko because it thrilled me as an Asian American spectator and I wanted to learn how to "be" Asian American in that particular noisy and choreographed way. Taiko is now one place I feel "at home" as an Asian American — usually. Its charged space, whether the rehearsal room or the outdoor festival performance, is the site of more than one kind of homework. In writing about it, I address its multiplicities, and Chapter 9 more than any other moved me into the practices of performative ethnography: the *Real Politik* of taiko as a site of Asian American performativity necessitated a new kind of writing (for me). T/here, subject/object, all became a matter of motion. One could say that this is what happens when all these contentious issues are brought home to roost: the performativity of the practice evinces — demands — a different kind of scholarship. As Phelan muses (1998: 13):

> What exactly does it mean to write performatively? … It is an inquiry into the limits and possibilities of the intersections between speech and writing. … This is the lesson of performance itself — the ability to realize that which is not otherwise manifest. Performative writing seeks to extend the oxymoronic possibilities of animating the unlived that lies at the heart of performance as a making.

This is more than a matter of emulation. Without collapsing all into performance and performativity, it is possible to situate the processes of performance and representation in the writing itself and to thus take the materiality of intervention seriously. Writing is always about other writing, but performative writing sets up a longing for the thing itself, a desire to see it enacted, the possibility of experience. Della Pollock refers to performative writing as "the constitutive form of unrealized democracies" (1998: 78). Performative writing in the service of Asian American ethnography is thus doubly, triply, about the emergence of new social possibilities.

From "Asian American Music" to Performance in Asian America

I have little interest in asserting a new category of "Asian American music." Indeed, my subtitle ("Asian Americans Making Music") is a deliberate attempt to shift the focus from categories to processes. Furthermore, quite a bit of work exists on music in Asian America but very little of it is inflected with the issues or methodologies foregrounded in Asian American studies. To put it another way, a lot of research has been done on Asian music in America and most of it treats the performers or the performance event as artifacts of authentic Asian practices. Still, such work paves the way for this book in a very real sense.

I have spent the last decade doing research on music and Asian Americans, but I don't think that this needs to be a bounded area of research, i.e., a new area studies in music. Joseph Lam has written, "Many musicians, audiences and scholars, including those who are sympathetic to Asian American causes, would doubt if Asian American music exists" (1999: 29). The taxonomical problems of ethnomusicological study are highlighted every time the Society for Ethnomusicology prints a new directory and tries to thematize its members' interests. If anything, I have gravitated toward the position that any music being performed or created by an Asian American is Asian American music, and I don't think this is as dissembling as it might seem. Rather, I want to understand why some Asian Americans make music, and what sounds they make and for whom. This is a very different question from the more common one of *whether* Asian American music exists.

The ghostly presence in all this is the unruly category of "American music," which has gone through significant critical change during the last fifty years. The study of American music, generated and defined by scholars like Oscar George Theodore Sonneck, H. Wiley Hitchcock, Charles Hamm and Richard Crawford, has been marked by impassioned attempts to explore the very limits of national vs. cultural identity and the formation of new sensibilities. The problem of origins has loomed. Academe wasn't (isn't) politically ready to regard Native American music as quintessentially "American music," but everything (everyone) else came from somewhere else. The early study of American music was focused on explaining that, although opera and hymnody came to the U.S. from western Europe, it was "American" rather than "European" once generated on this continent. Looking back, it's clear that the stakes had as much to do with the ongoing project of defining the American nation-state as it did music, but the formation of the Sonneck Society for the study of American music in 1975 was an important historical moment.[1] In its efforts to define Americanness, race, gender and sexuality were avoided. The academic study of jazz, and particularly jazz as defined and performed by African Americans, was slow to become a legitimate field of scholarly inquiry within American music. Indeed, moving away from a great-man approach to music history (e.g., composers, notated music, high art identifications, etc.) was a long process. The arrival of new educational ideologies of multiculturalism in American higher education in the late 1980s and early 1990s helped evince a sea change in American music studies by bringing the matter of ethnicity and national identity into view. In other words, race studies and minoritarian approaches to culture have been slow to find a place within the study of American music. George Lipsitz argues that there have always been two different American studies, one institutional and the other an "organic grassroots theorizing about culture" (2001: 27), and that the latter has consistently driven the former in often unacknowledged ways. He suggests that the tensions between American social movements and the (re)definition of American studies is, in fact, the lifeblood of this area studies, but American *music* studies has been slow to write this into its own histories. Meanwhile, academic positions in American music have become code for several things, sometimes overlapping, sometimes not (e.g., popular music studies, jazz studies, African American music studies, African American scholars, etc.). Certainly such positions are not intended to attract Asian American studies scholars focused on performance.

Is there something out there that ought to be called Asian American music? For me, part of the discomfort of the question lies in mainstream confusion over what Asian Americans are. We know that there is African American and Mexican American and Jewish American music; we're pretty sure there's such a thing as "White" music, though we rarely call it that. We know that a House Committee investigated a large number of Asians and Asian Americans for allegedly illegal contributions to the Democratic Party (though virtually no one besides Asian Americans questions this). We know that a headline shouted "American Beats Out Kwan!" after the Winter Olympics in Nagano. Nuclear physicist Wen Ho Lee is still in solitary confinement as I write. Americans are definitely not at all sure what the difference is between Asians and Asian Americans and thus have no idea what Asian American music might be. Lisa Lowe has written at length about how "the American of Asian descent remains the symbolic 'alien', the metonym for Asia who by definition cannot be imagined as sharing in America" (1996: 6). Asking whether there "is" such a thing as Asian American music has never struck me as the most useful question to pursue; I don't think it deserves a lot of attention because I think it's dangerously close to asking whether there is such a thing as an Asian American, i.e., an American who's Asian. It also diverts attention and scholarly energy into defending the idea rather than getting on with the more important work of showing what it is and how it functions. Still, I realize that my chosen research topic needs explaining, as the very explanation has a pedagogical function that goes far beyond music. Americans tend to recognize and to deny (all at once) their understandings of how American music is racialized and ethnicized.

Only a few scholars are engaged in research on what might be called Asian American music, including Su Zheng, Joseph Lam, Susan Asai and four extremely promising graduate students. A number of other scholars have done extensive research on immigrant Asian music in the U.S., including, again, a number of promising graduate students; none of these scholars described their subjects as Asian American because they were asking other equally important questions. George Yoshida's *Reminiscing in Swingtime* (1997) is virtually unique. A combination of archival research, oral histories and memoir, the book is a consideration of how and why big-band jazz was so popular among Nisei in the internment camps. Dense with photographs and names of musicians, Yoshida's book offers a moving account of Japanese American involvement in American popular culture. Sansei jazz composer Mark Izu has since written a multimovement multimedia work titled *Last Dance* that featured a jazz orchestra and Yoshida himself reading passages from his memoirs as images of Japanese American big bands in the camps were projected above the ensemble.

Work on Asian immigrant music cultures is especially rich. Jairazbhoy and DeVale's collection, *Asian Music in North America* (1985) is generally marked by a salvage conception of such music but is nonetheless important. Scattered articles address Japanese and Korean music in the U.S. (Asai 1995, 1997; Sutton 1987). Chinese immigrant music has attracted a fair amount of attention at this point in promising ways. While Ronald Riddle's pioneering study of Chinese opera and music clubs in San Francisco was generally focused on the genres as traditional holdovers, he recognized that second-generation American-born Chinese were drawn to music clubs out of a self-conscious interest in ethnic identity (1983: 223–24), and thus nods in the direction of Asian American cultural dynamics. Casey Man-Kong Lum's and Su de San Zheng's works stand out for their use of new theoretical frameworks and the ways that these suggest new objects of study. Lum's *In Search of a Voice: Karaoke and the Construction of Identity in Chinese America* (1996) and Zheng's dissertation, "Immigrant Music and Transnational Discourse: Chinese American Music Culture in New York City" (1993) focus on Chinese immigrant music-making in the New York metropolitan area and both focus on the complexities of relative generation, class and region of origin as vectors of difference within the ongoing construction of "Chineseness" through music-making. Rather than focusing solely on "traditional" music, both venture into contemporary terrains, from karaoke to avant-garde composition, and the resulting picture shows diasporic Chinese engaged with transnational flows of aesthetic and material capital.

The major arrival of Southeast Asians following 1975 has prompted a new body of work on Vietnamese, Lao, Hmong and Cambodian music in diaspora. Several ethnomusicologists — notably Amy Catlin (1985, 1987a, 1987b), Sam-Ang Sam (1991) and Phong Nguyen (1990) — focus on Southeast Asian refugee music; their work, though invaluable, tends to center on "traditional" genres and treats them as Southeast Asian rather than Asian American. Adelaida Reyes's book, *Songs of the Caged, Songs of the Free: Music and the Vietnamese Refugee Experience* (1999a) stands out for its compassionate consideration of the effects of traumatic relocation on two generations of Vietnamese composers, performers and audiences; in putting immigration at the center of her study, Reyes makes traditional and popular Vietnamese music speak to broader issues of diaspora.

To summarize, existing work on Asian music in the U.S. is characterized by two contrasting approaches. Some scholars treat music as a pocket
of traditionality and essentially present the artifact as "Asian music." Others take a completely different path by asking how issues of movement and
diaspora can be considered through performance practices. These contrasting approaches situate "the music" in significantly different ways: the
first regards the sounds and practices as something isolatable and the second extends the central ethnomusicological proposition — that music is
culture — into questions of cultural movement and transformation.

Veins of literary criticism and historical work in Asian American studies
are very much part of the background for this book. Work on Asian American theater, film and cultural performance has fundamentally shaped my
intellectual frameworks, as have Asian American critical responses to orientalist film, television, music and theater (Moy 1993, Hamamoto 1994,
Hisama 1993, Kondo 1997, W. Lee 1999). Josephine Lee's (1997) and
Dorinne Kondo's (1997) work on Asian American theater has been a particular inspiration. Both offer new critical strategies for interpretation and
both consider the performative effects of liveness. Lee considers the radical
presence of the Asian American body in performance and its interface with
"basic gut reactions" to race. She argues that:

> The "liveness" or "presence" of theater suggests an immediate, vis-
> ceral response to the physicality of race; the embodiedness of the-
> ater is experienced or felt, as well as seen and heard. The physical
> response of the spectator to the body of the actor complicates any
> abstraction of social categories. ... Literature and cinema or elec-
> tronic media ... may be somewhat abstracted, divorced from the
> actual body. Theater is less capable of a divorce from the body.
> (1997: 7)

Lee extends these questions into a consideration of Asian American
spectatorship, and her reworking of feminist models of spectatorship
interfaces with my own interest in matters of consumption, reception and
the audience. Lee's arguments creatively problematize the binary dynamic
of the White audience and the Asian American desire "for stage presentation to validate, through public performance, a vision of authentic reality"
that walks a tightrope between solidarity and the elision of difference (57).
Kondo traces these issues through slightly different vectors. She theorizes
liveness through the politics of pleasure and interpretation through the
gesture of intervention and both lines of argument meet in her consideration of consumption. Ultimately, Kondo locates the responsive power of
her subject matter in relation to orientalism. She writes, "I am concerned
primarily with what I call counter-Orientalisms: specifically, the ways in
which Asian American theater and Japanese fashion might mobilize this
subversive potential" (1997: 10), and she positions all this within histori-

cally constructed transnational power structures of production and consumption, arguing that it is naïve to imagine a pristine social space beyond the reach of commodity capitalism. She is particularly fascinated by the possibility of "complicitous critique" (144–152), that is, the critical response that recognizes its imbrication in the "constitutive logic" (151) of the commodity. Over and over again, she argues against an immobilized Asian/American subject done in by the inherent contradictions of critical intervention in a world where hegemony and resistance are constantly interpolated.

Lee and Kondo both address the mechanisms by which theater enables (or makes visible) social change. Lee emphasizes visibility over intervention: she concludes, "If race and ethnicity are changing social formations, then theater can assist us in understanding certain dimensions of these formations and their contexts" (1997: 217), thus locating theater as primarily reactive to other cultural constructions. Kondo takes a distinctively different tack. She submits that performance and critical ethnographic writing share the potential for creating new social spaces via narrative; these spaces may take the shape of new social realities, including disciplinary transformation. "Going home" by writing or performing what you know not only "represents" community but creates it as well (1997: 205). Both are thus loci for critical new awarenesses and bring this into being, into existence; narrative is a generative site and cultural production is always a space for social possibility, never pure but always full of promise.

Overview

This book is not a comprehensive survey of Asian American music; rather, it is shaped by broad questions around the cultural politics of performance that I address through ethnographic work. Most of the material arises from extensive fieldwork (interviews, concert attendance and producing, etc.) and in-depth contact with particular performers over some years' time. The book falls into three large sections. The first section focuses on diasporic Southeast Asian performance in the U.S. and addresses issues of change and transformation through often troubled contact with Anglo Americans, African Americans and Latinos; the second section addresses the dynamics of public presentations in differentiated social environments; and the third section focuses on second-, third- and fourth-generation Asian Americans experimenting with the African American genres of jazz and hip-hop. Throughout, I treat interethnic contact as a constructive force in performance.

There is so much more that could be included. South Asian American music, from *bhangra* to hip-hop crews to Vijay Iyer's contemplative jazz piano compositions, is flourishing. A book could (should!) be written on Filipino American music, or even on Filipino American musical activities in the Bay Area alone. It troubles me that only one Asian American woman

(Miya Masaoka) is featured here, though there are real reasons for this — the Asian American music scene is dominated by men. Asian American student organization culture nights are sites of flamboyant attention to performance and its promise of new social formations. And so on.

Working on this book has allowed me to explore different ways of bridging my research and my role(s) as a member of the Asian American community. I have been deeply involved with Asian American issues for many years, at several schools and in several communities. Although I am of Chinese and European descent, my research has been focused on Southeast Asian music and performance, in Thailand as well as in immigrant America. I draw on all these strands of Asian-ness in my work and research: that is, Asia as learned (I am not Southeast Asian) and as experienced (through fieldwork and personal history). George Lipsitz notes that, "Scholars in ethnic studies and American studies can sometimes become weighted down by what they know" (2001: 138), and it is true that to be reminded over and over again that Amerika and its identifications are founded on fearful asymmetries is hard work. But I take heart from Ruth Behar's observation that the discipline of anthropology emerged from the self-evaluation of the 1980s and 1990s "at once more vexed and more sure of itself" (1996: 163), and, in many ways, this project has done the same thing for me. I hope this work speaks to intersecting audiences. It adds to the growing body of scholarship in cultural studies and anthropology that focuses on performance and popular culture as sites of agency and cultural production. I mean for it to serve as a model for how performance studies and ethnomusicology might intersect more closely. Naturally, I am directed toward scholars and activists in Asian American studies. Finally, I have tried to extend current academic discussions of multiculturalism and interculturalism: I suggest that the intersecting landscapes presented here are deeply, fundamentally constitutive of emergent (Asian) American cultures and practices.

Endnote

[1] See American-music.org for more on the Society for American Music and its history.

2
History, Memory, Re-Membering

When I lam, people remember the past.

Khamvong Insixiengmai

The poem is not a vehicle. It is an act of transportation ... The poem, made up of breath, blows us away — to everything that is not "us," to everything by which an "us" is created. Writer to reader, self to another self, living to the dead, city to another city, city to nature, today to yesterday, this world to other worlds, sound to silence to sound.

Eliot Weinberger (1988: 6–7)

History is lost to me.

Genny Lim (Jang 1997c)

I begin with the matter of looking back. In this chapter, I am thinking about journeys — my own into Asian American studies; the pathways that refugees follow to the U.S. from Cambodia, Laos and Vietnam; the Chinese immigrants who disembarked at Angel Island; and the songways that channel memory and historical understanding. The aftermath of the Vietnam War brought waves of Southeast Asian refugees into the United States who have not yet acquired the aura of nostalgia and romance that Ellis Island has for Euro-Americans descended from earlier immigrants. Meanwhile, Angel Island has accrued real emotive force for many West Coast Asian Americans. Emigration and the movement across time and space carries its own logic of history-making. I focus here on the re/casting of arrival and looking back.

Fig. 2.1 Khamvong Insixiengmai in 1988. (Photograph by René T.A. Lysloff.)

Khamvong Insixiengmai, one of Laos' premier *maulam,* or narrative singers of *lam (*the action of singing poetry and executing stylized dance movements*)* is the carrier of histories both beautiful and traumatic. (Figure 2.1) A professional, he has always supported himself by performing, and his patrons have been powerful and highly placed. His life history and his cultural roles in Laos and in the United States speak powerfully to the experiences of Southeast Asians in diaspora.

Khamvong[1] grew up in Savannekhet, a district in southern Laos. Neither of his parents were singers but he was fascinated by the *maulam* performances he saw as a child and began studying poetry with local monks at age thirteen or fourteen. He entered the Fine Arts Department school (*Krom Sinlapakaun*) as a teenager and received a degree in Lao song and dance. He had already won a number of *maulam* contests by the time he graduated and (by his own admission) was well known as a performer before he was twenty years old. When he was twenty-one (in 1968, a tumultuous year in many parts of the world), he was drafted and sent to work for the National Radio Broadcast as a singer. When the Pathet Lao and North Vietnamese seized power in 1975, he was assigned to the military radio station, where he sang propaganda songs.

Khamvong escaped from Laos to Thailand in 1979 and arrived in the United States a year later. He lived for a time with his cousin Bountong Insixiengmay[2] in Kentucky. By 1981, he had resettled in Minneapolis, then the heart of the Lao community in the U.S. He met folklorist Cliff Sloane through the Lao Association Cassette Project and was recorded by him in a friend's living room in 1982. The resulting cassette, *Thinking of the Old Village,* contained three *lam* composed and performed by Khamvong describing life in Laos under the Pathet Lao. Then one of the few recordings that featured a single Southeast Asian refugee musician, it made Khamvong known to American ethnomusicologists. Khamvong was performing frequently by that time, both within the Lao community and sometimes beyond it, e.g., at the 1983 conference at Kent State University on Lao and Hmong music in the United States. He moved to Fresno, California in 1984, where he still lives at the time of this writing, performing regularly on the radio and at festivals. In 1987, he was invited to perform at the World Music Institute in New York City; Khamvong and several friends drove across the U.S. for the occasion, visiting Lao friends all along the way. I spoke with him in 1988.

"With My Pen and My Paper, I Wrote This *Lam* for You": Khamvong's Creative Process

I begin by trying to understand Khamvong's creative process not to make him seem any more foreign or strange than any other Asian American but to suggest that, for me, beginning to understand how his ideas of originality and innovation were *not* located in ideologies of the humanistic individual was a formative experience. Trying to understand made me into an ethnographer and I mean that in several ways. Listening to Khamvong talk and sing began to teach me how to take such conversations seriously, you could say, and that is one thing ethnography *should* do: in engaging directly with people, you enter into an ethical contract to take them on their own terms as best you can, utopian though the task may be. I was in the middle of making myself into an area studies specialist at the time, taking graduate courses in Southeast Asian studies as I worked toward my doctoral degree at the University of Michigan, and preparing for further research in Thailand. Listening to Khamvong's music and to his explanations ultimately resituated my own relationship to Southeast Asian studies and to the troubled history of area studies, though it took me quite a while to realize this. Perhaps I shouldn't be surprised that Khamvong's narratives seized me in the way they did, as I now suspect that my interest in Southeast Asia has everything to do with growing up during the Vietnam War. As a graduate student, I had no models for thinking critically about the ways that Southeast Asian area studies were so deeply shaped by particular historical moments and specific political concerns. Indeed, the famous and well-established Center for Southeast Asian Studies at the University of Michigan (where I spent so much of my time as a grad student) was one of some nine such centers created at major universities during the 1960s with Department of Defense funding in order to generate cultural "experts" who could advise the government on its deepening involvement in the war. Still, writing about Khamvong for my master's thesis now looks to me like my bridge into Asian American studies. Although I approached Khamvong and the *maulam* tradition as if they were both purely Lao, it was, in fact, the affective power of Khamvong's representation of diaspora and relocation that spoke to me from the beginning, and his work changed how I thought of "Southeast Asia" as a place. Talking with him and thinking about his work resituated Southeast Asia as t/here, a cultural space both Asian and American.

Translation is central to ethnographic work. In this chapter, your access as reader to Khamvong's thoughts takes place via a complicated process of trilingual conversation and translation, but the trope of translation runs even deeper than that. The ethnographer takes experience and encounter and re-presents them, transforms them, refashions them. You don't and can't have access to someone else's experience, only to a representation of it, and the process that brings it to you is deeply translative. This is inevitable. It is a challenge. It is a process profoundly different from interpreting texts, though ethnographers have learned much from textual criticism since the 1970s. To reject ethnography as too damaged by its colonial origins to be of any use at the turn of the millennium is a sweeping and dismissive response to difficult matters. The artifact that the ethnographer creates may be a text, but it emerges from relationships with real people and an accountability that is potentially life changing. In talking with Khamvong, I thought I was making myself into a Southeast Asianist, but looking back, I see that I was becoming an Asian American working in Asian American studies — though I didn't realize it at the time.

There were as many language abilities as there were participants in the conversation. Lao and central Thai are mutually intelligible (up to a point). I speak central Thai, but not Lao. Khamvong is a native speaker of Lao, but spoke little English at that time; he was familiar with central Thai and occasionally substituted Thai words for Lao when he suspected I wouldn't understand. Khamvong's longtime friend and manager, Thongthip Rattanavilay, was also present: Thongthip is a native speaker of Lao, but spoke good central Thai and fairly good English. Bounxeung Sinanon, Khamvong's *khaen* player, spoke only Lao and so idiomatically that I had trouble understanding his interjections and comments. (Figure 2.2.) Despite all this, the conversation proceeded pretty smoothly and we spent most of our time discussing fairly detailed aspects of the *maulam*'s art. All of the following quotations from Khamvong are my own translations.

What goes on in the mind of a musician who is making or creating music? This question has been addressed in a number of studies, but one

Fig. 2.2 Bounxeung Sinanon in 1988. (Photograph by René T.A. Lysloff.)

of the most rewarding ways of finding out is to ask the musician and then consider closely the way she or he talks about musical activity. Music-makers' conceptions of what they are doing is nearly always interesting because the terminology and metaphors that appear in discourse about music can have startling revelatory power. The fact that many cultures have no generalized word for "music" is one example. The ethnomusicologist Charles Keil strongly advocates coming to terms with new systems of musical thought through language, and writes that "the equivalent of an esthetic or "ideology of expression" is … implicit in any language, if we choose to interpret it as such" (1979: 26). A large body of work suggests that musical and everyday discourse can overlap in ways that illuminate wider cultural patterns of perception.[3] Terminology or metaphors that are music-specific help to define the boundedness of music as an activity, whereas terminology that overlaps with, but is not specific to, musical activity may indicate the confluence of certain domains. Judith Becker (1979 and 1981) and A.L. Becker (1979 and 1982) have argued that Javanese music, text-building and time-reckoning closely resemble one another. In a now-classic essay on a Javanese wall calendar and its evocation of the world of gamelan, A.L. Becker suggests that (1987: ix):

> This is the way cultural coherence works: a few deep metaphors
> bind various things together, make them resonate and mutually

reinforce each other, and make the world seem orderly, reasonable, and harmonious.

Similarly, Lakoff and Johnson have noted that:

Our conceptual system is not something we are normally aware of. In most of the little things we do every day, we simply think and act more or less automatically along certain lines. Just what these lines are is by no means obvious. One way to find out is by looking at language. (1980:3)

So I talk with musicians and performers. I try to find out not only "what" they are doing but I also attend to how they say it and to whom, and when, and I try hard to listen between the lines and through the deep resonance of metaphoric constructions. The conversations create bonds of friendship, responsibility, obligation, investment. The following discussion is drawn entirely from a taped interview with Khamvong Insixiengmai in February 1988.[4] Months later, after listening to the taped conversation many times and finally transcribing it, it became apparent to me that Khamvong's vocabulary and discourse about the creation and performance of *maulam* texts reveals a basic orientation toward two different creative processes: one that might be called "literate" and one that might be called "oral," although these labels are deeply interconstitutive.

I sought out Khamvong for several reasons. When I first heard his tape, "Thinking of the Old Village," I had never heard *maulam,* but I was immediately impressed and interested in it. I was also moved by its narrative power; Khamvong's words address the Southeast Asian refugee experience with an eloquence that is undeniable. Khamvong's poetry was created and performed by a Lao for other Lao and it was created by a man whose career has been built out of the skillful manipulation of words (Audio Example 2.1 and Appendix). Last but not least, I wanted to talk with Khamvong because I learned (from Cliff Sloane, the tape's producer) that his taped performance had involved the use of written texts that Khamvong had prepared beforehand. (Figure 2.3.) Although previous studies show that *maulam* have employed the written word as a means of transmission for a long time, I was curious to see how a particular singer might talk about the relationships between writing, memory and the improvisatory process of performing.

Powerful constructions of nostalgia drive all of this. Traumatic relocation sets up a particular relationship between refugee and homeland even as it forces the refugee to become culture-bearer and culture-maker all at once. Certainly these directives are in all of us all the time already, but the refugee is immediately invested with responsibilities both terrible and wondrous, as well as a heavy self-awareness. The refugee must re/create the homeland as an act of self-preservation and can't phone home for advice

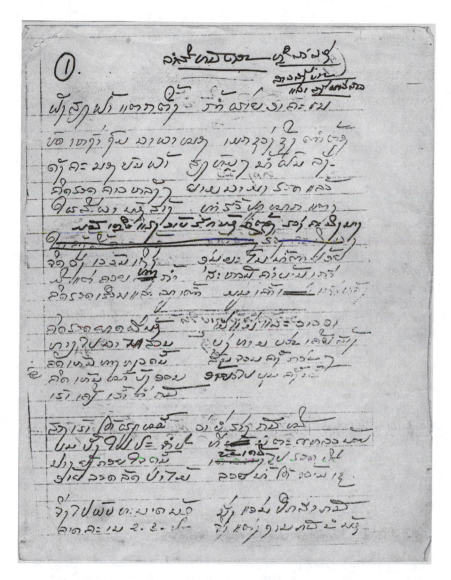

Fig. 2.3 The first page of Khamvong's handwritten text for "Thinking of the Old Village."

or materials. The memory of home is created and recreated, asserted and valorized and home-as-place is re-placed by powerful imaginary and phantastic performatives. Adelaida Reyes has written about how Vietnamese immigrants in the U.S. created a definitive immigrant culture industry, particularly in Orange County, and how its expressive media (radio, popular music, TV, etc.) were focused with wrenching urgency on a Vietnamese homeland that did and didn't, does and doesn't, exist (Reyes 1999a). The long-term construction of the refugee Khmer court dancer as nostalgic emissary for a Cambodia refuting the horror of killing fields is central to sentimental American understandings of the Southeast Asian refugee experience. Anthropologist Marilyn Ivy describes nostalgia as "an ambivalent longing to erase the temporal difference between subject and object of desire" (1995: 10). For Lao, Hmong, Khmer and Vietnamese refugees, the homeland that is longed for no longer exists: the presence of socialist and Communist governments acts as a kind of irrefutable boundary between then and now. Yearning for the place of the past is no maudlin exercise but rather a very necessary exertion of presence and will. The performative means for creating and sustaining nostalgia thus bears attention.

Khamvong used two different verbs to talk about the way he creates poetry. Consider the following explanation. I knew that he had gone to New York City the previous year to perform at the World Music Institute and I knew that our mutual friend, ethnomusicologist Terry Miller, had later asked him to sing about his trip. I asked Khamvong if he had had to write out his song text first, or if he had just gone ahead and sung. Khamvong's answer and his account of Miller's response encapsulate his conceptions of these two separate-but-relative processes:

> Dr. Miller asked me to tell about my performance in New York ... I didn't compose (*taeng*) it, I went ahead and performed (*lam pay day*). Dr. Miller recorded it and said, "*Khun* Khamvong, you have a good brain. You have the ability to compose (*taeng*); you have the ability to perform (*lam*)."

These two verbs, *taeng* and *lam,* represent two abilities, two skills, two kinds of training and two ways to create performances. Khamvong is proficient in both and is very proud of it. A closer look at the two words begins to point out certain divergences.

The verb *lam* is more musically restricted in meaning than the verb *taeng.* For performance, it means the action of singing poetry and executing stylized dance movements while accompanied by the *khaen.* (Figure 2.4.) A dictionary that provides definitions of Northeastern Thai terms in Central Thai (*Phacanaanukarom phaak iisaan-phaak klaang* 2515/1962: 350) gives the primary meaning of *lam* as "a kind of singing in which the *khaen* is an element." Mary Haas's Thai-English dictionary (Haas 1964: 483-84) provides a similar definition for the word *lam* followed by two others: (1) a classifier[5] for boats, ships, airplanes; for long objects, approximately cylindrical in form, as a plant stem, a beam of light; (2) courseway, passageway.

Lam ton thus means the trunk of a tree and *lam nam* means a water passage. The underlying metaphor of a course or passageway is dominant

Fig. 2.4 Bounxeung Sinanon playing the khaen in 1988. (Photograph by René T.A. Lysloff.)

in all these words; although boats, ships and airplanes can be "approximately cylindrical" in form, they are also things that follow a course. Lakoff and Johnson (1980: 10–13), drawing on Michael Reddy's work, have identified a "conduit metaphor" found in many languages, including English, which is often used in language about language or communication; the conduit metaphor often flags a kind of meta-language. Expressions about communication are frequently encapsulated as metaphoric acts of sending idea-objects that are contained in linguistic expressions. Similarly, *lam* goes out from its performer like a passageway from one place to another, or from performer to audience. It could be said that *lam* (as sung) flows forth as a stream (of sound, in this case) that follows a strict course of poetic rules and *khaen* patterns.

Conceptions of song as a path are not unique to Lao music. This metaphor appears in musical cultures all over the world, and usually implies connections between music (particularly song) and the spirit world. Marina Roseman has written how certain individuals among the Temiar of upland Malaysia are gifted at dreaming songs that cure illness; while sleeping, such a person's unbound spirit will encounter a spirit-guide who teaches him a song. But Roseman notes that there is no Temiar word for "song" (1991: 6):

> When I first heard mediums sing during ceremonial performances, I was told that they were singing: "*naung.*" *Naung,* I wrote in my notebook, must mean "song." When I asked what the female chorus, vocally responding to each line sung by the medium, was doing, they responded with the word: "*waedwad.*" That must be "choral response," I thought. One day, as I was walking with Temiars through the forest on the way to the rice fields, someone pointed out a path between the trees and commanded: "*Waedwad naung-na.*" What are these people doing talking about songs and choral responses out here, I wondered in surprise. What I had been told, they explained, was to "follow that path." I realized, then, that songs were paths and choruses were following the path.

The Temiar dreamer doesn't "sing a song," but rather follows the spirit-guide along a path that happens to be musical. Later, when the song is performed in the world of human social interaction, the singers "follow the path described by the spirit-guide." Similarly, Steven Feld found that the Kaluli of the Papua New Guinea rain forest use song as a map that describes the passage of journeys (1982: 150–56). Unlike the Temiar, whose songs are paths between worlds, the songs of the Kaluli affirm and reinforce the singers' ties to the topography of their locality and to each other. Feld found that the word *tok* was part of a larger "verb morphology that creates poetic time and space" (ibid., 133), which grants songs great emotive power by situating them in local mountains, streams and garden sites that have strong personal meaning for the listeners. *Tok* means path, road (ibid.: 150–51):

> The device refers to the way that a song, from start to finish, projects not merely a description of places, but a journey. The song is successful when listeners are totally suspended into a journeying mood, experiencing the passage of song and poetic time as the passage of a journey. Many Kaluli men said … there would be no song without a *tok* … (I)t is the song's path that envelops the attentiveness of the listeners.

Think too of Aboriginal songlines and the way they collapse time and space: a songline isn't a *representation* of place but rather an enactment of it and vice versa; neither is the original. In short, song-as-pathway is explicitly constructed through language in more than one culture, and this conception is often central to its affective power, though its emotive associations are always culturally specific. I am not making a universalistic argument for music but rather want to suggest that music-making (particularly song) is often tied to senses of place and to ideas of communicative acts that are profound, right at the level of language. This power is intensified when the subject at hand is traumatic relocation.

The meaning of the Lao word *taeng* extends out even further than that of *lam*. Dictionaries of Central Thai, Northeastern Thai and Lao (Haas 1964: 210; *Phacanaanukarom* 2515/1962:185; Marcus 1970: 331) all show a cluster of meanings around the idea of decorating or embellishing something. "To compose" is part of this meaning, whether it is verse, prose or music. Haas defines the verb *taeng* as: (1) to fix up, beautify; (2) to ornament, decorate, adorn; (3) to compose (e.g., verse): *kaan taeng* = writing, composition (1964: 210).

A number of compound words using the word *taeng* extend the idea of decoration, including the expressions for "to get dressed," "to get married," "to confer a title," "to make up the face (with cosmetics)", etc. Expressions involving composition include *taeng phleeng,* "to write a song" and *taeng prayoot,* "to write a sentence." At the heart of all these expressions is the action of adding something on to a preexisting person or object, e.g., adding on clothes, adding on a person to another person, etc. Seen as composition, *taeng* takes on a special shade of meaning found in many Southeast Asian notions of creativity. Rather than make something utterly new and original (the kind of creativity romanticized and valorized in the West), to *taeng* a song or poem implies adding material on to preexisting material in such a way that the configuration is new but built on something old. The way to nostalgia is thus prepared through language.

It is clear from Khamvong's explanations that *lam* takes place in the world of sound and social interaction. In other words, it is a performance act that needs an audience.[6] Khamvong constantly refers to people who heard (*dayyin*) him *lam,* or who listened (*fang*) to him *lam*. The action of *lam* "goes out" from the performer: the auxiliary verb *pay,* "to go," is frequently found in conjunction with the verb *lam* in Khamvong's speech, as in "*phom lam pay day,*" "I-lam-go-able," or "I can *lam.*" *Lam* doesn't exist as an action until it has gone out and left its performer and the only way it can leave its performer is as sound.

The verb *taeng* represents a very different process. Unlike *lam*, it takes place in the silent realm of thought. Unlike *lam*, which goes out from the performer, the thoughts that lead to the action of *taeng* "come to" the creator. Khamvong emphasizes that he wasn't able to *taeng* poetry (*kawii* or *klaun*) until he was more than twenty years old, many years after he had first begun to *lam*. He then studied how to *taeng* poetry when he was a student at the Fine Arts Department of Laos, working under the guidance of his professors. Although he says he can now *taeng* poetry "comfortably," it still requires time, effort and, importantly, study. He sometimes uses books of poetic texts when he is trying to *taeng* something and he refers to "doing research" (*khon khwaa*) in books as a way of helping thoughts to come. He says:

> You have to study how to do it. After I was able to *lam,* I still had to sit at my desk and work at *taeng.* I'd think along (*khit taam*) various books, along various old stories. Sometimes I can think fast. But sometimes I have to think for eight hours a day before I'll know what it is (that I want to write) and then *bup!* I'll know. Other times I look at the verses that my professors gradually led me through: I'll take them out and look at them, take them out and look and study them little by little …

As an action, *taeng* takes place before *lam* (although Khamvong is quick to reiterate that he can *lam* without having to *taeng* first). But the process of *taeng* ends when the performance begins. Khamvong is very clear on this point: *taeng* helps to form *lam,* but not vice versa. When I asked him if he ever went back and changed a text after performing it, his answer was wonderfully evocative and, in fact, stresses the importance of speech acts and the sounded word in *maulam:*

> You have to change a text *before* going out to lam. If you changed a text after going out to *lam* it wouldn't have any meaning, because what's been said is said.

Literally translated, his phrase was, "Utterances in uttering already in speaking already" ("*khwaam waw nay waw pay laew nay phuut pay laew*"). Speaking (*phuut*) and uttering (*waw*), like *lam,* are acts directed outward; once they leave the actor, they are a *fait accompli* that cannot be changed or revised.

When Khamvong creates a text by the process of *taeng,* change, revision and reflection are integral to it:

> I sit and think and sometimes something will come into my brain — something that I never studied. So I'll write it down. After I've composed (*taeng*) it, I review it — I read it ten times over and if there's something that isn't so good, I'll improve it. I'll compose (*taeng*) new words and put them in. Then, when I'm sure of the words, I'll go out and *lam.*

Khamvong uses the single word *taeng* to describe several similar processes, although I have (rather uneasily) been translating it as "to compose." Sometimes *taeng* seems to imply writing; in other contexts, it suggests a performance prepared sometime before the actual performance; at other times (e.g., "I'll *taeng* new words and put them in"), it refers to the action of arranging the configuration of words. In many ways, *taeng* seems

Fig. 2.5 Khamvong Insixiengmai singing "Thinking of the Old Village" while—uncharacteristically—looking at his own handwritten text. Bounxeung Sinanon accompanies him on the khaen. (Photograph by René T.A. Lysloff.)

to approach "arranging" or "constructing" in meaning, or even "the decoration of preexisting material," since Khamvong doesn't "compose" new words as much as he tinkers with them and rearranges their configuration. (Figure 2.5.)

Although *lam* and *taeng* are essentially different processes, "thinking" (*khit*) and "remembering" (*cam*) are integral to both. A good memory is a prerequisite to being a good *maulam* and Khamvong's references to his own excellent recall are frequent. As a teenager, he says he was able to remember whatever he heard other *maulam* sing or read in books; this helped him when he began to *taeng* poetry around age twenty:

> I went and studied, I went and sought knowledge, I went and listened, I went and looked — and my brain was able to remember everything.

Thinking is a prelude to *lam*. Thoughts "arise and come to" the *maulam* (*khün maa*): Khamvong says "the thoughts come and then I can go *lam*" (*nük khün maa kaun lam pay day oey*). Memory is a prerequisite to being able to *lam* and it can be a substitute or alternative to *taeng*. In one case, he says he was able to *lam* for an hour by drawing on memorized material that he didn't *taeng* himself. Thinking, remembering and *taeng* are similar in that all three "arise in" (*khün maa*) the *maulam:* all are silent and internal and are manifested in sound. Silent internalization is a characteristic of all kinds of knowledge in Laos and Thailand; knowledge resides in the brain (*samaung*) and/or in the heart, and true knowledge is acted out in the world of human beings and social interaction. The actions of *lam* and *taeng* thus represent certain dichotomies that coexist relationally and dynamically. One is externalized, the other is internalized; one is performative, the other is meditative; one is sounded, the other is silent.

Memory

The themes of Khamvong's songs demand contextualization. Perhaps it is enough to present Khamvong as the epic singer of the Lao killing fields, but he has been more than that. Khamvong has been a civil servant, a propagandist, a singer of advertisements, a soldier and (in America) a mechanic. His life revolves around language and the skillful manipulation of words. It probably isn't coincidence that he has pursued a skill in the New World that requires few words at all; English has been difficult for him and the insides of cars must sometimes seem more intelligible. Khamvong's song "Thinking of the Old Village" (see Appendix A for the transcription and translation) concerns an enemy who incarnates evil. He calls them the communists, the devils (*maan*), the evil ones (*phuu raay*) — they have many names. They are Khamvong's fellow Lao, but their Otherness is so complete that they might as well be from another world. Khamvong's songs have no hero in the mold of Achilles, Arthur, or Roland. There is only an "I" who is and isn't Khamvong himself: a soldier who hates the Pathet Lao and their destruction of his homeland, a soldier who has slept in the forest with leaves for his blanket, a soldier who thinks mostly of the young woman he planned to marry but who is now lost to him through the course of events. Good and evil are so obvious as to be left unexplored: good is the way of life now gone forever and evil is the army that destroyed the old village. Death and destruction are addressed, but the relationship to the young woman is the lens through which everything is experienced and portrayed. The survivor knows only loss and memory becomes all.

Memory is of central importance to Khamvong. Tremendous value is placed on memory in Southeast Asia, particularly in the performing arts; one of the most frequent praises heard of skilled performers generally is that they have a phenomenal and accurate memory. Tambiah (1985: 121) has noted that in Buddhist cultures like those in Thailand and Laos, "knowledge implies and is wedded to practice and is intimately related to the capacities of the knower." Khamvong is proud of his ability to remember songs, stories and histories and he refers to it often. Speaking of memory, he frequently uses the word *khwaamsongcam,* an elegant extension of the everyday word *cam,* which simply means "to remember."

Khwaam is a bound prefix that makes verbs into nouns. *Song* is a bound verb most often used to indicate that the action is being performed by a royal person; as a verb in its own right, it means to stay the same or to stand still. When put together, *song* and *cam* suggest a kind of remembering that is clearly on a different plane from remembering to pay bills or to return library books.

What is memory for Khamvong and what kind of memory does he create in performance? Poet and critic Eliot Weinberger writes that the invention of memory and a past is the primary activity of most poetry.[7] He cites classical Chinese poetry as the example *par excellence*, a body of work containing thousands of poems "about remembering, and remembering those who, in history, are famous for remembering" (1988: 4). The disjuncture between past and present is necessary for poetry to exist: the poem is a piece of the past that is drawn into the present. For a poem to bridge that disjuncture is impossible, or possible only at the end of time:

> A poetry without its own archaic, that doesn't talk with the dead, that doesn't meditate on ruins, that doesn't know it is surrounded by others who contradict everything it says, that has no nostalgia — a poem, in other words, that is completed — can only exist at the end of Christian or Hindu or Confucian or Aztec time, when poetry will no longer be written (ibid., 7).

Similarly, the ethnomusicologist Philip V. Bohlman has considered the discursive force of "endism," that is, the "overwhelmingly Western" construction of the end of history, e.g., in millennial movements (2002: 8). He situates such "ahistorical teleology" in cultural anxieties over encounter and/or the future (6) and he examines the specific crisis in interpretation and representation that the music of the Holocaust poses for music historians (19–20):

> With the Holocaust, the civilization of the West did reach an endpoint. What the West had celebrated as its most glorious of humanistic traditions culminated in an endgame of mass destruction and even greater mass murder, all so that the historical claims to a thousand-year Reich, emulating the quintessence of Europe's centuries of formation, could eliminate those insufficiently European from Europe itself. The finality of the Holocaust was so complete that, even at the beginning of the twenty-first century, it remains an open question whether the teleological history of the West can be said to have recovered and to have begun again. From the eschatological dystopia of the Holocaust the teleology of modernism proceeded at best in fits and starts, which more often than not found nowhere to go in the era of endings that has characterized the half century leading up to the new millennium.

Bohlman argues that the Holocaust was, among other things, a key moment when the Western construction of otherness and selfness were played out with finality and that recourse to exoticism routinely has been the European response to the threat. Master narratives of history can be maintained only by removing certain others from them. As Bohlman puts it, "we explain the ruptures in the fabric of our own history by stuffing them full with exoticism" (27).

Khamvong responds to an equally final, traumatic version of history-making/history-ending by resorting to nostalgia. He meditates on his own kind of ruins. His poems celebrate and mourn the past, but their poignancy stems from an uncertainty about the placement of this past in time. Is Khamvong a poet at the end of traditional Lao time? Musically, culturally and politically, Laos has certainly reached a turning point. For the Lao now in exile, it must seem like the shift from one era to another. For Khamvong, who is conservative even by Lao standards,[8] the past is his life's work: his evocation of that other era assumes compelling power and, as Weinberger says of poetry in general (ibid., 3), "the present is always juxtaposed with the past. The present is either wanting ... or, at best, unstable ..." As narrator, Khamvong performs as if he stands on the island of the present, surrounded on all sides by a past he has relinquished with sorrow and anger.

Unlike Khamvong, whose role as the carrier of cultural memory binds him to history, most Lao have no great sentimentality for the old ways. The Lao have proven to be one of the least cohesive groups of Southeast Asian refugees in the United States (unlike the Hmong or Cambodians, who have tended to live together in communities, relying on cooperative associations). This tendency has obvious implications for traditional Lao customs and performance arts. Terry Miller (1985a: 108) has supported and encouraged Khamvong and other Lao performers but is resigned to the situation:

If I sound pessimistic about the future of traditional Lao music in the United States, it is because I am pessimistic. It has lost its cultural context, lacks cultural organization that might foster its continuation and is generally viewed as old fashioned. Unlike certain other Asians in the United States, such as the Koreans and Chinese who came gradually and voluntarily, the Lao came to escape calamity. Some, if not most, of the country's leading musicians came to America or to France. The Lao situation is, therefore, very different from those of the Chinese and Koreans whose cultures (including music) survive intact in the old country. A significant part of the Lao musical heritage now resides in the West, and its extinction would represent a serious loss for the Lao.

Khamvong is keenly aware of this possibility. He says,[9]

> Since coming to America, my *lam* have changed a lot. I used to *lam* about romance and politics and propaganda. Now I stress Lao culture, its customs. There's so much here in America that's new — the old ways could disappear. So that's what I *lam* about.

Khamvong's relationship to his work is different from the Chinese poets, who tended to seek places of solitude for their written meditations on time and history. Khamvong doesn't create artifacts: his meditations are meant to be realized in the world of social interaction. They are meant to be performed — they cannot exist as artifacts because they vanish, as all utterances do, as soon as they are uttered. They are ephemeral: they are created in interaction with the Lao audiences Khamvong feels closest to and with whom he fears to lose touch. Khamvong and his audiences create his songs together: like every epic singer, Khamvong adjusts his performance to his surroundings and his past to his present.

So Khamvong goes on, recalling a past that is painful but necessary to remember. By doing so, he gives it a place in history, a place that is of central importance to the Lao who fled to escape disaster. In a way, he is busy creating a contemporary origin myth, a tale of separation and emigration. As Khamvong says,

> We can't go back to the homeland. There is no Laos. So I *lam* tears. I *lam* sadness. I'm the one who *lam*s of our relatives, our families, our friends. ... Husbands came without their wives; wives came without their husbands. Nearly everyone in our great circle thinks of and misses someone who's still back in Laos. So I *lam* and I create poetry. Laos and America are distant from one another. Laos will never see the day when husbands, wives and children meet again. So I *lam* and I create poetry. Sometimes when I *lam*, people's tears flow. But other people concentrate, focus their thoughts (*tang sati*) on Laos, on times past. When I *lam*, people remember the past.

Angel Island: Reasserting the Performative

Khamvong is not, of course, the only Asian American whose performances are predicated on close and reflexive treatments of the past. Considering the ways that different scholars, writers, and stage performers address the contemporary moment in the Asian American experience allows me to take a step back and dwell for a moment on how certain key historical texts have offered models for bridging past and present. This issue is both related to the necessity of defining Here against There and Now against Then, and also provides me with a useful extended example of how textual and ethnographic inquiry can inform one another. Let me segue into it by way of Marlon K. Hom's *Songs of Gold Mountain* (1987), a groundbreaking look at a collection of Chinese "vernacular" poetry published in San

Francisco's Chinatown in 1911. Although Hom deals with the poems as texts, he notes that most are written in the style and form of Cantonese folk songs; though most were probably written as texts (possibly for a contest), they ride a dynamic line between literary text and performed practice. Hom argues that their critical commentary on immigration is evidence of an emergent Asian American sensibility (Hom 1987: 73):

> The Cantonese folk rhymes on immigration in the 1911 anthology represent the earliest collection of published poems dealing with the Chinese immigration experience. They are different from the poems on the Wooden Barrack walls (at Angel Island). Not only do these rhymes protest the harsh treatment at the Wooden Barracks; they also show that Angel Island with its Wooden Barracks was not a euphoric Ellis Island for the Chinese immigrants. Instead, it was a contradiction to the principles of liberty that testified to injustice. This criticism, so pronounced in these rhymes, reveals that the Chinese immigrants did have an appreciation of the American principles of justice and democracy. They expected to be treated on that level and they believed that they should be accorded such rights. This was, I believe, the first crude sign of their Americanization.

I would extend this assessment to suggest that the importance of these poems lies partly in their imaginative genesis as performance: the movement from "song" and "poem" is dynamic in this genre. Hom notes two literary genres that were popular among Chinese immigrants, both based on song traditions. *Gamsaan go* (or *Jinshan ge*), "Gold Mountain songs," were written in the style of oral narratives, with rhyme and syllable schemes borrowed from folk song genres (Hom 1987: 39). *Muk yu go*, "wooden fish songs," were originally rhymed narratives performed in a rhythmic chanted style; texts written in this style were tremendously popular in San Francisco's Chinatown in the late nineteenth and early twentieth centuries (Hom 1987: 47–48 and 47, fn. 67).

Hom's book on the *muk-yu* poems and song texts published in San Francisco's Chinatown in 1911 and 1915 documents remarkable examples of poems written by Chinese immigrants to California. A significant number, probably by male writers, are in the persona of the wife left behind in China, registering the nonimmigrant wife's frustration and loneliness. Whether actually written by women or not, such song texts represent the flip side of immigration — the family left behind — and point to immigrant interest in and consumption of such texts. As Hom writes (1987: 43–47, 63–66), some of these texts may have been imported from China for publication in the U.S., but most provide "aesthetic echoes and records of the immigrants' own sentiments" (1987: 69) and some were even exported back to China (52). Similarly, Su de San Zheng's work on an elderly Chinese immigrant in New York City composing such songs in the

1980s–90s documents the continued importance of *muk-yu* as a Chinese performative practice of reflecting on the experience of immigration (Zheng 1992).

With this background in mind, I return to matters of performance and the performative via a consideration of how Gold Mountain songs have been redefined by contemporary Asian American performers. The Angel Island poems — Chinese American artifacts of central historical importance — have been reinvigorated through (and as) performance by two different artists, and their efforts are a window on the cultural politics of Asian American performance. The poems carved on the walls of the Angel Island detention center in San Francisco by Chinese immigrants between 1910 and 1940 were discovered in 1970 by a National Park ranger who intuited their importance. Their preservation became key to arguments for making the center a national historical site. Bringing the texts off the page and out of silence makes important points about the power and potential of performative practices for Asian American memory and the making of alternative histories.

In the early 1970s, Bay Area poet Genny Lim got involved in local efforts to find out more about the poems, and her resulting research and oral history work led to two publications, a co-edited book presenting translations of about one hundred of the poems (Lai, Lim and Yung 1980) and a play, *Paper Angels* (Lim 1993). The book, *Island: Poetry and History of Chinese Immigrants on Angel Island, 1910–1940*, is a fairly straightforward compilation of the poems in both Chinese and English translation, interspersed with excerpts from interviews with former Angel Island detainees, and historical background and photographs. The play, however, attempts something more daring: Lim's attempt to bring the poems to life via the stage is a gesture that cuts to the heart of how and why performance creates new social possibilities. I focus here on her use of dramatic practices beyond quotidian dialogue. *Paper Angels* takes place in the Angel Island Detention Center in 1915; it provides a window into the histories and motivations of seven detainees (four men and three women). Moving between English and Cantonese, "the dialogue" performatively explores the question of voice and identity as the detainees wait and wait and wait, killing time by talking with each other, rehearsing and resenting their necessary "paper" identities and undergoing interrogation by detention center inspectors. The interrogation sequences are particularly important. The performative effect of listening to English or Chinese and waiting for translation creates a cumulative, itchy impatience over the ponderousness of the process that mimetically reproduces the detainees' feelings in the watching and listening audience. The play opens with the following "prologue" (Lim 1993: 19):

Inspector: How old are you?
Interpreter: *Nay gay daw suey?*

Applicant: *Yee sup.*
Interpreter: Twenty.
Inspector: When were you born?
Interpreter: *Nay gay nien chut-sai?*
Applicant: *Bot ngut sup-chut, yut bot gow um nien.*
Interpreter: August 17, 1895.
Inspector: Where were you born?
Interpreter: *Hai bien shu chut-sai?*
Applicant: *Chew Kai Choon.*
Interpreter: Chew Kai village.

While I believe that the supposed incomprehensibility of the Cantonese sets up a powerful and deliberate audience response, Lim offers a slightly different but not contradictory explanation for her use of spoken Chinese in the play. She notes, "English is not my inherent language. Even though I'm American born I come from a bilingual bicultural context. The English language is limiting for me. To break out of that construct I integrate music, movement, voice, poetry and visual art, which bring in the Cantonese feeling" (Uno 1993: 14). Thus, as the play proceeds, she incorporates chanted poetry, American folk songs sung by Chinese woman detainees, poetry (from the barracks walls) read aloud by its "writer" and a Chinese women's work song about sewing. For instance, one of the main characters, Lee, is described as "a high-strung young poet with naïve delusions of life. He wants very much to be western" (Lim 1993: 18). In the very first scene, he carves a poem on the barracks wall as two fellow detainees quarrel out of boredom and frustration. The other two men derisively call him Li-Po (a famous poet of the eighth century), sing a "filthy peasant rhyme" at him (22–23) (much like some of those found in the 1911 collection addressed by Hom), and, when he drops his "coaching book" by mistake, they quickly burn it to protect him from deportation. Lee accepts their help but says,

> (*resentfully*) I am Lee Sung Fei, not (*gesturing at the burnt contents in the spittoon*) this Moy Fook Sing or whatever his name is! I am from Shekki not Sunning. I am a scholar, not a merchant's son!

In a subsequent scene, the poem on the wall becomes a haven, a refuge, as two men take desperate measures. One is deported for liver flukes (a common Chinese ailment legislated as a convenient rationale for sending immigrants back to China) and the other makes a reckless attempt to escape. In deciding not to follow suit, Lee responds through his poem:

> (*returns to his poem and reads*)
> There are tens of thousands of poems composed on these walls.
> They are all cries of complaint and sadness.

The day I am rid of this prison and attain success,
I must remember that this chapter once existed.

In the play's final scene, Lee is putting the finishing touches on his poem when he is informed that he and his wife have been given permission to enter the U.S. The poem's defiance and its promise of memory thus becomes the frame for the experience of entry, the subversion of the system through the institution of paper sons and immigrant determination. It is important to understand that this is a "real" poem — one of many on the walls of Angel Island — though its anonymity is refuted by Genny Lim through her play. At another level, the entire play is an amplification of the poems that inspired her to write the play in the first place: the poems' intensity, poignancy and defiance led Lim to want to reiterate and magnify them in a different register.

Jon Jang (who makes several appearances in this book (see Chapters 10 and 13 and Figure 2.6.) has taken the poems further in two separate works, *Island: The Immigrant Suite* No. 1 (Jang 1997c) and No. 2 (Jang 1996). The two suites could not be more different — one is in Jang's "post-modern jazz/improvisational" language, whereas the other is closer to the modernist style of late twentieth-century art music; both feature a female vocalist, but one is performed entirely in English by a Chinese American and the other entirely in Cantonese by an immigrant. Both feature the Angel Island poems, though, and the political critique that they offer is essentially the same.

Island: The Immigrant Suite No. 1 features Genny Lim performing her poems and poems by Angel Island detainees with the Jon Jang Octet, an ensemble of piano, saxes, *pipa, erhu,* cello and multiple percussion. (Figure 2.7.) The five-movement work features three of Lim's poems and two from Angel Island. Lim is well known in the Bay Area for her poetry addressing the Asian American/Chinese American experience and her "readings" of her own work are close to performance art. She and Jang are longtime friends and collaborators and Jang left her ample room in this work to play with recitation styles.

The work is "about" multivocality in a number of ways. The octet is a mixture of Western and Asian musical instruments and a mixture of Chinese, Chinese American and White American musicians. As in many of his works, Jang placed Chinese musicians specializing in traditional Chinese music alongside American jazz musicians, encouraging each to perform in the ways they know best but also asking them to respond to the encounter by borrowing from each others' musical languages. The two Chinese musicians, Min Xiao Fen on *pipa* and Wang Hong on *zhonghu, erhu and guanzi,* thus spend a certain amount of time playing "Chinese" music, but they do more than that as well. Several of the featured American musicians specialize in free improvisation, so Jang incorporated this into the work, moving back and forth between "composed" music and free improvisation

Fig. 2.6 Composer Jon Jang. (Photograph by Michael Sexton.)

(this musical/political dynamic is explored further in Chapter 12). At the end of the second movement, "First Interlude/Yellow Woman," for instance, saxophone player Francis Wong takes off into an improvised solo that wanders into territory he explores elsewhere (again, see Chapter 12): for a moment, he riffs on the Chinese national anthem, "Chi Lai," and then ironically finds himself in "The Star Spangled Banner." The musical language of the work as a whole is, then, not only quite varied but is also Jang's and not-Jang's, in that he opens up spaces for sounds over which he has no control, and the resulting mix is multivocalic to say the least.

The progression of the poems through the work sets up a dynamic of return and defiance. The first poem, Lim's "Burial Mound," is in "her" voice, the voice of a Chinese American evoking her great-grandfather and meditating on the mountain locations of the railroad workers' graves, and this becomes a metaphor for locating history (Jang 1997). The movement opens with a "straight" instrumental introduction in traditional *naamyam* style, followed by Lim singing, "Oh! Great-grandfather!" She sings the

Fig. 2.7 Cover of Jon Jang's Island: The Immigrant Suite No. 1. (Reproduced with the permission of Flavio Bonandrini and Soul Note.)

poem twice. The first time, she is accompanied only by Francis Wong on solo sax and the two unmetered contrapuntal lines create a feeling of introspection:

> History is lost to me,
>   just as yellow skin erodes
>   Black hair becomes white frost
> Sturdy as yoked oxen,
>   they drove the spike, hauling rail,
>   still their jaws locked and
>   their hands froze
> Wind sweeps the summits and
>   an occasional beating of wings
>   startles memory

The second time, the instrumental accompaniment is a spirited, upbeat combination of cymbals, sax and *er-hu* and Lim's singing becomes strongly rhythmic. (Audio Example 2.2.) Lim's delivery of her poem "Yellow Woman" in the next movement is closer to "reading," moving into song at the end of each stanza. Instrumentally, the movement alternates between traditional Chinese melodic fragments (played mostly on *pipa* and *er-hu*) that are interrupted by the "Western" instruments interjecting dissonant or disjunctive comments. The *pipa* then has a long solo passage in which it plays in the traditional narrative style depicting battle scenes, accompanied by urgent percussion. This poem too is from the perspective of a latter-day Chinese American and opens with a chanted evocation of ancestral labor:

> I am the daughter of
>   seafarers, gold miners, quartz miners
>   railroad workers, farmworkers
>   garment workers, factory workers
>   restaurant workers, laundryman
>   houseboys, maids, scholars
>   rebels, gamblers, poets
>   paper sons ...

At the end of this verse, Lim's chanting shifts to blues-inflected song and this too "speaks" a certain sensibility — the meeting ground of the Asian American and the African American and the implicit historical critique contained in the act of participating in an African American musical genre. These moments, brief as they are, offer a kind of melodic punctuation that closes each verse. Lim chants over a foundation of ponderous sustained chords that rock, stepwise, up and down, creating a feeling of endless work. (Audio Example 2.3.) The middle of the movement is an extended free improvisation (referred to above) featuring Wong over driving percussion.

The third movement is built around a poem from Angel Island, "Random Thoughts While Staying in the Building," beginning with a reference to "Island," as Angel Island was called by Chinese immigrants. It opens with a quiet sax ostinato that continues through Lim's delivery of the poem:

> For days I have been without freedom on Island.
> In reduced circumstances now, I mingle with the prisoners.
> Grievances fill my belly; I rely on poetry to express them.
> A pile of clods bloat my chest and I wash it with wine.
> Because my country is weak, I have become aware of the laws of growth and decay.
> In pursuit of wealth, I have come to understand the principles of expansion and diminution.
> While I am idle, I have this wild dream
> That I have gained the western barbarian's consent to enter America.

Lim enacts the despair in this poem by "reading" it with a flat resignation, imbuing the last words, "enter America," with a quiet longing. (Audio Example 2.4.) The fourth movement is a reprise of "Yellow Woman" and the fifth is an Angel Island poem, discussed in more detail below because Jang's fascination with it has led him to use it in both suites.

Island: Immigrant Suite No. 2 was performed by the renowned Kronos Quartet with Cantonese opera singer Eva Tam. Broadcast live in the Bay Area on May 4, 1996, it is as yet unreleased. Before rehearsing the work with the Kronos Quartet, Jang took lead violinist David Harrington out to Angel Island to see the poems. Harrington said, "I couldn't believe what I was seeing there — and the fact that I didn't know anything about it and that I've lived here for many, many years, was shocking in itself." Jang explained the five-movement work as follows:

> This is part of my musical language, which is based on the reconstruction of Chinese sorrow songs, within a modern jazz or new music context, but from a Chinese American perspective. ... The way these poems are performed, they blur the boundaries between recitation and song — sometimes the poems are performed as spoken, or sung, or something in between. ... The first three movements express the sadness, loneliness at being confined in the wooden building. The latter movements are mainly expressions of defiance — in fact, the last movement is a line taken from the Tang dynasty, that the Chinese continue that legacy and put it in the early twentieth-century context, and now I think it is very contemporary to today, in terms of all the anti-immigrant legislation and this climate of immigrant-bashing and so forth. So the last movement says that it's up to all of us to roll back the wild wave...

Each of the movements draws on one poem, if not several. The singer ranges from *muk-yu* style singing, to *naamyam* (or *nanyin,* a Cantonese narrative song form) style singing, to Cantonese opera singing. At one point in the final movement, the singer shouts in Cantonese, "Stop Prop 187! H.R. 2202!" To grasp Jang's musical decisions, one must understand how he deploys cultural reference and borrowing in service of the political. Jang is familiar with traditional Chinese musical forms but does not simply replicate them. Even when he brings traditionally trained Chinese musicians into his works (as he has on many occasions, in many pieces), he draws on their expertise and training *and* asks them to try new things. In drawing on various Cantonese singing styles in *Immigrant Suite No. 2,* he is not offering the listener an "authentic" experience. He writes, "As a third generation Chinese American artist, I cannot express or musically "replicate" the experience of this first generation of Chinese poets" (Jang 1997c, liner notes). Rather, he "builds on" their tradition, using poetry and music to speak to "the present human condition" in an idiom that blends Then and Now, Here and There. The experience of listening to the Kronos Quartet play is both moving and disorienting (and I mean that in both senses). If you didn't "know" it was the Kronos, you might think it was several *er-hu* players riffing on Chinese melodies in a sometimes dreamlike and sometimes aggressive manner. Their "straight" rendition of Cantonese *naamyam* accompaniment in the second movement is replaced in the third movement with urgent fragmented phrases that shift restlessly between "Cantonese" styles and more dissonant modernist art music language, which is in fact foregrounded in the fourth and fifth movements as the emphasis shifts from nostalgia to defiance. Importantly, the musical styles in which the poetry is heard remains Cantonese throughout, embodied sonically in Eva Tam's voice. Jang employed a number of different musical valences in his writing for the quartet, and his ability to produce the musical language of Western modernist late-twentieth-century composition commands a certain cultural capital that is hard to articulate because it is refracted through Cantonese sensibilities. It's not a matter of arguing that *Suite No. 2* is "more" or "less" Western or Cantonese, or that it is "Asian American" because it puts the two into conversation. Jang was able to write in a way that the Kronos Quartet found interesting and this moved his work (at least temporarily) into a different milieu: from the Bay Area jazz scene to a top-billed string quartet, from a collaborative, semi-improvisational jazz idiom to a written score.

Both suites end with movements devoted to the same poem, Poem 39 (Lai, Lim and Yung 1980: 88):

> Twice I have passed through the blue ocean, experienced the wind and dust of journey.
> Confinement in the wooden building has pained me doubly.
> With a weak country, we must all join together in urgent effort.
> It depends on all of us together to roll back the wild wave.

Jang recontextualizes the last line, deliberately making "the wild wave" a metaphor for the anti-immigrant hysteria of the mid-1990s. He was well aware that the poem's author probably meant something rather, but not entirely, different. It was common Chinese poetic practice to create intertextual depth and nuance by referring to classical works in clever or evocative ways; the last line is a quotation from an essay by Han Yu (768–824 A.D.), a Tang dynasty official, whose phrase, "To return the violent wave that had fallen" meant to make an effort to restore declined fortunes (Lai, Lim and Yung 1980: 88, fn. 45). Quite a few of the poems at Angel Island refer to China as a "weak country," expressing despair and resentment that it had so little political clout with the U.S. In *Suite No. 1*, Lim reads the poem in English and the movement is startlingly short (only one minute and forty-eight seconds long): she "reads" the poem, the ensemble plays a four-phrase melody based on Chinese materials (with Lim joining in wordlessly halfway through) and the movement ends. (Audio Example 2.5.) The parallel movement in *Suite No. 2* is also quite short. The poem, read in Cantonese, is framed by loud, furious, chromatic string lines surging through asymmetrical meters that change every few measures, creating an effect of anger and off-kilter effort. (Figure 2.8.) Jang's double setting of this poem presented different challenges to him as a composer. As he put it, the final movement of *Suite No. 1* ran the risk of being too easily identified as "political" partly because of Genny Lim's vocal presence:

> I did not want the music to sound like an agit-prop cliché. With the *zhonghu* playing a melancholy Chinese sorrow song, the feeling is reflective and heroic. Francis (Wong) said this reminded him of the heroic soundtrack music in Bruce Lee films.

Jang was also aware that he was writing for different "worlds." Making strategic decisions about musical style led him in a different direction in *Suite No. 2*:

> I also think that agit prop music is more expected in the "jazz" world than the "classical" music world. I wanted to make a subtle statement without making any heavy-handed overtures...

The final movement of *Suite No. 2* is quite explicitly a critique of xenophobic legislation: its subtitle is "Stop Anti-Immigrant Exclusion Laws!" Jang notes that the challenge lay in creating a sensibility of protest in the instrumental parts while also foregrounding the virtuosity of the Kronos Quartet. All this stacks up to a challenge for any composer.

The political gesture of writing a work for string quartet and Cantonese opera singer — so appealing to me — created production problems that Jang managed to work around, though with certain implications. I had imagined the visual and sonic impact of Eva Tam's presence on stage with the quartet: she is a strikingly beautiful and androgynous woman, unquestionably Chinese. She dresses like a man and her voice is commanding — it has the deep resonance and volume of the best Chinese opera singers. The critical gesture of envoicing the poems through the person of a contemporary Cantonese immigrant (and a gender-bending one at that) appealed to me politically in any number of ways. But in the end, Eva Tam did not perform live with the Kronos Quartet — ever. The practical concerns of touring won out: another artist means additional expenses (artist fee, hotel, airfare); had she been unavailable for any one performance, finding another Cantonese opera singer would have been difficult. Her part was therefore prerecorded: she recited the poems that Jang had chosen and he cued her entrances and anticipated her phrasing and pacing. Her voice is thus a phantom presence in both the broadcast premiere and in the score: note that the vocal part is almost entirely undesignated, enigmatic, in Jang's written score. Quite literally, there is a ghost in the machine. In another way, though, her voice dictated the entire performance. Jang told me that for the first two movements, he wrote the string

Figure 2.8a Excerpt from Jon Jang's score to *Island: The Immigrant Suite No 2*, excerpt from Movement V (pp. 19–21 of the score). (Reproduced with the permission of Jon Jang.)

quartet part based on her phrasing and pacing. In perhaps the most basic way, then, Tam's performance of the poems generated the rest of the piece. The quartet performed the work with a click track that enabled them to coordinate their live playing with her recorded voice. I had imagined an

Figure 2.8b

encounter that didn't happen, or rather, an encounter that happened only sonically, musically. Jang notes that Tam attended the premiere but as an audience member and this final distancing of the poems from her voice saddens me the most of all.

The political economies that allow me to allow *you* to hear (or only see) Jang's music is also part of the poems' transformations. Jang's longtime

Figure 2.8c

commitment to recording his works on independent labels (e.g., Asian Improv aRts, Soul Note, etc.) enables the continued circulation of those recorded sounds through legal relationships that permit him a certain control over his music. Getting permission from Soul Note to include excerpts from Jang's *Immigrant Suite No. 1* was thus relatively easy. Jang's opportunity to write a work for the Kronos Quartet (well known for their

Figure 2.8d

interest in commissioning new and "unusual" works) not only led him to write for perhaps *the* quintessential high art ensemble — the string quartet — but also put him in different relationship to the performed sounds of his own music. The Kronos Quartet is a business entity that commands control over its musical products, both written and recorded. *Immigrant Suite No. 2* is as yet unreleased by the Kronos Quartet, so I couldn't get permission to include excerpts from the recorded broadcast of the premiere performance though I am able to include parts of the score here. The poems are thus embedded in new webs of ownership. First inscribed anonymously on the barracks walls, the poems are not only protected by the U.S. government but are also owned by it. It was never Genny Lim's or Jon Jang's intention to own the poems — indeed, the idea is completely counter to their political and creative motivations — but Lim's publication of the poems (Lai, Lim and Yung 1980) and her musical collaborations with Jang implant the poems in new works. Jang's work for the Kronos Quartet puts the poems into a new, rarefied system of ownership.

The question of cultural authenticity surfaces in this book in a number of different chapters. As an ethnomusicologist working in a poststructuralist ethnographic milieu, my intention is not to locate authenticity but to position expectations of it and I am particularly interested in assertions, like Jang's, that it's not there for the having. Performance (whether musical, dramatic, or both) "does" something to the poems. I doubt anyone would argue with that. The ways that performance foregrounds questions of cultural and historical location and the means by which one can "hear" this (or not) is the question. The unruliness of performance immediately raises issues of the audience. The Chinese immigrants who wrote and read the poems on the barracks walls knew that the words were for and by them; they must have been all too aware that their language was both an obstacle and a private place, a mark of their Otherness and the sound of home. Jang's and Lim's recastings of the poems play with language as a site of inscrutability and defiance. Hearing the poems move through different bodies (Chinese American actors, a Chinese American poet, a Chinese immigrant) opens up their meanings and renders them intelligible to new audiences even as these transformations create new vectors for political intervention. Island is the imaginative and performative bridge to Asian America. Focusing on the Angel Island poems and their transformations by Genny Lim and Jon Jang offers a look in miniature at the salient themes of this book: history, diaspora, immigration, the discursive construction of memory across generations, the emergence of new Asian American sensibilities and the role of performance in all this.

Asian American Memories

The place of memory in Asian American experience is vexed, risky. For second-, third-, fourth-, fifth-generation Asian Americans, arguing against a blood understanding of "home" is central to asserting Americanness. For Southeast Asian immigrants, coming into conversation with "the Asian American" runs the risk of denying very real connections to places/spaces they left under duress and, in diaspora, they reconstruct these spaces nostalgically, sometimes angrily and always sadly. In the past few years, I have seen young Filipino/a Americans and Vietnamese Americans move into newly vocal positions of authority within the Association for Asian American Studies. The annual conference is suddenly full of panels addressing these specific Southeast Asian American histories, and more than a few job announcements have appeared calling for specialists in Southeast Asian American studies. The Southeast Asian American has a nicely challenging role within Asian American studies, forcing a reconsideration of class and diaspora that has proven useful (if sometimes painful) for the field; Chinese American and Japanese American experiences can no longer be treated as emblematic of "the" Asian American experience.

Within academe, the young scholars working in this new area often speak out loudly, challengingly. Beyond, Southeast Asian American communities continue to struggle for place, space, a foothold. Thinking about forced diaspora brought me into Asian American studies, but this small movement pales in comparison with the fierce demonstrations outside a video store in Little Saigon in the summer of 1999, when its owner insisted on his right to display a North Vietnamese flag. Vietnamese/Americans from all over Southern California descended on him and his shop, furious. Memory wasn't, isn't, won't be merely evocative for them. If my memories of war, filtered through television and the newspapers, were as formative as I think they were, then the impact of Southeast Asia on Asian America must be written carefully. Thus ethnography: this multi-ethnic Chinese American is determined to learn something about Asian America by talking with Southeast Asian immigrants. From Fresno to Philadelphia to Orange County, I try to follow the songlines.

Endnotes

1. I refer to Khamvong Insixiengmai as "Khamvong" throughout not as a sign of familiarity but because this is the practice in Lao and Thai; one simply doesn't say "Mr. Insixiengmai," though one would normally precede a person's given name with a title, honorific, or kinship term (e.g., "older sibling," "uncle," "Mr.," etc.).
2. Bountong is also an accomplished singer of *lam* who now lives in Murfreesboro, Tennessee. He was recorded by Jacques Brunet on "Traditional Music of Southern Laos," Unesco Collection Musical Sources, Art Music of Southeast Asia, IX-4, Philips 6586.
3. The idea that language reflects and even forms a speaker's view of the world is not new. Benjamin Whorf and Edward Sapir set the stage for linguistic work in this area; Michael Silverstein (1979), Paul Friedrich (1979), Joshua Fishman (1982) and George Lakoff (1987) have more recently extended this approach to language. A few ethnomusicologists have taken a close look at the discourse surrounding musical acts. Keil's discussion of Tiv musical terminology is especially evocative. Ames and King's *Glossary of Hausa Music and Its Social Contexts* (1971) and Faruqi's *An Annotated Glossary of Arabic Musical Terms* (1981) are probably the most detailed studies of their kind to date, although they focus on terminology rather than discourse. Roseman (1986) explores the metaphors of the path and the journey in her work on the curative dream music of the Temiar. Stone's work on the Kpelle (1982) and Feld's study of Kaluli aesthetics (1982) use specialized musical vocabulary as a lens through which to experience performance events and indigenous aesthetics; both will be returned to later. Seeger's discussion of two Suyá Indian song genres (1979) addresses the ceremonial contextualization of song by explaining why the genre known as *ngere* is best translated as a "communicative act" rather than "song," "dance," or "ceremony."

4. Some general considerations are necessary to contextualize the conversation. It was the first (and, to date, only) time Khamvong and I had met. Khamvong and his *khaen* player were wearing suits and ties for the occasion and Khamvong knew only that I was a scholar and a friend of *Acaan* Terry Miller's who had come a long way to see him. The tone of our discussion was therefore somewhat formal, though it became less so as it went on.

5. Classifiers are a class of words that are grammatically necessary for any construction involving amounts or numbers. There are hundreds of classifiers in Lao and Thai that offer fascinating insight into worldview because they indicate the ways that people, animals, objects, etc., are culturally grouped. A few classifiers exist in the English language, e.g., a *flock* of geese, a *herd* of sheep, a *ream* of paper, etc.

6. Bauman (famously) refers to "the emergent quality of all performance" (1977:37–38): The emergent quality of performance resides in the interplay between communicative resources, individual competence, and the goals of the participants, within the context of particular situations.

7. In March 1988, I attended a symposium on cultural poetics (*Sulfur Live: A National Symposium on Poetry and Poetics*, Eastern Michigan University, 25–26 March 1988) where I heard Eliot Weinberger deliver a paper that indirectly illuminated aspects of Khamvong's art I had been trying to articulate for myself. Mr. Weinberger generously sent me a copy of this essay though it is as yet unpublished. I refer to this paper frequently because it speaks to Khamvong's cultural role more eloquently than anything else I have encountered, even though it addresses neither Khamvong nor Asia but rather poetry in its largest cultural sense.

8. Terry Miller, among others, has suggested that "popular" and "traditional" are not as dichotomized in Southeast Asia as in the West. Discussing Lao popular music in the United States, he says (1985a: 107): "Lao audiences do not see the issue as either traditional or acculturated.... Even the most traditional Lao singers, like Khamvong, will sing to the accompaniment of an electric combo or include a popular rendition of lam saravane."

9. All quotations in Khamvong's own words are from an interview with him in Fresno in February 1988, held at the home of his longtime friend and manager, Thongthip Rattanavilay. I have translated his comments from Lao into English throughout this essay.

3

Taking (to) the Street: Cambodian Immigrants in the Philadelphia Mummers Parade

A great city is nothing more
than a portrait of itself,
and yet when all is said and done,
its arsenals of scenes and images
are part of a deeply moving plan.

— Mark Helprin[1]

I have always loved cities. I like to live in them, to walk in them and ultimately I find them good to think in, despite their sometimes tragic land-scapes. I returned to Philadelphia in 1993 after many years away, and I was immediately seized by the identity politics of the Asian American in this large East Coast city; living in Center City, I couldn't help but consider both ethnicity and the streets as loci of control, redefinition and cooption. As a one-time resident of Philadelphia, as an Asian American and as a scholar of Southeast Asia and performance studies, I have found myself fascinated by the events I will address here, ever since I first heard of them. We are, of course, in the middle of an extended historical moment in which refugees from the war in mainland Southeast Asia are performa-tively and politically positioning themselves *vis-à-vis* other Americans, and I find myself compelled to witness these moments as they pass. This is, then, one scene among many.

The Mummers Parade is quintessentially Philadelphian. Parades and events that festivalize cities can both disrupt and reinscribe the power dynamics that grant any city its distinctive character. On almost every New Year's Day since 1900, White male working-class Philadelphia has adorned itself in satin, sequins and feathers and strutted up Broad Street to the sound of banjos. As a festival event, the parade can be interpreted in any number of ways, but it definitely enacts race, ethnicity, gender and class. It is a moment, reiterated every January 1st, when the mostly Italian American working class of South Philadelphia takes to the streets and sweeps en masse up the city's main artery to the symbolic center of this landscape, City Hall.

The Philadelphia Mummers Parade: Histories, Geographies

The first official — that is, city-sponsored — mummers parade in Philadelphia was held in 1900, but mumming and its attendant social structures were well established in South Philadelphia by the 1870s.[2] As a tradition, mummery stretches back to medieval Europe.[3] The Philadelphia mummers parade has direct historical connections with these traditions, but its distinctive character is the result of more than a century's cross-fertilization with other twentieth-century festival traditions including Mardi Gras and Brazilian carnival. In its history since the Civil War, Philadelphia mummery has been consistently associated with the working class, white immigrant groups and South Philadelphia neighborhoods. Today, the Mummers Parade has an elaborate social structure of different clubs and categories, and participation in the parade is contingent on strict rules and regulations defined by the Mummers Association, the official body that governs the parade. Although the clubs clearly play a variety of roles in the texture of South Philadelphia social life, and although they perform in different contexts throughout the year, the club members themselves are single-mindedly directed toward the parade. This is the high point of their year: this is the whole reason for their being. The parade is thoroughly reified, like any ritual, as its own purpose. The rhythm of the year is centered on New Year's Day. One way or the other, mummers are always directed toward New Year's Day and the parade; by January 2nd, postmortems are already leading to plans for the next year's parade. It's hard to articulate the centrality of this event for these South Philadelphia neighborhoods. In the week or so before Christmas, there is a nearly tactile energy and excitement in the air of the Italian market: by that time, many of the merchants — most of whom are mummers — are up late every night at their clubs, finishing costumes and rehearsing.

The parade as an annual moment of class and ethnic definition is shaped at a fundamental level by the social space of the neighborhoods that house many of the clubs. Although I have thus far generically referred to this area as South Philadelphia, the mapping of this imagined space is far more detailed than that. For many Philadelphians, the phrase "South Philadelphia" conjures up images of poor working class African American neighborhoods. The South Philadelphia of mummery is a rather different area. Sometimes referred to as "the Italian market area," the market itself is actually on its northwest boundary. (See Figure 3.1: the market is on the lower right-hand corner of the map, near G5.) Now known as Pennsport, this neighborhood is bounded on the north and south by Washington and Snyder Avenues, and to the east and west by the Delaware River and Fourth Street. The Mummers Museum is a local landmark (at Second and Washington), and over thirty mummers' clubhouses are found in this area (Heavens 1993). Notice that this neighborhood is barely — actually, mostly not — on the "Visitor Map" to which I am referring: it is literally on the edge of the Philadelphia packaged for tourists. This rowhouse neighborhood is closely knit, working class and largely Roman Catholic; many of its approximately ten thousand residents have lived there all their lives, and houses are rarely advertised for sale, instead passing from older to younger members of families (Heavens 1993). In the eighteenth and nineteenth centuries, this area was known as "the Neck," and even more specifically "the Swedish Neck": today, it is populated not only by Italian Americans but also by Philadelphians of Irish, Polish and Lithuanian descent. The geography of the neighborhood shapes, and is shaped by, mummery: Second Street, known as "Two Street" by those in the know, is the festive heart of pre- and post-parade revelry. The museum is on Two Street because of this tradition, not vice versa. During the weeks before the parade, mummers' string bands practice their routines under the Interstate 95 overpass that separates Front Street from Columbus Boulevard, redefining the landscape and soundscape of the Neck.

Before 1900, each mummers association held its own parade, usually in its own neighborhood, and local merchants would vie to attract the mummers to their shops with huge spreads of food. Mumming in the streets was locally based and in fact locally contained — a performance *by* locals *for* locals. Although Philadelphians from other parts of the city knew about the working class practice of New Year's masquerading, it was regarded by outsiders as quaint if safely contained and disruptive if not. When mummers roamed beyond their own neighborhoods, the quaint became threatening. An account from 1881 in a local magazine reports how costumed men and boys wandered the streets of lower Philadelphia all night on New Year's eve; note the metaphorical language of the following excerpt (quoted in Welch 1970: 36):

> This custom, doubtless a remnant of the Old English Christmas "mumming," grows year by year in Philadelphia and the mummers, becoming bolder, penetrate as far north as Chestnut Street.

Such "bold penetration" of social space was worthy of mention: to go "as far north as Chestnut Street," some thirteen blocks and fifteen minutes' walk from Washington Avenue in the Neck, was a significant social journey.

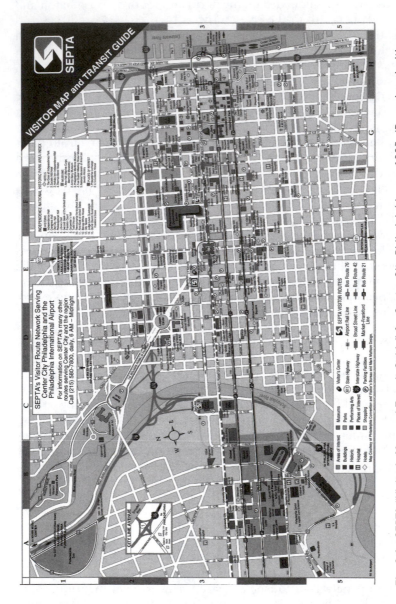

Fig. 3.1 SEPTA "Visitor's Map and Transit Guide" for Center City Philadelphia, ca. 1995. (Reproduced with permission of Christopher C. Salvatico and the South Eastern Pennsylvania Transit Authority.)

How, then, did the Mummers Parade end up on Broad Street, far outside its home neighborhoods? The disruption of Philadelphia's social landscape couldn't, obviously, occur gently or easily. Disruptive elements were essentially tamed. By 1899, the south Philadelphia parades were so well established that a local newspaper writer proposed a big Mummers Parade to mark the city's turn-of-the-century celebrations. He suggested an official reception for the mummers at City Hall on New Year's Eve, with fireworks and City Hall brightly lit; on New Year's Day, the official parade would be sponsored by the city, and cash prizes awarded. The Mayor not only agreed, but the City Council contributed $5,000 in prizes. Significantly, the mummers' associations initially reacted quite negatively: one historian notes that "they resented city interference with their Parade" (Welch 1970: 43). After many meetings, the clubs and the city came to an agreement, and the parade has, at least officially, been a civic-sanctioned event ever since.

The parade can be interpreted as a celebration of White working class identity, with an ongoing relationship of contestation with the city as a civic institution. This is typical of urban festival events in general: their histories are almost always stories of pendulum swings between control and disruption, cooption and subversion. Nor are these either/or propositions: urban festival events often contain all these elements at any given moment, and at any level of social analysis, whether at the level of street interaction or of government institutions (Falassi 1987: 2–3).

But the Mummers Parade is also part of a centuries'-old conversation about Otherness and intercultural contact. In medieval Europe, mumming revolved around Otherness of many kinds: Turks and Saracens figured prominently in the mumming of the Crusades, and cross-dressing by men as animals and women explored constructions of gender. In nineteenth- and twentieth-century America, Mardi Gras and the Mummers Parade have been predicated on what might politely be called reversals and inversions — or more directly seen as imbued with identity politics — as festivalized moments in which race, ethnicity and class meet head on. In New Orleans, the *krewes* of White male society parade through the streets during Mardi Gras as African warriors, blackface minstrels, Arabs and Turks, at the same time as African Americans and Black Creoles mask subversively as "Indians" (Lipsitz 1990: 233.253). In the 1994 Philadelphia Mummers Parade, I watched a phantasmagoria of invented ethnicity parade across my television screen. Some of these orientalized Others are doubly or even triply mediated. What are we to make, for instance, of a club whose costumes and music are based on Disney's *Aladdin*?

Riding hard on the heels of these rites of Dionysian orientalism are the cultural politics of city ordinances attempting to control racist representations and to remove class and race barriers to participation.[4] The Mummers Parade has a troubled history of race relations. The use of blackface, long a staple of mummery, was banned just before the 1964 parade after bitter public battles among the NAACP, the Common Pleas Court of Philadelphia, the Philadelphia Bar Association's Panel on Community Tensions, and the Mummers Association.[5] The Mummers Association maintained that the basic issue was one of censorship and freedom of expression; the NAACP saw it differently. Tensions were so high that three thousand police officers were assigned to the 1964 parade. Many of the mummers' string bands refused to play as they marched through the African American districts of South Broad Street; other mummers wore blueface, greenface and purpleface to subvert the ban. One of the comic clubs staged a sit-in in the middle of the street, chanting, "Negroes sat down in City Hall, we'll sit down here," and thus briefly coopted the theater of civil disobedience. At the end of the parade, several clubs marched back down Two Street chanting, "The Democrats own Broad Street; we own Second Street" (Welch 1970: 152–54).

In short, the sounds and sights of the mummers clubs have complex overlapping histories of ethnic stereotyping and representation. Deeply reframed as fun and fantasy, the mummers' costumes and performance themes could be seen as a performative means of containing the Other through parody. But all of this runs more deeply still, because the mummers' perception of themselves as engaged in subaltern resistance is profound. One of the major books on the history of the Mummers Parade, *Oh! Dem Golden Slippers*, by folklorist Charles Welch, is a valorization of mummers' resistance to real and imagined efforts to contain their activities. Anything that speaks of "The City" has prompted resistance, and this is at least part of the mummers' paradoxical history of portraying themselves as Others even when faced with the real thing, as I will explain.

Bold Penetrations

By the mid-1980s, however, the Other had in fact begun to penetrate Pennsport and the Italian market area. As the second wave of post-war Southeast Asian immigrants arrived in the U.S., this neighborhood attracted large numbers of Vietnamese and Cambodians. When I left Philadelphia in 1983, the market was dominated by Italian Americans; when I returned ten years later, every third or fourth shop was run by Southeast Asians or Koreans.[6] By 1993, the greater Philadelphia area was home to over eight thousand Cambodians, and one of two areas of concentration within the city was in Pennsport. In 1987, the Cambodian Association bought the site of a former Presbyterian church and established a Buddhist temple in the heart of Pennsport, at Third and Greenwich Streets (Heavens 1993). In 1993, a troupe of Cambodian American performers participated in the Mummers Parade, and this, to say the least, bears examination.

My account of these events is not ethnographic: I have reconstructed my own version of what I think happened, but I wasn't there, and if an

ethnographic account is to be written, it is up to any of the actual participants to do so, whether the Cambodians, local folklorists,[7] or mummers. I
will deal with this event as an allegory in James Clifford's sense — as a par-
able, a story with an underpinning in moral play, a story we tell ourselves
about ourselves (Clifford 1986). The parade is, among other things, a metonymic representation of ethnic relations in South Philadelphia, and I
want to examine the self-conscious reading of the parade as allegory by the
participants and the media.

When ethnic groups interact across lines of race and class in urban contexts, it is rarely by chance. The Palelei Cambodian Buddhist Temple is two
doors down from the Golden Sunrise Fancy Club house, but this alone
doesn't mean that the two groups would have ever encountered each other
without a go-between.[8] The Cambodians and the mummers were literally
brought together, not by neighborliness but by the Philadelphia Folklore
Project, an independent public folklife agency that had conducted long-
term projects with both groups of performers.[9] Several years before,
researchers with the Project had worked closely with members of Golden
Sunrise and produced a videotape on their tradition of fancy costume-
making (Noyes, Greenberg and Kodish 1990). In the 1990s, the Project
began to support activities by Cambodian artists and performers in the
Pennsport area.[10] Introducing the Cambodian performers to the members
of Golden Sunrise was a self-conscious effort to create bridges between
communities through the performing arts. Debora Kodish, the founder
and director of the Project, took one of the Khmer performers, a young
woman named Leendavy Koung, to the Golden Sunrise clubhouse in February 1992 and introduced her to Palma Lucas, the club's chief costume-
maker and mother-in-law of the club's captain. The initial point of contact
was apparently aesthetic: Khmer dance drama costumes are in some ways
remarkably similar to mummers' costumes — both are brightly colored
and covered with sequins. Leendavy was immediately taken by the mummers' costumes, and reacted with pleasure to a familiar aesthetic of sparkly
busyness.[11]

After this initial contact, it was many months before the two groups
actually discussed the idea of including Cambodian performers in the
parade. Meanwhile, Leendavy and her father, Koung Peang, a highly
respected artist and performer, were intensely busy with their own activities, supported by the Philadelphia Folklore Project. During 1992–93, the
Project invited Koung Peang to teach a weekly class in the traditional
Cambodian arts, in which he covered drawing, painting, mask-making,
beadwork and costume design, and eventually music, dance and acting.
His students were Cambodian young people from the area. Although the
class was initially process oriented, it eventually became clear that Koung
Peang had more specific goals in mind. He began to prepare his students
for a performance of *lakhon bassak*, a uniquely Khmer form of dance
drama that combines Chinese, Vietnamese and Khmer elements into a

lively form of working class theater. What had begun as an open-ended arts class became training for a performance of "Tipsongva," a traditional Khmer story involving a princess and her involved rise to the throne.[12] Bill Westerman, a Project staff member, remembers how he realized that Koung Peang had more ideas still (Westerman 1994a: 15):

> Koung Peang asked me in an interview in the early fall [of 1992] if the American New Year's [mummers'] parade was open to participation by a Cambodian arts group. At this point a combination of things occurred which changed the focus of the class for good. Attention shifted away from a process-oriented art class with no definite end-product or outcome, which seemed to have been an issue for Koung Peang if unspoken at the outset, towards preparation for concrete performances ...

Koung Peang knew of his daughter Leendavy's visit to the Golden Sunrise clubhouse, of course, but it was his idea to actually participate in the parade — and on Khmer terms. Koung Peang had his own reasons for wanting to participate in the parade. It seems likely that he was less interested in the parade's history and meaning for Philadelphians than he was in its importance as a stage. This is not to say that he was *unaware* of the parade's form and function, either: like his daughter, he was pleased by the aesthetic crossover between the spectacle of mummery and *lakhon bassak* as well as certain similarities between the parade and Cambodian New Year's processionals, known as *chayyam*. In short, Koung Peang apparently identified points of contact *with Khmer traditions*, and not vice versa.

What about the other parties involved? Debora Kodish, the Project director, was of course a key figure: she "pushed the idea of a merger" between the Cambodians and the mummers, as one newspaper article put it (Hollman 1992b), because she was ideologically and emotionally committed to community bridge-building through the arts. And while the members of Golden Sunrise, without such activist intervention, might never have met their Cambodian neighbors, let alone invited them into the parade, they too recognized the social worth of such a gesture. David Shuster, the captain of Golden Sunrise, initially left it up to the club members to decide collectively whether to invite the Cambodians to participate under their sponsorship. One newspaper article (Hollman 1992b) states that:

> Shuster figured he might have to sell the idea (to the club members), but it really wasn't necessary. Other club members were just as excited. They had a tradition of innovation to uphold. As any self-respecting club member will tell you, the first female to march in a "handsome" costume — those elaborate, sequined outfits with huge, ponderous backpieces — marched with the Golden Sunrise fancies.

In other words, certain members of Golden Sunrise saw their club as emblematic of innovation and change in mummers' traditions — and this represents one school of thought in the contentious world of mummery, where tradition and change are in constant conflict. Golden Sunrise had already stretched the rules by costuming a woman; they were pleased to see themselves as innovating by including yet another kind of outsider in the tradition.[13]

It was agreed that the Cambodians, calling themselves "The Cambodian-American Arts Group," would compete in the Special Mention category. In the marvelously arcane, rule-bound world of the mummers competition, any club in the Fancy Costume Division must compete in nine established categories. These categories have long histories. The Captain is a category unto himself, but he can be attended by up to nineteen Juveniles, or young club members; the Handsome Costume is traditionally a huge frame suit that can use wheels but not any motors; the Fancy Trio must include three identically costumed members and so on. The Special Mention Category, however, is the most flexible. Although a Fancy Club must include at least one group in the Special Mention category, they can have up to nine. The more competitors in a category, the greater chance the club has for winning prizes and points, but the greater the outlay of money. On the other hand, competitors in the Special Mention category don't have to be official club members,[14] so it was ideal for the Cambodians. They didn't have to be club members (in fact, I don't think this was even discussed): they only had to be registered with Golden Sunrise as fellow competitors. They were a low risk for the club since no outlay of club funds was required, but Golden Sunrise stood to gain from any points that might be earned.

Still, it's important to examine the nature of the cross-cultural contact between the two groups. The Cambodian group marched separately, under the sponsorship of Golden Sunrise but apart from the club's acts. Most of the Cambodians and mummers didn't actually meet until just two weeks before the parade, and representatives of Golden Sunrise didn't even see the Cambodians in rehearsal until two days before the parade, on December 30th, at the temple; this was their first (and as far as I know, only) visit to the temple. Nevertheless, the newspapers and television news teams, always looking for new ways to do stories on the Mummers Parade, were quite taken by the idea of Southeast Asian participation, and a number of articles and human interest spots appeared in the days before the parade. All emphasized the bonhomie and cooperation among the groups and the Cambodians' commitment to tradition. None of the newspaper photographs showed the Cambodians and mummers together, however: after decades of photographing mummers, the reporters were more interested in capturing the newcomers, and the Cambodians were consistently represented as vividly exotic and tradition bound. On New Year's Eve, for instance, two photos appeared in *The Philadelphia Inquirer*, one showing Koung Peang intently painting a student's face into a warrior king's frown, the other showing "two young Cambodians," nameless, masked and costumed as the Khmer hermit-teacher and his clown-servant (Hollman 1992b). Although the media was *taken* by the idea of cross-cultural fertilization in the Mummers Parade, the Cambodian performers themselves were depicted in newspaper photos not as innovating and adaptive, but as isolated and timelessly Asian.

Before dawn on January 1st, the Cambodian troupe gathered at Koung Peang's house to dress; several blocks away, the Golden Sunrise clubhouse was in a similar state of intense activity. When they got in line at Broad and Snyder Streets, the starting point of the parade, some members of Golden Sunrise were concerned that the Cambodians would be cold in their thin costumes and offered sweaters — and that was pretty much the extent of their interaction during the event itself. Several miles and many hours later, Golden Sunrise was declared the winner of the Fancy Costume Division with a total of 1,330 points and a cash prize of $7,834.[15] The Cambodian troupe earned a $350 prize that Golden Sunrise gave to them directly.

The structure and the spectacle of the parade are also part of its politics. Almost every year, *The Philadelphia Inquirer* publishes a map of the parade route in the New Year's Day edition. Along with the locations for fast food restaurants and portable toilets, the so-called "performance stops" are usually marked, five in 1993. These indicated where each group was to stop and do its choreographed number (in contrast to moving along the parade route). The first four stops were for the crowds; the fifth and final stop was at City Hall for the judges' stand. Television cameras are always stationed up and down the parade route and roaming reporters are everywhere, interviewing as many octagenarian mummers as they can find. Still, at least two thirds of the television broadcast is always from the "Mayor's and TV booths" at City Hall. Television broadcast has, over the years, begun to shape the event at a basic level. Clubs save their best performance for City Hall, not only because this is where they are judged but also because this is when they are most likely to appear on television. In 1994, for instance, Golden Sunrise had so many acts that it was on the air for nearly forty minutes. For the parade-goers, however, the event at street level can have a certain ennui. Clubs aren't "on" for the whole parade: they save themselves for the designated performance stops and the TV cameras. Near the performance stops, parade marshalls may keep groups as much as several blocks apart so that their music won't sonically overlap. While the television broadcast of the parade is filled with non-stop chatter, performances, interviews and commercials, the streetside experience of the event is quite different and demands considerable patience.

I don't have television footage of the 1993 parade (I wasn't yet in Philadelphia), but I watched Golden Sunrise compete in the 1994 parade. The conventions of television coverage were essentially identical, I've been told, to the year before. The club's costumes and themes were different, but the club members were mostly the same, and their theme was, once again, an extended reimagining of race. Titled "Out of Africa," the Captain's performance — the first and most important of any club's competitive categories — featured more than forty club members (adorned with beads, feathers, tinsel and sequins) who danced as "Africans," their faces painted into multicolored masks. The prelude to their act featured prerecorded music, generically described by the newscasters as "authentic African drumming," which segued into "new wave music"; the club members waved their spears and stomped through their choreography, beads swinging. Several television cameras caught it all, complete with closeups and special attention to the Captain's ("the African chief's") presiding role.

The footage from 1993 was apparently similar in both coverage and detail: Golden Sunrise's acts, especially the Captain's performance, were given much airtime, but the Cambodians never appeared on television at all. I think it is safe to say that Cambodians all over Philadelphia had their VCRs set on "record." But the Cambodian troupe simply never made it onto the air.[16] This was partly bad luck; as Palma Lucas from Golden Sunrise told me, you never know whether you'll get on TV, because the parade goes on through commercial breaks. Also, there are two judging stands, A and B, at City Hall; the club captains and the other high-status acts are judged at the A Stand, which is given far more airtime than the B Stand, where the Special Mention and Juvenile categories are judged. The Cambodians performed at the B Stand, and never appeared on television.

Nevertheless, I know what the Cambodians looked like because they videotaped themselves.[17] Throughout the parade, the performers handed a video camera back and forth among themselves. Their footage shows them walking along Broad Street behind a Golden Sunrise act comprising large bat-like creatures: the Cambodians, by comparison, look strikingly human and unchoreographed, betwixt and between fantasies. Their costumes were simplified adaptations of Khmer stage costumes. Several performers were dressed as the main characters in "Tipsongva"; others wore masks from the *Reamker,* the Khmer version of the *Ramayana,* and a small army of monkey-warriors plus a hermit-teacher thus accompanied Tipsongva. But the collision of such stories (and worlds) is common in much Southeast Asian drama, and one could indeed say that it was central to the entire parade. At the conclusion of their two-and-a-half-mile walk up Broad Street, the Cambodians lined up in front of City Hall, waiting to perform at the B Stand where they were to be judged, and stood in anticipatory silence, bombarded by the band music from the act before them. Their judged performance differed significantly from the slick choreography of the Golden Sunrise Captain, whose precision movement was borrowed from football halftime shows and Broadway musicals. In comparison, the Cambodian performance involved multiple worlds and multiple choreographies. The monkeys and demons of the *Reamker* battled it out while, in another era, Tipsongva confronted an enemy king and engaged him in a stick fight. At least three things were going on at once. The musicians kept up a steady pattern of drums, gongs and cymbals; the camera peered over the shoulder of a drummer, Cambodians gazing at Cambodians. Koung Peang led the dancers into a closing cadence with his hand cymbals, bringing all simultaneities to a halt.

Agents, Ironies and Otherness

Parades and urban festival events can disrupt or reinscribe a city's patterns of power and authority. The Mummers Parade may have begun as a nineteenth-century working class reclamation of street space, but the parade in the late twentieth century is something else again, an exercise in hypercontrol, metacontrol, from both within and without. The parade speaks order and centralized control even as it enacts a working class taking of the street. And yet, the paradox isn't. It's a taking *to* the street that also constitutes *taking* the street — an act of wresting control and authority — yet the frame that allows it also controls it.

The Cambodians' participation in the parade meant something different to nearly everyone involved. The media, delighted to find such a harmless, depoliticized symbol of multiculturalism, played up the Cambodians' Otherness in pre-parade articles. But when it came down to the crucial decisions of who got airtime, the Cambodians were invisible. The members of Golden Sunrise, while meaning well, were operating under a similar model of multiculturalism that acts as a leveler of difference: they grasped at what sameness they could, making much of the similarities in costume-making and in the value placed on tradition and its transmission to the next generation. Koung Peang, too, was interested in samenesses — but only up to a point. He has no investment in the rhetoric of multiculturalism. He was simply determined to do what he does — to perform *lakhon bassak* — and he had a performer's eye for finding the best venue he could. Essentially, he did the parade on his own terms. But then, so did the mummers. One could also say that the Cambodians were absorbed into the baroque play of Otherness that defines the parade as a whole. So was the whole experiment a kind of parallel play, an exercise in hyperfestivity where anything can mean anything?

I would argue that media coverage of Southeast Asian immigrants in the 1990s is largely depoliticized in Philadelphia, perhaps more broadly on the East Coast in general. There is a world of difference between newspaper articles on Southeast Asian diaspora populations and, say, the coverage of Korean Americans during the 1992 Los Angeles riots (see Palumbo-Liu 1994 for a discussion of this). Southeast Asians may present an ongoing challenge for cities and social services, but I sense that, as the war recedes into history, they are less and less a reminder of a troubled political past and more and more perceived as generic Asians in the imaginary of the city. The specific socioeconomic problems they face are quite real, but I suspect that the moral reminder they pose to memory is less and less present.

For now, the Otherness of African Americans has been carefully contained by the issue of blackface — which, since it's banned, is a problem solved. "Out of Africa" therefore isn't a problem. Its exuberant excesses aren't racist because there's no blackface in sight. Something similar happened with the Cambodian American arts group: they were rendered invisible by the surrounding excess. They were so outlandishly, gaudily real that they simply became another Other among many, and the rhetorical force of their realness lost its subversive potential.

It was all supposed to happen again in 1994 and I was standing by, batteries charged, hoping to capture it. The members of Golden Sunrise had reserved a slot for the Cambodians in their program — the same place in their Special Mention category. On their terms, it had been a successful experiment, and they were happy to give it another go. But the Cambodians never quite got it together. It had been seven months since their last *lakhon bassak* performance; they couldn't get rehearsal space at the temple or, in fact, anywhere; several dancers had moved away; everyone was busy. On January 1st, Golden Sunrise marched without them. But Palma Lucas, already planning next year's costumes, says she would hold the slot. Leendavy Koung said she envisioned a group of Cambodians from all over the U.S. — the best of the best, a huge group of performers, maybe some Lao and Vietnamese performers, too. She said she wanted to apply for grant money to bring the performers to Philadelphia for New Year's Day 1995. But Leab Koung, who played the character Tipsongva, is no longer with us — she died at the hands of an angry South Philadelphia boy in 1996 in a moment still too painful for me to write about here. I can almost accept this phantasmatic tradition of mummers whose faith in their own subversiveness renders their hegemonic control of Others (whether real or a year in the making) quite invisible. I can also picture a crowd, a horde of Southeast Asians, dancing up Broad Street. But they will be so secure in their own authenticity that they will need no irony to make sense of their place in the event.

Endnotes

1. From *Winter's Tale*, p. xi. New York: Harcourt Brace Jovanovich, 1983.
2. See Welch 1970: 21–43 on the early history of the mummers' associations and parade. Susan Davis' *Parades and Power: Street Theater in Nineteenth-Century Philadelphia* (1986) looks closely at parades, and effectively demonstrates that the city's parades have almost always involved tensions of class relations and the control of public space.
3. The practice of masquerading around Christmas and the New Year dates back to at least the fourteenth century, and in England, men dressed as clowns, animals and women were going from house to house, performing songs and short skits in return for food and drink, by the fifteenth century (Welch 1970: 5). A vivid account of Christmas mummery can be found in Thomas Hardy's *The Return of the Native* (Book Two, Chapters 4 through 6), set in Dorset between 1840 and 1850. A group of laborers, all men, prepare a performance of the traditional play, *Saint George*, with a cast of characters including Saint George, the Valient Soldier, the Saracen, the Turkish Knight, the Doctor and Father Christmas. According to Hardy, their wives and daughters help make their brilliantly decorated costumes, and the men rehearse their lines before walking to the home of the local landowner, where they perform the play for the enjoyment of guests at the annual Christmas party. Afterward, the hosts insist that the mummers stay for dinner, but class conventions place them in an anteroom, where they can see the party but are not part of it.
4. The Mummers Parade isn't the only civic festival event in which ethnic representations have been contested. Just before the 1992 Carnival season in New Orleans, the New Orleans City Council passed a civil rights ordinance forbidding discrimination on the basis of race, creed, color, religion, national origin, ancestry, sex or sexual orientation, age, physical condition or disability; it specifically addressed "clubs and membership organizations that, under City law, enjoy a specially protected privilege of parading during the restricted Carnival parade season" (Vennman 1993: 77, 90–95).
5. I know of only one discussion of the ordinance, in Welch (1970: 136, 150–59), but this description is at best a beginning. Welch's study is as much a fan's account as a historian's, and his evaluation of the parade's cultural politics is limited. His examination of the blackface debate and the introduction of women into the parade is, tellingly, in a chapter titled "Don't Rain on My Parade," which describes various obstacles that mummers have faced over the years — bad weather conditions, black resistance to racist representation and women's participation all fall into this category. While Welch recognizes the possibility of racism, his own loyalties clearly lie with the mummers and their emphasis on freedom of expression, and his discussion of the debates in 1963–64 thus have an odd noncommittal tone, ultimately celebrating the mummers' resistance to this and any ordinances designed to control their activities.

   In a newspaper article about a mummers' club ritual visit to the grave of James A. Bland, composer of what became the mummers' theme song, "Oh! Dem Golden Slippers," the reporter (Hollman 1992a) notes: "Critics have found exquisite irony in the notion of white Mummers making an anthem of a song written by an African American. After all, they will tell you, the history of Mummery is replete with examples of prejudice and racism."

   "Oh! Dem Golden Slippers" was first heard in the parade in 1905, introduced by a minstrel performer (Welch 1970: 123). In fact, the not-so-distant echoes of the minstrel show can be heard in the music of the mummers' string bands, one of the four basic categories for competition in the parade. String bands are a clear descendant of minstrel bands, emphasizing steel-string banjos and, more recently, sax, accordion, glockenspiel and snare drum. More accurately, the late twentieth-century string band is an odd pastiche of minstrel influences (i.e., the banjo), swing bands and marching bands. Welch (1970: 120) notes that the standard string band instrumentation is banjos (in a 1:4 ratio to other instruments), saxophones (also 1:4), eight accordions, two glockenspiels, one bass drum and one snare drum; other instruments, including violins, clarinets, guitars, mandolins and trumpets, may be added.

6. I don't know of any sociological or demographic studies addressing this change, but I would guess that the area attracted Southeast Asian immigrants for several reasons. First, the Chinatown area north of Market Street is already crowded and rentals, whether commercial or residential, are quite high. Second, the Italian market area was already well established as a center for fresh produce and market retail business. Finally, property values are low: the median Pennsport home price in 1993 was $50,000.

7. Bill Westerman and Debora Kodish (Director, Philadelphia Folklore Project) were closely involved with these events and have written a number of reports about the performance activities of the Cambodian community in Philadelphia. I am completely indebted to their work and to their generosity in sharing their accounts, materials and memories of these events. In no way do I mean to usurp their right to tell this story more completely; indeed, I await that more complete telling, because Bill and Debora are inspiring examples of public-sector folklorists who take their responsibilities as cultural workers vey seriously indeed. The Philadelphia Folklore Project publishes a newsletter that contains reports and information on the Cambodian community through the 1990s, and as far as I know, this community work continues.

8. This is not to say they weren't aware of each other. Local residents were quite aware of the temple's presence: when the Cambodian Association bought the property in 1987, the Pennsport Civic Association met to discuss how the temple might affect the neighborhood. Later, neighbors called for more discussions when they realized that the temple had a dormitory to house guests; their understanding of the temple's social functions didn't align with Cambodian customs in which temples are both public and private space. Furthermore, the local Cambodians knew about the Golden Sunrise clubhouse and had even been curious about the frantic pre-parade activities they saw on their street (Hollman 1992). Still, language and race barriers might not have been breached without outside influence.

9. The Philadelphia Folkore Project is described as follows in the program notes for a Cambodian dance drama performance (Koung and Westerman 1993): "About the Philadelphia Folklore Project: We are committed to paying attention to the fundamental ways in which people organize, understand, and share their experiences and knowledge.... We see folklife traditions as basic ways of representing diverse truths and perspectives, critical resources for exploring our own experiences and, ultimately, as powerful means for controlling our own destinies. We're seven years old this year — and we're an independent folklife agency with local roots, scholarly perspectives, activist programs and a commitment to taking arts and culture seriously. We assist artists and communities, conduct research, develop exhibitions, offer public programs, workshops and technical assistance, maintain an archive, and issue publications and resources."

10. To date, the Project has curated a major exhibit of Khmer art by Philadelphia artists ("Giants, Kings, and Celestial Angels: Teaching Khmer Arts in Philadelphia," shown at the Fleischer Art Memorial and at the Philadelphia Museum of Art in 1993); has published several working papers on Khmer oral histories and *lakhon bassak*, a form of dance drama; has issued a videotape life history of Leendavy Koung titled *Welcome to Philadelphia: Arts of Being Khmer in Philadelphia*; has sponsored a Cambodian arts class; has co-sponsored a production of *lakhon bassak*; and is in the process of publishing a monograph on the *lakhon bassak* tradition in Philadelphia.

11. My account of the 1993 Mummers Parade is based on a number of conversations with several people: Leendavy Koung, a staff member and researcher at the Philadelphia Folklore Project and daughter of Koung Peang; Debora Kodish, founder and director of the Philadelphia Folklore Project; Bill Westerman, a staff member and researcher at the Philadelphia Folklore Project whose extensive involvement with the Project's Cambodian work led to his participation in the 1993 parade; and Palma Lucas, costume-maker and designer for the Golden Sunrise Fancy Club. I am grateful for their time and patience in answering my many questions, and especially to Debora Kodish, who I hope will eventually write her own account of these events.

12. In the next six months, "Tipsongva" was performed in a number of different venues for contrasting audiences. In November 1992, a few scenes were performed at a Project-sponsored community concert. On January 1st, 1993, the class-turned-troupe marched in the Mummers Parade; in April 1993, they performed at the Buddhist temple for the Cambodian community (this performance was a benefit for the temple, which was partially destroyed by fire in March 1993). Of all the performances, this most closely resembled a performance in a Cambodian context. In May 1993, a final performance was given for a mostly Anglo-American audience at a local art center (the Painted Bride Art Center in Philadelphia, a gallery and performance space committed to avant-garde and multicultural performance). The program notes (Koung and Westerman 1993) were published by the Philadelphia Folklore Project.

13. Interestingly, the Philadelphia Folklore Project videotape documentary on Golden Sunrise (Noyes, Greenberg, and Kodish 1990) describes the club as working "within a more traditional framework," and contrasts its "traditional motifs" with the tradition-stretching frame suits of another club, the Oregon Fancy Club. In general, the Fancy Clubs are seen by mummers as the most "traditional" of the four categories of competition — that is, the Comics, the String Bands and the Brigades are perceived as more open to change. Fancy Clubs take considerable pride, for instance, in their rules concerning costume-making: everything must be made by the club members themselves, who spend much of the year designing and realizing their ideas without help from "professionals."

14. Golden Sunrise club memberships are $20 a year, and voting privileges aren't given until the third year of membership; if members win prizes, the money goes to the club, not the individual competitors.

15. The cash prizes and points were gathered from nine categories of competition. The Golden Sunrise costume themes and categories were as follows (from Macklin 1993): Captain — David Shuster, $1,818; Handsome Costumes — "Devil with a Blue Dress," $720, "Iron Butterfly," $610, and "Spirit of Trinidad," $250; Fancy Trios — "Galaxy," $700, "Slippin' and Slidin'," $600, "Just Clownin' Around," $400, "Bee-U-Tiful," $250; King Clowns — "Toyland," $550 and "Winter Wonderland," $300; King Jockeys — "Over the Rainbow," $350, and "Let Freedom Ring," $200; Handsome Trims — "Jitterbugs," $650, "Papillon," $350; Special Mentions — "Geisha God," $625, "Alien Fish," $575, "Xanadu," $550, "Rags to Riches," $500, "Lady in Red," $450, "Sor Sdey Chnom Tmey Happy New Year" (The Cambodians), $350, "African Princess," $300, "The Wizard and His Crystal Ball," $200, "Carousel of Numbers," $200, "Midnight Lightening," $150, and "Inca Warrior," $75; Trio Pantomime Clowns — "Demons in the Dark," $275 and "Hot, Hot, Hot," $200; and Juveniles — "Struttin'," $170, "Mummer Fountain," $150, "European Clown," $130, "Cleopatra," $120, "The Dragon Fly," $120, "Centipede," $100, "Jungle Drums," $100, "American Heritage," $75, "Puss 'N Boots," $75, and "The Littlest Mummer," $50.

16. Bill Westerman, a Philadelphia Folklore Project member who played gong for the troupe in the parade, said that at certain points in the broadcast you could *hear* the gong cutting through other bands' music.

17. My thanks to Bill Westerman for sharing this video footage.

4

Karaoke, Mass Mediation and Agency in Vietnamese American Popular Music

In the spring of 1993, Pomona College — a small liberal arts school on the eastern edge of the greater Los Angeles area — held its annual Asian Pacific Islander Week, a week-long festival celebrating Asian and Pacific American culture. At noon on April 2nd, students, staff, and faculty gathered in a courtyard outside a dormitory and sat on the grass in the spring sun, eating lunch and watching as a group of teenagers set up a large sound system and casually tried out hip-hop moves on a small concrete stage area.

A good half hour after the scheduled starting time, music suddenly began to blare out of the sound system, and a crew of about ten young people — all dressed in baggy jeans and oversize tee-shirts, many wearing baseball caps on backwards, all Filipino American — strolled out and began to dance. The music came from a small sound booth at the back of the stage area, where the DJ stood and put on various LPs, occasionally scratching, adroitly bringing in and fading out different grooves for the dancers. After more than ten minutes of freeform hip-hop, the leader of the troupe finally appeared — La Quian,[1] a Filipino American rapper. Tall, commanding, La Quian rapped (in English) for almost an hour as his DJ laid on grooves and the dancers spun and strutted behind him. (Figure 4.1.) At the end of the hour, La Quian closed with the following words:

> They call me the La Quian
> The son of Raul (?)
> [*an unintelligible line*]
> Under a tree
> And with the freestyle/And in the meanwhile

Fig. 4.1 La Quian performing at Pomona College, Claremont, California, April 1993. Note his DJ, Jim, behind him. (Still from a videotape by Deborah Wong.)

So check it out
Oriental/Instrumental
Fundamental/Call me frontamental
Hip-hoprisy/If I go to college
Just to suppose/I seek some knowledge
With my dancers/They know how to house
I'm a [*unintelligible*] /Just wait out and out
So I step/Step to my right
I step to my left and then I touch my bicep
[*unintelligible phrase*] 'cause I go from the miiiiind
[*several unintelligible lines*]
Get the microphone/And I know what's up
[*an unintelligible line*]
But I'm not Vanilla[2]/I'm the man from Manila
Not Michael Jackson but yes I can tell ya
[*an unintelligible line*]
I want the microphone/And yes, I'm an agent
An Asian/Not a Black sensation
Got the microphone/So what's up with that
That blow your mind/Yes I can see
The A to the R to the N to the G
And if you know I can also do my thing/Do the swing
And I said like a sting/
Like a song like a [*unintelligible*] /Rhythm like a [*unintelligible*]
Cause you know/So so so
Big-big-bagow/Big-big-bagow
I come from the Riverside/Front end of the town

The side of the river/The river of the side
Get the microphone and I can satisfy
My my my/Just like Johnny Gibb (?)
Like Steven Segal[3]/I will be hard to kill
[*an unintelligible line*]
Make like this[4]/So I got to kick it
So what up, Jim/So give me some five
[*unintelligible*]/We come from the Riverside
[*unintelligible*] you know/[*unintelligible*] the microphone
And ya know
Nineteen-ninety-three/My name is La Quian
I want to thank all of ya'll [lovin'?]
For payin' attention to me/Give me your love
And all the Asians/Asian Pacific Islander Week
Good luck/And I'm out
Peace/And I'm out

With that, he saluted the crowd with a clenched fist and strode off the stage, followed by his crew.

This chapter reflects my ongoing interest in how Southeast Asians mediate their lives with music. Like people everywhere, Southeast Asians create, react to, interact with, and appropriate mass-mediated musics; they are enthusiastic participants in the transnational distribution of Western popular musics, and they support thriving popular music industries of their own. I am interested not in what mass-mediated musics do to people, but in what consumers and performers can do with such musics. Mass-mediated musics provide all-too-fertile ground for Marxist takes on the asymmetrical relationship between the multinational music industry and a Third World that is often depicted as passive and disempowered.[5] The power relationship is certainly there, but the ground-level reception of mass-mediated musics can be a site of real contestation and redefinition — and I demonstrate this by taking a look first at La Quian and then at karaoke, a genre that might seem emblematic of the disempowered actor and the reified, global techno-musics that take the people out of performance.

La Quian's performance had certain broad similarities with karaoke, but I want to look at what he was saying before I consider how he chose to say it. In the four short minutes of rapping just described, La Quian deliberately positioned himself in a number of telling ways. He is very clear about who he is: he's Filipino, he's Asian, he's not Vanilla — i.e., he's not White. Despite his chosen performance genre, he's an Asian, not a Black sensation. He's from Manila, he's from Riverside (a city on the eastern edge of the greater Los Angeles area). He's an agent (not a passive spectator). In short, he outlines a tangle of ethnicities and localities, all defining precisely who he is and who he isn't. The problems of positionality are fascinating — though, of course, they aren't problems for La Quian. If rap is the genre of young African American urban men, what is it doing in the mouth of a young Filipino American? Does he have any right to it? La Quian inserted himself into not only the genre but into actual recordings, too: his performance was a palimpsest of live spontaneous utterances and borrowed recorded sound. He positioned himself as a live landmark in a landscape of mediated sounds. His performance was a *tour de force* not only of mass-mediation but of liveness too, and the end result was powerful, confident, and highly entertaining.

All this suggests it's worth considering how the interaction of the canned and the live messes up and redefines our notions of the authentic in performance. While mass mediation is often considered a hegemonic force, people can (and do) reclaim mass-mediated musics for their own purposes, and I have seen how Southeast Asians consistently and enthusiastically put liveness back into genres that seem to epitomize the hegemonic evils of the transnational music industry. Obviously this happens all over the world, but the greater Los Angeles area is a particularly rich site for such performance activities because of its intensely immigrant character.

Karaoke in Diaspora

Karaoke first appeared in a Japanese bar in Kobe in 1972; the first karaoke machine (for 8-track tapes) was put on the market in 1976, and the rest is history. *Karaoke* is one of only a few Japanese words (along with *sushi, teriyaki, kamikaze,* and *ninja*) to enter the English language. *Kara* means "empty," and *oke* means "orchestra." The compound word itself is wonderfully evocative — it joins the central Japanese aesthetic of emptiness (e.g., *karate,* "empty hand") to the archetypal high-culture Western music ensemble, the orchestra. The word's interculturality and the full-circle return of *oke* to the English language point to the transformative power of intercultural performance.

Since the early 1970s, karaoke has gone through a series of cultural and technological transformations and has spread all over the world. Karaoke is especially popular in Asia, including Japan, of course, but also in Hong Kong, the People's Republic of China (Huang 1991), Taiwan, Korea, Hawaii (Harada 1992), and virtually every Southeast Asian country. Akiko Otake and Shûhei Hosokawa (1998) have written about the spread of karaoke through East Asia, paying careful attention to its different meanings in Taiwan, Hong Kong, Vietnam, Korea, and Okinawa due to the historical specificities of their relationships to Japan (as former colonizer and as twentieth-century economic powerhouse). As they point out (1998: 194):

[there is a] triangular connection between Japan, the West, and 'East Asia' (excluding Japan) with respect to the phenomenon of 'global karaoke'. Japan is ambiguous in the sense that it is geographically situated on the fringes of East Asia and has much more biological, historical, and cultural affinity with Asia than with the West, but at the same time in terms of the economy it is closer to and much more competitive with the West than East Asia. The triangle we are dealing with has much to do with the triple interconnected processes of Japanization, modernization and Asianization.

They argue that the specific public spaces created by karaoke in each country/culture are deeply shaped by this triangular relationship. While attending closely to the specificities of karaoke cultural practice, they provide an analysis of karaoke as a set of practices informed by complex historical and economic processes which are interconstitutive with matters of class, nation-building, economic imperialism, and "modernity." They point to embedded inter-Asian relationships wherein "Japanese consumer technologies are trying to promulgate in Asia neither a 'Western way of life' nor a 'Japanese way of life' but a Japanized version of the 'American way of life' …, that is more simply 'Japanese middle-class material life'" (1998: 197). When karaoke is exported to other Asian countries, a kind of "double domestication" thus takes place.

Interestingly, karaoke has been slightly slower to take off in Anglo-America (Armstrong 1992), but "karey-okie," as it's pronounced by most non-Asian Americans, is found in more and more bars. In fact, the transformation of *karaoke* into "karey-okie" points to the genre's transnational movement and a second intercultural transformation — a kind of full-circle imaginative return, in which *orchestra* becomes *oke* becomes "okie."[6] Rob Drew's ethnographic examination of karaoke in American bars (primarily on the east coast) is focused on karaoke as "a local music" that is central to "everyday, collective life" (Drew 2001: 15-16). Ultimately most concerned with the ways that karaoke is community-building, Drew stays (mostly) at the ground level of karaoke practice but thereby follows the threads connecting the industry and the world of mass-produced popular music to the intimate, particular settings of bars where enthusiasts define their own terms for pleasure (126). While it is not his purpose to compare karaoke in America with its praxis in any other part of the world, Drew offers a number of telling comparisons to karaoke in Asia and particularly in Japan, especially the American emphasis on using karaoke to feel like a "star." He writes, "Whereas in Japan, karaoke is seen as many things — a skill, an etiquette, a cultural emblem, a health aid, a purification rite, an aphrodisiac — in the United States, it is seen overwhelmingly as one thing: a chance to 'be a star'" (13). In critiquing the peculiarly American rhetoric of stardom, individuality, and celebrity, Drew is able to focus on karaoke as a local practice without disregarding its intersections with the inter/national.

Karaoke in Asian American communities is another story. Casey Man-Kong Lum's book, *In Search of a Voice: Karaoke and the Construction of*

Fig. 4.2 Storefront in a mini-mall in Little Saigon, Westminster, California. Note that karaoke is prominently advertised. (Photograph by Deborah Wong.)

Identity in Chinese America (1996) follows the use of karaoke through several different diasporic Chinese communities in the metropolitan New York area and shows how the practice is as much a way of maintaining differences between older Cantonese immigrants, recent Taiwanese arrivals, and so forth; his study amply shows how language, relative generation, class, socioeconomic status, etc. are played out and asserted through participation in karaoke. Whether of East or Southeast Asian origin, when Asian Americans (especially first generation) talk about karaoke, their faces light up. Karaoke is fun. Karaoke is a social ritual of great satisfaction and it can negotiate the potential wasteland between being Asian and being Asian American.

This last point assumes a special importance in the Vietnamese communities of Los Angeles. After 1975 and the end of the Vietnam War, the United States became the new home for hundreds of thousands of Southeast Asians. Unlike immigrants from China, Japan, the Philippines, and Thailand who generally came to the United States voluntarily (for reasons of economic opportunity), the Cambodians, Laotians, and Vietnamese who managed to gain entry were political refugees, cut off from their original countries. Now concentrated in California (especially in Fresno and Orange County), these communities have had a doubly difficult task. Like most immigrant communities, they work hard at maintaining tradition, but, economically cut off from their homelands, they have had to create a

Fig. 4.3 U-Singalong, a karaoke store in Little Saigon, Westminster, California. (Photograph by Deborah Wong.)

contemporary sense of self, too, and this has meant creating an immigrant popular culture.[7]

At least eighty-five thousand Vietnamese now live in the greater Los Angeles area (Pearlstone 1990: 93), and most are concentrated in the Orange County cities of Westminster, Garden Grove, and Santa Ana. These sprawling suburban cities are the center of the Vietnamese community in America and are characterized by one mini-mall after another, each filled with huge Vietnamese supermarkets, travel agencies, gold shops, restaurants, and music stores. In the music stores, cassettes, CDs, and laser discs line the walls and spill out of bins. Most are produced in Orange County; until the late 1990s, very few were imports from Vietnam, and those were usually black market dubbings. Most stores stock a few traditional genres (especially *cai luong*, or opera) but are otherwise devoted almost entirely to southern Californian, Vietnamese American popular music.

A good portion of any Vietnamese American music store is given over to karaoke. Karaoke material is available in a variety of formats, and this is usually prominently advertised in store windows (see Figure 4.2). Some stores even specialize in karaoke (see Figure 4.3). In addition to recordings, such specialty shops also carry karaoke equipment, and lots of it. As one clerk cheerfully said to me, "Lots of stuff in here that the government doesn't know about!" Any such store is a beehive of activity on a weekend afternoon: several customers will be gathered around a monitor playing the latest karaoke laser disk, others will be bargaining for a lower price on a pile of videotapes, and others still will be intently listening to a clerk's description of the latest laser disc combiplayer, remote mike, or package deal.[8]

Technology is at the heart of the karaoke phenomenon. Not surprisingly, Japanese equipment dominates the market: the stores in Orange County are full of Sanyo, Nikkodo, JVC, and Sony hardware, each model newer and more sophisticated than the last. Unlike the rest of the audiovisual industry, which is explicitly focused on reproductive quality, karaoke technology is primarily directed toward social accessibility and the people who use it. Consider the progression of karaoke technology over the past twenty years: after the first 8-track karaoke tapes, audiocassettes, videotape, CDs, laser discs, and now DVDs have successively cornered the market. The first karaoke machines were essentially glorified tape players, first of 8-track and later cassette tapes; a typical tape contained four songs and eight tracks, i.e., each song twice, once with the solo vocal part and once without. The performer either sang from memory or read from special books of lyrics. By the late 1970s, however, video karaoke was introduced: the song lyrics unrolled in front of a series of romantic backdrops. This new visual element created a significantly different performance environment: instead of looking at the singer, the audience tended to watch the video. As one electronics industry executive said, "Sometimes people felt uncomfortable singing in front of other people, but videos helped eliminate that tension" (McClure 1992: K3). The president of the Karaoke International Singalong Association described the change in audience dynamics even more succinctly: "With the lyrics on TV, the whole room gets to watch, and they get sucked into the experience" (McGowan 1992b: K2).

In 1978, home-use karaoke machines were introduced, but were still expensive enough that most karaoke singing continued to take place in bars. In 1982, Pioneer introduced LaserKaraoke, the first laser disc machine, and despite dire predictions that its costs could never compete with the VCR and videotape market, it took off almost immediately because of its accessibility: unlike the constant rewinding and fast-forwarding required by videotape, laser discs permit random access, allowing performers to select songs quickly and easily. In 1985, the first home-use LaserKaraoke machine appeared, and it is now estimated that there are some 450,000 such machines in Japanese homes alone. As users grew to like the possibility of performing in an intimate environment, public performance possibilities changed accordingly, and in 1988, the first "karaoke boxes" were introduced in Japan: at certain karaoke establishments, customers could rent small private rooms with karaoke equipment and have parties with a few select friends, but on better equipment than they might be able to afford at home. In the interests of affordability, "CD + G karaoke," or compact discs with graphics, was popular in the early 1990s, offering good sound quality and random access while projecting the song lyrics onto any TV monitor. DVDs have become common since the late 1990s.

Initially a form of public entertainment, karaoke has been designed for increasingly intimate environments. Karaoke bars and "boxes" exist in southern California, but karaoke machines for the home now command a large part of the American market. A small advertisement in the *Los Angeles Times* stated, for instance, that "We can turn your VCR/Cassette/CD/ Laser Player into [a] Karaoke Machine with Karaoke Mixer ($159.00)." In fact, the preferred venue for Vietnamese karaoke is restaurants, which I argue are public extensions of the home.

Like most Southeast Asians, many Vietnamese regard eating as an activity that should be social and affordable. Most Vietnamese American restaurants in Orange County are thus significantly cheaper than their Western counterparts and are geared toward fairly large groups of people — families and, later at night, groups of male friends. Most restaurants now have a laser disc karaoke machine and a large screen that can be seen easily from any table. My observations from here on are based mostly on evenings spent at the B. B. Q. Banh Mi So Mo restaurant in Pomona in the mid-1990s. Pomona is a small city just inside the eastern edge of Los Angeles County; it is about twenty-five miles from the Westminster/Garden Grove area but has a sizable Vietnamese population. Though not in one of the most densely-populated Vietnamese areas, the restaurant had mostly Vietnamese customers and did fairly good business at the time when I went there frequently.

By late afternoon or early evening, the karaoke machine in B. B. Q. Banh Mi So Mo restaurant was on constantly whether anyone chose to sing or not. Unlike karaoke bars, where patrons pay by the song and have to meet a minimum tab (usually $10), karaoke is free in most restaurants. The B. B. Q. Banh Mi So Mo restaurant didn't have a liquor license; in fact, the owner of the restaurant said he bought the karaoke setup to attract more customers, and he felt it had done just that. During the early evening, most of the tables were filled with extended families, but by eight or nine o'clock, most of the customers were men who sat and smoked, ate snacks, chatted, and sang karaoke.

Informal, amateur singing of popular music is common in social gatherings of many Asian cultures. Think of Imelda Marcos crooning into a microphone at countless diplomatic dinners. Chinese wedding banquets often feature singing by the bride, groom, and their family members; I am told that this is common in Java as well. I have been on countless long-distance bus trips with Thai university students and faculty members where nearly everyone got up, one by one, and sang a song into the bus P.A. system to pass the time. Common to all these settings is an emphasis on participation rather than skill: while good singing is admired, bad singing isn't maligned. The point is simply to take part — to demonstrate good humor and good manners by taking one's turn, as well as by expressing appreciation of other's singing. Karaoke thus falls neatly into a performative niche already well established in many Asian societies.

The customers at B. B. Q. Banh Mi So Mo restaurant who chose to sing were almost entirely men. Although some women sang, this was fairly unusual and usually involved middle-aged women in large family groups. Vietnamese women simply don't gather in public, though they do socialize in same-sex groups in the home; male social life, on the other hand, often involves informal evening gatherings in restaurants and bars. Vietnamese women of several generations have told me that female socializing at home can revolve around karaoke evenings: one woman told me that she and her female relatives periodically get together and pool their individual collections of karaoke laser discs. Such gatherings are usually noisy events full of laughter, food, and conversation. Men and women follow distinctively different karaoke practices in many places in Asia and by extension in diaspora. In her essay "Karaoke and Middle-Aged and Older Women," Shinobu Oku (1998) writes that Japanese karaoke coffee shops are popular with blue-collar housewives who come to sing *enka*, a popular music that draws on many elements of Japanese traditional music. Oku suggests that it is not karaoke in and of itself that appeals to these women but rather its intersection with this particular kind of music and its location in daytime, public spaces that could not be more distinct from the nighttime bar environment of white-collar male office workers. Rob Drew takes this further, though speaking in more general terms (2001: 87):

> The enviable vitality of Asian karaoke seems to hinge upon a segregation of the sexes that renders interaction between them moot. There are two karaokes in Japan. By night, businessmen gather at high-priced bars where the only women admitted are hostesses paid to coddle male patrons. By day, housewives, working women, and young people frequent "karaoke boxes," multiroom arcades where small groups rent rooms and machines by the hour for private use. Male bars are crowded, shadowy, brimming with drink and vice; female boxes are sheltered, brightly lit, alcohol free, and closely policed.

Drew then notes that men tend to dominate karaoke singing in most American bars, both in sheer numbers (generally 2:1) and in presence, e.g., men frequently sing alone but most women prefer to perform only with a partner, often a man.

Male socializing around karaoke in Vietnamese restaurants is a much more restrained affair. At B. B. Q. Banh Mi So Mo restaurant, a circle of regulars — male friends in their thirties — stopped in almost every night

Fig. 4.4 Three friends at B.B.Q. Banh Mi So Mo Restaurant in Pomona, California, singing karaoke. (Still from a videotape by Deborah Wong.)

for an hour or two; they invariably sat in nearly total silence, smoking continuously, staring at the karaoke screen, and passing the microphone around the table. In fact, part of the pleasure of the evening seemed to lie in the routine itself: night after night, these friends sang songs from the same laser discs with no apparent loss of enjoyment, though the occasional new laser disc met with keen interest. Despite advertisements that invite karaoke enthusiasts to experience what it's like to be a star, for these men, the pleasure of karaoke performance seemed to lie in a very different place. If they experienced flights of fancy as they held the mike, such fantasies were contained in a frame of male reserve: the singers remained seated at the table, and expressed no emotion beyond slightly pained expressions during the sadder love songs. Technical skill was irrelevant, and neither applause nor boos punctuated any performance, no matter how excruciating. Though a friend might be holding the mike, other men at the table would sing along silently, moving their lips but making no sound. The performance experience was solo, but it occurred within a circle of cigarette smoke and restrained male camaraderie (see Figure 4.4).

Most Vietnamese American videotapes or laser discs featured a series of scenes over which the lyrics unfolded. At their most bland, these visual narratives were merely panoramic shots of nature — rivers, meadows, waterfalls, etc. More often, though, the visuals followed a character through a minidrama. One videotape of a song about a man away from his sweetheart, for instance, showed a young soldier stationed along the Vietnamese-Cambodian border, alternately walking on patrol, stopping to reading his sweetheart's letter, and gazing soulfully into the distance. This example was filmed in Vietnam, which brings me to an important point: karaoke material was being filmed by Vietnamese Americans in both Vietnam and southern California. Regardless of where it is filmed, these karaoke narratives had a strong and integrated aesthetic sensibility of softness and restraint. Markedly unlike the fast cutting and juxtapositions of American MTV, Vietnamese American karaoke videos (like so many music videos in Asia in the 1980s and the mid-1990s) often featured extended pans, liberal use of slow motion, and many soft-focus shots.[9]

Some songs were so popular and well-established that they existed in several karaoke versions, highlighting an important aspect of Vietnamese American karaoke videos: they provided a performative frame for exploring immigrant identity. One such song, "Bai Tango Cho Em," or "A Tango for You," was available in at least two different karaoke versions, issued by different companies. "Bai Tango Cho Em" is literally a tango, sung in Vietnamese but driven by classic tango rhythms. Its lyrics are intensely romantic and, although the song can be sung by either a man or a woman, it is actually a dialogue between two lovers. The frequent references to sadness and melancholy are typical of Vietnamese love songs and classical poetry: love tinged with melancholy is central to the aesthetics and poetics of romance (see Figure 4.5 and Track 6).

One karaoke version of "Bai Tango Cho Em"[10] was laid over a visual narrative of life in old Vietnam: a young woman, dressed in traditional Vietnamese clothes, was seen in a series of scenes, absorbed in daily village life — washing clothes by the river, feeding chickens, praying at the family shrine, greeting her grandmother, and going to the market (see Figures 4.6 and 4.7). This film was in fact shot by Vietnamese Americans in Vietnam but produced and distributed in California; as far as I know, it was intended solely for an immigrant market and was unavailable in Vietnam.

A second version of "Bai Tango Cho Em," released by a different company,[11] followed a teenaged couple through an idyllic afternoon in southern California. It opened with the young woman strolling down a suburban street and then knocking on the door of a typical southern Californian ranch house; her boyfriend answers the door, they embrace, and they then wander through sunlit gardens and the oceanside boardwalk at Long Beach (see Figures 4.8 and 4.9).

Why would this song be set to such contrasting narratives? One version offers a vision of the past — a way of life now nothing but a memory to most Vietnamese Americans, and nothing but hearsay to any Vietnamese American under twenty years of age. The other is squarely placed in the world of the Southeast Asian diaspora — or rather, a utopian vision of the refugee experience. The second version, marked by sunlight and affluence, is a sedate fantasy of demure romantic love in which teenagers hold hands and go for long walks in slow motion in the California sunshine.

Why a tango? Tangos made their way from Argentina to European nightclubs, from there to colonial outposts like Vietnam,[12] and from there to the karaoke of Vietnamese immigrants. In this present context, the tango has a complex emotional landscape indeed, and is in some ways a

"Bai Tango Cho Em" (translated by Mai Elliot)

(**Man**)
Tu' ngay co em ve
Since you came back to me
nha minh tran anh trang the.
My house is filled with moonlight
Dong nhac tinh da tat lau.
Love was absent from my heart for a long time
Tuon trao, ngot ngao nhu giong suoi.
And now it overflows like a rushing stream
Anh yeu phut ban dau, dep nghieng nghieng dang em sau.
I loved you the first moment I saw you move in sadness
Trong mat em buon ve mau.
With sadness quickly clouding your eyes
(**Woman**)
Anh o'i co khi nao, lan gap day cho mai sau
Could this meeting last forever
Tieng dan hoa em ai.
The sound of music, harmonious and soft
(**Man**)
Nhip bu'oc em them la lo'i,
As you move ever more gracefully
Cung dieu buon cho'i vo'i,
The sad melancholy tune hovers in the air
Doi tam hon rieng the gio'i.
Our two souls are lost in their own world
(**Woman**)
Minh diu sat di anh,
Hold me tightly as we dance
De nghe lan ho'i chay, trong tim nong nan.
So I can feel the burning of your passionate heart
(**Man**)
Tiec th'o'ng chi, khi tro'i rong thenh thang.
Why regret anything when the sky is limitless
Vu'o'ng van de roi, mot do'i cu'u mang.
Why harden ourselves with any cares, for they will remain with us all our lives
Gio' minh co nhau roi, do'i dep vi tieng em cu'oi,
Now that we're together, your laughter makes life beautiful
Vu'ot ngan trung, qua be kho'i.
We'll journey a thousand miles and cross a deep ocean
Dat diu cung ve can nha mo'i.
And hand in hand we enter our new home
Ta xay vach chung tinh,
We'll build a wall of everlasting love
Nhieu chong gai co tay minh,
We'll overcome all obstacles
Xin ca'm o'n do'i con nhau,
We're thankful to be together
Ghi sau phut ban dau,
We'll engrave the memory of our first meeting on our hearts
Bang bai Tango cho em…
With this tango dedicated to you

Fig. 4.5 Lyrics and translation of "Bai Tango Cho Em," translated by Mai Elliot.

Fig. 4.5 Still from a karaoke videotape of "Bai Tango Cho Em." Filmed in Vietnam, this opening scene shows a young woman washing clothes by the river. In English, the lyrics read, "The sound of music, harmonious and soft/As you move ever more gracefully."

Fig. 4.6 Still from a karaoke videotape of "Bai Tango Cho Em." The young woman walks through rice paddies on her way to the market. The lyrics read, "Hold me tightly as we dance/So I can feel the burning of your passionate heart."

Fig. 4.8 Still from another karaoke videotape of "Bai Tango Cho Em." The young Vietnamese American couple strolls through the campus of California State University, Long Beach. The lyrics read, "Why harden ourselves with any cares, for they will remain with us all our lives."

Fig. 4.9 Still from karaoke videotape of "Bai Tango Cho Em." As the couple strolls along the boardwalk at Long Beach, the young woman puts her arm around her boyfriend. The lyrics read, "Now that we're together..."

postcolonial artifact with a new spin. Ethnomusicologist Adelaide Reyes, who has done extensive fieldwork on Vietnamese music in refugee camps, New Jersey, and in Orange County (Reyes Schramm 1991, Reyes 1999a and 1999b), suggests that dancehall numbers of Latin American origin — e.g., tangos, cha-chas, and boleros — have special meaning for Vietnamese immigrants. The musical life of post-1975 Communist Vietnam is shaped by government regulations and, for some Vietnamese of the diaspora (especially the middle- and upper-class Vietnamese who emigrated immediately after 1975), Western-influenced popular musics represent a pre-Communist past. As Reyes writes, tangos

> ... are part of a pre-1975 Vietnamese past, [a] symbol of a pre-Communist period which immigrant Vietnamese wish to retain as [a] marker of who they are vis-à-vis other Vietnamese and vis-à-vis the American host country. Whatever the ideological force of these dichotomies might be, the relevant point is the new multiplicity of function. In the American context, these appear to be community- and identity-directed in a situation where the Vietnamese are confronted by their own heterogeneity on the one hand and their relations with American society on the other (Reyes Schramm 1991: 97).

In other words, a tango can evoke a particular past as well as create an immigrant Vietnamese present. In this context, a tango speaks the past in a way that lends sense and order to the borderlands of the diaspora. It is a frame for a particular historical moment, a momentary stopping-off point maintained in the face of tremendous odds. Anthropologist James Clifford suggests travel is the central metaphor of the colonial and postcolonial eras and he reflects on the narrative force of the migrations and immigrations that, indeed, created the Other. He says, "If contemporary migrant populations are not to appear as mute, passive straws in the political-economic winds, we need to listen to a wide range of travel stories" (Clifford 1992: 110). Vietnamese karaoke is a travel story *par excellence*, always told in the first person, and this brings me to some closing thoughts on karaoke as a cross-cultural phenomenon and on its specific importance for a refugee Southeast Asian people.

Cultural studies theorist Jody Berland has proposed that the study of transnational cultural production must involve not just the song and its audience (for instance) but also the study of the space it inhabits and establishes. She suggests that

> ... the production of texts cannot be conceived outside of the production of diverse and exacting spaces: that much of the time we are not simply listeners to sound, or watchers of images, but occupants of spaces for listening who, by being there, help to produce definite meanings and effects (Berland 1992: 39).

Karaoke presupposes and is structured around an empty space, a place meant to be filled by a live, not-canned person whose performance will merge with the package, a person who fills sonic and social and historical space, and whose performance becomes larger than life. Or is the technological frame so imbued with power relations that the performer is necessarily co-opted? As the ethnomusicologist Charles Keil admits in his important article on mediated and live musics in Japan (Keil 1984: 92),

> Until a few years ago my position on all the electronic media was basically Luddite, a desire to smash it all on the grounds that it substituted machines for people, replaced live music with canned, further alienated us from our already repressed sensoria, [and] enabled capitalists to sell us back our musical and emotional satisfactions at a profit.

Obviously, I don't think karaoke is the latest insidious step in a long, drawn out process of transforming consumers into the dupes of transnational industries and technologies. Rather, it is one of many examples of how people reclaim the mass media and make it their own again. "Mediated musics, sounds schizophonically split from their sources" (Keil 1984: 91) have been around for over a hundred years, since Thomas Edison first invented wax cylinder recordings — or even, one could say, since the invention of the telephone. Karaoke is one way that people ensure performative possibility and their own active participation in this process. In her study of lip-synching, Nora Beck cites Lipsyncha, a popular nightclub lip-syncher in New York City who insists that "we are not impersonators, we are song interpreters" (Beck 1992: 2). Craig Rosa, a Rocky Horror enthusiast and participant, notes that the interplay of the live and the canned is central to any showing (or should I say performance?) of The Rocky Horror Picture Show, which he calls "one giant carnivalesque karaoke." Why should canned performance make us so uneasy? Why should mediation diminish the value of an event? Rosa muses that

> There is… something unsettling about the live being not yet completed and the mediated being finished. Maybe it is the sense that the mediated is being reduced to the mechanically registered and reproduced. It is like saying that the finished painting is less interesting than the performance of the painter painting. We're missing a beat, if not the boat.[13]

If anything, karaoke takes the very notions of live and canned and messes them up, makes them relative. Performance studies theorist Sharon Mazer suggests that we compare karaoke to the pleasures of watching puppet theater: the puppet, she says, "makes manifest the distinction between alive and not alive because it verges on but never attains the status of 'living.'"[14]

Steve Wurtzler outlines a wide variety of performance practices located somewhere between the completely live and the completely mediated (1994). Karaoke hinges on the fact that it's not all mediated, not canned — is, in fact, alive.

Karaoke in Asian American Los Angeles is not a single phenomenon but has acquired profoundly different meanings in different communities. In the new Chinese immigrant communities of Monterey Park and Alhambra, for instance, karaoke bars have become associated with crime and drugs. During December 1992 to January 1993, the City Council of Alhambra denied karaoke permits to several Chinese American restaurant owners and eventually passed an emergency measure freezing the issuance of such permits for forty-five days ("Karaoke Permit Rejected," 1992). One article ("Limits," 1993) states that "Karaoke has come under fire from police and residents who worry that it attracts illegal activities, including violent crime, prostitution, and alcohol abuse."[15] Nor is karaoke necessarily a unidimensional site for the exploration of ethnic identity: second- and third-generation Japanese Americans in Los Angeles now use karaoke as a means for learning their parents' or grandparents' language (Tawa 1992). Clearly, karaoke is whatever its performers make it, and not vice-versa. Karaoke is a template for performative possibility. When La Quian (to return to my beginning) so emphatically defines himself through rap, he doesn't steal grooves as much as he transforms them. When Vietnamese Americans sing karaoke tunes in a Pomona restaurant, they freely range between possible selves: for a few moments, they can be transported back to an imagined Vietnam that no longer exists, or they can project themselves into uniquely immigrant versions of the California dream. Either way, it seems to me, these technologies offer a means by which Vietnamese Americans create a moment, however fleeting, and insert themselves into it.

I've got the microphone, I *want* the microphone, and yes, I'm an agent. La Quian might not articulate it as I am, but he knows about agency, its power, and its potential. His rap is emphatically about the eye/I, the process of defining a self. In performance, his hands are constantly in motion: one grips the defining microphone, the other points again and again to himself. *I* have the microphone, *I'm* an Asian, *I* will be hard to kill. But this is of course only half of the dialectic. As often as he gestures toward himself, defining and positioning himself, he then points to the audience — the defining listener. That La Quian locates himself through a mass mediated genre isn't merely a detail — it's a deliberate positioning that draws on and simultaneously reinscribes the power of the genre as defined by African American performers. La Quian ≠ Ice Cube ≠ Vanilla Ice, any more than Vietnamese Americans become French colonials or Argentinian gauchos when they sing tangos. To return to Clifford's trope of travel, we must look here at the "different modalities of inside-out connection, that the travel, or displacement... can pass powerfully *through* — television, radio, tourists, commodities, armies" (Clifford 1992: 103). The oppositional voice of African American rap not only passes powerfully through La

Quian but is transformed in the process into something consciously Asian American, directed (in his Pomona College performance) to a self-consciously Asian American audience.

If I present La Quian as an exuberant stealer-of-sounds, as a voice deliberately positioned vis-à-vis other voices, am I guilty of "the optimistic attribution of agency to consumers... and the tendency in cultural studies to celebrate fragmentation" (Grossberg, Nelson, and Treichler 1992: 3)? Perhaps. I do celebrate La Quian's agency, and the agency of Vietnamese American producers and consumer-performers who construct a past and present for themselves through mediated song. But I don't see the process as fragmented. Neither the tango nor rap are monolithic genres that carry a core of essential meaning through their transnational journeys, nor do they fragment a spurious reality. If anything, the mass mediation that carries them from one transfiguring consumer to the next encourages — no, invites — constant transformation.

Acknowledgments

I want to thank a number of people for help with this chapter: the members of PERFORM-L, an electronic discussion group on performance studies, whose spirited, month-long discussion of karaoke provided me with much grist for the mill; a number of Asian American students and faculty members at Pomona College who responded to an early version of this paper and who shared their own experiences of karaoke; Mai Elliot, for her translation of "Bai Tango Cho Em"; the manager and patrons of B. B. Q. Banh Mi So restaurant, who graciously allowed me to intrude on their meals and karaoke performances; various merchants in Little Saigon who took the time to answer my questions; Andrew Weintraub, Jerry Irish, and several other friends who kept an eye out for interesting articles on karaoke; Greg Booth, who organized the panel that prompted this study; Kathy Bergeron and René Lysloff for their thoughts and suggestions; graduate students and faculty members in the music departments at the University of Pittsburgh and UC Berkeley who offered comments on a later version of this essay; and finally, all the friends who good-naturedly accompanied me on my outings to Vietnamese restaurants.

Endnotes

1. *La quian* = "big," "large." His given name is Lakandewa de Leon; in the late 1990s, he was a graduate student in the Asian American Studies program at UCLA, where he wrote his master's thesis on hip-hop.
2. Vanilla Ice.
3. The star of such action movies as *Under Siege* (1992), *Above the Law* (1988), and, of course, *Hard to Kill* (1990).
4. His DJ.
5. See Manuel 1993, "Introduction: Theoretical Perspectives," pp. 1-20, for a good overview of such theories.

6. I experienced considerable indecision in spoken presentations, unsure whether to pronounce the word "karaoke" or "karey-okey," since the latter word and its attendant implications point to precisely the kind of transnational performatives I'm interested in here. In the end, I went with "karaoke," since that's how it is pronounced by most Southeast Asians.

7. U.S. trade sanctions against Vietnam were lifted in 1994 and had begun significantly to change the Vietnamese American music scene in Orange County by 1999-2000. Popular music imported from Vietnam raised contentious issues for Vietnamese Americans. Young people flocked to it while the older generation regarded it as an arm of the Communist government; local radio stations largely refused to play it even though it sold very well in stores. Imported CDs cost as little as $2 whereas those locally-produced were $8-12. Local companies found they couldn't compete: whereas about thirty Little Saigon record companies dominated the diasporic Vietnamese market for many years (reaching a peak in 1995), eight companies had closed by 2000 and more were in trouble. This chapter thus depicts an ethnographic present and a historical moment that has already passed. See Marosi 2000 for more.

8. Otake and Hosokawa briefly address karaoke in Vietnam, noting that "pirate karaoke" is not only widespread but that it coexists with large, beautifully appointed karaoke restaurants in, for instance, Ho Chi Minh City (1998: 185-86). They describe this as a contrast between 'high' and 'low' karaoke, because small private karaoke bars are perceived as trying to evade taxes and having close associations with the underworld. Furthermore, the karaoke materials themselves are often pirate versions (usually of videotapes).

9. Having made these generalized comparisons, I hope someone will be inspired to look more closely at Asian music videos. For insightful essays that problematize my overly general stylistic characterization of American music videos, see Andrew Goodwin's and Lawrence Grossberg's essays in Frith, Goodwin, and Grossberg 1993. Goodwin ("Fatal Distractions: MTV Meets Postmodern Theory," pp. 45-66) argues that MTV music videos are, and aren't, ideal postmodern texts, and Grossberg ("The Media Economy of Rock Culture: Cinema, Postmodernity and Authenticity," pp. 185-209, especially 187) suggests that there is no "clear single aesthetic" that unites, say, the videos featured on MTV, VH-1, BET, Nashville, etc.

10. From a videotape titled *Karaoke 1: Vietnamese Hit*, produced by Thu Thu Productions, 4213 Rosemead, #C, Rosemead, CA 91770 tel. (818) 286-3148.

11. From a videotape titled *U-Sing-Along Karaoke: Doi mat ngu'o'i xu'a*, produced by U-Sing-Along Karaoke Superstore, 9020 Bolsa Ave., Westminster, CA 92683, tel. (909) 895-2686.

12. Two movies set in French Indochina, *The Lover* (1992) and *Indochine* (1992), each contain tango scenes.

13. I've borrowed Rosa's comments from a posting on PERFORM-L in November 1992.

14. Again, Mazer's comments were posted to PERFORM-L during the same period.

15. According to one member of PERFORM-L, karaoke has similar associations in Taiwan, and members of the Taiwanese military are forbidden to patronize karaoke bars.

5

Pham Duy at Home:
Vietnamese American Technoculture
in Orange County

*"It's all so hard to explain! But through the book, and through the
CD-ROM, you can understand me."*

—Pham Duy in conversation, 1995

*It is no longer possible for a social analysis to dispense with indi-
viduals, nor for an analysis of individuals to ignore the spaces through
which they are in transit.*

—Marc Augé (1995: 120)

This chapter is an extremely localized consideration of one musician and a
representation of one piece of music. Ethnographies of the particular offer
special rewards as well as a corrective to certain habits in cultural studies.
My consideration of the Vietnamese composer Pham Duy[1] in the context
of Vietnamese American[2] technoculture is self-consciously placed at the
intersection of cultural studies and ethnography, i.e., I work within an
expectation of cultural construction amidst the free flow of power, but I
believe that the best way to get at its workings is through close, sustained
interaction with the people doing it and an obligation to address their
chosen self-representations.

I begin with the assumption that technology is a cultural practice and
that an examination of technological practices in context is the only way to
get at what technology "does." Far too much of the literature on technology treats it as something outside of or beyond culture, or simply valorizes

it as a force with specific effects and outcomes (such as cultural gray-out). I assume, on the other hand, that any technology is not only culturally constructed but that its uses are culturally defined as well; the "same" technology can thus have very different uses in different societies. A certain body of thought views technology as inherently destructive to "tradition," but I regard this too as a cultural belief system rather than a given; if anything, I err in the other direction, assuming that technology carries with it the potential for democracy and community building.

Current work on communication and technology is increasingly informed by cultural studies and anthropology, and "the hypodermic needle theory" of mass communication and its effects is now routinely cited and discarded. In a discussion of audience studies and its contentious interface with cultural studies and ethnography, communications theorists James Hay, Lawrence Grossberg, and Ellen Wartella (1996: 3) note that "the one general area of consensus across this range of shifting, occasionally contradictory positions was their rejection of the "hypodermic needle" conception of communication which assumed (some long time ago) that audiences were passive receptors — tablets on which were written media messages." Cultural studies provides effective tools for getting at agency without ruling out the possibility of coercion but rather treating it as one dynamic among many. Undoubtedly, technology and the media have effects, but new theoretical models enable considerations of multidirectional results in which production and reception are no longer constructed as binaries or as mutually exclusive.

I focus here on an example of localized production that raises interesting questions about reception. In his groundbreaking book on Chinese American karaoke, Casey Man Kong Lum notes that most media studies have focused on texts "such as television programs, popular magazines, and romance novels [that] do not involve their audiences in the process whereby their semiotic resources are produced" (1996: 16). Without ruling out the possibility that audiences can read against a text, Lum argues that "audiences are certainly limited in the extent to which they can negotiate meaning because they interpret on the grounds built by others" (ibid.). While I think one can locate the production of semiotic resources nearly anywhere, it is not helpful to simply level the field in reaction to earlier models that locked making and receiving into particular sites. There are always reasons for locating cultural production in particular places, and the Vietnamese composer Pham Duy has reasons for turning so singlemindedly to local, family-based output.

Television is one of the major forms of technoculture that has undergone extended cross-cultural study. In the West, some theorists have argued that television causes social isolation and alienation, but the American anthropologist Conrad Kottak has countered that considerable ethnocentrism lies behind studies like the Annenberg School of Communication's project finding that heavy television watching leads to the "cultivation effect," wherein viewers begin to believe that the real world is similar to whatever they see on television (1990: 11). While this may be true for Americans watching American programming, Kottak maintains that television watching in Brazil follows different patterns, whether in the cities or in remote rural areas. He and his research team found, among other things, that many Brazilians watch TV in groups — not alone in their homes — and that, in rural areas, people with TV sets in their homes are expected to open their windows so that neighbors can watch from the street (Pace 1993). Furthermore, television clearly expanded Brazilians' understandings of regional and social differences within their own country as well as their knowledge of the rest of the world; Kottak concludes that (1990: 189):

> Brazilian televiewing *expresses and fuels* hunger for contacts and information. ... Our village studies confirmed that television can (1) stimulate curiosity and a thirst for knowledge, (2) increase skills in communicating with outsiders, (3) spur participation in larger-scale cultural and socioeconomic systems, and (4) shift loyalties from local to national events.

Overall, Kottak finds that "TV is neither necessarily nor fundamentally an isolating, alienating instrument" (1990: 189). If it is isolating and alienating in the U.S., then this is a particular cultural response to the technology.

Similarly, ethnomusicologists have addressed particular technomusical artifacts as expressions of localized community issues and concerns. Mark Slobin's work on sheet music as a cultural technology for Jewish immigrants (1982) was an important first step toward conceptualizing the physical products of music cultures as expressions of local conflicts and challenges. More recently, cassette culture has attracted a lot of attention. One body of work treats cassettes as physical texts that can undergo cultural analysis (Wong 1989/1990, 1995; Manuel 1993); another followed Slobin's lead and focused on localized cassette industries for issues of identity work (Sutton 1985, Castelo-Branco 1987). The shifting space between production and consumption has also been redefined. Popular music theorist Steve Jones (1990) addressed how the accessibility of cassette recording puts production into the hands of nearly anyone, thus generating a "cassette underground" of popular music that rejects the values of the music industry. Ethnomusicologist Amy Catlin refers to Hmong American practices of recording young women's courtship songs on cassette (a traditional practice maintained in the diaspora) and circulating them widely — between Rhode Island and California, for instance — and notes that some young women no longer rely on matchmakers but make and distribute the tapes themselves (1992: 50, 1985: 85 for a photograph). Anthropologist Susan Rodgers (1986) considered the role of cassette recordings of music drama for the Batak of northern Sumatra, concluding that the tapes are "cultural texts" in which the Batak both confront and mediate issues of kinship and ethnic identity. More recently still, some ethnomusicologists have begun to consider how cassettes are used, regarding them as sites for social action based in local concerns (see Greene 1995 and 1999 for detailed ethnographies of cassette use in a Tamil Nadu village). In short, the material basis of certain music technocultures — cassettes in particular — have been treated rather differently over time in response to changing theoretical landscapes. Significantly, research has addressed urban popular musics as well as rural "traditional" musics, finding redefinition through local use in both contexts.

Locating Little Saigon

I have been fascinated by Little Saigon ever since I first visited it in 1991. Little Saigon is the largest Vietnamese community outside of Vietnam and is the unofficial capital of the Vietnamese diaspora.[3] Located in the contiguous suburban towns of Westminster, Garden Grove, Midway City, and Santa Ana in Orange County, California, it is a site of intense mediation. By mediation, I refer to all the forms of technoculture found in everyday life, and I use the term to point to the ways technology is culture; culture is always mediated (i.e., dialogically shaped and filtered), but I am here concerned with the roles of technology in shaping Vietnamese American memory and political resistance. Driving along the broad suburban thoroughfares of Little Saigon, you can't miss these characteristics of the community: its strip malls are full of video and music stores devoted to Vietnamese American singers and songs. Every mall has at least one if not several stores stuffed full of cassettes, CDs, videotapes, and laser disks[4] (Figure 5.1). I touched on the centrality of mediated music to Little Saigon in the previous chapter, and this chapter extends those arguments by taking a look at a rather intense site of production (and thus complementing my consideration of karaoke as both consumption and production).

Adelaida Reyes (1999a: 152) suggests that the Vietnamese American music industry has changed culture practices, writing that "for most Vietnamese, the love for music has been deflected from performing to listening. As one Vietnamese put it, their musical life is now lived largely through audiocassettes." She looked briefly at the Orange County industry and found that most recording artists were their own producers, doing all their own marketing and distribution (1999a: 157). She describes the process as follows (ibid.):

> Once the recording and duplicating are finished, they contact the dealers to announce the availability of the new product. Some of the dealers are large audio stores but many are small establishments — bookstores or specialty shops. Artists distribute and sell locally, nationally and internationally. It is a tremendous amount of work

and Pham Duy considers himself lucky because he has family members who share the work: he "creates"; his son [Duy Cuong] is the "fabricateur," running the publishing and recording enterprises; his daughters are singers; and his daughter-in-law travels abroad to manage the distribution which is worldwide.

Reyes also provides a fascinating glimpse of cross-cultural negotiations she witnessed between a Vietnamese singer and an American sound engineer during a recording session in a professional studio (1999a: 153–55). The singer was there to overdub a pre-prepared tape of American instrumental musicians playing the accompaniment and was thus locked into given tempos unless the tape was played faster (thus raising the overall register). At one point, the sound engineer tried to dissuade her from the expected Vietnamese practices of sliding into pitches and ornamenting her line. Reyes suggests that their interaction mirrored Vietnamese/American cultural negotiation more broadly, noting that "There were no overt conflicts. There was considerable but not total loss of control on the part of the recording artist" (1999a: 154).

Little Saigon has a fascinating immigrant mass media industry in its own right, but it is also a terrific site through which to consider theories of mass communication. To oversimplify, one of the perennial questions in media studies is who drives whom? Does the mass media drive people, or vice versa? Neo-Marxist theorists assert that media technologies create and sustain hegemonic holds over communities and populations, but cultural studies theorists look for fissures that suggest otherwise. I fall in the latter camp, not so much out of any romantic, totalizing belief that the lumpen proletariat ought to have a voice, but because I think both theoretical stances help us to see certain political realities: they help us to understand the consequences of certain technologies as well as to see how envoicing can happen (when it does), sometimes despite tremendously powerful counter-assertive forces. In *Big Sounds from Little Peoples,* Wallis and Malm argue that the multinational music industry has been very difficult to resist, noting that "Governments will ... have to create systems for redistributing money to cover the expenses involved in keeping local music life alive and flourishing" (1984: 322). While issuing a stern warning about the might of multinational industry, Wallis and Malm maintain great optimistic belief in cultural response, taking pains to avoid demonizing technology: "Whichever way it goes, technology will play an important role. But technology alone will not determine the outcome. People and governments do that" (1984: 324). I will follow their lead and start by discarding the equation that technology = hegemony: technology is culture, and culture is shaped by resistance as well as acceptance. We also need to look hard at what we call resistance, to be sure we see the messy internal politics that can grant resistance an even more interesting profile.

I consider a single technocultural artifact here as an example of these issues, and turn now to Pham Duy, one of Vietnam's preeminent composers; any Vietnamese or Vietnamese American would not only know his name but would probably be able to sing at least one of his songs. Adelaida Reyes (1999a: 68) writes,

> I have not met a Vietnamese who did not know the name Pham Duy, Vietnam's best known composer, and his use of folk and traditional materials in the music he created and performed — music subsequently heard all over Vietnam as a powerful rallying cry around Vietnamese nationalism during the war against the French.

Pham Duy was born in North Vietnam in 1921 and emigrated to the U.S. in 1975; he is seventy-seven years old at the time of this writing and lives in Little Saigon (Midway City). He is a noted composer of songs as well as a folklorist: his book, *Musics of Vietnam* (1975), is one of the few extended English-language overviews of Vietnamese music. Pham Duy's life covers all of the momentous events of twentieth-century Vietnamese history. He fought against the French in the 1950s as a member of the Viet Minh (the Vietnamese resistance) and later fell out with the Communists over ideological matters;[5] his songs are still banned in Vietnam as a result. His name is inextricably linked to the creation of Vietnamese "new music" (*nhac cai cach*, "reformed music," or *tan nhac*, "modern music"), created in the 1920s–40s by Vietnamese composers well-versed in Western musical vocabularies and instruments but wanting to reinvigorate Vietnamese music. Ethnomusicologist Jason Gibbs (1997: 9–10) notes that "this reformed music was not clearly defined, but was generally used to denote the new western-style music composed by Vietnamese," and suggests that it led to the Vietnamese adoption of the artistic figure of the composer. Gibbs also notes that many of the Vietnamese composers associated with this movement made a point of studying traditional Vietnamese folk musics (Gibbs 1998) and that part of their motivation was to change the rather low regard in which many traditional musics were then held.[6]

Pham Duy is an out-going, energetic man, fluent in French and English as well as in Vietnamese; he constantly goes on lecture tours to Vietnamese communities in the U.S. and in Western Europe to promote new projects. He is very comfortable making public presentations and he clearly enjoys talking about his work; he is well known and admired for his promotional skills. He has lived in the Little Saigon area for almost twenty years. He is extremely resourceful and has continued to compose and to make sure that his music gets disseminated. A fiend for music technology, his home on a quiet residential street near the main drag of Little Saigon is also his studio and his business. He has state-of-the-art computers (a PC, a Macintosh, and a PC laptop), several MIDI-keyboards, and any number of DAT recorders. At one point I asked him why he thought that the older genera-

Fig. 5.1 Pham Duy packaging cassettes and CDs of his works in his home. (Photograph by Deborah Wong.)

tion generally doesn't explore new forms of technology, and he retorted, "Because they are fools! But I am a workaholic, a computerholic." A self-taught computerholic, he composes using a synthesizer and creates computer-generated sheet music that he publishes; he is well-versed in HTML software and designed his own web page, which is constantly growing (http://www.kicon.com/Music.html, then follow the links to Pham Duy's pages). With the help of his wife and their adult children, he records and packages cassettes and CDs of his works which are distributed to countless shops in Orange County and far beyond (Figure 5.1).

Pham Duy's is one of many Vietnamese American home music businesses in Little Saigon, though it is certainly one of the most technologically sophisticated. This is significant because Little Saigon is the center of the Vietnamese American mass media: if you buy a Vietnamese American cassette anywhere in the U.S., it was almost certainly produced in Westminster, Garden Grove, or any of the townships that constitute Little Saigon. Vietnamese American newspapers, videos, and television news programs are also disseminated nationwide out of Little Saigon. The community is marked by a stunningly varied local mass media that permeates the area.

In fact, a major Internet project in Garden Grove has a central role in the Vietnamese diaspora. Some work in cultural studies has questioned whether virtual space is "real" social space, but this simply is not an issue for many Vietnamese Americans (and indeed for other immigrant communities, especially those created by forced migration). The Vietspace World Wide Web site (http://www.kicon.com) was created in 1996 and was logging over 10,000 hits a day in 1998; it has become "one of the premier meeting places — a 21st-century town square — for a worldwide community of refugees spread across thousands of miles," according to an article in *The Los Angeles Times* (Tran 1998). The site was created and is maintained by Kicon, a multimedia software company in Garden Grove that is owned and run by Vietnamese Americans. Although there are dozens of other Web sites devoted to the Vietnamese community in diaspora, Vietspace is certainly the most extensive and the most up-to-date as it is revised daily. It contains postings of articles from Vietnamese newspapers, wire reports from Vietnam, and radio broadcasts from the Vietnamese station in Westminster, all downloadable for free via audio and video hookups; samples of music videos, film clips, and songs by Vietnamese artists (including Pham Duy) are available as well as a virtual art gallery of paintings by well-known Vietnamese artists. Most importantly, a missing-persons page allows Vietnamese to search for parents, children, friends, and colleagues who were separated after 1975: some people post photographs along with their personal information, and a number of reunions have resulted. In short, the site creates real connectedness, not simply imagined community, and is a vital link between far-flung members of the Vietnamese community in the U.S. and beyond.

Still, questions of access and its relationship to socio-economic class must be asked for any form of technology, including the Web. In some ways, the Web is remarkably open and democratic; in other ways, it is linked to hardware that is not widely available in public institutions and which still requires a significant outlay of money. The Vietnamese American community is markedly differentiated and does not have unilateral access to mass communication forms. The major line of demarcation in Vietnamese American identity is relative generation and after that, arrival date in the U.S.: the refugees who arrived between 1975 and about 1979 were largely middle- to upper-class Vietnamese whose connections to U.S. governmental officials facilitated their emigration; some were able to bring financial reserves with them. These immigrants founded Little Saigon and continue to play a leading role in (especially) the business life of the community. The second wave of emigration was characterized by many so-called boat people who left Vietnam under dire circumstances, often enduring years of relocation camps (in the Philippines, Thailand, and Hong Kong) before resettlement in the U.S. or elsewhere; this group has found it harder to find a foothold in relocation, as many left Vietnam with few personal resources. Other differences include religion: Vietnamese can be Catholic, Buddhist, or Methodist, and the churches have become community centers for distinct groups of Vietnamese. Finally, respective generation creates fundamental lines of difference within the Vietnamese community, as the second generation and members of the 1.5 generation (those who were born in Vietnam but emigrated to the U.S. as children or young adults) are often more acculturated to American society and will ideally have different opportunities available to them. All these factors have effects on access to new forms of mass communication technologies. The newspaper article cited above contains a telling anecdote about an elderly Vietnamese man in Toronto who "made a ritual" (Tran 1998) of going to his son's home each morning and waiting for the son to log on to the computer so that he could listen to a radio program from Little Saigon posted to Vietspace; his son was his link to Internet access. Missing from the picture of a mediated Vietnamese America are the Vietnamese who can't yet afford a computer or the monthly fee for a browser (like several Vietnamese American undergraduates I know in nearby Riverside, California where I teach). The community is thus heavily mediated (and mediating), but unilateral contact and participation in new forms of technology cannot be assumed.

Voyage through the Motherland on CD-ROM

Pham Duy has consistently experimented with different technological forms. Indeed, he has participated in virtually all of the major forms of twentieth-century mass communication. As a young man, he left his home in North Vietnam to travel as a *cai luong*[7] singer in a troupe called the Duc Huy Group, touring Vietnam from north to south from 1943 to 1945. He was the first to sing the so-called "new music" (*nhac cai cach*) for Radio Indochine in Saigon in 1944 on a twice-weekly program. Indochine was the first radio station in Vietnam, established by the French but featuring programs in French and Vietnamese from the beginning. Pham Duy was thus in on the ground floor of this fundamentally important form of mass media and he quickly became well-known through it. He joined the Vietnamese resistance (Viet Minh) in 1945 and broadcasts in which he sang his songs, many about a free Vietnam, were a regular feature of the Viet Minh clandestine radio, transmitted from a cave just outside Hanoi in the north. He writes, "a gun in one hand and a guitar in the other, I went to war with songs as my weapon" (1995: 25) (Figure 5.2).

He is very forthright about the role of the political in his life and work, and he doesn't see its centrality as unusual. He said to me, "In Vietnam, everything — music, poetry — has to do with politics. You cannot avoid it. If you didn't have this situation in Vietnam, you wouldn't have *me*."[8] The "modern music" style in which he writes has an inherently political base, as its genesis was in Vietnamese intellectuals' rejection of French cultural hegemony. Although its Western influence is obvious to a Western

Fig. 5.2 Pham Duy during the mid-1940s in Vietnam, as a singer, composer, and performer for the Viet Minh. (Reproduced with the permission of Pham Duy.)

ear, the fact that it was written by Vietnamese for Vietnamese listeners means everything for its followers. Its anticolonial ideological foundation had a powerful effect on Vietnamese audiences in the 1930s, as Pham Duy has written in his autobiography (1995: 18):

> Modern music … had [a] strong psychological impact upon the mentality of Vietnamese youth. Gone were the patriotic songs written to ancient Chinese or French tunes, poorly made up, too simple and very much unpolished. The new musical language provided musicians with better means to express emotions and sophisticated feelings. Many realised how powerful music can be and used their songs to stir patriotic sentiment especially among the youth, who would play the key role in the fight against the French colonialists.

Since his arrival in the U.S., he has formed several production companies, including "Pham Duy Enterprises" and "PDC Productions," named for himself and his son (Pham + Duy + Cuong). Duy Cuong came to the U.S. at the age of twenty-one in 1975; he is very adept with new forms of

Fig. 5.3 Duy Cuong and Pham Duy side by side on an album cover for an edition of *Con Duong Cai Quan.* (Reproduced with the permission of Pham Duy.)

music technology (even more than his father, as Pham Duy readily admits), and the two have collaborated extensively. I have long been fascinated by musicians' home studios as actual sites of cultural production (see Chapter 10). Duy Cuong's skill with music software is the other half of Pham Duy Productions, their joint business. He works in a Macintosh platform, using Sample Cell II as his main program for mapping, and numerous other programs for sound editing, including Sound Designer II, Alchemy, HyperPrism, Infinity Looping, Wave Convert, TimeBandit (for changing a tempo without changing pitch), HyperEngine, Medicine (which allows him to see sound waves and to visually edit them), and Sound Edit. His rack mount hardware, set up in his study at Pham Duy's home, lines one wall of the room and includes lots of MIDI sampling processors, e.g., Proteus I and II, Proteus World (for samples of non-Western instruments), two versions of Rack Mount with numerous piano samples, Vintage Keys (with samples of other kinds of keyboards), Music Workstation, a CD writer, and his latest purchase, a 24-bit mixer with a fiber optic cable connecting it to his computer's CPU. He creates the finished albums, working closely with his father; no mere sound engineer, he is a collaborator of the closest kind (Figure 5.3).

When Pham Duy first began releasing his music in California (shortly after 1975), he used cassettes and continues to do so, but he was also the first Vietnamese American to issue his music on CD; CDs are now ubiquitous in the community as other production companies picked it up once it became clear that they sold. His first CD-ROM appeared in 1995 and is centered on a song cycle whose title is variously translated as either *The Mandarin Road, The National Road,* or *Voyage through the Motherland* (*Truong Ca Con Duong Cai Quan*) and contains elaborate discussions of his life and work. *Voyage through the Motherland* is arguably Pham Duy's most famous composition. It was composed between 1954 (the year that the Geneva Accord divided Vietnam into two countries) and 1960 and has since come to symbolize a united Vietnam, especially for the Vietnamese now abroad. The work features three large sections (titled "North," "Central," and "South," for the regions of Vietnam) and a total of nineteen songs; the piece depicts a traveler journeying from north to south Vietnam along the Mandarin Road, a highway that runs the entire length of the country. Each movement draws on folk regional melodies, giving the work tremendously strong affective power for Vietnamese Americans who thus hear it as a nostalgic affirmation of a single Vietnam and, simultaneously, as a strong statement against Communism. When I played Duy Cuong's symphonic arrangement of his father's piece for the undergraduates in my course on Southeast Asian musics in 1992, for instance, the three young Vietnamese American women in the class all asked if they could copy the tape, saying that they wanted to listen to it again and again (Audio Example 5.1). The work is deeply symbolic, but it arose from Pham Duy's personal experiences. He writes (1995: 68) that he has walked the length of the route four times:

> In my life, ... I have walked on "the mandarin route" four times. The first time when I was a singer of a drama and music troupe [*cai luong*] touring from Hanoi to Saigon. The second time when I left the south to come home after the return of the Expeditionary French Corps in Vietnam in 1945. The third time when, after a few months of training in Hanoi, I went back to the South, joining the resistance. Then in the fall of 1946, when I was slightly wounded, I left ... to return to Hanoi.

He notes that he began work on the piece in 1954, just after "the great nations of the two capitalist and communist forces agreed, through the Geneva Conference, to divide Vietnam in two parts" (1995: 68). He heard the news while on a ship, en route to Paris to study at the French Institut de Musicologie. He writes in his autobiography that he "decided to protest" this political outcome with his music, through the piece that eventually became *Voyage through the Motherland.*

This work is well known in the different Vietnamese American communities. Adelaida Reyes (1999a: 84-88) describes its performance during a New Year (Tet) celebration in the Vietnamese American community of Woodbridge, New Jersey in 1984, recounting its arrangement by a local Vietnamese musician into a musical, complete with costumes, scenery, and slides of Vietnam projected onto a screen. Working from the melodies alone (the event took place before the creation and dissemination of Pham Duy's published score), this musician harmonized it and created a production that emulated Broadway musicals, particularly *Nicholas Nickleby,*

Fig. 5.4 Cover of CD-ROM edition of *Voyage through the Motherland (Truong Ca Con Duong Cai Quan)*. (Reproduced with the permission of Pham Duy.)

which he had studied closely through tapes. This example — let along Pham Duy's and Duy Cuong's numerous rearrangements and reissues if the work — suggest that "the piece" has undergone repeated reimagining, and that this process often takes place through other forms of media and technology.

The CD-ROM of this work is remarkable in a number of ways: it surrounds a single musical work with a number of other histories and leaves it (like all CD-ROMS) up to the user to choose his or her own route through it. It is a profoundly historical document and it is also intensely multi-media. Among other things, it represents a web of mass-mediated histories and exemplifies Little Saigon's status as the mass media center of Vietnamese America (Figure 5.4).

The CD-ROM album was a group effort, the first of a partnership that may result in five to ten more CD-ROMs of Pham Duy's work. The music and the entire content of the CD-ROM are Pham Duy's, including the choice of images. The actual programming and design were done by Bui Minh Cuong, a staff member at Coloa, Inc., the company that produced the album.[9] The music was arranged for MIDI by Duy Cuong, who has arranged most of his father's albums after Pham Duy has written the lyrics, melody, and harmonic progressions.

The web site for Coloa, Inc. contains the following description of the CD-ROM:

The CD-ROM contains:

- A multimedia presentation of the 11 pieces in the "Con Duong Cai Quan" cycle in which images of historic Vietnamese landmarks, beautiful scenery, bustling cities, quaint towns, and the Vietnamese people and their multifaceted character, will guide the user through the flowing lyrics of the songs.
- Included are multilingual musical narration and song lyrics presented in Karaoke form, in Vietnamese, English and French.
- The adaptation by Duy Cuong of this musical work "Con Duong Cai Quan," recorded in high fidelity stereo audio. Also included other Pham Duy's songs in MIDI formats.
- Video clips of 1954 division of the country
- Several of Pham Duy's songs performed by Thai Thanh, Khanh Ly, Ngan Khoi Chorus, Bich Lien…
- Commentaries and critiques on Pham Duy's work by Tran Van Khe, Nguyen Ngoc Bich, Annie Cochet.
- Moments with Pham Duy
- An autobiography of Vietnam's prolific composer Pham Duy that will have rare insight into his life from the Khang Chien period, through his Tinh Ca works, up to his latest "Hat Cho Nam Hai Ngan" (Songs for the 21st Century). The presentation will be in Vietnamese, English and French.
- Press footage and reviews of "CDCQ" beginning from the '60's to present day. Some of the articles are translated to Vietnamese, English and French.
- Glimpses at many famous Vietnamese composers, poets and writers who were Pham Duy's contemporaries and how they influenced his music. Included in this section are photos of Van Cao, Vu Hoang Chuong, Dinh Hung, Duong Thieu Tuoc, Han Mac Tu, and many more along with their selected works.
- A short electronic book of "My Country Once Upon a Time," in which PD describes in depth his life journey from his involvement in Khang Chien to his travels throughout VN. Photos of historical landmarks and significant places and cities provide a colorful pictorial guide through VN's past.
- Complete index and references with hypertext jumps that allow quick and easy access to authors, cities, publications, etc…
- Complete music notes of the whole *CDCQ* work that is printable.
- Bibliography and discography of other works by PD provided.

Though centered around the one long work, the CD-ROM obviously contains extensive related information. It is all in Vietnamese but many sections are available in English and French translation (accessed by clicking). An extensive biography of Pham Duy featuring lots of photographs provides a colorful look at his life. The short biographies of his musical con-temporaries (both singers and composers) offer an overview of the most famous Vietnamese musicians of the twentieth century. *Voyage through the Motherland* appears in two different mediums. First, the complete musical score in Western notation (done in music notation software) affords the possibility of playing the piece oneself (e.g., on piano). Second, a MIDI karaoke version of the work invites the viewer to participate by singing along while looking at photographs of Vietnamese landscapes and histori-cal sites that fade in and out while song lyrics unfold with the music.

In yet another section, extensive cultural and historical information appears about each of the regions and cities referenced in *The Mandarin Road* — and as the piece covers virtually the entire country, this section is essentially an introduction to the culture and history of Vietnam (all in Vietnamese). The bibliography and phonography of Pham Duy's work maps out a career that spans Southeast Asia, Europe, and the U.S. Last but not least, the section offering numerous reviews and discussions of *Voyage through the Motherland* is staggeringly transnational in scope: the maga-zine and newspaper articles are in Vietnamese, English, and French; the video excerpt from a television interview with Pham Duy was originally broadcast on Little Saigon TV (showing Pham Duy and a commentator strolling through a park while chatting in Vietnamese); the videotaped excerpt of musicologist Tran Van Khe talking about Pham Duy was shot in Paris; and finally, the video clips of *Voyage through the Motherland* being performed by Vietnamese Americans were filmed in San Jose and Little Saigon in 1993–94.

This overview is only an indication of the kinds of items found on the CD-ROM album — there is much more, and it takes a viewer many hours to go through the entire document. I am particularly fascinated by the choice of a karaoke version rather than something more "complete," though vocabulary is a problem in trying to articulate the difference between this and any version *not* requiring participation. A karaoke ver-sion builds in the expectation of interactive involvement, much like CD-ROM technology in itself: both are "activated" by participation. As I argued in the previous chapter, karaoke is central to many Vietnamese American social events, from weddings and other parties to informal socializing in restaurants; the Vietnamese American music industry pro-duces hundreds of karaoke videotapes (and many, but fewer, laser disks) every year. One of my Vietnamese American students once invited me to his home for lunch, and the meal was followed by a karaoke session featur-ing a videotape from Little Saigon that alternated songs in English and Vietnamese, though all were American pop songs; we passed around a microphone that both amplified and added reverberation. Karaoke is cen-tral to Vietnamese American social life, so it is no surprise to find it on Pham Duy's CD-ROM, a strategy meant to encourage interaction beyond clicking the mouse.

Furthermore, the CD-ROM is replete with references to other forms of media — television, radio, etc. — and this is no surprise, as twentieth-century forms of mass communication tend to refer back to or even to subsume the forms preceding them, thus creating links both metaphorical and actual. For instance, when CD-ROM drives are used to play audio CDs, the software is designed to look like a CD player on the monitor screen. In this case, the references link Pham Duy's work to the bigger mediated picture presented by Little Saigon: clips taken from the Little Saigon television station's programs are part of the connection to a community that exists partly in geographic and social space (in Orange County) as well as in virtual and mass mediated space. I don't want to call this an imagined community, as much as it lends itself to Benedict Anderson's powerful construction, because Vietnamese Americans don't seem to see it as imagined but rather as part of a larger political stance of resistance to the current Vietnamese government.

On the CD-ROM, Pham Duy addresses the importance of computer technology to his work in the U.S. *Voyage through the Motherland* was released on compact disk (CD) in a symphonic version on synthesizer, and an interview with Pham Duy about this earlier release is included on the CD-ROM. The interviewer asked him under what circumstances the work was composed, and after some explanation about the historical context, Pham Duy turned to its new, resourceful arrangement in an American context, saying:

> My son (Duy Cuong) and I completed *Con Duong Cai Quan* in eighteen months using computer technologies. It would not have been a feasible task had it not been for the use of the Music Sequencer software. It is very costly to use a real symphony orchestra concert to compose. An orchestra can cost 260,000 dollars to perform. As a refugee, I don't have that kind of money, and therefore, had no choice but to use computer as a means to compose. The software help us to acquire all acoustic sounds, ethnic sounds and electronic sounds. One may deem these sounds are artificial, but it could not be done otherwise since I have only limited monetary resources. Had I been a musician in a prosperous country with strong cultures, I would have had a symphony orchestra concert at my disposal.

And yet, Pham Duy's and Duy Cuong's commitment to exploring new forms of media technology is more than just financial resourcefulness. Pham Duy and Duy Cuong each said to me several times that they regard computer and sound technology as a means to cross over generational interests and concerns, to "bridge the gap" between the Vietnamese who grew up in Vietnam and those who grew up in the U.S. Duy Cuong said that they rely on the computer and its associated technologies both "to

preserve the musics of the past *and* to bring that music into the present."
Clearly, Pham Duy and Duy Cuong don't use technology only as a means
to an end; rather, they reflect on its cultural role in their community and
make the most of its possibilities.

Pham Duy's CD-ROM in the Vietnamese American Community

Looking at a product alone provides a limited picture; by itself, a product
is not a technoculture but comes to life only when it is used and thus
embedded in particular practices. Any technological object — a cassette, a
musical instrument, a computer, etc. — only has meaning in the context
of praxis. Considering any of these things as autonomous objects is in
itself a cultural practice, e.g., the turn-of-the-century Sachs-Hornbostel
organological scheme for classifying instruments tells one more about the
German scholars trying to organize a basement full of musical instruments from all over the world than about the people who actually played
the instruments. Understanding Pham Duy's motivations and intentions
in authoring the CD-ROM is certainly part of the picture but not all of it,
and yet getting at reception is one of the most difficult and untheorized
areas of ethnomusicology and performance studies (and completely over-
emphasized in marketing and advertising, both dominated by the late
twentieth-century aesthetic of overdetermination). John Mowitt is one of
few critical theorists to focus on electronic reproduction and reception. He
argues that focusing solely on production obscures the shaping force of
reception (1987: 177):

> If recording organizes the experience of reception by conditioning
> its present scale and establishing its qualitative norms for musicians
> and listeners alike, then the conditions of reception actually pre-
> cede the moment of production. It is not, therefore, sufficient
> merely to state that considerations of reception influence musical
> production and thus deserve attention in musical analysis. Rather,
> the social analysis of musical experience has to take account of the
> radical priority of reception, and thus it must shift its focus away
> from a notion of agency that, privileging the moment of produc-
> tion, preserves the autonomy of the subject.

In the case of Pham Duy's CD-ROM, the conditions and "radical priority"
of reception are a diasporic Vietnamese community that believes it will
return home and which is dedicated to reproducing the place itself and its
metonymic relationship to cultural memory. Mowitt points out that in
electronic reproduction, "the production and reception of all music is
mediated by the same reproductive technologies" (1987: 194), i.e., electronic media carries with it political implications for control and channeling. The Kicon web site and Pham Duy's CD-ROM are clearly dedicated to

the cultural maintenance of memory and are predicated on the expectation of similar priorities on the part of its audiences, but that audience produces, in turn, Pham Duy and the Vietnamese web specialists who create mediated community. Mowitt argues for an "emancipatory dialectic of contemporary music reception" (1987: 174) which acknowledges the institutions that generate social memory and experience, describing a "socio-technological basis of memory" that has certain political ramifications; I suspect that this is taken for granted by the Vietnamese American cultural producers who work so passionately to reestablish community through technoculture.

In June 1995, just after the CD-ROM was released, I had the opportunity to join an audience listening to Pham Duy. Pham Duy invited me to come watch him present the album to the members of a Vietnamese music club in Little Saigon, less than a mile from his home. Completely in his element, Pham Duy talked to some fifty Vietnamese American audience members ranging in age from their twenties to fifties and including an approximately equal number of men and women; he addressed the process of putting this well-known work onto CD-ROM and then the room was darkened and a video projector threw the monitor image of the CD-ROM program onto a large screen at the front of the room. Pham Duy sat in the front row, watching the screen and commenting through a microphone on what went by; Bui Minh Cuong, the engineer from Coloa, Inc. who designed the CD-ROM, sat at the computer and silently ran through the contents of the album, clicking the mouse in response to Pham Duy's narration and commentary. The presentation took about forty-five minutes; when the lights were turned on, Pham Duy and Bui Minh Cuong went up to the front of the room and took questions from the audience.

The MC first apologized for problems with the sound blaster on the computer used during the presentation (not the engineer's own) and then said, "Please encourage Pham Duy's efforts to help the Vietnamese community by buying the CD-ROM or encouraging others to buy it." The first question from an audience member was exactly what I would have asked: "Why do you think technology is important for the Vietnamese?" Pham Duy answered at length:

I consider myself the first [Vietnamese] person to have made a CD. I did it for the community — I didn't mean to sell thousands or millions of them. Now the different music stores, Lang Van, Lang Vo, and others have come out with a million CDs and have squashed us! But at this point I can only count five people who work on CD-ROM — it's not too crowded.

Walking on my way to exercise, I say to a friend, "Please come see my CD-ROM this afternoon!" [He answers,] "What is a CD-ROM?" Which means he doesn't understand what a CD-ROM is. I am really happy that I jumped in, and I guarantee that I will open up a new way for many other people to jump in, too. I think that we only need to have lived in America for two years to adopt this technology. If we lived in America for twenty years and didn't adopt this technology, we would do better to have stayed home. If we have technology going hand-in-hand with art then we can do much better, for the sake of Vietnam. I really hope Vietnam will change quickly so I can give a hand to Vietnamese culture.

The audience member and Pham Duy each assumed that technology had a specific importance for Vietnamese Americans beyond its obvious uses and focused instead on *the* driving question for Vietnamese Americans of a certain generation, i.e., how can Vietnamese culture be "helped," maintained, preserved, defined in an American context? All other questions move out from this central concern. A doctor in the audience then stood up and offered his thoughts on the relationship between technology and the Vietnamese community:

I don't have any question, but I do have some suggestions I want to share with everyone today. About five days ago I read a San Francisco magazine article saying that we Americans should use CD-ROMs for educating the young, so I feel very happy and proud to see that Pham Duy has put his music on CD-ROM. … Pham Duy, you have filled a need of the Vietnamese people living in America with the new technology. This could be a great and effective benefit to the Vietnamese people living in America. The young will follow your CDs and thus understand Vietnamese culture and the history of our country. We will all understand it because he uses both the Vietnamese and English languages [in his CD-ROM]. In my family, I can see that the computer is not only for adults and students but also for my grandchildren, only six, seven, eight years old, who already play on the computer every day. I only use my grandchildren as an example, but I think that the thing this musician [Pham Duy] has given us will continue for a thousand generations. The musician [Pham Duy] deserves our congratulations and respect.

The doctor thus acknowledged that CD-ROM technology has the potential to bridge the perceived generation gap between those brought up in Vietnam and those not; he celebrated its new importance for its role in cultural maintenance. Pham Duy modestly acknowledged the doctor's praise by saying that half the congratulations should go to the engineer, Bui Minh Cuong, because he wouldn't have known what to do without him. "This is a very helpful marriage between technology and art," he said.

The MC then said that they were out of time but noted that Pham Duy would be going on tour to Washington, D.C. and to Paris the next week to promote his CD-ROM, and urged the audience to learn the new technology, to "jump in." He then announced contests for writing awards in the local newspapers and an up-coming meeting of the club to introduce the Internet. He said:

> What is the Internet and how can we access its programs? What are the dangers and how can we avoid them — the good of the Internet and the bad of the Internet? A group of Vietnamese engineers will discuss this and will show us how to get on to the Internet. This is one of the fastest modern ways to make contact and to send information — it is super fast.

He then thanked everyone for coming and the session ended.

Brief though it was, I found this exchange fascinating for its assumptions: technology was not celebrated simply for what it was or for its perceived modernity. Rather, everyone tacitly agreed that it was a new way to uphold and to preserve cultural information and memory. Whereas fear of cultural gray-out is a common middle-class American intellectual response to the expanded role of technology in everyday life, the music club audience was closely focused on the specific ways emergent technologies could help them to cohere as a community with ties to another culture. Nor did they discuss CD-ROM technology in relation to matters of cultural assimilation: if anything, a marked confidence in maintained Vietnamese identity characterized the discussion.

Places and Non-Places in the Vietnamese Diaspora

I am fascinated on two counts by French anthropologist Marc Augé's little book (really an extended essay), *Non-Places: Introduction to an Anthropology of Supermodernity* (1995). Written in the style used by so many French intellectuals — intimate, poetic, yet assertive — the book outlines the growing presence of "non-places" in our lives, that is, supermarkets, airports, hotels, cash machines, and freeways, sitting in front of a television set or computer, all described by Augé as having no "organic" social life. He sees these non-places as a consequence of supermodernity, his term for the cultural logic behind late capitalist phenomena. "Non-places" are distinguished by Augé against "space"(1995: 77–78):

> If a place can be defined as relational, historical and concerned with identity, then a space which cannot be defined as relational, or historical, or concerned with identity will be a non-place. The hypothesis advanced here is that supermodernity produces non-places, meaning spaces which are not themselves anthropological places and which... do not integrate the earlier places: instead these are listed, classified, promoted to the status of 'places of memory,' and are assigned to a circumscribed and specific position.

Augé writes that supermodernity is the "obverse" of postmodernity (1995: 30) — the other side of the same coin — and that excess of time and space is its defining characteristic, an "overabundance of events" brought about, among other things, by technology run amuck in a postindustrial world. Augé is particularly bothered by the way that other social spaces are brought into the home by television, creating a "spatial overabundance" (31) of overlapping places. He has a great nostalgia for what he calls "anthropological place," even while recognizing that it is an "invention" and "fantasy" (75–76). He provides an intellectual history of place and space (referring to de Certeau among others) and notes that he would "include in the notion of anthropological place the possibility of the journeys made in it, the discourses uttered in it, and the language characterizing it" (81). He argues that space, however, is defined by movement and travel, even (85–86)

> a double movement: the traveller's movement, of course, but also a parallel movement of the landscapes which he catches only in partial glimpses, a series of snapshots piled hurriedly into his memory and, literally, recomposed in the account he gives of them, the sequencing of slides in the commentary he imposes on his entourage when he returns.

Spaces are thus empty, solitary, ahistorical, shifting. Augé is most all concerned with spaces that become non-places in the context of supermodernity: over and over again, he evokes "transport, transit, commerce, and leisure" (94) as the effects of supermodernity and the forces that create certain spaces/non-places and shape individual's relationship to them. The user of a non-place or a traveler through it enters into a certain contractual agreement to allow his or her identity to be defined by the space. Augé sums up these conditions by asserting that "the space of non-place creates neither singular identity nor relations; only solitude, and similitude" (103).

I have gone into Augé's argument at some length because it offers a compelling model for misunderstanding Pham Duy's CD-ROM. I can't help but try to read Pham Duy's activities through Augé's concerns, as I am fairly certain that Augé would consider Pham Duy's CD-ROM a nonplace, presumably read in solitude, driven by supermodernity. Augé says that in non-places, "there is no room for history unless it has been transformed into an element of spectacle, usually in allusive texts" (103-4), and thus invites us to regard the CD-ROM as a collection of spectacular, nostalgic texts, inviting a certain gaze but offering little more than similitude. Augé does not address the politics of class or movement and travel: his travelers are unmarked, and his example *par excellence* (at the beginning of the book) is a French businessman going to his cash machine, driving along the freeway to the airport, and boarding a plane. Middle-class travel through supermodern non-places is thus presented as emblematic, but, at this point in my essay, its problematic relationship to the forced, traumatic migration of Vietnamese refugees is obvious and troubling. Pham Duy is both forthcoming and reflexive about the place of travel and movement in his life. I asked him why several of his major works are song cycles about roads and epic travel (*Voyage through the Motherland, Song of the Refugee's Road*, etc.) and he answered:

> I am the old man wandering, the old man on the road. It is my destiny and the destiny of my people — always moving. The Jews and the Chinese went everywhere, but slowly, gradually. The Vietnamese went all at once — in one day, one hour! *Viet* originally meant to cross over — like an obstacle — to overcome. So this is the essence of the Vietnamese spirit. Now *Viet* just means 'people,' though its real meaning is 'the people who overcome, who cross over.'

Pham Duy thus theorizes the place of movement in his own work as well as in his culture, putting it in the context of historical comparison and the memory implicit in language. Augé renders difference invisible by flattening out travel and thus establishes universalized non-places by unthoughtfully making the businessman's plane flight and the refugee's journey equivalent. In a conversation with James Clifford, Stuart Hall refers to "the fashionable postmodern notion of nomadology" (Clifford 1997: 44), the theorized uprooting of peoples from fixed time and place. By inference, mass communications technologies are part of the apparatus of supermodernity that create non-places.

Music technocultures are considered "real" social spaces by many Vietnamese Americans. Arguing the matter in the abstract, or without an explicit consideration of history and cultural politics, has, it seems to me, little point; I have chosen here to work at a closely local level — some might feel overly local — but I think this is the only way to get at the social workings of any music technoculture. Pham Duy's work could be seen as a concerted attempt to create not only places but "places of memory" that fill a particular role in Vietnamese American culture. Clifford writes (1997: 250), "People whose sense of identity is centrally defined by collective histories of displacement and violent loss cannot be 'cured' by merging into a new national community." Pham Duy's places of memory stand between four different sites: a nation-state that he and many overseas Vietnamese refuse to recognize (the Socialist Republic of Vietnam), the united but colonized nation of pre-1954 Vietnam, the divided Vietnam of 1954–1975, and the diasporic communities of overseas Vietnamese in the U.S., Australia, and France. Vietnam does not stay put as a spatial or temporal location in any political terms, and landfall in the U.S. or any other overseas Vietnamese community hasn't resolved the problems of place for many Vietnamese, especially those of Pham Duy's generation. Little Saigon is almost certainly a different place for the Vietnamese American undergraduates now taking my classes than it is for Pham Duy. Clifford has eloquently argued for treating travel as a major condition of the twentieth century rather than an anomaly in relation to historicized places (1997: 3):

> During the course of [my] work, *travel* emerged as an increasingly complex range of experiences: practices of crossing and interaction that troubled the localism of many common assumptions about culture. In these assumptions authentic social existence is, or should be, centered in circumscribed places — like the gardens where the word "culture" derived its European meanings. Dwelling was understood to be the local ground of collective life, travel a supplement; roots always precede routes. But what would happen, I began to ask, if travel were untethered, seen as a complex and pervasive spectrum of human experiences? Practices of displacement might emerge as *constitutive* of cultural meanings rather than as their simple transfer or extension. ... Virtually everywhere one looks, the processes of human movement and encounter are long-established and complex. Cultural centers, discrete regions and territories, do not exist prior to contacts, but are sustained through them, appropriating and disciplining the restless movement of people and things.

But even as I feel that I understand something better about the Vietnamese predicament by reading Clifford, I must acknowledge that this explanation would be unacceptable to Pham Duy and many overseas Vietnamese. The route to the U.S. would be readily traded in if possible; the route of the Mandarin Road constituted Pham Duy's understanding of Vietnam as a place; the route chosen by a reader through the CD-ROM is understood to communicate that dedication to place. The technomusical artifact is thus metaphorical for so much, all at once, that it forces us to confront the supermodernity of the angry refugee.

Until recently, Vietnam was a non-place for overseas Vietnamese: it was not to be returned to, politically beyond reach, and morally repugnant. However, the resumption of diplomatic relations between Vietnam and the U.S. has changed everything. Vietnamese Americans can and do return to Vietnam, though most only for visits. Duy Cuong recently spent over two years in Vietnam (1995-97) sampling the sounds of Vietnamese instruments to bring back to Little Saigon for digital editing and reproduction;[10] these sounds are an integral part of his latest project with his father, *Minh Hoa Kieu* (The Tale of Kieu), a song cycle telling the quintessentially Vietnamese story of the young woman Kieu. Pham Duy could not return to Vietnam for twenty-five years; indeed, the present government continues to ban his songs despite their continued circulation through pirate cassettes, often brought by overseas Vietnamese, and his visit in 1999 was controversial. Duy Cuong painstakingly weaves the sampled sounds of Vietnamese musicians into the song cycle, over and under the voices of the Vietnamese American singers who sing the main parts. The resulting pastiche could be seen as a postmodern collapsing of past and present, Here and There, but Duy Cuong's purpose is to establish something authentically and unequivocally Vietnamese; as his father said, Duy Cuong is a "fabricateur," but this implies not artifice but rather the technowizard who maintains the past and its places by pulling them into the present.

The proliferation of technologies and their affordability and accessibility to consumers of any sort, including immigrant communities, poses a challenge to theories of mass mediation *and* of travel. Localized uses of technology in Orange County are tied into a diasporic community that has increasingly strong ties to its origin country as economic relations open up again.[11] We must be able to move theoretically from Pham Duy's study and kitchen table to Little Saigon's shops and TV stations, to Vietnamese American communities in other parts of the U.S., to Paris, and indeed to Vietnam itself. This transnationalization of the local is far from coincidental — it is central to Pham Duy's sense of purpose. This producer and his product encourages us to theorize the movement of power and agency through different registers of place.

Acknowledgments

I am not a specialist in Vietnamese culture, so I am thankful for the help and advice I found along the way. Pham Duy was extraordinarily generous and patient, spending long hours over numerous interviews explaining his work to me; my thanks also to his son, Duy Cuong, for a fascinating tour of their home studios, and to Duy Cuong's wife, Phoebe Pham, for help with translation. My student Duc Van Nguyen selflessly provided a detailed translation of the question-and-answer period described above. Jason Gibbs kindly shared his work on Vietnamese popular song history and provided detailed feedback on this essay. I have learned much from Adelaida Reyes's inspiring work on Vietnamese music in diaspora. As always, René T.A. Lysloff provided comments and feedback that made all the difference.

Endnotes

1. Pronounced "Fum Tzooee."
2. I use the term "Vietnamese American" throughout this essay as an attempt to stand outside the terminological identity politics of Vietnamese outside Vietnam. Some prefer to be called "overseas Vietnamese," or *Viet Kieu,* "Vietnamese citizens residing abroad."
3. Though not incorporated as a township, the area is recognized by a highway sign reading "Little Saigon" near the exit off the 22 freeway in Orange County.
4. See Lull and Wallis 1992 for a discussion of the presence of popular music in the Vietnamese American community in San Jose, California.
5. As Pham Duy describes it, his songs about the personal sufferings and tragedies of the common Vietnamese people led to his parting ways with the Viet Minh. In his autobiography (1995: 40), he writes: "I had sung about the glory, now I sang about the tragedy — to the stern disapproval of the Viet Minh leaders who saw these songs as negative and potentially damaging to the spirit of the Resistance. I was let known of their disapproval in subtle but no uncertain terms, to which I simply did not agree, and did not even care. It was not my desire to be moulded [sic] into a war-glorifying propaganda machine. ... My unyielding attitude had put me at odds with the Viet Minh leaders and would see me leaving the Resistance movement not long after."
6. Since the 1950s, a further development along similar lines has emerged from the Vietnamese conservatory system, called *nhac dan toc cai bien,* "modernized traditional music." Its blending of Vietnamese musics with European art music and Western pop is discussed in Arana 1994.
7. This is a form of music drama with historical relationships to Chinese opera and to other Southeast Asian forms of music drama.
8. All quotations from Pham Duy are from interviews I had with him at his home in 1995, 1996, and 1998.
9. The CD-ROM is available for $29.95 from Coloa, Inc., which can be contacted at PO Box 32313, San Jose, CA 95132, (e-mail) nxbcoloa@aol.com; (Web site) http://members.aol.com/nxbcoloa/page1.htm.
10. Duy Cuong's wife, Phoebe Pham, was sent to Vietnam by the advertising company that employs her. They lived in Hanoi from June 1995 until December 1997 and Duy Cuong set up a studio using the computer he brought from home in the U.S. He sampled over eighty different Vietnamese instruments and singing styles, asking musicians to play single pitches as well as entire pieces. He recorded them on a professional DAT recorder and then edited them on the computer, taking out the sounds of street noise. He told me that he kept in the additional sounds that make the samples sound "human," e.g., a flute player taking a breath; he even edited this back in so that the sample wouldn't sound "too electronic," as he put it. He has no plans to copyright or to package the samples, saying, "They're all here [on my computer], and that's good enough." He emphasized that many of the musicians were old and hard to find, and thus feels that his archive of samples represents a record of traditional Vietnamese musics that would be hard to match.
11. See fn. 7 in the previous chapter.

II

Encounters

6

Making Space, Making Noise: Locating Asian American Resistance in the Festival

(Self) Representation

I'm tired of policing representation. This is such a large part of multicultural education, and of course I feel compelled to speak against the images and performatives that contain Asian Americans, but sometimes it's hard not to feel fatigued. This book is deliberately focused on Asian American representational practices rather than on the old and tired orientalist practices that have shaped mainstream perceptions of Asians in the U.S. Nonetheless, allow me to present two performatives, one after the other, to suggest that matters of representation and self-representation are policed with difficulty.

I was surfing late-night TV in April 1995 and I caught Jay Leno at the end of his monologue announcing that the Dancing Itos were back. That froze my finger on the remote, as you can well imagine. Five Asian American men dressed identically in judges' robes, black beards, and glasses swept onstage, lifted their robes revealing high heels, stockings, and garter belts, and danced the can-can to the delight of the audience. I was both charmed and stupefied, and watched for the next few nights to see if the Dancing Itos would make a reappearance. They did — the next time, they did a conga line through the audience — and I was more and more perplexed by the implicit racism of their act. Were the Dancing Itos simply a spoof of authority and celebrity? Would *any* judge presiding over this trial-of-the-century be danced across Jay Leno's stage, lifting his robes and flashing his gams?[1]

There were, of course, quite a number of spin-off performances from the Simpson trial, and too many of them were directed at Asian Americans who had a role in it.[2] In a trial already astonishing for its racist drama, Judge Lance Ito was the subject of one of the most astonishing public performances of institutionalized racism — Senator Alfonse D'Amato's infamous interview on the Howard Stern show, in which he "imitated" Judge Ito via an exaggerated Japanese Hollywood-movie accent (which Ito, as a Sansei, or third-generation Japanese American, doesn't have).

Cultural performance, social drama, and real life intersect in the popular imagination at a very immediate level. Mediated events of all kinds, from national elections to local tragedy to scholarly research, are produced and consumed at the level of both performance and reality:[3] the divider between real and not-real is wonderfully insubstantial these days, and I must say I enjoy this ludic quality to "news" even as I get more and more impatient with the resulting superficiality of most news coverage. More dangerously, however, play/performance is increasingly central to discussions of race/ethnicity, and this requires some thought. Why was Senator D'Amato trying to performatively transform Judge Ito into a World War II Japanese movie villain? Race is now discussed by social and natural scientists as a cultural construct, not a biological reality, and yet race and ethnicity are consistently collapsed and made equivalent. Indeed, race and ethnicity are increasingly treated as "fact" yet, at the same time, as cultural performance — as "only" performance, or "mere" performance — thus divesting them of their "deadly serious" intent, as George Lipsitz has called it (1994: 71). Cultural performances are perceived and constructed by communities as real but not-real, and the ways in which such social dramas relate to resistance and reinscription is well worth consideration. This chapter is part of a broader examination of how Asian American performance events (re)structure social space and performatively construct a pan-Asian American identity. Let me move into this via a closer look at the Dancing Itos.

The Dancing Itos are five Asian American men.[4] They first appeared on *The Tonight Show* on March 2, 1995 after Jay Leno, as *People* magazine put it, dreamt up "the giddiest act so far in the media circus surrounding the O.J. trial" (Pitzer 1995: 108). The dancers were hired through a Los Angeles talent agency and appeared on the show a number of times. They always wore glasses, beards, black robes, and additional details fitting the evening's theme. One night they came out as the Village Itos, one wearing a Plains Indian headdress, others a police hat, a hardhat, etc., and performed "O.J.L.A." to the tune of "YMCA." On another night, they did the conga line mentioned above, led by Charo. They always danced a demasculinized body, with feminine erotic moves (flashing legs, bumping butts, etc.), and for this Asian American viewer, there was the uncomfortable familiarity of seeing a feminized Oriental body on stage. At yet another level, the Dancing Itos performed the tired dialectic that all Orientals look the same; they become the five Chinese brothers, as the composer and musician Fred Ho said to me.[5] Is this self-representation? A parallel: in mid-nineteenth century America, African Americans participated in minstrelsy, a genre created by Whites in blackface. At what point does appropriation become transformation and at what point reinscription or, as Gayatri Spivak says, "a kind of ventriloquism that then stands in for free will" (1992: 798)?

Tricia Rose has pointed out that some groups (like Public Enemy) manage "to retain the mass-mediated spot-light on the popular cultural stage and at the same time function as a voice of social critique and criticism" (1994: 101). I can't help but feel that the Dancing Itos failed to arrive at critique. I find myself going over and over the shape of various defenses: it's OK because they're all Asian American; it's OK because Judge Ito "has watched [their] routines with delight" (Pitzer 1995: 109). The mass-mediated spotlight shines bright, and now it's Asian Americans doing their own acting bits on a post-*Miss Saigon* stage. So why do those five feminized Itos all look the same?

My second example of an Asian American social performative is smaller and fiercely, beautifully local yet in that same mass-mediated spotlight. On Saturday, May 6, 1995 the Coalition of Asian/Pacific Americans of New York City sponsored the 16th Annual Asian Pacific American Heritage Festival in Union Square Park. When I arrived there around noon, I found that one end of the Square was crowded with rows of tables featuring different Asian American organizations — everything from social service and legal agencies to community arts and culture groups. One table immediately drew me. It featured a large oversized black and white photograph of Senator D'Amato with a red circle over his heart. For a dollar, you were given three darts and were invited to take aim. It was simple but elegant. Obviously, it drew on a long performative history of doing damage via representations: sticking pins in dolls, hanging someone in effigy. But it also allowed Asian Americans to do things that they don't usually do — to take up weapons, for one thing. This strikes me as an utterly successful performative moment, small as it was. It seized a mass-mediated event and asserted local agency; it worked at the level of you, here, now, and also at the level of organized resistance; it put a dollar in the coffers of that resistance; it posited an Asian American you, but allowed for other actors; it was violent but played off the violence of representation. The next year, the same group had a new display inviting performative reactions to the latest racist legislator, City Council member Julia Harrison, whose comments on Asian immigrants had inflamed the Asian Pacific American community (Figure 6.1). This time two interventions were solicited. You could take a beanbag from a small pile at the bottom of the display and toss it at Harrison's mouth (which was filled with a patch of Velcro), or you could help yourself to a whistle alongside the poster and "blow the whistle on racism." Below the beanbags, a notice read, "RACISM LIVES from D'Amato to Harrison — 95–96. Same Shit! Different Year!"

Fig. 6.1 Poster display pillorying New York City Council member Julia Harrison, 1996. (Photograph by Deborah Wong.)

Small successes, large failures. Can self-representation only work in localized gestures? I wonder if smallness is the chief place where resistance can happen. In my students' papers, I read, over and over again, thoughtless powerful phrases like "mainstream society," "larger society," and "dominant society." I don't know where that large overbearing social river is, but we speak ourselves into smallness as if it were the only valence where we're audible. The D'Amato dart board and Harrison beanbag/ whistle invitations to action were small moments in a larger event which was in itself a small moment in the time and space of the city. I turn now to a consideration of that festival as critique, resistance, and complicity, and I will try to theorize its successes and failures.

Sherry Ortner has suggested that resistance studies are generally marked by "ethnographic refusal," that is, a refusal of thickness and a refusal to engage with "the logic of a group's own locally and historically evolved bricolage" (1995: 174, 176). The flattening-out or, as Ortner puts it, the "sanitizing" of the subaltern position compromises the importance of studies that highlight "the presence and play of power in most forms of relationship and activity" (175-80). Resistors are necessarily up to more than "simply producing a virtually mechanical *re*-action" (177); they engage not only with that-which-they-resist but also with each other, and their messy, even inconvenient, internal politics must be addressed if we are to avoid romantic totalizing gestures that are themselves a theoretical stance of privilege. In that spirit, I want to look at the 1995 (and to some extent the 1996) festival in New York City and to critique its ideological underpinnings as well as to salute its affective reality. The seven hours I spent in Union Square Park in 1995 surrounded by Asian American faces and bodies were tremendously affirming; the visceral, affective power of Asian Americans gazing at Asian Americans is something I have yet to theorize because I'm so caught up in its experiential reality. Still, we need to think hard about the metaphorical impact of celebration versus resistance, looking out versus looking in, and I offer these thoughts as suggestions for how we might continue to refine available frameworks for self-representation.

The APA Heritage Festival in New York City

The annual Asian Pacific American Heritage Festival is sponsored by the Coalition of Asian Pacific Americans, and its purpose is explicitly celebratory rather than activist.[6] I will return to the dialogic distinction between these two stances later. The Coalition's primary purpose is to organize the festival, which has become such a large event that it takes all year for its volunteer members to pull it together. Figure 6.2 is a photocopy of a page from the 1995 festival program, providing the structure and membership of the Coalition and its committees. Cynthia Wong, then a graduate student in ethnomusicology at Columbia University, was closely involved with the Coalition and served on no fewer than five of its committees. She warned me to be careful about how I portray the Coalition, saying that it is not a political group but rather a means for bringing together different parts of the Asian American community.[7]

Coalition of Asian Pacific Americans

1995 Steering Committee
Cyril Nishimoto
Chairperson

Julie Azuma
Christopher Chen
Rob Dobkin
John Eng
Kuen-Hee Han
Rose Han
Minnie Hong
Laura Isler
Kitty Katz
C.N. Lee
Corky Lee
Lily Lee
Sue Lee
Winnie Lee
Felicia Lin
John Louie Jr.
John Moy
Ginny Myung
Peter Ong
Barbara Tran
Bertrand Wang
Henrietta Whitcomb
Cynthia Wong
James Yee

The Festival is produced with the generosity of the following sponsors and friends.
AT&T-Corporate Sponsor
NYNEX-Corporate Sponsor
Asian American In Harmony underwritten by
  Anheuser-Busch
Manhattan Community Arts Fund
The Former Governor's Asian American
Advisory Committee Associate Sponsors
Flyer and poster underwritten by Citibank
Neighborhood sponsor

Friends of the Festival
Nobuko Kuzuoka
David Hayase
Tamio Speigel
Midori Lederer
Nobu Miyoshi
Meriam Lobel
Emi Akiyama
Walter & Michi Weglyn
Arun Aguiar
Nobuko "Cobi" Narita
Joan-Shigekawa
Timothy C. Burica
Cyril Nishimoto

Speical Thanks
Asian New Yorker
Asian American Arts Alliance
City of New York Parks and Recreation
The Coffee Shop
Community Board #5
David J. Louie Agency Inc.
14th St. Local Development Corporation
Union Square Community Coalition
Japanese American Social Services Inc.
New York Newsday
Japanese American United Church
John Louie Jr.
John Moy
June Lee
Ilene Curtach
Marilyn Abalos
Cobi Narita

Working Committee
In Harmony Theme
John Eng
Henrietta Whitcomb
Cynthia Wong

Site Logistics
Corky Lee
Ginny Myung

Performance Program
Producers:
Barbara Tran
Bertrand Wang

Program Advisor:
Chuck Lee

Stage Manager:
David Chin

Community Outreach
Rose Han
Cyril Nishimoto

Media Public Relations
Kitty Katz
Corky Lee
Felicia Lin
Cynthia Wong
Rob Dobkin
Lily Lee

In Harmony Exhibition
John Moy
John Louie Jr.
June Lee
Sue Lee

Writers
Marilyn Abalos
John Eng
Cynthia Wong

Fundraising/Advertising
Christopher Chen
Kuen-Hee Han
Cyril Nishimoto

Booket
Editor:
John Louie Jr.

Cover Design:
Ramon Gill

Production:
Julie Azuma
Naomi Azuma
Rose Han
Kitty Katz
France Metz

Photos:
Kitty Katz
Corky Lee

Writers:
Cynthia Wong
Fred Ho
Marilyn Abalos
John Eng
Chuck Lee

Finances
Julie Azuma
James Yee

1995 Asian Pacific American Heritage Festival   3

Fig. 6.2 Page 3 from the program notes of the 16th Asian Pacific American Heritage Festival, Saturday, May 6, 1995, listing the working committees of the Coalition of Asian Pacific Americans and acknowledgments.

Bert Wang, an activist and a rapper (he is half of an Asian American rap duo called Yellow Peril) agreed with Cynthia Wong's description of the group but took it further. Bert, like Cynthia, is closely involved with the Coalition; after Yellow Peril performed in the festival in 1994, Bert was "recruited," as he put it, to help with programming, and he was half of the program committee for the 1995 festival. Bert is also involved with other Asian American community groups, including the Chinatown Workers Association, which (as he put it) "is as grassroots as it gets."[8] The Coalition and the festival aren't "grassroots" to his mind, partly because of its patronage but also because of its aesthetics and ideology:

> It's mostly just Asians getting together to be Asian, not in any real political way. All kinds of different groups come together there. They have corporate sponsorship, you know. I wouldn't say it's community activist (laughs). Is this going to get me into trouble? I mean, community people are there — there's nothing stopping that. But I don't know. It's very celebratory, very 'feel-good', very quote-unquote 'cultural.'

For Bert, community activism is in a different sphere from corporate patronage and the "cultural"; in fact, "the community" seems for him to *imply* the noncorporate and the political, whereas the "cultural" is apolitical. Fred Ho, a New York-based Asian American composer and musician, takes this even further, suggesting that the festival's message and purpose is deliberately nonconfrontational:

> Well, [the Asian Pacific American Coalition isn't] a "real" coalition — its main thing is to put on the festival every year, and even around the festival, the themes have tended to be lowest common denominator — you know, safe kinds of themes. They don't really address burning social issues like immigration and the attacks on immigrant rights. They don't deal with issues affecting the Asian American community.[9]

Again, Ho's very language suggests that "the community" is something separate from the Coalition, and his comments point to the main problematic behind "ethnic" festivals: the reliance on "lowest common denominator" points of contact.

The 1995 festival ran from noon till 6 p.m. and featured continuous performances on a stage at one end of Union Square Park. Although the annual festival always emphasizes performance, the 1995 theme focused on music and was titled "Asian Pacific Americans in Harmony." Different organizations' tables were cheek by jowl along the sidewalks that crosscut the park, but the most concentrated activity was by the stage, which had about a hundred and fifty folding chairs set up in front of it and a big amplification system that carried the sounds of the festival well beyond the perimeter of Union Square Park. Figure 6.3 provides a list of the performers. Bert Wang, who performed and MCed in addition to serving on the program committee, said they made a strong effort to come up with a

PERFORMERS 1995
ASIAN PACIFIC AMERICAN HERITAGE FESTIVAL

TI-HUA CHANG, REPORTER, NEWS 4 WNBC
REGIE CABICO, PERFORMANCE ARTIST
BERT WANG AND JOHN STEWART, YELLOW PERIL

PERFORMANCES:

AKIRA TANA TRIO / ACANNATUNA MUSIC
Born and raised in California, Akira Tana earned degrees from Harvard University and the New England Conservatory of Music. Since coming to New York in 1979, he has worked with such jazz greats as Sonny Rollins, Zoot Sims, Sonny Stitt, Al Cohn, George Coleman, Hubert Laws, Milt Jackson, Art Farmer, Paquito D'Rivera, Dizzy Gillespie, Lena Horne and the Manhattan Transfer. An active teacher and clinician, Tana is an adjunct professor at Queens College and Mannes School of Music in New York. He co-leads a group called TanaReid with bassist Rufus Reid, they have 4 C.D.'s released. For bookings and information contact: TanaReid Productions or Acannatuna Music 212 662-7476 or fax 865-3580.

BANGLADESH INSTITUTION OF PERFORMING ARTS
(BIPA) is a Bangladeshi group of singers and musicians who are committed to promote Bengali music and culture not only in our community but also to interact with American mainstream culture. Our repertoire includes classical, folk and ethnic songs and dances. Bangladesh is only 22 years old but our culture goes back hundreds of years. Like any other ethnic community in the mosaic culture city New York, we Bangladeshi are proud of our own rich culture and heritage. Contact: Selima Ashrat 718-544-7817 or Annie Ferdous 718-859-6287.

REGIE CABICO
Regie Cabico is the winner of the 1993 New York Poetry Slam, a road poet on Lollapalooza and the opening act of MTV's Free Your Mind Spoken Word Tour for which he stars in a 30 second poetry video on MTV. His work can be heard on several spoken word compilations including "Grand Slam: Best of the National Slam" vol. 1 (Imago) and "Relationships from Hell" (Caroline). His poetry and criticism appears in IKON, The St. Mark's Poetry Project, Red Brick Review, Aloud: Voices from the Nuyorican Poet's Cafe and The Name of Love, among many others.

THE CENTER FOR KOREAN AMERICAN CULTURE, Inc.
The Center for Korean American Culture was founded in 1990 to empower and recognize American citizens with Korean heritage. CKAC recognizes Korean American bilingual and bicultural reality. Through various performances and community outreach forums and workshops, CKAC promotes a pride of heritage. CKAC is actively seeking and building a network of leaders in the Korean American community. CKAC offers traditional culture to Korean Americans and other ethnic Americans to promote better understanding of the people of Korean ancestry. Emphasizing the "group- dynamic- focused" aspects of traditional culture, CKAC works closely with various community organizations to promote racial harmony and unity in the United States. Contact: 718-539-6469.

EAST OF THE SUN
East of the Sun: Their sound crosses all the international borders and can truly be considered "Universal Music". The group has created their own unique "music" form from an electric mix of musical influences comprised of traditional Japanese folk, American jazz and contemporary music. Contact: Kuni Mikami 212-967-8038.

THE GEORGE GEE ORCHESTRA
The George Gee Orchestra was the first big band to play on MTV and has made numerous television appearances including an NBC TV movie, Entertainment Tonight and Live with Regis and Kathi Lee. Unlike most of the big bands that perform in New York City, The George Gee Orchestra plays not only for listening enjoyment -"We play for dancers, there is nothing hipper than a floor full of grooving dancers boogying to the swinging sounds of a classic big band." With a long list of performance credits including The Apollo Theater and The Waldorf Astoria, The George Gee Orchestra is currently appearing every Tuesday night at the Metropolis Jazz Club on Union Square, as they have been doing for more than 6 months.

THE JAPANESE FOLK DANCE INSTITUTE OF N.Y. -MOMO SUZUKI
The Institute promotes and keeps alive interest in the traditional folk dance of Japan. The Japanese folk performing arts evolved out of the daily lives of people in the local communities. Handed down from generation to generation, these performances can be seen in many Japanese festivals and popular events. They are the prototype for the Kabuki and Noh plays and strongly reflect the spirit and characteristic nature of each region. The folk arts are a valuable means to understanding Japanese culture. Contact: 212-982-6952.

KINDING SINDAW (Dance of Light) GROUP.
Director Potri Ranka Manis is a member of the Maranao tribe from Mindinao in the southern Philippines. Her father was a sultan. This traditional folk dance has been handed down from generation to generation amongst family members. Today the group will be performing "Afir Afir," a Maranao fan dance imitating the movements of the butterfly; "Langka Kuntaw," a Moro Nation martial art in dance form; and "Pamansak," a court dance from the Tausug tribe which is a Pangalay variant demonstrating the movement of the bird atop the kumpit, an indigenous boat. Contact: (212)982-2158.

NGARYEA KHOE
Ngaryea Khoe, lyric-coloratura soprano, conductor of the CMA-Hai Yun Chorus and the Faith-Vow-Deed Buddhist Chorus is a frequent soloist with major music groups in the New York metropolitan area. She has performed a diversified repertoire ranging from opera, oratorio, art songs to traditional and contemporary Chinese vocal works at Lincoln Center, Merkin Center Hall, Weill Recital Hall to CAMI Hall. A recipient of many music scholarships and a vocal competition winner, she has devoted much work since 1980 to promote Chinese vocal works to the New York audience as well as bringing the western music repertoire to the Chinese community. Contact: 201 387-8935.

RUTGERS UNIVERSITY WU SHU KUNG FU CLUB
RUWSKFC was founded by Sifu Leon Peng in 1988 as a channel to promote not only Asian martial arts, but also to promote Asian cultural awareness to the Rutgers community; a community of 40,000 students, faculty and staff. The words "wu shu" means martial arts and "kung/gung fu" means man capable of work or skills. Aside from martial arts instructions, RUWSKFC also provides field trips to New York and Philadelphia Chinatowns, sponsors Asian movies and cultural food festivals to its members and guests. Contact: Leon Peng 908-545-1201.

SOH DAIKO
Thundering. Primal. Raising spirits. The drums of Soh Daiko pound out their unique brand of drum folk music with startling intensity. Established in 1979 at the New York Buddhist Church, Soh Daiko is the first taiko group on the east coast, taking as its name the ancient, pre-Buddhist meaning "peaceful, harmonious drums." The name reflects the spirit of dedication and cooperation that has enabled Soh Daiko to flourish from it's beginnings. Today's performance is funded, in part, with public funds from the New York State Council on the Arts. Contact: Choony Lee 212-965-7054 or Merle Okada 718-939-1546.

TEA CLUB
Donna, Stan, John and Ed are Tea Club.
Drink Up.
Contact: Donna 212-533-6793 or Stan 212-683-1508

VIVI formed in NYC
A Japanese hip pop band formed by Japanese American musicians with backgrounds of jazz, funk, rock, classics and Japanese music. They have performed at The Limelight, The Pyramid, and other local clubs in New York City. For more information and upcoming gigs, contact: Eisuke Kotanu 212-673-5028.

TERRY WATADA
Terry Watada is a singer/songwriter who has seven albums of his music in circulation. His songs center on Asian North American issues. He has performed various venues from San Francisco to Vancouver, Canada to New York. His latest album features New York musicians John Seetoo and Bill Asai. It is called "The Art of Protest". Contact: Terry Watada at 99 Ivy Avenue, Toronto, Ontario, M4L-2H8 Canada or 416-465-7688.

YELLOW PERIL
Yellow Peril combines cutting edge hip-hop and rap beats with samples of traditional Asian music producing a unique sound and style. With a funky blend of "in your face" politics and humor, Yellow Peril provides a fresh perspective for Asian American issues and concerns traditionally neglected by the larger society. Kicking Asian self awareness, Yellow Peril's rhymes cover everything from Asian American history to media portrayals of Asian Americans to "Kung Fu" cinema. Yellow Peril is available for performances, lecture/workshops and combinations of the two. Yellow Peril advocates for strong knowledge of self, Asian American history and justice for all oppressed peoples. Contact: Bertrand D. Wang 718-330-0931 or John A. Stewart 609-936-9752.

Fig. 6.3 Insert from the program notes of the 16th Asian Pacific American Heritage Festival, Saturday, May 6, 1995: list of performers and MCs.

program that was diverse on a number of counts — in terms of different Asian ethnicities, different musical genres, and in terms of contrast and programmatic movement. It wasn't hard, he said, to solicit acts; towards the end, his "phone was ringing off the hook."

Note that, out of fifteen acts, only five were self-consciously "traditional" and folkloristic: the Bangladesh Institution of Performing Arts, the Center for Korean American Culture, the Japanese Folk Dance Institute of

N.Y., Kinding Sindaw Group, and Soh Daiko. All five featured (mostly) amateur performers and appeared in traditional dress. The other ten acts drew on popular and art music genres, including jazz (Akira Tana and the George Gee Orchestra), performance art (Regie Cabico), new music (East of the Sun), art music (the soprano Ngaryea Khoe), alternative (Tea Club), pop (VIVI), folk-rock (Terry Watada), and hip-hop (Yellow Peril). The Rutgers University Wu Shu Kung Fu Club ended the day with a parody of Chinese kung fu movies. Bert emphasized that the program committee made a strong effort this year to encourage the participation of non-traditional Asian/Asian American performance groups.[10] He noted that "there are other ways of expressing ourselves" as Asian Americans besides traditional genres.

Matters of Asian American performance and identification are complex, however. Not all Asians in America choose to self-identify as Asian American: the "Asian American" is an emergent identity involving a choice to identify across particular Asian ethnicities in resistance to the cultural politics that have made race a shaping social force. To identify as Asian American suggests some consciousness of the Asian American movement and activism. Only a few of the performers at the festival self-presented as Asian American (e.g., Terry Watada and Yellow Peril); others were more directed toward specific Asian ethnic groups (especially the folkloristic troupes); some made no reference at all to their race or ethnicity. George Gee, a big band conductor, is frequently referred to as a perplexing example (See Figure 6.4). Gee is Chinese American but has never particularly emphasized his ethnicity; he's essentially a swing band performer who is Chinese American. Should he be regarded as a performer of Asian American music? [See Figure 6.5]. Should Yo-Yo Ma? Asian Americans disagree on this point; such performances don't seem to be self-consciously informed by any sense of ethnic identity, yet doesn't it matter, at some level, that it's an Asian American producing those sounds?

The main point is that the six hours of music heard in Union Square Park was, and wasn't, Asian American music. This is clearly not a matter of semantics, at least to Asian American musicians. Whether there is "an" Asian American music, or even Asian American *musics*, elicits strong opinions. With the assistance of Fred Ho, Cynthia Wong wrote a long article for the festival program notes providing a history of Asian Americans and music; she told me that one of the first matters she and Fred had to get straight between them was whether the essay would be about Asian Americans and music, or Asian American music. They opted for the former, and the final endnote, after ten packed pages of information, is tremendously revealing of the tensions surrounding the production and ownership of such musics. It reads:

> *A note from the authors*: This article is meant to be a general description of the contributions and participation of Asian Pacific

Fig. 6.4 George Gee leading the George Gee Orchestra in 1996. (Photograph by Deborah Wong.)

> Americans in the field of music. It should not be taken as a reflection of the authors' perspective or position of what Asian Pacific American music is (Wong and Ho 1995: 20).

What seems to be a distancing move (even a disclaimer) could be read another way, as a deliberate attempt to open up the area under examination and to shy away from the categorizations that the essay seems to beg. Nor do the two authors allow themselves to be positioned. Rather, their closing note reopens the category they seem to have asserted, and allows for multiple interpretations of the complex musical histories they describe.

I now turn to two acts in the festival and will try to use them to illustrate the variety of voices the festival was able to support. One act was short, loud, and (as it turns out) extremely ephemeral, and the other was stationary, silent, and carefully researched. Both stood as representative moments of Asian American musics. Let me focus briefly on one group that performed because it was the most emergent (if emergence is a matter of degree). Tea Club was an Asian American alternative rock band; I use the past tense because by five months later, they had disbanded (two of the four band members had moved to San Francisco) (Figure 6.6). The festival was only their second gig; their first had been the night before.[11] Their set was loud and sprawling and somewhat unrehearsed. They experienced bumpy moments when communication broke down among them: an amp blew out, transitions went awry and, once, a song ended more suddenly

Fig. 6.5 George Gee leading the George Gee Orchestra in 1996. (Photograph by Deborah Wong.)

than any of them, clearly, had expected. When all else failed, one or another band member would turn to the audience, hold up an imaginary tea cup, and say, "Drink up!" The idea of a Asian American mad tea party was incredibly appealing to me, and I spoke later with the band's bassist, Ed Lin.[12]

Dick Hebdige has suggested that in British contexts of the 1970s, punk stood in dialectical relation to reggae[13] — that it was one kind of an "open dialogue" between "an immigrant culture with a strong 'ethnic' character and the indigenous working-class culture which technically 'encloses' it" (Hebdige [1979] 1993: 68), that is, between Black Jamaican immigrants and the British white working class. Similarly, the emergence in the 1990s

Fig. 6.6 The band Tea Club in performance on May 6, 1995. (Photograph by René T.A. Lysloff.)

of white alternative rock is probably (at some level) a response to the commercial and social success of African American hip-hop. Asian American alternative rock of the 1990s of course speaks in still other directions. Obviously much more could be said about all of this, but Hebdige's observation that contemporaneous musics are sometimes speaking to each other about class and ethnicity is well taken.

Tea Club's noisiness and disorderliness stood out at the festival. They were preceded on stage by a pop group of Japanese nationals, and Lin told me they were intimidated by the other group's "tightness." Yet in other ways, Lin was also proud of Tea Club's feistiness — when I told him I thought his group was easily the festival's noisiest and most raucous band, he said, "Cool! Thanks!" I asked Lin, who was twenty-six years old at that time, why he was drawn to alternative rock, and he said it was an inevitable process that began in high school:

> I could relate to it the most, 'cause when I was growing up the 80s there were groups like Def Leppard, there was Yes making a comeback…there was just all this *garbage* coming out. And I couldn't relate to any of it. And I heard Hüsker Dü's "New Day Rising," and the Clash, and I could relate their music to a lot of the *hate* that I

felt. So I guess that's how I really got into it: the *hate*! (Laughs) Like, hating society. Sick of always trying to be happy, always having to tell people, "Have a nice day!" I grew up in 5 or 6 different places in New Jersey, and being the only Asian around, I was always subject to a lot of abuse. I can't even think of a day that went by when someone didn't call me a chink or something. All these kids who thought they were so cool and everything — who were going out to see Van Halen and Def Leppard and Quiet Riot — you just listen to these groups' music — they're wearing leather and think they're so bad and everything, but they don't even curse in their songs, they don't really have anything constructive or *de*structive to say...

To what extent was Tea Club an Asian American band? Ed explained that they came together through secondary friendships, and says that although they didn't decide to form "an Asian American band," its ethos was strongly informed by Asian American experience. All of the band members are involved in other Asian American arts and activist groups. Tea Club performed four songs, all original. Composition was collaborative: Stan and Ed, the lead and bass guitarists, would come up with the chord progressions and riffs, and Donna would "go through her notebook" of poetry and lay lyrics over their guitar work. The fourth and final song that Tea Club performed at the festival was "Alien," which Ed saw as playing off the double-think of immigrant as extra-terrestrial; Donna's lyrics were "I'm an alien!," uttered repeatedly in a despairing tone over Stan's and Ed's power chords.

A second presentation at the festival offered another perspective and another take on cultural ownership. A large poster exhibit on "The Musical Heritage of Asian Pacific Americans" was on display on the west side of the park. Each panel featured a different Asian American musician, with photographs and a short bio. The exhibit was clear and attractive, and was designed by several members of the Coalition. A number of musicians were profiled in it, including Toshiko Akiyoshi, Billy Asai, Terumasa Hino, the TanaReid Ensemble, George Gee, Fred Ho, Cecile Licad, Chee Yun, Midori, Sarah Chang, Yo-Yo Ma, the Tokyo String Quartet, Seiji Ozawa, Kent Nagano, the Children's Orchestra Society, and the Ahn Trio.

The opening panel (Figure 6.7) posited "a specifically Asian Pacific American identity" but "musical expression" is explicitly accepted as multiple and diverse. Notice too that Asian American musical "presences" as well as "production" are acknowledged — i.e., a wide range of musical activities were recognized. The poster exhibit could be seen as a self-conscious attempt to define a corner of music-making, and even a gesture toward institutionalizing it as a history while still insisting on its variegated nature. Still, as a defining statement, I find these five sentences fascinating for the line they walk between trying to define and trying to leave open what Asian Pacific American musical activities might be.

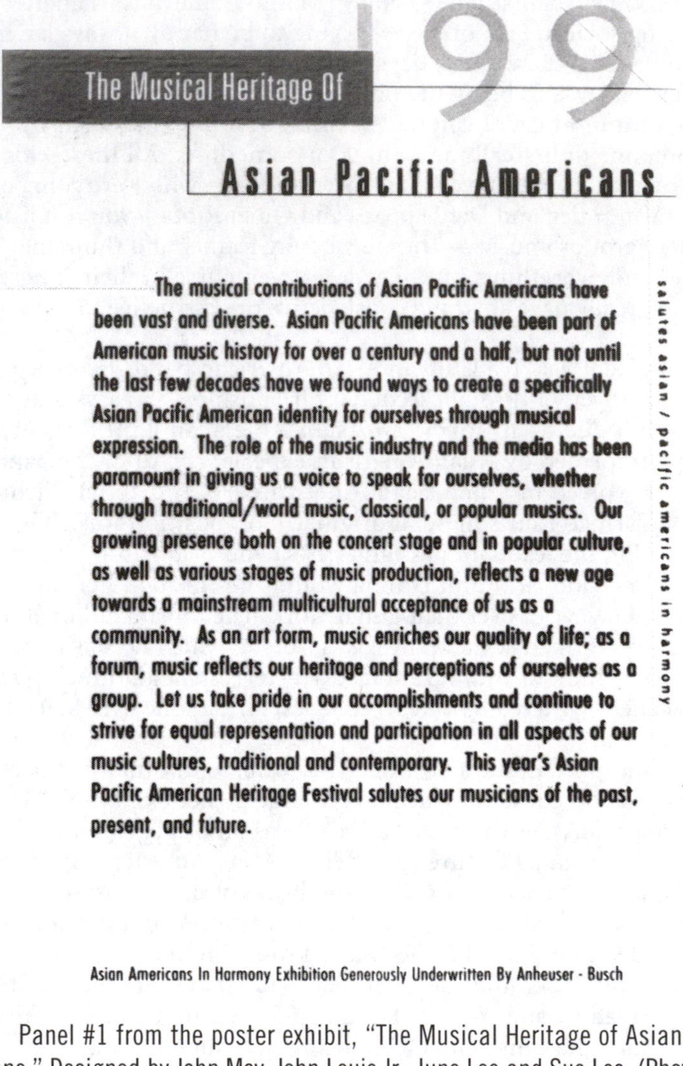

The Musical Heritage Of 199

Asian Pacific Americans

The musical contributions of Asian Pacific Americans have been vast and diverse. Asian Pacific Americans have been part of American music history for over a century and a half, but not until the last few decades have we found ways to create a specifically Asian Pacific American identity for ourselves through musical expression. The role of the music industry and the media has been paramount in giving us a voice to speak for ourselves, whether through traditional/world music, classical, or popular musics. Our growing presence both on the concert stage and in popular culture, as well as various stages of music production, reflects a new age towards a mainstream multicultural acceptance of us as a community. As an art form, music enriches our quality of life; as a forum, music reflects our heritage and perceptions of ourselves as a group. Let us take pride in our accomplishments and continue to strive for equal representation and participation in all aspects of our music cultures, traditional and contemporary. This year's Asian Pacific American Heritage Festival salutes our musicians of the past, present, and future.

salutes asian / pacific americans in harmony

Asian Americans In Harmony Exhibition Generously Underwritten By Anheuser - Busch

Fig. 6.7 Panel #1 from the poster exhibit, "The Musical Heritage of Asian Pacific Americans." Designed by John Moy, John Louie Jr., June Lee and Sue Lee. (Photograph by Deborah Wong.)

Allow me to use this poster as a springboard into a broader consideration of the rhetorical framework of the festival and a consideration of it as a site of cultural production. The multiculturalism industry is of course alive and well these days, and for those of us committed to, and invested in, an activism and educational imperative located in sites of difference and inequity, the challenge is to maintain a particular stance of multiculturalism that resists efforts to contain and domesticate it. The poster exhibit panel stated that Asian American musics and musicians reflect "a new age toward a mainstream multicultural acceptance of us as a community." The intentions of this statement are deep and community-based and impassioned, and my intention here is not to reject its problematic rhetoric but to propose other ways of producing community-based action that don't compromise that community's diversity or ignore the inequities that, in turn, produced it. To put it another way, I admire what the organizers of the festival have accomplished, and I offer these thoughts as one effort out of many to keep prodding at the ways we collectively create community through such events.

"Community" is a sticky concept in Asian American studies. Asian American communities are notoriously threaded through with differences of ethnicity, region of home country, class, and generation. Communities' realities lie in the imagination — occupying the same space–time continuum is only one of many ways that communities can exist — and the effort to performatively create an Asian American community of New York City is a self-conscious attempt at a pan-Asian coalition. Chinatown and Flushing are real Asian American communities, certainly, but a pan-Asian American community is something that can only exist fleetingly, in the context of the one-day annual festival. It *is* important for Asian American bodies of different ethnicities, ages, generations, classes, genders, religions, sexualities, and political persuasions to gather in the same space, and perhaps the only way for this to happen is through the ephemeral reality of performance, in a space which would normally be empty of Asian Americans. Urban planners have methodological frameworks for analyzing urban emptinesses like vacant lots, abandoned buildings, squares, and parks; emptiness is "culturally created and socially meaningful," writes urban anthropologist Gary McDonogh. Such spaces aren't social vacuums but rather "zones of intense competition: the interstices of the city" (McDonogh 1993: 13). City parks, squares, and plazas are empty spaces meant to be filled with certain kinds of people and activities. The Asian Pacific American Coalition has to rent a public space for its annual festival — it has to seek out empty space that is affordable and accessible to it. In the past, the Coalition held the festival outside at Lincoln Center, the sacred center of European high art culture, and found that the audience was mostly tourists; the decision to move closer to Chinatown was a deliberate effort to place the festival closer to a different kind of symbolic center. McDonogh argues that empty public spaces can, up to a point, be

> an anomalous form of space in which conflict is grappled with
> rather than avoided … Such spaces … form the heart of grass-roots
> citizens' movements. When an empty space fills, its actors contra-
> vert its social construction or planned meaning. Hence it provides
> a place from which to protest a city and society as a whole, whether
> by rioters in eighteenth century Paris or by the assembled civil

rights marchers on the Washington Mall in the 1960s or by the pro-
testers in Tiananmen Square in 1989 ... Whether vacant, open, or
razed, empty spaces thus play crucial roles in the fabric of the city
(McDonogh 1993: 14–15).

When the planned emptiness of Union Square Park is filled by Asian
Americans, even for a day, *something* happens, but to what extent does it
"contravert" the social fabric of the city? The annual festival disrupts *and*
reinscribes relations with a dominant culture in ways that are partly
thought through and partly not. In other words, I think the festival plays
into and against dominant culture at the same time.

Much of this relates to the rhetoric of ethnic and multicultural festivals
in general. American ethnic festivals have a strong narrative thrust that is
nearly impossible to neutralize. Most are held outside the geographic
boundaries of the communities they supposedly showcase, moving people
and their activities — often performance — into a museum-like dynamic
of exhibit and gazer. The very politics and proxemics that create, sustain,
and contain urban ethnic neighborhoods are deliberately domesticated by
taking the actors out of their environments and putting them into "public"
— i.e., empty and depoliticized — spaces. The Asian Pacific American festival plays into this at yet another level because the effort to create a sense
of pan-Asian community precludes the use of neighborhoods with specific
ethnic Asian identifications (like Chinatown).

American ethnic festivals also rely on a kind of multicultural rhetoric
that I find particularly damaging to Asian American activism, which is
especially vulnerable due to its built-in problems of difference that create a
centrifugal pull against coalition. This vision of multiculturalism, which
purports to have replaced earlier metaphors like the melting pot and the
mosaic, promotes cultural pluralism but one with a strong pull toward the
center. David Palumbo-Liu has addressed this problematic in his introduction to *The Ethnic Canon,* a collection of essays focused on the history and
practice of creating a multicultural curriculum by constructing canons of
American ethnic literatures. He calls this "the liberal argument for multiculturalism," noting its drive toward a normative pluralism in which cultural differences are expected to arrive at a kind of "conflict management
formula" (Palumbo-Liu 1995: 10). As he puts it, "the ethnic text [is]
reduced to a pretext for the pluralistic argument that all cultures share certain expressive values," and thus "vacate[s] the term "multicultural" of its
progressive intellectual, pedagogical, and social goals" (ibid., 2). The counterhegemonic potentials of such texts are undermined, neutralized, and
rerouted. Rather than trying to move these texts into canonic formation,
or trying to place them on shared platforms of difference and resistance
(which is in itself a neutralizing move), Palumbo-Liu proposes a "critical
multiculturalism," which would explore "the fissures, tensions, and sometimes contradictory demands of multiple centers, rather than (only) cele-

brating the plurality of cultures by passing through them appreciatively"
(ibid., 5). The urge toward celebration is thus revealed as a hegemonic
strategy of containment, in which difference (in true late capitalist style) is
made "not only unobstructive, but attractive" (ibid., 5), a "diverting spectacle within the dominant mythology from which it in part emanates"
(Hebdige [1979] 1993: 94). A critical multiculturalism, on the other hand,
"should be always in revision and contestation" (Palumbo-Liu 1995: 14)
— should be in constant movement against stabilization, against particular relationships with the hegemonic that are the *modus operandi* of representation. As Palumbo-Liu suggests, once minority discourse is "visible as
a represented and representative object," it is open to control and indeed
to canonization (ibid., 17).

All of this brings me back to my original questions — whether an Asian
American self-representation is possible and whether the Asian American
festival event is a performative of self-representation. I recall Bert Wang's
assessment of the festival as a "feel-good" event, and now see this as an
extremely astute identification of the festival's strengths as well as its vul-
nerabilities. The festival does feel good. But this is partly the relief that
comes when you stop banging your head against the wall — a temporary
release from the everyday racist gaze of the city. Shouldn't it feel good to
get away, even for a moment, from what Lani Guinier has called the tyranny of the majority?[14] But it's also partly the ease of entering into a seduc-
tive master narrative of equality-in-difference. By relying on a comfortable
pluralism that reaches back into normative difference for meaning, it
seems to me that the festival walks a dangerous line between assertion and
cooption. How can the essential ferment of "an" Asian American community, with all of its internal politics and its uncrossable lines of internal difference, resist a hegemonic encouragement to celebrate itself?

In 1996, the festival was moved from Union Square to the outdoor
plaza at Lincoln Center in an attempt to put it in a more "central" location.
The result was mixed. Certainly the site of Lincoln Center suggested a set
of associations with the high art establishment on New York City as well as
a subversion of its elitist space. The overall feeling of the event was quite
different from the bustling, small town environment of Union Square the
previous year. The open concrete plaza at Lincoln Center was a bit empty
and forbidding, and it didn't help that that day in May was overcast and
chilly. Between the weather and the location, fewer people came. The stage
was a formal bandshell, much better from a production standpoint (great
acoustics, better lines of sight, etc.) but it enforced a large proscenium spatial separation of performers and audience. When the Mountain Brothers,
a three-man Chinese American hip-hop crew from Philadelphia (discussed in more detail in Chapters 8 and 10), came on, they were a bit
dwarfed by the expanse of the empty stage (Figure 6.8), and the nuances of
their introspective style (Figure 6.9) were hard to appreciate. Some audience members got as close to the stage as they could, dancing right up

Fig. 6.8 The Mountain Brothers onstage at the 1996 festival at Lincoln Center. (Photograph by Deborah Wong.)

against barricades keeping them a good thirty feet away from the performers (Figure 6.10). But the spectacularized "uptown" space of Lincoln Center, far from any appreciable Asian American neighborhood, made the celebratory frame of the event even more apparent, and the small attendance made the gesture seem all the more limited.

I come back, as I do again and again, to Henry Giroux's ideal of cultural workers — activists, teachers, artists, community workers, etc. — who take seriously the responsibility of encouraging many sites of cultural production. Central to Giroux's work is the call to insert "the primacy of the political and the pedagogical" (1992: 5). The idea is to close the distance between theory, pedagogy, and activism, and to place the interrogation of representations back in the hands of those affected by them. Cynthia Wong and the Asian Pacific American Coalition are doing that; the performers who get on stage at the festival are doing that; perhaps even the New Yorkers who walked through Union Square Park on May 6th could be seen as doing that. But it's a steel frame that holds them all in place, that allows them to occupy an empty space for an afternoon, that allows a moment of collective difference. And that's the problem: I don't want to forget that contradiction, or to indulge in a forgetful *bonhomie* that translates into normative pluralism. I don't think celebration is a safe place, yet. Working toward "a mainstream multicultural acceptance of us as a community," as the poster exhibit suggested, is too sadly compromised.

Fig. 6.9 Chops from the Mountain Brothers performing onstage at the 1996 festival at Lincoln Center. (Photograph by Deborah Wong.)

Tricia Rose has pointed out that "attempts to delegitimate powerful social discourses are often deeply contradictory" (1994: 103), and the festival was no exception. How can we allow for voices that speak the language of corporate multiculturalism, yet resist becoming ventriloquists? Giroux insists that "cultural workers must take responsibility … for the knowledge they organize, produce, mediate, and translate into the practice of culture" (1992: 175). Do we simply allow for the contradictions — allow complicity and reclamation to coexist — and have faith that critique will emerge? The very process of organizing and translation — translating alternative rock into an Asian American performative, for instance — is surely an act of critique in itself. Still, Rose goes on to note that "These contradictions are not reducible to the pitfalls of limited vision … but, instead, characterize the partiality and specificity of cultural struggle" (ibid., 104). The Dancing Itos may indeed compromise the possibility of critique even as they sharpen up our ability to see power moving through performing bodies. An Asian American figure of authority like Judge Ito must still be

Fig. 6.10 Three audience members dancing to the Mountain Brothers' performance, getting as close to the stage as they can. (Photograph by Deborah Wong.)

contained and controlled; the multicultural showbiz of the festival is deliberately depoliticized at the corporate level, but the darts still fly on the ground. These contradictions indicate that something important is going on. Small successes. Connect the dots and something else begins to take shape, through performance, through the dizzying contradictory movements of cultural workers who won't agree.

Acknowledgments

This essay was written for the symposium, "Sounding the Difference: Musics and the Politics of Identity in America," held on 14–15 October 1995 at the Department of Ethnic Studies, University of California, Berkeley. I would like to thank Tim Taylor for inviting me to participate and for organizing this event.

Endnotes

1. Several members of the on-line discussion group of the Association for Asian American Studies were very helpful as I prepared this section on the Dancing Itos, sharing their interpretations and providing leads for more information. I want to thank Sylvia Kwon, Darby Li Po Price, Traise Yamamoto, Christina Woo, Darrell Hamamoto, and Robert Lee for their thoughts and suggestions. I should note that many of these electronic colleagues did not think that the Dancing Itos were a racist or derogatory act.

2. Dennis Fung was even the butt of racist performatives by the Simpson defense team, whose members passed out fortune cookies at a press conference saying, "We had *Fung* in there today."

3. One of the more bizarre examples I've encountered was a "documentary" on Donald Johansen's discovery of the skeletal remains now known as Lucy, which took the current fascination with re-enactments even further: Johanson re-enacted himself. Johansen not only narrated the documentary but was filmed striding through the Rift Valley and "finding" a bone fragment.

4. Guessing from their names, Nito Larioza is probably Filipino American, Tym Buacharern is probably Thai or Lao American, Danny Lee is probably either Chinese or Korean American, Hoang Ho is probably Vietnamese American, and although I have no idea what Michael Gregory's ethnic background is, he looks Asian (Pitzer 1995).

5. Personal communication, 26 September 1995.

6. Personal communications, Cynthia Wong (24 September 1995) and Bert Wang (26 September 1995).

7. Personal communication, Cynthia Wong (24 September 1995).

8. Personal communication, Bert Wang (26 September 1995).

9. Personal communication, Fred Ho (26 September 1995).

10. Fred Ho, who was on the festival's program committee in the early 1980s, remembers that earlier festivals also included Asian American popular culture acts. In 1994, for instance, Margaret Cho (of the ill-fated and probably ill-conceived *All-American Girl*) did a stand-up routine, and an Asian American juggler appeared.

11. At an open house of the New York City Asian American Writers Workshop.

12. The two band members listed in the program (Donna and Stan) have moved from New York to San Francisco. All of Lin's comments are from an interview conducted on 9 October 1995.

13. Hebdige's discussion of dialectical white-Black movements in popular music styles ([1979] 1993: 68-70) speaks to the inevitable issue of Asian American musical "intrusions" into genres associated with White or Black origins.

14. *The Tyranny of the Majority: Fundamental Fairness in Representative Democracy*, by Lani Guinier. New York, NY: The Free Press, 1995.

7

Listening to Local Practices:
Performance and Identity Politics
in Riverside, California

If reception is the most under-theorized area of performance studies, then I am doubly at a loss when trying to explain refusal. How can we theorize audience resistance to a performance, or the audience that refuses to attend? That audience — the one that stays home — executes a different intervention, an intervention of denial that is itself perhaps an affirmation of the performative. Refusing to take in the performative is perhaps the only effective means for eluding transformation. Performance studies has no apparatus for dealing with an audience that closes its eyes and ears; indeed, it is shot through with progressive yet sadly romantic ideals of community. *The Drama Review* regularly carries work focused on community theater and the theater of resistance. How (or even whether) "the community" engages with the performative is another question. Such methodology presupposes a community of the oppressed — a community in such duress that it is willing to engage with the possibility of transforming itself.

But consider an audience that is angry or bored or offended or distracted. This too is reception: resistance of this sort is perhaps the strongest expression of agency. Noncompliance is the most difficult gesture of all to parse as it closes up at the moment of interrogation. This chapter is, then, an ethnography of reception with a critical edge: in considering unwillingness and repudiation, I will not offer a relativist apology but instead will move toward strategies of engagement and pedagogy.

139

Miya Masaoka is an Asian American musician and performance artist whose performance at the Unnatural Acts conference, hosted by the University of California, Riverside on April 11, 1997, created a situation rife with sensationalism and anxiety as well as pedagogical possibility. Various responses to Masaoka's performance suggested that gender, sexuality, and race intersect in ways neither subtle nor abstract for many UCR students and Riverside residents. I will consider how performance might have a pedagogical function in a conservative city and will arrive at these strategies through an ethnography of an event and its reception.

As an ethnomusicologist studying performance, I prefer close ethnographies of particular people in particular circumstances because they are a crucial kind of resistance to the generalizing pull of performance studies scholarship focused on cross-cultural universals. Interpenetrating relationships of class, race, ethnicity, gender, sexual orientation, etc., are made most visible through close ethnographic work. I also want to take ethnography further into a process that connects scholars to communities and thus creates conditions of accountability and responsibility — conditions refused until recently, but which we can make pedagogical in the broadest sense, as cultural work (Wong 1998).

Let me enlarge on each of these points. Taking local lives and local practices seriously is an effective means to reflexively address problematic histories. Anthropologist Lila Abu-Lughod (1991) has persuasively argued that "ethnographies of the particular" can subvert the process of 'othering' (1991: 149).[1] Carefully noting that she does not suggest reversing older practices by simply "privileging micro over macro processes," she points out how anthropological methods for generalizing about cultures are intrinsically related to scholarly epistemologies of objectivity, speaking what she calls "inevitably a language of power" (ibid., 150). Instead, Abu-Lughod proposes what she calls tactical humanism — that is, a self-conscious attempt to write "against" anthropological generalization by strategically focusing on the local, the particular, the individual. Such a humanistic gesture is tactical, to her mind, because it recognizes humanism's problematic history as a means of celebrating the essentialized individual. Rather, Abu-Lughod calls for the use of humanism as a moral force and as a local language, or one might say, a language consciously made local by mindful writers. As Abu-Lughod says, if Western positionality cannot be escaped, then "our writing can either sustain it or work against its grain" (ibid., 159). Abu-Lughod's two ethnographies, *Veiled Sentiments* (1986) and *Writing Women's Worlds* (1993), provide vivid models for tactically humanistic ethnography by addressing particular women's worlds and experiences.

The younger discipline of Ethnic Studies, however, took on issues of difference from the beginning (in the 1960s), largely in reaction to the political sensibilities of certain constructions of history. The incursion of feminist theory in the 1980s and 1990s into Ethnic Studies is one of its major second-wave changes. Although theorizing race, ethnicity, and class was the focus of the first decade of work in Ethnic Studies, more recent theoretical influences have led to methodological shifts that theorize race, ethnicity, class, gender, and sexual orientation as interconstitutive. Contemporary Ethnic Studies thus more broadly addresses the social construction of difference. Introducing gender and sexuality as central to identity work has essentially transformed Ethnic Studies as a field. Reflecting on this change in Asian American studies, sociologists Michael Omi and Dana Takagi (1995: xiii) write that:

> While Asian American scholars took exception with feminist scholarship and practice which rendered race invisible, failed to grasp the unique circumstances of families of color, and marginalized the role of women of color in scholarly and activist organizations, the overall insights of feminism dramatically reshaped intellectual and political practices within Asian American Studies.

Acknowledging the complexity of academic accountability to the communities it touches can be painful. American Ethnic Studies — as contrasted to area studies and even to so-called American studies — has embraced accountability and made community links central to its purpose. In a 1995 issue of *Amerasia Journal* (then the leading scholarly journal of Asian American studies), editor Russell Leong summarized this problematic in no uncertain terms (Leong 1995: ix):

> Academic pimping ... involves the following: utilizing the communities' "bodies" as informants, studying, collecting and using community culture as material for research, publishing essays, articles, and books based on the above — without giving anything back. As rewards for such intellectual production that is actually based on the labor, experiences and expertise of others (often free), academics get tenure, promotions and royalties from books, article reprints, access to special grant monies for scholars, attendance at symposiums, and so forth. ... Rarely is the work translated for the broader public. Seldom is such work transformed into active political or cultural strategies.

Connecting with community has taken two forms. Many Ethnic Studies scholars in the academy have committed themselves to responding to the needs and directives of communities while also trying to share the largesse of their own position and privilege. In California's public universities, for instance, many of us share a keen awareness that our students *are* members of those communities: if we provide access to certain ideas and experiences, we directly impact the future of those communities by allowing its members a broader range of political possibilities from which to choose.

This is not abstract. Many Asian/Asian American undergraduates, for instance, arrive at UCR with little sense of their place in American ethnic politics let alone a sense of themselves as Asian American *as well as* Chinese American, Vietnamese American, or Korean American. The pedagogical process of asking them to make informed choices about identity based on history, culture, and experience is no simple thing. Certainly our students come to us with experience — they are not blank slates. The important thing is that they leave the university with some sense of how their experiences connect to, or fail to connect, with broader social and political forces. And yet, all this must be inflected with a consciousness of what Patti Lather calls "post-critical pedagogies," i.e., an attempt to activate agency as well as to produce knowledge. As Lather writes (1992: 122),

> [Critical] pedagogies have [too often] failed to probe the degree to which "empowerment" becomes something done "by" liberated pedagogies "to" or "for" the as-yet-unliberated, the "Other," the object upon which is directed the "emancipatory" actions. It is precisely this question that postmodernism frames: How do our very efforts to liberate perpetuate the relations of dominance?

Accountability is thus two-tiered. Accountability to the community, certainly, but also a commitment to continuously question the dyadic relationship between community and academy.

If the ethnography of performance were joined to the progressive political agenda of Ethnic Studies, much could happen. If we seek to understand the mechanisms of the performative, then this particular disciplinary coalition can lead to a kind of politically performative scholarship.

Why present and discuss an Asian American woman performer? Miya Masaoka is almost the only Asian American woman I will address in detail in this book because she is one of very few Asian American woman jazz and avant-garde musicians working in an idiom explicitly constructed as Asian American. I can't help but feel uneasy about her lone female presence even though it's a fact of Asian American musicianly demographics. The historian Gary Okihiro writes that in Asian American studies,

> Women's recentering, their inclusion within our 'community of memory', has only just begun. ... [R]ecentering women positions gender as a prominent social category in determining relations of power and trajectories of social change — race and class are neither the sole nor principal determinants of Asian American history and culture... (1994: 91).

I am not engaged in a kind of first-wave feminist salvage work: I am not writing women or even this woman back into historical reality. Masaoka is busily creating her own Asian American historicity — she doesn't particularly need me to explain what she's up to. Instead, I will address how gender and ethnicity combine powerfully in Masaoka's explorations of the Asian and the Asian American. This performer is keenly aware of the politics of representation: to some extent, she makes this awareness part of her presentation of self.

So I am left with the question of how to present a responsible reading of her to any audience, whether Asian American or not. In fact, I think I failed this exercise in April 1997 when Masaoka came to UCR at my invitation and gave a performance that packed our recital hall for many wrong reasons. I hope to recuperate that extended, compromised moment by doing a better job here — that is, I hope to transform past clumsiness into something pedagogically useful, through re-examination. Elizabeth Ellsworth has criticized the tendency of critical educators to "operate at a high level of abstraction" and the preponderance of journal articles on education that, "although apparently based on actual practices, rarely locate theoretical constructs within them" (1992: 92). She further wonders whether the use of "code words" like "critical" and "social change" veil the political agenda of critical pedagogy, and I will here question whether my own "posture of invisibility," i.e., my assumption that my agenda in producing this event would be self-evident, was naïve and ultimately ineffective, leaving the event open to conservative reinterpretation (1992: 93).

(Figure 7.1). Miya Masaoka is a *Sansei* (third-generation Japanese American) born in 1958; she lives in San Francisco. She is a musician, composer, and performance artist. Her chosen instrument is the Japanese *koto*, a 21-string zither with a long and venerable history. Masaoka has extensive training in traditional Japanese music; she is the director of the San Francisco Gagaku Society, an ensemble that performs the ancient music of the Japanese courts. She has a master's degree in composition from Mills College and is a full-time professional performer. She plays jazz and new music on the *koto*, and recorded a solo compact disc titled *Compositions/Improvisations* in 1993. This album was released by Asian Improv Records, a non-profit label dedicated to Asian American new music, and Masaoka is at the center of this circle of activist musicians in the Bay Area.[2] Masaoka has written that, as a Japanese American composer, she has had "no choice but to construct my own musical reality" (Masaoka 1996: 8). She is keenly aware of the cultural politics surrounding her use of the *koto*, and the possibility of being accused of inappropriately drawing a non-Western instrument into modernist Western traditions of new music. Rather, she justifies the intercultural nature of her activities by saying:

> …for me, being of Japanese heritage and born in America, biculturalism and transcultural identity have always been basic to my existence; it is this hybridity that engenders and perhaps necessitates a new cultural expression for me (ibid.).

Fig. 7.1 Publicity photograph of Miya Masaoka playing the *koto*. (Reproduced with the permission of Kim Stringfellow, © Kim Stringfellow.)

I met Masaoka in April 1996 when I helped arrange a three-day residency for her and her Asian Improv colleague Mark Izu in Philadelphia. At that time, I was a member of an Asian American community arts organization called the Asian Arts Initiative, and I spent three days driving Masaoka and Izu around the city, taking them from one lecture-demo to another at different schools and community centers. In short, I got to know Masaoka and her music quickly and intensely, and I liked what I saw and heard. I was intrigued by the diverse influences and ideologies at work in her music: the traditional Japanese, modernist, *avant-garde* art music,

Fig. 7.2 Publicity photograph of Miya Masaoka's legs with hissing Madagascar cockroaches. (Reproduced with the permission of Lori Eanes.)

jazz, etc. I also learned that Masaoka was closely involved in several community-based arts projects in San Francisco.

During our free time, Masaoka told me about her performance art work, especially two works in progress. *Bee Project #1* (performed the following month in Oakland) involved 3,000 live bees, violin, percussion, and *koto;* the sound of the bees was amplified and run through MIDI interface; the human performers responded to the resulting sounds. Another piece, titled *Ritual,* featured Masaoka, a number of Madagascar hissing roaches, and a mixed soundtrack of *koto* and hissing roaches: Masaoka was to lie nude on a table with the roaches crawling over her body while the soundtrack played and a video projector showed close-ups of the insects. (Figure 7.2). We talked about *Ritual* in some detail, as she was in the process of finalizing it; she told me it was to be the first of a series of performance art pieces addressing the Asian American body, and she asked if I could suggest any readings about the body, identity, and performance. I suggested Judith Butler's *Bodies That Matter,* which she consequently read. Fast forward a year: I had relocated to University of California, Riverside and was involved in the Unnatural Acts conference; the organizers — Sue-Ellen Case, Susan Leigh Foster, and Philip Brett — asked if I could suggest someone for an evening performance and I offered to bring Masaoka to UCR. Arranging it with Masaoka, I asked if she might put together a program of solo *koto* works plus the performance art piece *Ritual,* and she agreed.

All this was routine enough until the week before the performance, scheduled for April 11, 1997. I made sure that publicity announcements got out, arranged for a poster, and attended to all the details surrounding the recital hall. The performance was advertised as "Miya Masaoka in Performance: Hissing Madagascar Roaches and the *Koto* Monster," so perhaps it's not surprising that the Riverside County newspaper, *The Press-Enterprise,* called me a week before the event. They ran a preview story three days before the performance, based on a telephone interview with Masaoka.

Almost immediately, telephone calls started flooding in to the music department, UCR's University Relations office, the Dean, the Chancellor — but especially to the music department. Many of the callers simply expressed disapproval, others disgust and outrage. Two days later, a letter appeared on *The Press-Enterprise*'s editorial page from Robert Wild, a UCR professor emeritus of physics. (Figure 7.3). (His "brother professor" Bill Reynolds was formerly a professor in the music department, once the department chair, now deceased.) "The community" was up in arms over Masaoka and her roaches.

Ashamed for UCR

■ UCR has been embarrassed and harmed beyond measure by the UCR Music Department. "Hissing Madagascar Roaches and the Koto Monster" (Entertainment section, April 8) is a despicable act which would be "at home" in a porno movie — not in Watkins Recital Hall. Gordon Watkins would be appalled that this disgusting act was in the hall bearing his name. My "brother professor" Bill Reynolds would not have let it happen in his Music Department.

What I don't understand is why Chancellor Ray Orbach's staff didn't bring the matter to his attention. I feel certain that neither he, nor none of the previous UCR chancellors, would have allowed these "14 cockroaches" to perform in Watkins Hall. I am ashamed for UCR.

R. L. WILD
Riverside

Fig. 7.3 Letter to the editor from community member Robert Wild, *The Press-Enterprise.* Reproduced with the permission of *The Press-Enterprise.*

Who *is* "the community" in Riverside, California? In 1992, the population was 238,000 of whom 60.5% were White, 26.5% were Latino/a, 7% were African American, 4.9% were Asian American, and .9% were Native American. Riverside is the county seat and the largest city in Riverside County; it is about sixty miles east of Los Angeles and the river in question is the Santa Ana River, which is mostly if not completely dry for much of the year. The city was established after the introduction of citrus trees in the nineteenth century transformed the region — in fact, UCR was once an agricultural college, and a multitude of courses are still offered in soil, insects, and worms. Much of the Latino/a population of the city originally arrived to work as laborers in the citrus groves; the latest waves of laborers are indigenous peoples from Mexico and Central America. Still, the Anglo population is by far the largest. UCR is one of the smallest UC campuses with only 9,000 undergraduates, many of whom come from Riverside or Orange Counties, many of whom are the first in their families to attend college. UCR's undergraduate population is dominated by Anglo- and Asian/Asian Americans. Out of 8,381 students in 1998, the undergraduate population was 42.8% Asian/Asian American, 28.6% White American, 19.9% Hispanic, 2.5% 'other', 5.5% African American, and 0.6% Native American ("Self-Study Report": 95). In short, student demographics do not by any means reflect the city's demographics.

While I would not describe UCR's undergraduates as particularly radical or even liberal, the faculty and curriculum have repeatedly attracted the attention of the community, and the dismay of the more conservative community has often found a forum in *The Press-Enterprise*. In May and June 1996, for instance, faculty approval of a new minor in Lesbian, Gay, Bisexual and Transgender Studies caused a major stir in the local newspaper. The Unnatural Acts conference has prompted community outcry several times. In short, "the community" expects something between titillation and the offensive from UCR.

Professor Wild's reference to pornography was echoed in many of the phone calls taken by music department staff members[3] and thus evoked previous controversies. By Friday (the day of the performance), the calls were more focused. One woman caller told the secretary answering the phone that the chairperson of the music department (Philip Brett) was "no better than a pimp standing out on University Avenue." Another warned that if Masaoka disrobed on stage, he would effect a citizen's arrest on the spot. Others called to threaten disruptions. While most of the phone calls were apparently from community members, UCR students, faculty, and staff were also intrigued, but in other ways. I assigned concert attendance to the undergraduates in my class, "Music and Gender in Cross-Cultural Perspective," and they reported that prurient curiosity was inspiring many of their friends to attend. They assured me that I could expect a full house.

By the evening of the performance, we had arranged for three rather than the usual solo security officer and university legal counsel had advised us that the legal definition of "public lewdness" is that no warning is extended to potential viewers. We therefore posted notices outside the recital hall stating that the performance would involve nudity, thus protecting the school and enabling security officers to remove anyone causing a disruption. (Figure 7.4). Watkins Recital Hall seats two hundred and eight people, and it was packed by 7:45. I might add that this was unprecedented: the usual chamber music concerts held in this hall generally don't draw hordes of people. The student ushers were so unprepared for the phenomenon of a full house that I had to tell them to close the doors.

Backstage, Masaoka was excited and bemused but not at all worried. She said her performance of *Ritual* in San Francisco hadn't attracted one tenth this attention, nor was it regarded by the press as controversial. In short, she was simply pleased at the turnout. I, on the other hand, was tense and perplexed, feeling that the situation had somehow gotten out of hand and wondering how I might have better handled it. I had seated sympathetic friends and colleagues in the front row to form a kind of supportive barricade, but it was clear that the second row was lined with conservative community members: they had arrived together — in fact, they were nearly the first people in the recital hall doors, and they looked both grim and … prepared, like they had a plan.

Meanwhile, the excited buzz of undergraduate conversation filled the air. I scanned the audience, at once ashamed of my own attempts to identify troublemakers yet compelled to try. I'd say there were three categories of audience members: outraged community conservatives, curious undergraduates, and faculty members and Unnatural Acts attendees ready for a tussle over First Amendment rights and censorship. That middle-aged White man with the crew-cut, for instance, sitting right beside the steps up to the stage: was he in position to disrupt the performance? In my role as producer/panopticon, I found myself wondering if every unsmiling, middle-aged White person in the audience represented conservative middle America and was further distracted by my own readiness to profile.

**THE "HISSING MADAGASCAR
COCKROACHES" AND
"THE KOTO MONSTER"
PERFORMANCE
BY MIYA MASAOKA
WILL INVOLVE NUDITY.
IF YOU THINK YOU WOULD
BE OFFENDED BY THIS
PERFORMANCE,
PLEASE DO NOT ATTEND.**

Fig. 7.4 Warning notice posted at Masaoka's performance.

And in the end, nothing happened. Or rather, Masaoka gave a stunning performance. The first half of the program featured solo *koto* pieces, some using digital processing and computer interface, one about the Japanese American internment camps based on a poem by Lawson Inada. Masaoka spoke to the audience between numbers as she retuned her instrument, explaining each piece, explaining that the "*koto* monster" was her *koto*-plus-sound-technology, a monstrous and often fractious combination. By the second and third pieces, it was clear that many audience members were responding to her virtuosity. During the intermission before *Ritual,* the sense of anticipation was stronger than ever. When everyone was reseated, I went out and (following Masaoka's instructions) explained the technology behind the piece and asked for the audience's silence and concentration, noting that the piece was quite solemn. The curtains opened to reveal a dimly-lit stage with Masaoka's nude body, absolutely still, stretched out on a white-shrouded table in its center. The video projection started, filling the back of the stage with such extreme close-ups of her body that precise anatomical locations were unreadable. In the wings, I punched the "start" button on the CD player and the amplified sounds of hissing Madagascar roaches moved stereophonically across the hall. Asian American graduate student Yutian Wong, dressed in black, appeared on stage right and slowly struck two Tibetan hand cymbals together. Another Asian American student assistant emerged from stage left bearing a box in her hands: she solemnly approached Masaoka and slowly, carefully, began to take Madagascar roaches out of the box, one by one, placing them on Masaoka's body. The roaches sluggishly explored her arms and legs until all thirteen were on her body—and then the assistant began to gather them up, one by one, putting them gently back in the box and finally walking off stage with them. The video ended; the soundtrack ended; the curtains were pulled closed. The piece had lasted fifteen minutes, and nothing had happened. After a long moment of silence, the audience began to applaud. Masaoka pulled on her clothes and went out to bow, announcing that the roaches were for sale if anyone wanted an easygoing pet.

I would like to turn to three textual renditions of *Ritual,* one by Masaoka herself, another by undergraduates in my class who wrote reports about the event,[4] and the third by writers for *The Press-Enterprise.* Despite their *Rashomon*-like mosaic, each points to ways that reception can be shaped or resisted, and each suggests pedagogical possibility.

First, it is important to consider that Masaoka offered her own explanation of *Ritual* in her program notes. (Figure 7.5). That explanation arose from her creative and political interest in performing the body as well as my earlier suggestion that she read Judith Butler. Masaoka found that Butler's use of performance as a central trope fit perfectly with her ideas. The resulting exegesis of *Ritual* is Masaoka's:

UNIVERSITY OF CALIFORNIA,
RIVERSIDE
AS PART OF THE
UNNATURAL ACTS CONFERENCE

HISSING MADAGASCAR ROACHES AND THE *KOTO* MONSTER: MIYA MASAOKA IN PERFORMANCE

FRIDAY, APRIL 11, 1997
8:00 P.M.
WATKINS RECITAL HALL

Fig. 7.5 Program notes from Masaoka's performance.

The *Ritual* is an offering to begin considering the relationships between and the social construction of the body, race, and performance. Recent theoretical work by critical theorist Judith Butler suggests that bodies tend to indicate a world beyond themselves, beyond their own boundaries, a movement of boundary itself. Bodies cannot be said to have a signifiable existence prior to the mark of their gender; the question then emerges, how do we reconceive the body no longer as a passive medium or instrument on which cultural meanings are inscribed? The body can, for example, be thought of as a machine, a work of art, an object of desire/revulsion, a site for hegemony or control, or all of these in fluid and simultaneous flux. The bare skin is the border between our interior self and the exterior world while symbolizing cultural representations and triggering cultural memory, illuminating the contradictory nature of female bodies, male bodies, Asian bodies, and even Japanese bodies. This piece addresses issues of power, control, and the social construction of race and eroticism in performance.

In short, Masaoka had rather specific ideas about what her piece "meant," even though its meanings didn't lie at the micro-level of, for instance, what the roaches might symbolize. Why she chose the language of critical theory to convey her explanation is another question. At the very least, we can assume it fit her thoughts, since she was already planning the piece and thinking about the body as a cultural construct when she asked me for reading suggestions.

What caught the eye and ear of *The Press-Enterprise,* on the other hand, was the possibility of revulsion — insects and nudity were all too easy to sensationalize, and Masaoka's phone interview was easily manipulated to point up the vacuousness of contemporary art: she'd originally wanted rats, the roaches didn't "mean" anything, etc. Yet I'm not quite ready to dismiss the newspaper as a rather desperate small-town rag, either. Rather than simply cry irresponsibility (the expected language of liberalism), I have to consider that *The Press-Enterprise* fulfills a pedagogical function (though not the one I wish it did). It filled Watkins Hall, to be sure, and in all fairness I should say that the front page article the morning after the performance was fair and level-headed (even though penned by one of their sports writers). Still, "the community" had the last word a few days later, again on the editorial page (Figure 7.6). Despite her venom, I find Alta Armstrong's letter interesting because she keeps coming back to the issues I too am concerned with, teaching and education. Never mind that her use of the possessive "our" is unthoughtful (or that *my* music department has nowhere near a million dollars in either annual budget or endowments). Armstrong's evocation of tax dollars emerges from a peculiarly American idea, a democracy of the imaginary, in which education is ownable through taxes. Indeed, any number of irate callers asked how *their* tax dollars could be supporting *that.* The controllable commodity trope is a pedagogical model that we need to engage with as educators, and we further need to engage with the paradigm of commodity capitalism that lurks behind it.

The undergraduates in my music and gender class went into the event with more information and more directives than other audience members. For one thing, they knew they had to write a short report on it, and I had provided specific questions they had to answer — so in some ways my efforts to shape their reception of the event were quite coercive. Of course they had read all the pre-performance newspaper materials, and they knew that the roaches had arrived by FedEx that morning, and they knew the event was potentially explosive, so I think it's safe to say that they went with a certain excitement and a sense that they had the inside scoop. I was keenly interested to see what they had to say about it in their papers.

Armed with the concept of the male gaze, most of the students addressed audience expectations head on. A few were honest enough to admit their own expectations were low: as one woman wrote, "For me, [performance art] conjured up images of people dressed in freakish costumes running rampant about the stage and screaming." One student wrote that during intermission the audience got quite "rowdy" because they "couldn't wait to see the 'naked chick.'" Another noted that "the auditorium was completely packed — with fans, horny male onlookers, [and] just plain curious folks." Yet another flatly stated that "one of the primary

Education at its worst

■ How can this be at our UCR? What are they doing at our university? Our tax money paid for this million dollar-plus Music Department. This cannot come under education! It can't even be entertainment. This is not acceptable education. . . .

How can "Unnatural Acts Conference" with "hissing Madagascar roaches" all over her nude body teach our children anything? With close-up video screens so everyone can get a good view.

This is sick, sick, sick. . . .
ALTA ARMSTRONG
Hemet

Fig. 7.6 Letter to the editor from community member Alta Armstrong, *The Press-Enterprise*. (Reproduced with the permission of *The Press-Enterprise*.)

reasons the hall was so packed ... was because people knew there was going to be nudity. ... Many men anticipated this performance as they would a live stripper in a bar."

These comments confirm what was evident to anyone in the audience: many of the spectators came to be shocked or titillated or at least to witness controversy — or perhaps even to see *others* reacting outrageously to the performance. All this points to the spectacle of controversy and the spectacle of titillation. In other words, these audience members came to see something happen *around* the performance (e.g., a citizen's arrest of the nude performer) or to see a nude body (as opposed to its performance).

Many of the students openly acknowledged that they ultimately found *Ritual* a bit dull to watch. One man wrote that "the piece [lost] its initial level of excitement for me because it [was so] repetitive. The cockroaches really did not move very much." Others unembarrassedly wrote that they weren't sure what it all meant: "I must admit, I felt confused. I had no idea what to think of it," one woman wrote.

Despite their ready admission that interpreting the piece's "meaning" was a challenge, most of the students had a lot to say about its sexual politics. Part of their assignment was for them to consider whether a reversal of the performer's gender would change the piece and its reception. One student suggested that "there is a difference in the way society views the male body and the female body. Women have always been suppressed and held to a standard of virtue, [so that] revealing the body is still considered a degrading and shameful act." One woman wrote that "a woman's naked body is the universal symbol of sex. A man's naked body doesn't have quite the same connotations. A woman has traditionally and historically been seen as a tool for man's pleasure ..."

All of the students addressed the de-eroticization of Masaoka's body. "She was not viewed as a sex object after the performance," wrote one. "The entire scene created a mood that shifted [us] from lust [to] disgust, and the feeling of being in a morgue," another noted. "What was to be an object of desire — the nude female body — was now a source of repulsion," one woman wrote. And all of them got the bigger point: "[Masaoka] challenged notions of sexuality and gender and tested the comfort level [of] her audience. ... She attempted to disrupt and dispute, but she also showed how these constructed roles are still rigid as evidenced by those who took offense [at] her program."

As pleased as I was by the honesty and thoughtfulness of the student papers, I was struck by the absence of any reference to Masaoka's race or ethnicity. Certainly the students noted Masaoka's connection to the *koto* through heritage, but no one even speculated about how sexuality and the body are racialized. Certainly, we were only several weeks into the course and hadn't yet addressed in any depth how race, gender, sexual orientation, class, etc., intersect in most forms of performance, nor had I explicitly told them to consider race and ethnicity. Masaoka herself made only passing reference in the program notes to her body as Japanese. But three of the four students from whom I've drawn most of these comments are Asian American (of Thai and Philippine descent). In fact, several of the students made universalizing gestures, suggesting that *Ritual* transcended the body, gender, and race. As one student wrote, "[Masaoka] was trying to show us that race, gender, and color should not matter because they are not significant."

In short, I was nonplussed by the students' *and* the public response, because race and ethnicity evidently disappeared into the display of the female body — and I had conceived of the event as Asian American in focus and message. Masaoka's racial politics were absorbed into the politics of the body. And I was caught off guard.

Introducing Masaoka as a campus event was as challenging as introducing nonWestern literature into the college curriculum. As an ethnomusicologist, I feel it's my responsibility to produce several performance events every year that will present cultural counterpoints to the usual roster of orchestra and choral concerts; such events complement the curriculum in ways that reflect *praxis,* doing. Whether I help present a xylophonist from Ghana, a Javanese *gamelan* ensemble of American undergraduates, or Miya Masaoka, some educational gesture *beyond* presentation seems necessary if "understanding" is the goal. Having said that, I immediately wonder why a Brahms symphony is somehow considered more transparently understandable when in fact it begs the same question of how the moment of reception can be made pedagogical. Such moments don't just happen, but on the other hand, I wonder whether — or to what extent — they can be controlled, because my interest in having an audience see beyond its preconceptions isn't disinterested at all; in the case of Miya Masaoka, for instance, I wanted them to see certain things and not others.

Masaoka's exposed racialized gendered body Othered her more profoundly than I could have foreseen. How might I have "taught" her to the audience, to local newspaper critics, to the students in my music and gender class? Considering how she might teach a novel by R.K. Narayan to non-Indian students, Gayatri Spivak worries that the book easily becomes a "repository" for "postcolonial selves, postcolonialism, even postcolonial resistance" — that the novel (or any cultural performance) can be too easily read as "direct expressions of cultural consciousness, with no sense of the neocolonial traffic in identity ..." (Spivak 1996: 239). Similarly, Masaoka's public reception as Woman Exposed blew away the traffic in identity that she clearly sees as central to her purpose. Ethnic politics vanished into her overwhelmingly female body.

One woman, one event, one community. I've carefully focused on the local and the particular as a means to think about pedagogy and the presentation of the Other. I am of course wondering if the absence of any discussion of race around this event is the result of studied fear — this did happen in California, after all, where even most conservatives know that race and ethnicity are topics to be approached carefully. Were discussions so single mindedly focused on gender and sexuality because that's what happens when people try to talk about difference — only one parameter can be handled at once? Everything else drops out of the picture. Edna Acosta-Belén notes that issues of gender have traditionally gotten lost in Ethnic Studies while Women's Studies has had a hard time dealing with race and class (1993: 177). Chandra Mohanty made this point in her already-classic essay, "Under Western Eyes," suggesting that the power of colonial discourses makes it difficult even for feminist scholars to get beyond universalizing frameworks (1995: 262). She writes:

> Thus ... in any given piece of feminist analysis, women are characterized as a singular group on the basis of a shared oppression. What binds women together is a sociological notion of the 'sameness' of their oppression. ... Thus, the discursively consensual homogeneity of 'women' as a group is mistaken for the historically specific material reality of groups of women.

Whereas the feminist attempt to get at gendered power relations leads to discursively constituted ideas of shared oppression, the same universalizing frameworks enable a misogynist and sexist reception of an Asian American woman performer as simply pornographic female display.

I should also point out that most of the public responses came from community members who were not at a performance that had yet to occur.[5] Still, I include them and their response as audience members in the broadest sense. As performance studies has taught us to look beyond the performance "itself" to the totality of the event, I consider this absent, offended critical group as an audience and their rejoinders as reception.

I have been concerned here with *praxis* in several ways. Patti Lather (1991: 11) suggests that "praxis is the self-creative activity through which we make the world." *Praxis* can be teaching, or theorizing in concert with others, or any kind of cultural performance. It is a moment when we learn, over and over again, how to turn critical thought into social action. Again, Lather (1991: 55) says that "theory adequate to the task of changing the world must be open-ended, nondogmatic, speaking to and grounded in the circumstances of everyday life."

It occurs to me that I haven't addressed the presence of another audience: the participants and attendees at the Unnatural Acts conference. They were there, too. And we were variously caught up in watching the audience and watching the performance and watching each other while preparing to prevent hostile audience members from disrupting the performance. I haven't theorized the vibrant, enthusiastic, stirred presence of these audience members, nor have I considered the presence of Marta Savigliano on my left and Liz Wood on my right as we watched from the front row. I haven't theorized the readiness of Unnatural Acts participants to fill that row forming a protective barrier. This *praxis* of participatory response was both reflexive and performative, and should be acknowledged even as I shy away from valorizing my own cohort.

Finally, I can't know whether "the community" had a *pedagogical* experience. The fact is, after all the hubbub preceding the performance, no one disrupted it in the end, and it I think we have to ask why not. Of course I (and doubtless many of the Unnatural Acts participants) try hard to believe in and to theorize performance as an activity creating environments that change attitudes and understandings.[6] Or that might change them. At some level, I have to admit I wanted "them" to get "my" interpretation of the performance, but at bottom how can one "know" what happened at the moment of reception? Its ethnographic unknowability irritates and challenges.

To close, I note that Masaoka recounted her Riverside experience to performance artist Guillermo Gómez-Peña, who is considering doing a spot on it in his performative editorial series for National Public Radio's *All Things Considered*. In other words, yet another representation of the event may be forthcoming, again by someone who wasn't there. Furthermore, Masaoka is now planning the second work in her series, "Asian Bodies in Performance," so it may well be that performers have the last word. Her new work is titled *What is the Sound of Ten Naked Asian Men?*, and will in fact feature ten Asian and Asian American men lying on ten different tables; each will have six audio pickups attached to different parts of their bodies. Masaoka's descriptive notes combine cultural theory, politics, and performance detail:[7]

> [The men] will be lying prone, and the amplified sound of their bodies, such as sounds of the stomach, swallowing, natural body shifting on the table, heart-beating sounds, etc. will be amplified and mixed by a sound technician. Later, in the studio, these sounds will be layered and manipulated via computer and digital signal processing. In addition, I will interview each of the ten men participants and the text will be taken from the interviews, recontextualized, fractured and interwoven to the soundscape. Naked men, particularly Asian men, are rarely part of the public and media imagination. By employing Asian naked men into a sound piece, I hope to confront this current invisibility of Asian, and Asian men in particular, in an upbeat and positive-Asian-male body kind of way.
>
> The goal of the series *Asian Bodies in Performance* is to question the preconceived notions of such social constructions as gender, ethnicity, and sexual orientation. To present the body as a passive canvas, as a passive medium or instrument for which cultural meaning is inscribed is to illustrate this point head-on.

Head-on indeed. As Philip Brett said to me on the afternoon of the performance, "I just don't understand it — *lots* of people have taken their clothes off in Watkins Hall. Tim *Miller* took off his clothes in Watkins Hall." The pornography of insects, of race. The pornography of the performative. I hope this chapter opens up broader questions of ethnography, identity, and community, but it also gestures toward the *praxis* (construction?) of the unnatural in a conservative environment.

Acknowledgments

I would like to thank Jan Monk, Kimberly Jones, and Sandra Shattuck for inviting me to participate in the Southwest Institute for Research on Women's 1997 Summer Institute at the University of Arizona, where I first presented this material. In Riverside, Traise Yamamoto, Paul Simon, Piya Chatterjee, Philip Brett, and René T.A. Lysloff provided thoughtful and spirited critique that helped me find the final shape of the essay. My thanks also to Maria Luz Cruz Torres for inviting me to present a version of this chapter in the colloquium series of the Department of Anthropology, UCR.

Endnotes

1. I would like to thank Tong Soon Lee for bringing Lila Abu-Lughod's "Writing Against Culture" to my attention.
2. Masaoka is mentioned briefly in Susan Asai's article on Japanese American music (1995: 447). Surprisingly, Asai notes that Masaoka's "interest in playing the koto is apolitical and is not intended as an expression of her Japanese heritage. She strives to compose music as a purely artistic endeavor, not meant to make a social or political statement." Masaoka may well explain herself in different ways to different questioners, but in my experience Masaoka explicitly links her musical activities to her Japanese American identity.
3. I would like to thank staff members Andrea Jones and Cindy Roulette for sharing this information with me.
4. I would like to thank the four students in my class who gave me permission to share their papers with you: Kit McCluskey, David Reyes, Michelle Phertiyanan, and Maria Porras.
5. I thank René T.A. Lysloff for this thought and for pointing out that this is *not* the same as John Pemberton's (1987) argument that Javanese don't "listen" to gamelan music.
6. My thanks to Philip Brett for arguing that this *did* happen.
7. Posted on Masaoka's homepage, http://thecity.sfsu.edu/~miya/bodies.html.

III

New Interventions

8

The Asian American Body in Performance

> *[O]ur major political preoccupations are how to regulate the spaces between bodies, to monitor the interfaces between bodies, societies and cultures, to legislate on the tensions between habitus and body.*
>
> —(Turner 1992: 12)
>
> *The body is the Achilles heel of hegemony.*
>
> —(Fiske 1989: 76)

Asian American and African American bodies have problematic relationships. I immediately think of violence: those terrible grainy images of Soon Ja Du shooting Latasha Harlins; Korean Americans arming themselves in Los Angeles. These recent memories lead almost immediately to others — the Asian-owned convenience store in the Black neighborhood — into a racialized loop of asymmetrical opportunities and surveillances. The Asian American cannot come into proximity with the African American without activating metaphors of encroachment and use — metaphors that are all situated in ontologies of embodiment.

Put simply, I'd like to offer some thoughts — explicitly, self-consciously Asian American thoughts — on cultural appropriation and the presence of Asian American performers in two traditions, jazz and hip hop, that have been racially constructed as African American. More broadly, I want to consider the relationships between the body, race, and performance, and the racialization of bodies *through* performance. The performances of those bodies in question have trajectories that reach into ideologies of labor in a late capitalist world. I especially want to offer some thoughts on the somatic process through which Asian American jazz musicians and rappers have sometimes been constructed as a problem — in short, as

161

inauthentic — and to propose some ways of rescuing such constructions by exerting what might be called a positive hermeneutics.[1]

This essay is in part a response to Ingrid Monson's trenchant exploration of ethnic authenticity in her article, "The Problem with White Hipness: Race, Gender, and Cultural Conceptions in Jazz Historical Discourse" (1995). Looking closely at the interface between Whiteness, Blackness, music, style, modernity, and cultural ownership, Monson reveals certain alignments of difference that have created possibilities for resistance and cooption in contrasting communities. Boldly focusing on the dangerous performatives through which White Americans have borrowed African American style and thus constituted rebellions of their own, Monson productively refigures naturalized connections between race, gender, and resistance. My essay might be considered a parallel conversation to hers — another encounter between bodies where performance is a constitutive moment for an activist response to racialized inequities.

The absent body in the Asian American/African American "problem" is of course White, always present yet rendered invisible by ideologies that create marked and unmarked categories. The larger, controlling cultural performances that place Asian American and African American bodies in conflict rely on what Peter McLaren has called "White terror" and its unmarked frameworks, its naturalized terms (1994: 59–62). To be an American and to think about race means engaging with Whiteness and all its performances, yet this encompassing racialization is perhaps the most undertheorized embodiment of all, and therein lies its power and narrative definition. In its most complete form, I might attempt that theorization in this chapter. But I choose not to reinscribe its historical power that directly; instead, I leave it in the wings, watching, defining, but deliberately unvisualized.

The Body Politic: The Body, Power, and Difference

There's a moment in *Yankee Dawg You Die*, Philip Gotanda's deeply reflexive play about Asian American representations in film, in which several bodies collide. Two Asian American actors, playing Asian American actors, break into a song and dance number from a famous World War II-era nightclub in San Francisco's Chinatown. As they do a soft-shoe shuffle, they sing about tea cakes, moon songs, and strolling down Grant Avenue, and they light into the chorus with "da da da da da, dah dah dah," the classic Oriental lick that any of us would recognize anywhere, in the soundtrack of any movie. The younger of the two characters suddenly stops in his tracks, looks at his companion, and says (Gotanda 1991: 21):

> Wait, wait, wait, what is this—WAIT! What am I doing? What is this shit? You're acting like a Chinese Steppin Fetchit. That's what you're acting like. Jesus, fucking Christ… *A Chinese Steppin Fetchit.*

This moment of recognition — forcing a character to see his own body moving through representations, of corporeally enacting the cultural memory of other racialized representations — is a key moment in a profoundly reflexive play. Seeing his own body evoke an African American body literally stops him in his tracks and stops the dramatic action of the play. The problem of impersonation opens up to him, to us, in all its regulatory might. This moment is emblematic of Asian American/African American encounters through other kinds of performance as well, and I mean to trace the ideological histories of some Asian American performatives that draw on African American forms. This will necessarily create some theoretical uneasiness over verbs. How to describe that ethnicized encounter? Do Asian Americans borrow, appropriate, incorporate, absorb, transform, evoke, or steal African American forms? Without retreating from the politicized nature of that encounter, I want to look closely at its character in jazz and hip hop. And, as Susan Foster has suggested,[2] to think about performance and difference without taking their corporeal histories into account is a particular kind of ideological denial, so I begin with the body.

Thinking about the body can take place only between two paradigms: the body as a site of regulation, or as a site where hegemony is evaded and resisted. Recent theory suggests that bodies are socially constructed, often through performance; that gender, sexuality, and race are interconstitutive and dialectically related; and that the performative reality of such interpenetrations is often deeply contradictory.

Foucault of course looms large in recent theories of the body. Though he never explicitly addressed race or performance, his positioning of the body between ideology production and the effects of ideological structures has had a profound impact on all subsequent theories of the body. He posits a "political economy" and "political technology" of the body (1977: 24–25) in which the state exerts or subtly brings to bear power and mastery over the materiality of bodies. In his view, knowledge is produced by power, not vice versa, and this enables his reworking of the Hobbesian body politic:

> ...[O]ne might imagine a 'political anatomy.' This would not be the study of a state in terms of a 'body' (with its elements, its resources and its forces), nor would it be a study of the body and its surroundings in terms of a small state. One would be concerned with the 'body politic,' as a set of material elements and techniques that serve as weapons, relays, communication routes and supports for the power and knowledge relations that invest human bodies and subjugate them by turning them into objects of knowledge (1977: 28).

The body, power and knowledge are thus directly linked, and the "anatomy" of power is not abstract at all, but rather material, situated in bodies.

To know a body is to produce the possibility of controlling, disciplining or instructing it.

Strongly influenced by Foucault, sociologist Bryan Turner has devoted several books to exploring the social constitution of bodies, particularly in terms of regulatory schemes such as science, medicine, diet and so forth. He points out that, "In addition to the metaphor of politics, the human body has been conceived either as a work of art or as a machine" (Turner 1992: 182). Although he too doesn't address race, he shows how public anatomical dissection, diet, and *anorexia nervosa* are all ideologically tied to concerns of class and social control, though in historically distinct ways.[3]

Foucault's linking of the body, discipline, and the fadeaway of its public spectacle marks an important moment in bodily history — in fact, in the history of bodily performance. As torture, execution, and even incarceration were slowly and methodically removed from the public gaze (beginning in the early nineteenth century), the theater of the disciplined body has been redefined. But it certainly hasn't disappeared. The social drama of the body is the focus of much interesting recent work that has prompted new ideas of performativity linking corporeality and social transformation. While Foucault located bodies in submission, scholars working in postindustrial, postmodern contexts look intently for signs of revolt, and performance has been identified by some as a means for locating agency.

Popular culture theorist John Fiske, for instance, has consistently regarded the body as an important site of reception and agency.[4] His recent work has focused on the material and social bodies of African American slaves, Rodney King,[5] homeless men watching (and responding "incorrectly" to) the movie *Die Hard,* Elvis, and Elvis fans. Fiske proposes a poststructuralist model for power and resistance based on dynamics of "locales" and "stations": localizing moves are cultural strategies for gaining control over "the immediate conditions of everyday life" while stations are the opposite but equivalent of locales, i.e., a physical and/or social space in which "the social order is imposed on an individual" (1993: 12). Though this model may at first glance seem uncomfortably structuralist (is the social order so easily, well, located?), Fiske carefully reroutes assumed connections between the social and the material body, suggesting that localizing moves afford the possibility of agency (ibid., 288):

> In slavery, the technologies of ... power were applied to the physical body; in "the new racism" their application is as much upon the social body. Environmental and economic racism work on the black social body as did the whips on the physical body. Retelling the atrocious narratives of slavery ... evokes shudders in the bodies of those who hear them. These shudders are experiences of affective intensity of the body's recognition that what it touches *matters,* and they are theoretically comparable to the homeless men's cheers at

Die Hard or Elvis fans' ecstasy, even though their intensity is of horror rather than pleasure. This bodily affect enables the power that oppressed the bodies in the narrative to be taken into the bodies of the listeners and turned against its origin.

Fiske is thus able to trace the channeling of power through time, through bodies, and to chart its transformation from imperializing power into localized agency. As I will suggest later, moments of performance could be thus seen as moves that establish important locales for reracializations.

While Fiske focuses on the body's relation to the enactment of power, Judith Butler posits gender, sex, and the body as exceptionally mobile constructions. Her work has tremendous potential for theories of racialization and performance. Refiguring sex and gender as discursive possibilities, Butler posits sex as an aspect of a "regulatory norm" that performatively moves the materiality of the body into expected shapes. Linking the body to discourse, she joins and extends Foucault and Derrida, focusing closely on the "reiterative power of discourse to produce the phenomena that it regulates and constrains" (Butler 1993: 2). Suggesting that sex is phantasmatic, she grapples directly with the "problem' of materiality, refusing to explain it away as "mere' discourse.[6] No mere construction, corporeality is rather "a process of materialization that stabilizes over time to produce the effect of boundary, fixity, and surface we call matter" (ibid., 9). Butler thus rescues the reality of the body from Derridean disappearance, placing it firmly at the intersection of power, control, performance, and agency. Refusing to romanticize performance as an enactment of agency and opposition, Butler instead insists on an intimate relationship between agency and control: "The paradox of subjectivation," she notes:

> ... is precisely that the subject who would resist such norms is itself enabled, if not produced, by such norms. Although this constitutive constraint does not foreclose the possibility of agency, it does locate agency as a reiterative or rearticulatory practice, immanent to power, and not a relation of external opposition to power (ibid., 15).

Most importantly, Butler makes the jump to race. In her discussion of passing (that is, the regulatory possibility of masking/performing race), she shifts her focus to difference, musing that feminist theorists have at times been overly intent on the social force of sexual difference. "This privileging of sexual difference," she notes, "implies not only that sexual difference should be understood as more fundamental than other forms of difference, but that other forms of difference might be *derived* from sexual difference." Instead, she repositions sexual difference within a broader sphere of relationships which must "be understood as articulated through or *as* other vectors of power" (ibid., 167). She suggests that homosexuality and miscegenation could be seen as analogous, as a "constitutive outside" to the normative, whether sexuality or race. In her analysis of Nella Larsen's novel *Passing,* the heroine's masked race, miscegenation and an attraction to another woman can be resolved only through death — through "the success of a certain symbolic ordering of gender, sexuality and race" (ibid., 183). Just as performativity assigns sex, gender, and sexuality to bodies, it also creates, maintains and transforms a racialized body. Racializing norms thus "exist not merely alongside gender norms, but are articulated through one another" (ibid., 182). As she puts it, whiteness is therefore not a form of racial difference (ibid.), and the performative creation of unmarked bodies constitutes "the currency of normative whiteness" (ibid., 171).

How then can we even begin to talk about race and the body? Having admitted that race is a social construct, how can we meaningfully look at its signs without reinscribing its violence?[7] In *The Body in Pain,* Elaine Scarry suggests that the body always creates narratives of time and place and that it is always political, whether in war or peacetime. Scarry muses that the body doesn't reflect winning or losing: "it is not (after a war) as though the winners were alive and the losers are dead," she says. Instead, she proposes "some surrogate form of objectification, … a vehicle of memorialization," such as a thread worn on the upper arm or a change in walking habits that might be adopted by both populations, winners and losers, to signify the past presence of war. Let me turn her proposal around and suggest that seeing racialized bodies is another vehicle of memorialization, though an involuntary one. If we defamiliarize the topography connecting body, race, class, gender, and sexuality, then race begins to look much more like a vehicle of memorialization dedicated to terror. The network of connections emanating out from race function to maintain some bodies as injured, in pain.

In other words, Scarry's extended meditation on the body at war can easily be read allegorically — if we read war as "a surrogate form of objectification" for the cultural maintenance of racial difference, then the mechanisms through which racialization occurs become clearer. As Scarry notes, "[i]njuring works in part by the abiding signs it produces" (ibid., 115). One might say that racialization is a convenient feedback loop, in which race is the sign that promotes past and continued injury by its very presence. Scarry says that one of the functions of injury is that it "provides a record of its own activity" (ibid., 116), which is precisely how a racialized body functions in, and is maintained by, the state. "Injuries-as-signs point both backward and forward in time," she says: they have a "reality-conferring" function (ibid., 121) that makes them unstable but nearly impossible to argue with.

Seeing performance and the body in dynamic relationship has emerged most strongly from medical anthropology. In the introduction to *The Performance of Healing,* Marina Roseman and Carol Laderman suggest that healing rituals are perhaps *the* performative of the body (1996: 3, 89).

After all, what other cross-cultural behavior is as rooted in the belief that performance, however defined, will fundamentally change the status of the body? Healing ritual, almost always performed, is directed toward physiological change — "real" change, often conceived as material change. In the same volume, Thomas J. Csordas, looking closely at Charismatic Christian beliefs about healing, notes that the performance of healing "works" in that context because (1996: 108)

> For Charismatics, efficacious healing is predicated not only on a cultural legitimacy that says healing is possible, but on an existential immediacy that constitutes healing as real. The immediacy of the imaginal world and of memory, of divine presence and causal efficacy, have their common ground in embodiment.

Performatives of healing can connect different spheres — e.g., cosmology, imagination, and the body. One might say that the most serious regard for the performative may be located in medical anthropology. The connections thus made between performance, change, the body, and social reality can be effectively extended into theoretical frameworks for race.

The injuries of race are acted out all the time in performance. In her marvelous ethnography of dance in small-town Greece, Jane Cowan shows us bodies in motion — men, women, dancers, musicians — and as she unfolds their dialectic relationships and their mutual dependencies, the constellation of instrumental music, Gypsies and the not-human emerges vividly, overshadowed somewhat by Cowan's interest in gender but striking nonetheless. Men lead the dance, women watch; men dance in public, women in private; women sing, men make instrumental music; instrumental music drives the dance. The musicians who specialize in instrumental music are in fact Gypsies — not-Greek, deeply Other — referred to by the Greek townspeople not as "the musicians" but as "the drums" (*daulia*), or "the instruments." In continuous dynamic interaction with the male dancers, these musicians are essential but held at arms' length, necessary but despised. Cowan mildly notes "the Greek contempt for Gypsies" and the Greek townspeople's "tendency to ignore the humanity of the musicians" (Cowan 1990: 102). Deeply suspect, the musicians are nonetheless the source of the most intense physical and emotional experience of dance (*kefi*): their music literally sends dancers into a heightened state, yet the money pressed upon them in the heat of such moments confers status not on them but on the giver: as Cowan puts it, the townspeople rarely remember which musicians were playing, nor do they see the bills as special evidence of the musicians' skill (ibid., 105–6). She says:

> I have stressed the hierarchical interdependence between Gypsy musicians and male youths in the performance of gender. These youths need the Gypsies' tunes in order to structure their dances

and, thereby, to structure their emotions. And they need to appear to dominate the Gypsies in order to enhance their own masculinity (ibid., 126).

Focusing all her analytical interest on gender, Cowan misses the chance to see racialization in process, through performance. It's clear from her energetic descriptions that the bodies in her ethnography are busily being engendered and racialized with great intensity, in performance. Men behave with physical abandonment while women enact decorum (showing enthusiasm only in their faces and gestures). The Gypsy musicians, however, "are always upright, physically composed, their faces often expressionless as they play" (ibid., 127). They are wordless, gentle, dignified, but not respected. Cowan translates their racialization as not-Greek into the language of gender:

> [T]he Gypsies' comportment is a total inversion of [the] explicit, stylized, slightly parodied sexuality [of Greek townsmen]. In a symbolic sense, then, the Gypsies appear not as feminine but as sexless, neutered men. In this play of gender, gender is a code of power as well as of difference.

> The symbolic position of the Gypsy musician in the performance is thus complex. He is at once, paradoxically, a man, a socially inferior and thus unsexed man, and an instrument. ... He is, through his music, the one who constitutes the performance itself, and at the same time his performance, according to [Greek townspeople's] norms, is and should be in a gestural sense invisible, neutral, without qualities, symbolically reflective. The performances of the [Greek] dancer and the Gypsy musician are a subtle, uneasy choreography of mutual interdependence (ibid., 127).

The musicking Gypsy body thus provides a record of its own activity by driving Greek dancers. The injury of race renders the Gypsy less than human, and Cowan's insistence on the deep relationality of all these performing bodies is astute despite her overly tight focus on gender. In fact, the Gypsy body as subordinate, as a body that serves and labors, has deep resonance with the performative constitution of other racialized bodies in other historical and cultural contexts.

I'm interested here in exploring two metaphors, that is, in seeing *and* hearing race in the performing body. The shaping presence of "visual economies" in ideologies of the body is undeniable. Much of Robyn Wiegman's book, *American Anatomies* (1995), is focused on making these economies theoretically visible: she suggests that race and gender have been rendered "real" via "naturalizing discourses of the body, ... discourses that locate difference in a pre-cultural realm whose corporeal significations supposedly speak a truth which the body inherently mean" (ibid., 4). Technologies of representation, she argues, have been technologies of vision which have fundamentally shaped contemporary cultural politics as well as "the investigative terrain of modern disciplinarity itself" (ibid., 3). Indeed, Weigman argues that color has been a visible economy since the late seventeenth century and the colonial encounter, and race has subsequently become overdetermined — the condition for subjection. The Western production of race emerged directly from imperialism and world trade; as such, the cultural reliance on visual signs of race is deeply situated.[8] Weigman insists that "we must take seriously the notion of race as a fiction ... in order to jettison the security of the visible as an obvious and unacculturated phenomenon" (ibid., 24). Race became an overdetermined sign through specific historical processes that joined scientific, industrial, and technological "revolutions' and constituted certain racialized bodies as subjects, as objects of knowledge (ibid., 36). The reliance on visible race was, and is, central to both an economic system and a representational economy. As Weigman explains:

> In Western racial discourse, for instance, the production of the African subject as non- or subhuman, as an object and property, arises not simply through the economic necessities of the slave trade, but according to the epistemologies attending vision and their logics of corporeal inscription: making the African "black" reduces the racial meanings attached to flesh to a binary structure of vision, and it is this structure that precedes the disciplinary emergence of the humanities and its methodological pursuits of knowledge and truth (ibid., 4).

Susan McClary and Rob Walser have argued that the visible sign of the Black body in performance has been central to American epistemologies of racial subjection. In their essay, "Theorizing the Body in African-American Music" (1994), they note that the body generally has not been "a prestigious topic among scholars of the arts" (1994: 75) because of the Cartesian mind/body split and the body's conception as precultural. McClary and Walser demonstrate how a chain of relationships — the body, to dance, to African and African American aesthetics connecting music and dance — has enabled a dismissal of African American musics from scholarly consideration. These perceived connections allow celebration-in-dismissal:

> African and African American musics [have been perceived] as sites where the body still may be experienced as primordial, untouched by the restrictions of culture. ......[T]he mind and culture still remain the exclusive property of Eurocentric discourse, while the

dancing body is romanticized as what is left over when the burdens
of reason and civilization have been flung away (1994: 76).

One way of resisting or intervening in this epistemology is to try to get
the body back into scholarship on Euro-American musics, or to focus on
"the more intellectual aspects of African-American music" (ibid., 77),
though, once again, the interventionist paradox of reinscription raises its
head. Still, I would like to engage with McClary's and Walser's suggestion
that:

> The challenge is to assess the international impact of African-
> American articulations of the body without falling into the usual
> traps — neither undervaluing physicality as a complex artistic
> terrain nor celebrating it as a site where one pushes reason aside
> to come in contact with (fantasies of) universal primal urges
> (ibid., 82).

In the remainder of this chapter, I would like to rise to that challenge by
looking at, and trying to hear, Asian American bodies articulated through
African American bodies, and even articulations of Asian American and
African American bodies that perform together, against/through/with
each other. Robyn Wiegman notes how the rhetoric of contemporary
identity politics has often elided and collapsed discussions of difference to
a consideration of "Blacks and women": this rhetoric "simply weds these
identity categories together, writing 'blacks and women' as the inclusivist
gesture of post-1960s politics" (1995: 7). Somewhat playfully, then, I will
turn my attention to a kind of body excluded from such gestures — the
Asian American man in performance — and I will consider how such
bodies sound as well as look.[9] The elision of music and the body (and race,
labor and the body) means that the musicking body is necessarily racialized. If these performing bodies necessarily enact historical memories of
subjectivation and injury (as I think they do), then I also mean to rescue
those memories by refashioning their labor as cultural work.

The Racialization of Jazz[10]

It is increasingly difficult to write or talk about jazz in unracialized terms
— or rather, to do so looks increasingly naïve, reconstituting jazz in a language too close to the discourse of art music to go unchallenged. Questions of who speaks, who ought to be speaking, and who's spoken too
much already, are more and more frequently cast in racialized terms.
These are by no means new issues. The first sentence of Amiri Baraka's
Black Music reads "Most jazz critics have been white Americans, but most
important jazz musicians have not been" (Jones 1967: 11). Though not
new, moving discursive discussions about race from a background mur-
mur into the front lines indicates that jazz has been reconfigured as some-

thing eminently worth owning. The tug-and-pull over ownership has centered on who's making the music and who's writing about it. Both arguments have been cast in Black and White terms; the racialization of jazz has been aggressively binary because it is a ventriloquist, metonymic stand-in for control over an American Elsewhere. The long history of Other colors in jazz — that is, Asians and Latinos — is consistently refigured as absence. If the very idea of an Asian American jazz is new or strange, this demonstrates — successfully — the American hermeneutics of race as binary: either/or, Black/White. Any other kind of jazz simply isn't.

Much writing on the cultural politics of jazz has indeed been produced by White men.[11] How Whites regard jazz has been of ongoing concern to White critics.[12] For instance, *Reading Jazz* (1993), edited by David Meltzer, is a collection of White writings that dramatically point out how nearly a century's worth of White musings on jazz have served as a lens on cultural mores and anxieties at different historical moments. Meltzer openly acknowledges his *modus operandi*: he admits that the collection "is a deliberate one-way street, a display of re-creation" (ibid., 30). Meltzer, a White poet and critic, has framed these writings with an impassioned, impressionistic "pre-ramble" in which he takes on the racialization of jazz in all its historicized might. "This [book]," he writes (1993: 4–5):

> is about the white invention of jazz as a subject and object. …
> While the music is the creation of African-Americans, jazz as
> mythology, commodity, cultural display is a white invention and
> the expression of a postcolonial tradition. … This is a source-book
> of forms of permissible racism.

Meltzer argues that consumers, fans, and critics have a different experience and in fact a different history from that of jazz performers (ibid., 21), and that the political economy of jazz and its artifacts are controlled by White consumer society. No liberal apologist, Meltzer points to the structural roles of capitalism in the racialization of jazz, and in talk about it. Control over the flow of material goods around jazz enables a kind of racist forgetfulness that allows jazz to be owned: "Jazz," Meltzer writes, "has entered the elaborate interweaving maze of the archive; it's fixed in an upwardly mobile museum culture; a branch of nostalgia and amnesia" (ibid., 29). The centrality of jazz in the Japanese American internment camps or the fame of San Francisco's Forbidden City are thus easily forgotten because those jazz sounds were neither produced nor heard by the right kind of Americans.

The very attempt to "get at" jazz is more and more consistently framed by jazz historians as an exercise in discursive representations.[13] Getting at race in jazz has been most creatively refigured by Gary Tomlinson (1992) and Ingrid Monson (1995). I will address Monson's argument for a racialized understanding of appropriation and participation below. Tomlinson focuses on African American theories of intertextuality and dialogics on music and thus disarms essentialist arguments for a core of African American identity in jazz. Rather than try to clear a space for himself or even for White historians, Tomlinson instead provides an argument that allows jazz discourse (whether musical or scholarly) to move beyond assertions of Black purity and nationalism. Vernacularism and Signifyin(g) create meaning by attempting to "keep sight, so to speak, of the other modes of thought around it by keeping them above [their] horizon" (1992: 66). Meaning thus emerges from engagement with difference, not retreat or isolation from it.[14] He outlines a resituated and re-racialized way of approaching jazz and, indeed, any form of located expression, allowing for encounter and dialogical complexity. Dialogics, he says:

> are unsettling precisely because it works against our natural impulse to be settled in the complacency of our own rules and terms. It threatens because it relinquishes the comforting idea of mastering a fully cleared space with open horizons in order instead to scrutinize uneasily the mysterious others crowding in on it (ibid., 93).

I turn now to some of those mysterious Others crowding in on jazz — Others who have always been there, always listening, participating, and consuming the musics imagined to be jazz. In the Bay Area around San Francisco, a small but widening circle of Asian American jazz musicians have been performing, composing, and recording since the mid-1970s; though they haven't been acknowledged in the racialized discourse of jazz capital, they themselves have placed ethnicity and identity politics at the center of their activities from the beginning. Mark Izu, Jon Jang, Francis Wong, Glenn Horiuchi, and Anthony Brown may not be familiar names to jazzheads, but are to those who follow Asian American arts and performance. All five are composers and performers; all five have recorded extensively, especially on the Asian Improv label, which is devoted to Asian American musical expression; all five have collaborated extensively with African American jazz musicians; and all five have been, and continue to be, involved with Asian American activism.

As McClary and Walser have pointed out, it is especially in African American musics that the body has been emphasized in order to enable its containment and dismissal. Jazz has been especially subject to location in an im/amoral body, a body beyond the control and humanity of culture. Still, virtually no criticism or scholarship has ventured beyond the African American or the White jazz body, maintaining instead two social anatomies in continual struggle with each other. Where might yet anOther kind of racialized body find a place where it is still allowed to produce jazz sounds?

These are precisely the kinds of questions that engage activist Asian American musicians. Most are involved with local Asian American community organizations. Their expressive activities are diverse: they perform in festivals and nightclubs; they manage recording companies; they compose the scores for (primarily) Asian American plays, films, and documentaries; they arrange for Asian musicians to visit the U.S. and to collaborate with them; and of course they teach. They try to shake up racialized and racist social structures through a variety of activities, but the connecting thread is an effort to use performance as a force in social transformation.

Collaboration with African American jazz musicians is explicitly important to many of the Asian American musicians. Jon Jang, for instance, studied with African American composer and performer Wendell Logan as an undergraduate at Oberlin College, where he was introduced to the identity politics of jazz. Francis Wong, Jang's longtime friend and collaborator, describes Jang's experience of the jazz culture wars as follows:

> [Jon had] experiences at Oberlin where people really tried to challenge that fact — students just couldn't get behind acknowledging that the [jazz] innovators were African American. You know, they'd be arguing with Wendell Logan and stuff like that. And I think there's also a basic playing off — like Jon said there were two big bands at Oberlin, one that was the official one under Wendell's direction that played interesting or creative music — Charlie Parker, and stuff like that — and then ... I guess some of the White students organized another band that featured mainly White arrangers. The thing is that that whole stage band movement — big band — in colleges is primarily White. I mean, a lot of it came out of the Stan Kenton thing, and then people made it business — like Sammy Nestico and a lot of these arrangers. So a lot of the White players really want to play that, and there wasn't an interest in learning from the [African American] masters, basically.[15]

According to Wong, Jang's interest in acknowledging and collaborating with African American musicians was thus established early in his career. Most of the long-lived Asian American jazz ensembles expressly include African American musicians. Fred Ho's group, the Afro-Asian Music Ensemble, has always been multiracial. Anthony Brown's ensemble, the Afro-Asian Eclipse, refers not only to Ellington's "African-Eurasian Eclipse" but also to Brown himself, who is half Japanese and half African American. James Newton, the well-known African American wind player who appears on many Asian American jazz albums, is a childhood friend of Brown's. The African American/Asian American musical encounter is thus self-conscious though, I hasten to add, it is imagined and pursued in different ways by different Asian American musicians. Many agree, though, that musical collaboration enacts political coalition as well as respect for the African American origins of jazz.

Non-Asian American musicians may not "read" or hear this music in the same way that an Asian American might. I once sat down with an African American musician friend and listened with him to part of Jon Jang's *Reparations Now!*, a multimovement "Asian American concerto for jazz ensemble and taiko" that addresses Japanese American political efforts to attain reparations from the United States government for unconstitutional internment during World War II.[16] Jang's ensemble, the Pan-Asian Arkestra, is multiracial though mostly Asian American, and its name alludes to Horace Tapscott's Pan African People's Arkestra. The name of the suite, *Reparations Now!*, is politically as well as musically referential, pointing to Max Roach's *We Insist! Freedom Now Suite* (which had addressed the racist administration of South Africa).

At the time I listened to this work with my African American friend, I found the music extremely exciting — it was stirring to me in ways that I was just beginning to articulate. A historian of African American popular musics and a gifted performer, my friend listened intently and provided a running commentary identifying all kinds of musical references to particular African American jazz musicians and even to famous performances of particular works. He was able to hear an intertextuality that was beyond me, and he was thus as engaged with the work as I but in a very different way. He wasn't listening blind: he knew that the musicians were ethnically diverse but mostly Asian American, and he understood the activist base to the work itself and more broadly to the musicians' work as a whole. At one point, however, he observed that the musicianship was technically good but "stiff" — that the musicians consistently maintained a rather close metronomic sense of the beat that "revealed" them as not African American.[17] He even stopped the tape at one point to demonstrate how an African American musician might realize a particular phrase with a looser, more fluid sense of rhythm and even timbre. I never felt that he was criticizing the Arkestra's technical skill or musicianship; rather, he was pointing out certain moments in which he felt he could hear the racialized conditioning of bodily and musical behavior. He didn't attempt to identify an Asian American sound — instead, he was hearing the absence of an African American musicking body, and this in itself was an assertion that such a body was somehow identifiable.

But what exactly *was* he hearing, and why? Rhythm, of course, is what Black bodies are supposed to have, and this innate quality has been mapped onto the African American body as surely as Reason has been central to the White cartology of Western racial theory. Ronald Radano (1993b) has outlined an archaeology of rhythm and blackness, suggesting that the connections between the two are deeply discursive. Getting through the representations that have constructed blackness to begin with is an exercise in racialization, he contends, and he opts instead to unpack a single allegorical category:

> … by focusing on a single discursive gesture, the value-saturated sign of rhythm, we can observe a formative device in the construction of musical blackness. Rhythm, as the central modernist figure of African American culture, has typically been inscribed as something beyond the grasp of whites; accordingly, it offers performers and insiders a powerful tool for inventing an exalted racialized space (ibid., 1–2).

Radano proposes that rhythm is "a fundamental discursive feature of modern racial consciousness" (ibid., 4) that, once established in the eighteenth century, has only been reworked, revised, and reinscribed through "countless manifestation" and many African American genres. Rather than try to assert the corrective power of specific methodologies (e.g., Signifyin[g]), he calls for "new listening practices (in the spirit of postmodern anthropology) that negotiate between the racialisms of black musical romance and our efforts to deconstruct them" (ibid., 10) — in other words, for closely located interpretations that enable constructive engagement with representations *and* resistance to them, history *and* our response to it.

I don't think my friend was deliberately or self-consciously clearing out an aural space beyond Asian American reach, nor do I think he was drawing lines in the sand. I think he heard what he heard, but the next step is, of course, to theorize what he thought he heard, or what he was expecting to hear and didn't. What he heard is beyond discussion at a certain level. When I told Francis Wong about the incident, he didn't try to "explain" the sound of the Asian American musicians on the album, nor did he try to move Asian American performers into a shared space with African American bodily experience. Instead, Wong said:

> Well, I don't have any problems with that, because people hear whatever they hear, you know. Eastern philosophy [suggests that] you can't second-guess someone's perception. If that's what he hears, that's what he hears. I don't have any issue with that.

Can one hear race?[18] I asked Wong if he could tell whether a musician was African American just by listening. Wong is articulate about the social and political dimensions of Asian American jazz, though the language he uses to describe the racialized musical encounter is a curious mixture of social activism and Western art ideologies. He said:

> **Francis Wong:** In the past, I used to try to think about that, but now I just kind of listen to [musicians'] influences.

Me: OK. Does that mean you can tell sometimes?

Francis Wong: Yeah, well, usually I can just tell who they are, at this point. After listening to the music for over twenty-five years, I can hear who they are or who they're coming from.

Me: Do you notice that more consistently with Black musicians, or White musicians, or even Asian American musicians?

Francis Wong: Well, it's still a pretty new thing with Asian American musicians, so it's a little harder. That's why it's not so much their color: you can hear what they *stand* for, you know. There's certain kinds of approaches that reflect more of a world view, I think.

Me: What do you mean?

Francis Wong: It's more about hearing how people think about creativity, how they think about spirituality — things like that. So you could maybe take it to the next level and say, well, they're probably Black, or they're probably this. But myself, I'm not as interested in doing that. That's not that important to me.

So Wong apparently once listened for race, but now hears particular histories and politicized, aestheticized stances; he hears what a musician "stands for," that is, *whose* influences sound through a particular performance. "Who they're coming from" is a matter of choice as well as personal history — he suggests that jazz musicians are well aware of who they're coming from, and that these aural autobiographies are constituted selectively, with emotional and political awareness. He resisted the question of whether race is musically audible, recognizing the essentialist shape of the question and answering, instead, that "playing" race is a matter of conscious choice; linking oneself to particular musicians represents a performative of political and ethnic coalition. We went on, and I persisted in posing essentializing questions:

Me: So sometimes, depending on who he or she is quoting from, or styling themselves on, or whatever —

Francis Wong: Sure, whatever tradition their feet are planted in.

Me: — will tell you something, sometimes.

Francis Wong: Yeah. You know if their music seems to be kind of heady, that doesn't mean that they're White — it just means that it's heady.

Me: Oh, really? "Heady' as in, like, abstract?

Francis Wong: Not necessarily abstract, but intellectual. I don't really look at abstract and intellectual as the same thing.

Me: What's "heady', then?

Francis Wong: Well, heady is to me, like, intellectual — you know, like they're thinking about the stuff too much.

Me: How can you tell when someone's playing in an intellectual way?

Francis Wong: Well, I think it's a lot of time like a lack of feeling, or it just doesn't have a grounded feel to it. So it can be pretty abstract

and still feel pretty grounded, you know. People always used to feel Coltrane was abstract, but I never felt his music was abstract.
Me: Really? You felt it was grounded?
Francis Wong: It was always grounded.

In short, Wong resists both of the ways that African American musicians have long been tied to their bodies. He disallows a simple, nativist explanation connecting rhythm or, for that matter, any specific musical behaviors to race: music may be produced by a body, but that body's racial history is not, to him, the source of its characteristic sound. He then resists the narrative force of the mind/body split, refusing to place headiness in White bodies.

Wong, Jang, and many of the other Asian American musicians oscillate between calling their expressive activities "jazz" and "creative music." In this, they quite deliberately model themselves on the Association for the Advancement of Creative Music (AACM) and its innovative mix of free jazz, avant-garde modernist improvisation, and Black nationalism. The inspiration for Asian Improv and the annual Asian American Jazz Festival also comes from the AACM: though never formally organized as a repertory group or an association, Asian Improv represents an effort to eke out an explicitly ethnic space in the recording industry, though in less nationalist terms than those espoused by the AACM in the 1960s and 70s. This particular mixture of economic self-determination and avant-gardism is the direct ideological legacy of the AACM. The Asian American musicians' connection to the AACM is sometimes enacted even more directly: Joseph Jarman (a founding member of the AACM) was the featured guest artist at the 1996 Asian American Jazz Festival in San Francisco, where he performed with Glenn Horiuchi and Francis Wong. Ronald Radano's thoughtful account of the AACM's formative years pinpoints some of the same ideological contradictions and challenges faced by these Asian American musicians thirty years later. He notes that (1993a: 104)

> ...it would be hard to ignore the contradiction between the musicians' efforts to distance themselves from Western artistic notions while simultaneously pursuing exceedingly Western, progressivist goals. There is no doubt that the AACM players embraced modernist ideas of style and greatness.

I must emphasize that the musical and ideological language of the Asian American musicians is based on a 1990s admiration of and delight in cultural hybridity, so their gestures toward an imagined Asia bear little resemblance to the Afrocentric purity and authenticity that AACM members sought to create. Yet the end results have interesting parallels. Just as the radical Black artists' "beliefs inspired something quite profound" (ibid.), the Asian American musicians' respectful use of the AACM's aesthetic language and musical styles relies on discomfiting notions of African American cultural authenticity even as it enables startling new sounds. That "the formation of grassroots organizations … could accommodate radical creative pursuits" (ibid., 77) while still asserting identity politics is the AACM's legacy. Sitting at Asian Improv's headquarters in San Francisco in May 1996, I listened to Izu, Wong, Horiuchi, Jang, and other Asian American musicians talk with Joseph Jarman and agree that neither identity politics nor "jazz" could contain their musical vision any longer though each were essential to their development as musicians, collectively and individually.[19]

For them, the use of the category "jazz" is both connecting and confining. The tie to African Americans is important to all of them, and jazz is the genre they have chosen to speak for and to that community. To some extent, jazz is valorized by the Asian American musicians as emblematic of African American experience, but illustrative of particular parts of that experience — as an expressive response to attempted subjectivation. As Francis Wong said to me:

> …some of it has to do with our own political maturity — [becoming active] in that period of the late 60s and the 70s, where there was a developing perspective about Black music and its relationship to the struggle for freedom and things like that. And the recognition that the major innovators in jazz were African American [was part of that]. So I think in that sense, in trying to both play the music and learn the music, there was an important emotional and intellectual desire to be connected to that tradition, in a very direct way.

The Asian American political identification with jazz is thus as an African American music. On the other hand, Asian American musical experimentation sometimes stretches beyond anything immediately recognizable as jazz, and Wong, among others, has noted the tug and pull between an identification with politically racialized music and an ideology of original, expressive creation. I have wondered, too, if this isn't a protective gesture, meant to insulate them from suggestions that what they're making isn't *jazz*. Radano suggests that "the development free jazz may be seen as a kind of dialogue taking place between white and black in the context of artistic modernism" (1993a: 109), but a modernism transformed by Black aesthetics. Similarly, the Bay Area musicians' "creative music" has emerged from an Asian American/African American encounter tempered by a politicized avant-gardism.

Monson (1995: 406) has described similar politics in the 1940s between the use of re-bop, be-bop, bop, and the term "modern music." Of all innovations in jazz music, bop was a supremely self-conscious response to jazz traditionalists. Monson notes that the use of the term "modern" had at least two associations. The "structural and artistic elements of the music itself" was impenetrable to many traditional jazz performers. (Interestingly, Louis Armstrong likened bop's utter strangeness to "Chinese music.") Second, bop's practitioners deployed its "modern" face as a political and social response to racist containment of jazz as entertainment. Instead, they insisted on bop's modern character, its status as "art," not entertainment; the body held at bay, the uneasy truce between resistance, self-determination, and reinscription. Rhetorically, at least, bop was cast in a radically intellectual mold. When Asian American musicians gesture toward their own "creative music," they too negotiate a new territory, in a language of newness — drawn from modernism — that introduces other depoliticizing ideologies.

Asian American jazz musicians approach the problem of White hipness in other ways, however. Tricia Rose has noted the phenomenon of "young white listeners trying to perfect a model of correct white hipness, coolness, and style by adopting the latest black style and image" (Rose 1994: 5). Any appropriation of African American expressive modes is fraught with problems; as Rose puts it, "Young white listeners' genuine pleasure and commitment to black music are necessarily affected by dominant racial discourses regarding African Americans, the politics of racial segregation, and cultural difference in the United States" (ibid.). Monson identifies gender and masculinity in particular as channels that mediate White notions of race, class, and African American cultural authenticity. Identifying African American musics as a source for Asian American expression becomes a way for Asian American musicians to rescue certain possibilities made so difficult by racializations that muffle and silence them. White hipness was (and is) an expression of imagined racial authenticity — an attempt to borrow racial markers in order to create White sites of rebellion and resistance. Identifying those racial markers is an exercise in reduction that, Monson says, "has caused many white Americans to perpetuate unwittingly primitivist assumptions about African American cultural authenticity" (1995: 422). Asian American jazz musicians approach this dangerous territory in yet another way. Whereas hip as a style became a marker for White liberal youth, Asian American musicians see their own activities as an expression of an important political moment when the Asian American movement emerged from Black activism during the Third World Strike at San Francisco State College in 1968-69 (Wei 1993: 15). Many Asian American musicians are overwhelmingly concerned with creating performatives of coalition and connection, and their historical awareness (unforgetfulness) of political indebtedness prompts their ongoing discursive use of (what they regard as) African American musical expressions. I would argue — more bluntly, less gracefully than Monson — that hipness is a top-down proposition. And yet, relative dominance and subjectivation is slippery ground. Who's on the bottom? Who's on first? The shape of the questions exposes their critical clumsiness. If hipness is a kind of slumming, i.e., a playacting of the privileged founded on essentialist, classist logic, are color-ful performatives of resistance then forever beyond the reach of anyone else? The notion of "people of color" is tricky on several counts and powerfully possible on several others. Grouping encourages totalizing gestures, but informed, unforgetful coalition is another story. As Anthony Braxton suggested, it's no longer hip to be hip anyway.[20] Perhaps we need to rethink the politics of appropriation in ways that will allow for combustion as well as colonization.

Racializing the Rapping Body

On October 29, 1995, I sat in the back room of a community organization's headquarters in Philadelphia and listened to the Mountain Brothers, a three-man Asian American hip hop group, answer questions about the performance they had just given. Their audience was a group of some twenty Asian American teenagers who had listened intently as the Mountain Brothers rapped over the "beats" they'd brought on a cassette. Chops (Scott Jung), Peril-L (Chris Wang), and Styles (Steve Wei) were relaxed and funny as the audience asked questions about how the rappers had gotten started, what their parents thought, and whether they'd gotten signed yet. A young woman asked:

> **Q**: What does "The Mountain Brothers" mean?
> **Peril-L**: It comes from a Chinese legend. But we're not real familiar with the details. *[everyone laughed]* The Mountain Brothers were a bunch of bandits that lived on a mountain. They stole from the rich and gave to the poor. Each one had special powers — there was actually one hundred and eight of them.
> **Q**: One hundred and eight mountain brothers?
> **Peril-L**: Yeah. There was actually a girl, too.
> **Styles**: There was a girl.
> **Chops**: She kicked some ass. *[everyone laughed]*
> **Peril-L**: They had these powers, and we just liked that. We extended the concept. *[He gestured toward Styles.]*
> **Styles**: The mountain is part of the ground, you know, but it's like taking it to a higher level. *[As he said this, he outlined a mountain with his hands, gestured upward, lets it go.]* But it's still part of the ground — it's still true to the ground — it still has its roots in the ground.

Styles' evocation of the trio's groundedness was a typical moment for the Mountain Brothers: easily explained but a bit esoteric, with much left unsaid.

Rap is a site where the body and ground (i.e., history, community) can come into conflict. It is one of the most transnational of popular music genres yet even outside the United States is perceived as closely linked to

African Americans. In a global context, rap is consistently associated with youth and social criticism, though the form that such criticism takes is extremely contingent. In American contexts, rap is performed by Whites, Latino/as, Native Americans, and Asian Americans as well as African Americans. Its bodily language, its sartorial style, its gender politics and its technological base all originated in African American performance practice.

Despite the international and interethnic spread of hip hop, matters of cultural ownership are constantly and passionately contested by some African American performers and producers. Tricia Rose has addressed these matters in the most depth and with the most consistent insight into African American youth culture and its aesthetics. Moreover, she has seriously engaged with the looming political problem of rap's transformations as it moves out of African American communities and into others. She allows for this movement within certain bounds. "To suggest that rap is a black idiom that prioritizes black culture and that articulates the problems of black urban life does not deny the pleasure and participation of others," she writes (1994: 4). Just as Dick Hebdige has used the idea of incorporation to describe the manipulation and absorption of subcultural elements by dominant institutions, Rose refers to the "bifocality" of African American culture in general, i.e., its long-standing ability to address, simultaneously, an African American audience and an enfolding White social framework (ibid., 5). The "ideological recuperation of black cultural resistance" is not a matter of semantics or subtle political analysis for many African American rappers: they are well aware of the potential for appropriation and, as Rose points out, "some rappers have equated white participation with a process of dilution and subsequent theft of black culture" (ibid.). Vanilla Ice is a particularly clumsy and specious example, though his fifteen minutes of fame suggest that White appropriations of Black authenticities continue to have ideological and commercial force. His fabricated childhood in the black inner city reduced the ghetto to a code for authenticity, a sign of hipness, and this naturally brought the wrath of the rap community down on him (ibid., 11–12). The appropriation of rap by other youth communities of color speaks in a very different direction, though. A horizontal identification along class lines has generally occurred without conflict or challenge from African American rappers. Vanilla Ice's error lay not only in race but in class, which may be a category that allows for no contingencies.

Ted Chung, a first-year undergrad at the University of Pennsylvania in 1995–96 and a Korean American DJ and MC, grew up in Los Angeles in a community that was half Asian American and half African American. The racial politics of rapping at Penn has been a source of amusement as well as concern to him. Performing in an environment that continues to be perceived in terms of Black/White relations despite a large Asian American student population has been a puzzle to him, but even more strange from his perspective is the relative lack of engagement between Asian American and African American students. He began to rap in the ninth grade; the hip hop group with which he continues to perform in LA is interracial, Asian American and African American. At Penn, his fellow MC is an African American student named Aaron Jones; the two of them host a weekly hip hop show on the university radio station, and they frequently DJ and MC together. I asked him if the two of them make their interracial partnership part of their performance in any way, at any level, and he responded that race matters, but a respect for and immersion in hip hop culture is the main thing for him:[21]

> **Ted Chung:** … I guess a lot of Asians around here never hung around with Blacks, but I'd have to say the majority of my friends at home — half my friends are Asian and half my friends are Black. I know I live in a world that's a little different from everyone else. I don't treat anyone different just because they're Black, or just because they're Asian. You know, if you rap, that's all I care about. You know, if you're White, if you're Black, Hispanic, Jewish — if you rap well, and you respect hip hop, if you're living it, then I'll support you all the way.
>
> **Me:** Do you and Aaron ever freestyle,[22] you know, about race? about ethnicity?
>
> **Ted Chung:** Oh, I see — you really want [to talk about] that racial thing! *[laughs]*
>
> **Me:** I'm really curious about it. I don't mean, you know, to keep bringing the conversation back to that…!
>
> **Ted Chung:** My partner's Black also, he goes to North Carolina Central right now, and whenever we went to talent shows, everyone would ask, well, how did you get an Asian kid and a Black kid to rap together.
>
> **Me:** So you've had these questions before.
>
> **Ted Chung:** Yeah, a million times.
>
> **Me:** *[laughs]* OK, good.
>
> **Ted Chung:** Yeah, we rap about it. We rap about it when we feel that people are watching out for that. I'm not going to say it because it's, like, nothing unusual to me, right. So I'm not going to say it just to impress you. But if I can feel that the crowd feels kind of funny about it … — then I'm gonna say it, so I could stick it in your face, so you're gonna be like, OK, I guess it's accepted.
>
> **Me:** So they have to deal with it.
>
> **Ted Chung:** Yeah. I'm not going to be, like, leaving you wondering whether or not him and I are really friends. I'll tell you straight out — like an Asian and a Black kid rapping together — but only for the means of like sticking it in their face, like, here you go, take it, you know?

In other words, Chung makes race an issue on a proactive basis, when he feels it's needed, and then does so assertively.

"Respect" for hip hop is frequently cited by rappers as an important issue. Few rappers describe hip hop as *only* an African American tradition, but many acknowledge its origin and vital location in African American communities. The Mountain Brothers' publicity packet, for instance, features the following statement, summing up some of the salient issues of hip hop authenticity, ownership, and participation:

> Because of [the Mountain Brothers'] dedication to the art, they (like the originators and true keepers of hip-hop) bring the kind of material that will add to hip-hop music, *not* steal from it or cheapen it. *No* shallow gimmicks, *no* karate kicks, *no* horror movie blood splattering, *no* "songs that sound like the group that went platinum," just straight up self truth. What the Mountain Brothers represent most of all is *a deep love, respect, and ability* for true "rewind the shit over and over in your walkman" hip-hop.

"The originators and true keepers of hip-hop" are of course African Americans, and the Mountain Brothers' ready acknowledgment of African American ownership *and* their own place in that "art" are up front and matter-of-fact. Even as they align themselves with African Americans, they dissociate themselves from Orientalisms and mass culture commercialism. They express "focused anger on vital issues." In other words, they eke out a space assertively their own, "a viewpoint which has yet to be represented in hip-hop," an Asian American voice and perspective.

The Mountain Brothers, Ted Chung, and Aaron Jones first encountered each other on College Green, an open public space at the center of the Penn campus. It was October 27th, 1995, the final day of Penn's Asian Pacific American Heritage Week, and much of that day was filled with Asian American performances on an outdoor stage in front of the library. A Japanese American folk-rock singer strummed on a guitar and was mostly ignored. Various student clubs — Thai, Filipino, Chinese, South Asian — performed traditional dances and drew their respective constituencies to the Green. A local Japanese American performer did modern dance. Hip hop ended the day. By the time the rappers came on, the student clubs were closing up their foodstalls and the crowds were waning.

My presence that day was neither accidental nor disinterested. Wanting to encourage a broader spectrum of Asian American performances and particularly eager to bring local nonuniversity Asian American performers onto the campus, I had arranged for the Mountain Brothers to appear.[23] Before they came on, though, two young men — Aaron Jones and Theo Chung — leaped up and took the stage, freestyling in such a spirited manner that the crowd began to gather all over again. It was the first time that day that an African American had appeared onstage. The student crowd laughed and cheered at their clever sexual jokes, and some began to sway and clap in time with the beat. Two young African American women suddenly climbed up on stage and demanded the microphones — they gave it back to the young men verse for verse, prompting pleased cheers from both women and men in the audience.

I was riveted, torn between capturing it all on videotape and wanting to simply experience the moment. During the 1995–96 academic year, Penn's undergraduate population was about 9,000 students, of which 0.17% were Native American, 5.5% African American, 4.0% Latino/a American, 18.1% Asian/Asian Pacific American and 64.1% White American. Between 1993 and 1995, the campus was the stage for some of the uglier racial performatives in the country, including the infamous water buffalo incident (which was a Jewish student's response to African American sorority sisters doing a stepping routine outside a dorm). Virtually any Penn student will tell you that the campus is deeply segregated, and that socializing across racial and ethnic lines is unusual and difficult. Seeing African American and Asian American students onstage together, in the context of an Asian American performance event, was thus a commanding sight.

By the time the Mountain Brothers came on, word was going up and down Locust Walk, the main crosswalk on campus, that *Asian* guys were rapping on the Green; by the time they finished up, the crowd included a group of local Asian American high school students who were on campus for the day. They wanted more, and asked for it. As the stage was struck behind them, all five rappers pulled into a circle and began to freestyle.

Clear differences in style and emphasis stood out in these moments. For one thing, Jones and Chung were much more comfortable with freestyling than the Mountain Brothers, but this is as much a matter of chosen focus. The Mountain Brothers are entirely directed toward getting signed and releasing an album, so all their work is carefully scripted; they never DJ, though they do perform at some parties. Jones and Chung have only just begun to think about recording; instead, their work is placed within the university party scene and some local clubs. They're used to performing spontaneously and responsively; their audience is integral to their resulting performance. Their interaction with each other is clearly central to what they do; they may cite its explicitly interracial character as an occasionally necessary performative, but in fact it's there continuously. They look at each other, they respond verbally to each other, they egg each other on in any number of ways. The more introspective nature of the Mountain Brothers' hip hop didn't come off as well in this context: although willing to engage with Jones and Chung, freestyling simply isn't what they do; all of them struggled with the beat at times, and, after a certain point, two of them weren't freestyling at all but instead uttered the texts of their set pieces. The Mountain Brothers' texts are in fact extremely complex, dense with metaphors and intertextual references and designed for repeated listening.

Yet, for the late afternoon audience gathered around them, that was less important than the fact that Asian American guys were rapping. The presence of Aaron Jones introduced a certain wariness that wasn't lost upon Chung. Months later, I asked him:

Me: So tell me about the crowd that day — it was almost entirely Asian American — there must have been about fifty Asian American Penn students standing around staring at the two of you. How was it?

Ted Chung: I mean, it's cool! I mean, any time they can get a chance to see that, you know… I mean, I think it's a positive thing. And you're always going to get people walk away from it, be like, jeez, I can't believe, like, that Asian guy raps, that's so stupid, that's for Black people. You know, you're always going to have that. So the more people you can — show that's more natural — it's GOOD to have the Mountain Brothers come out, and it's GOOD to have us come out, and whatever the groups, because in society, people take Asians — it's not even for granted — they take you — it's a subliminal thing, but like — they just don't want to accept you into anything. If you see a Black kid doing White music — if you can call it White music — like Hootie and the Blowfish, you know what I'm saying? People, like, accept it, they're like, it's cool that a Black kid would want to get into rock music. I mean, rock music's Black music anyways, but people forgot that.

Me: Right, right, right.

Ted Chung: People say that, but then, like, if you see an Asian kid doing rock music, then people are, like, what a stupid Asian kid, you know? There's just a certain negative vibe, and the more you stick it in their face, the more they're just gonna have to accept it.

Me: I see. OK. That sounds like a good strategy to me. I sensed a bit of caution from the crowd that day…

Ted Chung: There was …

Me: I wasn't sure where it was coming from, though. Part of it was that they didn't seem to know how to respond to you — I mean, they didn't seem to know enough to dance, to move their bodies.

Ted Chung: That's another problem. I don't think Asian people — at least at Penn — especially on the East Coast — because on the West Coast, hip hop — I mean, I'm glad I was born on the West Coast and lived there because hip hop is much more diverse. For example, I go to all the Pharcyde shows on the West Coast — and actually Tray from the Pharcyde is our group's manager — and we went to all the shows, and half, maybe a third of the audience is White, a third of the audience is Asian, a third of the audience is Black. I went to the Pharcyde show here two months ago, and it was ALL Black, you know it's MUCH more segregated over here. And all the Asian kids here — you know, if you go to the Asian frat dances that I DJ — like, if I play hip hop, they don't like that, you know? Whenever you go to any quote-unquote Asian party or Chinese Students Association you always hear, like, Euro music, techno. That's the kind of music that, like, I guess Asians are generally interested in. So they just didn't know hip hop, you know.

The East Coast/West Coast politics of hip hop are thus racialized in different ways. On the East Coast, at least in contrast to California, hip hop is strongly identified with Blackness, so much that Chung sometimes finds himself off balance, resisted in ways he's not used to. The manner in which his performance activities are collapsed into Blackness is both puzzling and exasperating to him, though not threatening; his sense of his own position in the tradition is quite certain.

What happens to race, voice, and the body in hip hop? Chung says that he uses his body in very particular ways when he raps: different parts of his body do different parts of the beat. One hand, as he explained it, "may be doing quarter note, quarter note, quarter note, the other is doing beats one and three, and my feet might do the *and-and-and* part of the beat." His hands operate in another way as well: when he points at the audience, especially during freestyling, it's to draw them in, to address them directly. His body is doing several things, then. It keeps the beat, and the beats within the beats, and it even enacts the relationships between some of those beats. In other words, his rapping body is rhythmicized in all the complex, driving ways that dancing bodies have always been. If African American bodies have been epistemologically confined to the physical enactment of rhythm, and if that embodiment of rhythm is directly keyed to historicized social interactions, then the insertion of an Asian American body into that discursive moment is troubling for some witnesses. The literal absorption of an Asian American body into an older conversation, and one so central to historical anatomies of White/Black difference, can't occur without challenge and confusion. Indeed, I can't help but wonder about the perceived Asian/Asian American predilection for techno, as if the coolie body were drawn to music evoking postindustrial technologies.

The possibility of racial impersonation is essentially at center stage in hip hop. If the body — any body — can rap, then where does African American authenticity lie? Take the case of Theo Mizuhara, a *sansei* DJ in Los Angeles: he's made his name by sounding Black (Della Cava 1996). "The king of LA drive-time" can be heard on 92.3 The Beat, and his voice has also been featured as the DJ in the film *Waiting to Exhale*; he's attracted spots for his show by Snoop Doggy Dogg and Ice Cube, and has appeared in music videos by Shanice (in whose "I Wish" video he appears as a rose-bearing suitor) and Easy E. His "tag", frequently uttered, is "No color line." In fact, his ethnicity was a station secret until a local TV station broke the news a year after he'd gone on the air. One magazine editor has dismissed Mizuhara as complicit with the tradition of "white jazz jocks and others, like Wolfman Jack, who played black music. Radio is a theatre of the mind" (ibid.). Mizuhara himself reacts to discussion of his color-crossing voice "with distaste and dismay," and doesn't think of himself as bridging race relations (ibid.). What does it mean to have a voice that passes? Mizuhara may insist on "no color line," but appears to have crossed it successfully and convincingly. Yet, when pressed to justify his radio presence, he too falls back on the language of cultural authenticity (Tazuma 1996):

> I'm being prejudiced against because I'm not Black. It's kind of crazy. ... The thing is that I understand. I may not agree. I may not think it's fair. Black people have been fucked with as long as they've been in the United States. They, I think, have been raped and robbed of their identity. I think they look at Black music as one of the last, maybe, unbastardized — to use a strong word — art forms that they possess, and they want to keep it as pure as possible. I understand that.

The coalescence of the Asian American and African American voice/body in hip hop is, for some, a newly threatening phenomenon. Asian Americans have traditionally been more easily absorbed into Whiteness. The American color line is Black and White, so an Asian American can be a banana (yellow on the outside but White on the inside), and a White rapper can be accused of posing as a Wigger (a White nigger) (Rose 1994: 11–12), but for Asian Americans to *choose* to move in the direction of color is literally unimaginable. When it happens, it's suspicious, uncomfortable, hermeneutically impossible. And when that bodily movement coincides with rap — one of the most oppositional performatives now at play — everyone's put on the alert except, perhaps, most hip hoppers themselves. Hip hop culture recognizes ownership, owns up to racialized authority, and yet allows encroachment on those terms. So Asian Americans rap and engage in a kind of racialized shape-shifting that's unsettling, not unproblematic, but inherently seated in identity politics. Asian American rappers are watched and heard with pleasure and discomfiture; the cultural tropes they rely on create a discursive environment in which, by rapping, they can't be White.

Somatic Society: Race, Performance and Cultural Work

What might an authentic Asian American cultural performance be, then? Locating an authentic cultural space from which Asian Americans might signify is no small task. Looking to Asian soundscapes has been a recurring experiment: Glenn Horiuchi incorporated his Nisei aunt, Lillian Nakano, playing *shamisen* into his "Poston Sonata"; Mark Izu has played the Chinese *sheng* in several of his jazz compositions; Jon Jang has made abundant use of Chinese musicians and Chinese melodies in his many works. As

Francis Wong has said, "I think you open yourself up to some problems if you just come in and take the form and you don't bring anything to it." The question remains, what *can* an Asian American bring to jazz or hip hop, and must it be Asian? Nisei Hollywood composer Paul Chihara, for instance, balks at drawing on Asian sounds in his scores. The musical sounds he remembers from his childhood years in the Minidoka internment camp were big band, and it's this soundscape that he deliberately chose to evoke in his score to the film *Farewell to Manzanar*.[24]

The problem of an authentic Asian American musical sound is, I think, directly related to the problem of locating an Asian American body *vis-à-vis* Whiteness and Blackness. Neither authentically Asian nor American, this body is held at arm's length by history, by legislation. Its Oriental ability to work is needed but suspect; in times of economic recession, the Asiatic body becomes a satisfying site for violence and refusal. If healing rituals are a central performative of the body, then performatives of racial violence are their inversion, equally dedicated to real, material change. Vincent Chin becomes a metonymic performance for holding back the yellow peril, for resisting the successful Oriental who labors unceasingly, perfectly, consumingly. Yet seeing Soon Ja Du shoot Latasha Harlins is shocking in a different way because it suggests the bottomlessness of the regulatory schemes maintaining race in America. The theater state is indeed terribly close at hand; the social drama of race is played out in endlessly creative and damaging ways. Just as every American of a certain age remembers where they were and what they were doing when Kennedy was shot, every Los Angeleno knows where they were when news broke of the verdict in the first Rodney King trial. Such moments are neither emblematic nor encapsulating; rather, they are constitutive sites for how racialized bodies come into being. Just as turn-of-the-century conceptions of the Asiatic body were a response to modernity and capitalist industrialization, the results of three large-scale American wars in Asia, coupled with an increasingly global economy and stepped-up Asian immigrations, has prompted a similar return to *fin-de-siècle* anxiety.

I suggested above that race is a constructed sign of historical injury that must be productively maintained and refashioned over time. The body won't stay still. I further suggest that the body is a somatic site for a society's most extreme visions of itself. Certainly it's difficult to forget the opening pages of Foucault's *Discipline and Punish*. The body is built up and broken down again and again, whenever the stakes are high. Race is not disinterested, let alone natural — it's hard work to maintain its categories. The Cartesian paradigm has tried to convince us that a psychosomatic symptom isn't real — not "really" of the body — but I suggest instead that the somatic realization of race is one of the great performative, destructive accomplishments of any society. Turning again to the anthropology of healing, I can conceive of performatives whose purpose isn't to "fix' race but rather to shift racialized materialities. Robert R. Desjarlais (1996: 159) notes that, among the Yolmo of Nepal, "Healing transformations take place not within some cognitive domain of brain or heartmind, but within the visceral reaches of the eyes, the skin, and the tongue." He calls for "less cerebral" models of healing, citing how a Yolmo shaman creates physiological change by altering a patient's sensory environment: the shaman's "cacaphony of music, taste, sight, touch, and wild, tactile images activates the senses and the imagination" (ibid., 160). Desjarlais suggests that the shaman "jumpstarts a physiology" (ibid.), and I unashamedly borrow from him to suggest that racialized performance has a physiology of its own that can result in social healing or disaster. By taking the body seriously, and by acknowledging its ongoing social construction, we are afforded the possibility of imagining other performatives. As Bryan Turner has suggested:

> We might define the somatic society as a social system in which the body, as simultaneously constraint and resistance, is the principal field of political and cultural activity. The body is the dominant means by which the tensions and crises of society are thematized; the body provides the stuff of our ideological reflections on the nature of our unpredictable time (Turner 1992: 12).

In bringing The Mountain Brothers to perform at Penn, I certainly hoped for a material response from the complex body politic of the university's undergrads. The cultural technologies that created racialized global flows of people represent a kind of cultural labor in its own right. Race might well be regarded as a condition for labor in a postindustrial world, the somatic indication of modernity's success. The question remains whether the reconfigured identities proposed by identity politics can move beyond the conditions that set it in motion to begin with. It's this juncture where hermeneutics and cultural work converge — where performance is operationalized.

Racial performatives like lynching or the exhaustive telecasting of the Simpson trial rely upon a hermeneutics of suspicion which allow surveillance to become direct, actual control over troublesome bodies (Gabbard 1995b: 17). One might say that the American culture wars from the Reagan era onward have hinged entirely on such a hermeneutics, where the very parameters of discussion have been defined as tightly as possible. Looking at performance, however, allows the formulation of a positive hermeneutics, or a glimpse of activities that redefine their own terms as they emerge. Theorizing race through performance might perhaps even be regarded as a tautology — a full circle reflexive look at that-which-is-made-through-performance.

What are the points of contact between these Asian American performers and nineteenth-century minstrelsy, Steppin Fetchit, or Al Jolson? As Asian American jazz musicians and rappers move toward Blackness, their self-conscious movement away from Whiteness is unequivocable. Passing and impersonation are, after all, performatives of privilege and longing. Impersonation takes place from the top down, and passing from the bottom up. When Asian Americans explore African American performance traditions, they describe their transit as lateral. Moving toward color can be a reclamation of race and labor; the laboring body instead discovers that it is engaged in the class-conscious cultural work of social and political transformation.

As Monson has noted, there exists "a range of options within which African Americans have situated themselves with respect to twentieth-century urban modernity" (1995: 419). I suggest that some Asian American men use performance to mediate ideas of Asian American ethnicity, and they too have a range of options between which they choose strategically. They draw freely and imaginatively on particular cultural forms for particular reasons. Jazz and hip hop speak in many directions and are radically contingent traditions, historically positioned at ground zero in the culture wars of the American twentieth century. These are not the only forms that Asian American musicians encroach upon and appropriate, but they are proving important sites for a certain recouping of race and ethnicity. The close alignment of these traditions with African American history, experience, and identity politics is not coincidental, nor is it unproblematic. Still, the choice to move away from Whiteness is a racial performative that is anti-assimilationist and potentially bridge-building.

The White musicologist Tomlinson writes that "Dialogical knowledge consists in this precarious maneuver of clearing space and building in it a discourse that never pushes other ways of knowing beyond its own horizon" (1992: 73). As an Asian American scholar, I want to believe that Asian American incursions into African American forms are conscious attempts to link different ways of knowing and reconfiguring race. This activation of the body politic is no small thing. If we regard these performers' efforts as pedagogical rather than appropriating, we can see anger, interrogation, coalition, action, revolution, in motion.

Acknowledgments

I would like to thank Irene Nexica and Marina Roseman for help and advice as I explored theories of the body. The graduate students in the Dance Program of the Department of World Arts and Cultures at UCLA and participants in the 18th Annual Dance Ethnology Conference, February 17–18, 1996, offered comments and made suggestions on an earlier draft of this essay; members of the Department of Music at UC Riverside also made useful suggestions on an earlier version. Ingrid Monson, Ron Radano, and Philip Bohlman offered detailed criticism of the best sort—the final shape of this essay owes much to their careful readings.

Endnotes

1. I'm indebted to Roger Savage for giving me the opportunity to think about a political hermeneutics, and for pushing me to engage with it even when I resisted.
2. Foster (1995: 11–12) writes that:
   ... the body shares with women, racial minorities and colonized peoples, gays and lesbians, and other marginalized groups the scorn and neglect of mainstream scholarship. The canonical thrust of Western scholarship has worked at every turn to deny and repress or else to exoticize the experience of these peoples just as it has dismissed body-centered endeavors and the participation of the body in any endeavor. The critiques of canonical scholarship established in feminist and queer theory, postcolonial and minority discourses of inherent racial, class, and gendered biases have immediate relevance for a scholarship of the body. These critical inquiries explicate techniques of dismissal used in canonical scholarship that find direct analogues in scholarly approaches to body-centered endeavors.
3. Turner suggests that theories of diet, for example, have almost always been tied to matters of class: the aristocratic body and the laborer's working body have been imagined through very different working metaphors, and the working class body politic has been conceived as a machine. Since the Enlightenment, ideas of diet have been closely tied to interests in working class efficiency: first developed for prisons and asylums, dietary regimes have been created to effect maximum efficiency through minimum sustenance — i.e., the working class body has been constructed as a site that can be maintained in many ways, including the materiality of its sustenance.
   Turner also suggests that *anorexia nervosa* stands in direct contrast to such dietary regimes of social control, though still rooted in matters of class formation and maintenance (1992: 214-28). He posits that anorexia is an "overdetermined disease, ... peculiarly expressive of the personal and social dilemmas of educated, middle-class women, because it articulates aspects of their powerlessness within an environment that also demands their competitive success" (ibid., 224–25). In essence, he suggests that the disorder may be pathological in nature but is still characterized by individual agency.
4. In his earlier work, Fiske connected the body and pleasure, suggesting that "bodily pleasures offer carnivalesque, evasive, liberating practices — they constitute the popular terrain where hegemony is weakest" (1989: 6). At that point, he conceived of pleasure as a kind of experience beyond the reach of dominant ideology, as "the least politically active" kind of resistance (ibid., 8). Analyzing surfing and video arcade games as social performances, Fiske described pleasure as a moment when "ideological subject reverts to the body"; he suggested that "t[he body becomes the site of identity and pleasure when social control is lost" (ibid., 93). His conception of pleasure as resistance, though, was rooted in a model of hegemony as homogeneous in character, and resistance (especially popular culture) as heterogeneous (ibid., 7-8). Rather than posit a body in interaction with dominant ideologies, Fiske froze it in an oppositional stance and invested it with a modernist individuality as a primary site of agency. His subsequent work is quite different, strongly inflected with poststructuralist theories of the body.
5. The body of Rodney King has prompted a number of scholarly and political responses, most notably in Gooding-Williams 1993.
6. Turner (1992: 41) is similarly unwilling to do away with the reality of the body:
   [I]t would be wrong to construe my sociology of the body as *merely* a social constructionist viewpoint. In arguing that the body is socially constructed (by language, ideology, discourse or knowledge), it has been assumed, wrongly in my view, that one could not in addition believe that there is such a topic as the phenomenology of pain. ... In short, I do not believe that reality is *discourse,* that is, I do not believe that social reality is merely an issue of representation.
7. This central problem has been acknowledged by many theorists. Wiegman (1995: 6), for instance, notes that "a politics based on identity must carefully negotiate the risk of rein-scribing the logic of the system it hopes to defeat."
8. See, of course, Said's *Orientalism* (1978) for more on these connections.
9. See C. Wong 1996 for more on issues of Asian American masculinity and performance.
10. I'm grateful for Andrew Weintraub's and Matthew Butterfield's bibliographic help in this section.

11. One of the most recent such books, *Jazz, Black and White* (1995) by White jazz critic Gene Lees, is the latest, rather clumsy attempt to write against race. Much of this rambling study profiles jazz musicians, mostly African American, and addresses in sympathetic White liberal mode the brutality of the racism encountered by African American musicians. At times, Lees' own role as empathetic White friend to these musicians is heavy handed; in that sense, he plays out White angst in awkward but well-meant terms. More damaging, though, is his final chapter, "Jazz Black and White," in which he takes on anti-White racism among African American jazz musicians, and suddenly one realizes that this is where he's been headed all along — the moment when he can take on the Black nationalist stance of Stanley Crouch and Wynton Marsalis. Lees complains that "anti-white racism is showing increasing signs of being institutionalized" (1995: 190), and proceeds to show how White musicians have been ignored, excluded, and expropriated from jazz then and now. In the end, the language of liberal humanism (can't we all just get along?) simply doesn't allow him to take Black nationalism seriously.

12. Frank Kofsky opens his book, *Black Nationalism and the Revolution in Music* (1970: 9-10), with the reflection:

    There is a curious dichotomy that reigns among white Americans. If they are in the jazz world proper, then they will tend to deny that, whatever else jazz *may* be, it is first and foremost a black art — an art created and nurtured by black people in this country out of the wealth of their historical experience. On the other hand, if they are not part of the jazz milieu, white Americans will automatically and virtually without exception assume that jazz is black—though not an art—and therefore, though this may go unstated, worthy of no serious treatment or respect.

13. Krin Gabbard's dynamic paired collections, *Representing Jazz* (1995a) and *Jazz Among the Discourses* (1995b), are devoted to a poststructuralist questioning of how jazz comes to carry meaning, presenting particular moments in jazz history as radically contingent. Gabbard himself directly addresses the political economy of writing about jazz, noting that "ever since the first serious writings about jazz appeared, critics have sought to become organic intellectuals, who would theorize themselves and the music into importance" (1995b: 7). Most of the case studies in these two volumes address the institutional structures and apparatuses surrounding jazz, with fascinating but often unexamined implications for race.

14. Tomlinson notes, too, the potentially transformative effect that Signifyin(g) can have on what it touches: by locating meaning in the interstices of place, expression, and movement, the nature of those materials shifts. "By naming [for instance] the black tradition from within itself we revise and rename all the other traditions with which it ... interacts," he says (ibid., 69). Presenting Miles Davis as a figure through whom African American and White critics (Crouch, Litweiler, Williams, and Baraka) have Signified their abiding concerns with jazz as they imagine(d) it, Tomlinson reconfigures Davis as problematically racialized and problematically true to the Signifyin(g) strategies of the blues.

15. From a telephone interview with Francis Wong in San Francisco, January 29, 1996.

16. This suite is on the album *Never Give Up!*, Asian Improv Records, 1989 (AIR 0007).

17. A year later, when I asked him if I could refer to his reaction in this essay, my friend, Charles Sykes, expanded on his original comments in an e-mail note as follows:

    I liken "stiff" to a metronome, an electronic one that plays an exact pulse. Music that grooves always seems to have a push and pull—there is a sense of the "beat," that constant, abstract metric pulse, but the groove is established on "top" of the beat (slightly before) or by "laying back" (slightly after the beat).

18. Hearing race in music is of course heuristically related to hearing sexuality and sexual orientation in music: both are ontologically grounded in a conception of difference *vis-à-vis* the normative. For a number of essays that explore (among other things) the problems of "hearing" sexual orientation, see *Queering the Pitch: The New Gay and Lesbian Musicology*, Ed. Philip Brett, Elizabeth Wood, and Gary C. Thomas. New York and London: Routledge, 1994.

19. I would like to thank Mark Izu for including me in this roundtable discussion during the weekend of the 1996 Asian American Jazz Festival, which he curated.

20. Personal communication from Anthony Braxton to Ronald Radano (to me).

21. All of Ted Chung's comments are from a telephone interview conducted in Philadelphia on February 1, 1996.
22. Freestyling is impromptu, improvised rapping that often takes place between two or more rappers in contexts of live performance; like the dozens and other forms of African American oratory, it can have a competitive frame. Each rapper takes a turn, rapping for a moment or two until s/he either hands the floor over to the next rapper or has it forcibly (verbally) taken away. Freestyling rarely appears in audio recordings or in music videos.
23. The Mountain Brothers' appearance at Penn was sponsored by the Department of Music, the Theater Arts Program in the Department of English, and the GSAC Multiculturalism Committee.
24. Interview with Paul Chihara in Pittsburgh, January 23, 1996.

9

Taiko in Asian America

Playing

When I began taking taiko classes in 1997, I had already wanted to learn taiko for many years. I had seen San Jose Taiko and San Francisco Taiko Dojo in concert performances and Soh Daiko in several outdoor festivals in New York City, and every time I saw these groups I felt as if I would literally jump out of my skin with excitement. Part of it was the unadulterated energy and power of the drums themselves, but much of it was seeing Asian Americans playing this forceful music and feeling it viscerally in my own body at the same time — this was central to my vicarious pleasure in taiko. Hearing taiko made me want to be able to *do* it: I have never been particularly athletic, but hearing and seeing taiko performed made me want to get beyond the vicarious to experience — made me want to be strong and loud like those Asian American musicians I so admired.

Much of this book has been written from my perspective as an ethnographer, which has included such roles as friend, sponsor, casual acquaintance, student, and fly on the wall. In this chapter, I write from experience, and I moved into passionate involvement with taiko for all the same reasons that I was drawn to write about Asian American musical activity in the first place. Much of my joy in taiko is related to its place in Asian American expressive culture, which does not preclude the presence of non-Asian Americans in its American realization — indeed, the group I belong to, the Taiko Center of Los Angeles, is explicitly multiethnic. The slippage between taiko as a specifically Japanese performance tradition, to its emergence as a Japanese American tradition, to its reformulation as a pan-Asian American tradition, to its placement as a tradition open to any participants from any background, is central to the place of taiko in America; I will address these multiple locations even as I try to make clear my own motivations in becoming a taiko musician.

I performed today. (But when is "today" in a written work, in a chapter that I will surely spend months working on, revising and revising again?) Today was a fall day in Riverside, California, and I played beside my teacher, Reverend Shuichi Thomas Kurai, in a demonstration concert for school children held at the Riverside Community College. At the time of this writing (1999), I have studied with Rev. Tom for two and a half years, almost exactly. I am barely intermediate in my abilities: I know some ten pieces and I am rarely put on a lead drum. When we played today, on a huge dark stage in an auditorium filled with some twelve hundred children, I immediately felt the same joy I feel every time I play taiko in public despite pre-performance anxiety over playing alone with my teacher. When I perform, I am someone else. My body changes, automatically: I stand up straight, I am alert, I am ready to spring into furious activity, I may be panting and sweating but I (try to) stay in control at all times. I am completely charged up but am relaxed at the same time, thinking not of myself but of how to stay in the group, with the group — how to be part of the whole. When the piece starts and I move out of *kamaete* position and shout "*Sore!*" and make that first contact with the drum head, a number of things come together all at once: the flow of *ki* out of my torso → arm → wrist → *bachi* → drum head → sound; an awareness of whoever I'm next to, and constantly monitoring whether they're on or off and where I should be in relation to them; my awareness of the audience, and playing out to them, with my eyes and with *kakegoe* and with my entire body. I am trying to let you in on my *experience*: I am trying here to make you feel what I feel, to know those moments of heightened heart rate and physical exertion and friendship that are all related to being Asian American and playing taiko.

(Are you distracted by the "foreign" terms? Do you want an "explanation," an ethnomusicological exegesis of those words with which you're not familiar? You will get it, in good time. The point here is that those words from an Elsewhere are now part of a particular kind of Asian American experience.)

At the time of this writing, I have performed perhaps fifty times in public: at street fairs, O-bon festivals, community celebrations, museum openings, etc., etc. — once even for a Japanese supermarket opening. Students of the Taiko Center of Los Angeles (TCLA) play constantly, and we have all gotten used to driving around the greater Los Angeles area for different performances. In my life as a professor and as a community activist, I constantly make decisions about where to go next, when to stand firm and when to give way; I am continuously in charge of things, whether students or activities. As a taiko student, I give myself over completely — to my teacher and to my fellow students. Both of these impulses are completely satisfying for me. In Thailand, my research on music and ritual focused on teacher–disciple relationships (Wong 2001) and I found that it wasn't uncomfortable or difficult for me for "give" myself to a teacher and to let go of the complicated ego that accompanies so much Western artistic activity; in Thai, performers actually say that a student must "give" him or herself over to a teacher's authority (they have several verbs for it) and this is viewed as an act of trust and respect rather than subordination, creating a bond with the potential for years of close association and mutual care. Vanishing into the act of learning music, first Thai and now Japanese, is deeply satisfying for me and involves an effacement of nearly everything that gets me through the day in my other life. That's part of my pleasure in it. The other pleasure is in becoming more than myself, i.e., becoming part of a group of other student musicians, some skilled, some less so.

We have just turned a corner: Rev. Tom has created a core group of some twelve students (including myself) who will do most of the public performances for the TCLA, and he wants to call the group Satori Daiko. *Satori* is the sudden illumination or enlightenment received in Zen Buddhism which is beyond communication or explanation; it can't be characterized emotionally or intellectually. It is repeatable, though, through practice — meditation — and this brings maturity to the practitioner. Some sects of Zen posit that it strikes abruptly and momentarily — indeed, this is central to one experience of satori; the sensation is a sudden absence of surging thought followed by a perfect, pure sense of self-nature. Soto Zen (Rev. Tom's sect), however, posits a gradually developing awareness that leads to satori.[1] In either case, satori is a peak spiritual state that is neither easily attained nor simply explained.

Rev. Tom is not in the habit of "explaining" things, and asking him questions may or may not result in answers. He is an accomplished teacher; one learns taiko in his classes, there is no question of that. It would be presumptuous to claim that I understand why he has given our group this name (indeed, I will have to work up to asking him about this), and it would be even more presumptuous to write that I "know" what satori is, but through playing, I might have a glimmering of what it could be like. The sudden flash of emptiness and joy always comes during performance — not in rehearsal, when I am thinking while playing. He always says, "Think during practice, but don't think when you perform. Just go out there and have fun." Does he mean what I am lucky enough sometimes to feel? I am not a Zen Buddhist, but if it's a good performance, I have that moment at least once, when movement gives way to an unbearable lightness of being, a long second of pure *ki,* and then I am plunged back into the body, thinking which round is this? pace yourself, don't give it all too soon! that place on my left hand is starting to blister again.

Rev. Tom

Shuichi Thomas Kurai is a seventh- or eighth-generation Zen priest. He is an Issei who says he thinks like a Sansei. He was born in 1947 in Katada village, Shima peninsula, Mie prefecture, Japan and grew up at a Soto Zen temple where his grandfather was the priest. He emigrated to Southern California when he was five years old; his father, Rev. Shuyu Kurai,[2] was sent to Los Angeles to serve as a priest at Zenshuji Soto Mission in Little Tokyo. His mother, Michiko Kurai (*nee* Kozaki) was born and raised in the San Jose area (in Los Altos); she was sent to Japan in 1937 when she was ten to get an education and after she graduated from high school, she taught as an elementary school teacher; her marriage to Rev. Tom's father was arranged. She lived in Japan for fifteen years, through World War II, and when the opportunity arose for Rev. Shuyu to do missionary work, she was eager to return to the U.S. Rev. Tom's mother is thus a Kibei Nisei — born in the U.S. and therefore a Nisei, but schooled in Japan (Kibei); as a result, she is completely bicultural and bilingual. Rev. Tom grew up understanding Japanese but not speaking it very well; his mother spoke English with him and Japanese with her husband.

The emphasis on relative generation is central to Japanese American identity and to Asian American location more generally. Indeed, the emergence of taiko in the U.S. is closely tied to Sansei — third-generation Japanese American — sensibilities. To be a Sansei in the Asian American movement means to be politically aware and to be willing to speak out (e.g., against internment and for reparations) in ways that the Nisei, the second generation, the first American-born generation, often found difficult if not impossible. One could say that the loud assertiveness of taiko is emblematic of Sansei outspokenness; the Nisei were more invested in big band jazz and baseball because their mission was to be American. Yes, this is over simplified: not all Sansei are politically involved and many Nisei fought for reparations; no one has a corner on anger or silence. Still, most Japanese Americans would agree that Issei-Nisei-Sansei distinctions are the bedrock of Japanese American identity and are states of mind as much as anything else. At this point, most of the Issei have passed on; the Nisei are increasingly elderly; the Sansei are increasingly middle-aged. Whether distinctive Yonsei (fourth-generation) and Gosei (fifth-generation) identities will emerge remains to be seen. Rev. Tom says he thinks of himself as Sansei though technically he is either Issei or Nisei-han, "half Nisei," or 1.5 generation (in current Ethnic Studies parlance). Rev. Tom's parents thought they would be in the U.S. for five years but this was extended to ten years, and at the end of that time, they decided not to go back to Japan. Rev. Tom grew up in Boyle Heights in East Los Angeles and then in Monterey Park; he went to Garfield High School, which he remembers as being about 90% Chicano; he says he had about thirty Japanese American classmates.

Rev. Tom isn't particularly easy to talk with. For one thing, he is constantly on the move; he teaches taiko at no fewer than six locations spread out over the greater Los Angeles region, so he is more likely to be driving somewhere than available for a leisurely conversation. When the Taiko Center of Los Angeles became his primary livelihood in 1997, his life became a masterpiece of scheduling; one afternoon when I was at his house, he was reading e-mail while the answering machine took a message and a fax came in, all at once, all related to up-coming taiko gigs. In short, he's a busy man and has little time for searching conversations. I "know" what I know about him through listening, playing, riding along in the van on the way to gigs, hanging out before/after/between gigs, and asking questions that occasionally get answered, as well as through one sustained interview, when we talked for an hour with the tape recorder running. His reticence isn't related only to time pressures. He simply doesn't operate in terms of explanations or question-and-answer, nor does he explain why he (usually) doesn't answer direct questions. During my interview with him, he came close to explaining the silence when I asked him whether he would characterize himself as a teacher emphasizing rigor or as one focused on experimentation:

DW: Where do you place yourself in the big continuum of possibilities? I mean, you do put a lot of emphasis on form and practice in your teaching, certainly.

TK: Uh huh, yeah.

DW: I'd put you closer to that end of things, but what do you think?

TK: Although I don't say specifically what my philosophy is, I'm always thinking that taiko is a way to improve your life.

DW: Oh?

TK: And to become a better person, through taiko. I don't say that too much —

DW: I don't think you've *ever* said it.

TK: I've said it in my newsletter a couple of times.

DW: That's true, yeah.

TK: I don't... I want people to find that out on their own.

DW: Why do you think that's more effective?

TK: Because that's what Zen is. You can't explain what Zen is, you can't read about it, you just have to experience it. And it was the same way in the relationship between my father and I — we hardly ever spoke about anything! We only spoke about trivial things, you know. I never got a lecture from him about what the meaning of life is, you know, or what Zen is, or what Buddhism is — *never*, not even once.

DW: He left you to figure that out yourself.

TK: Yeah! [*laughs*]

His father was a priest at Zenshuji Soto Mission for many years, but Rev. Tom never felt that his parents expected him to become a priest. In fact, he majored in landscape architecture and park administration at California Polytechnic State University, Pomona and, in the middle of all that, got drafted in 1970 and spent a year in Heidelberg, Germany before returning to the U.S. in 1972. In 1975, he took an Asian American Studies class at East L.A. College with Buck Wong and it changed the way he thought about things; he went back to school (at CSU Los Angeles) and took a number of Ethnic Studies classes. He got involved with Asian Pride, which evolved into Multicultural Pride, a division of Educational Participation in Communities (EPIC), a program that designed Asian American Studies curriculum for K–12 use. At that point, he had lost all interest in landscape architecture: "I wanted to do something that would get me in touch with people," he says. He joined Kinnara Taiko in 1976 as a way to explore Japanese culture and in 1980, he went to Japan and stayed for three years, teaching English to Japanese businessmen to support himself while studying traditional folk dance, *hayashi,* and taiko. He says it was the best thing he ever did. "I tried not have expectations — I thought I was going to find the Japanese side of me there, but I found the American side of me there, actually. I found out that I'm not Japanese; I'm Japanese American."

I am trying to "explain" what makes Rev. Tom tick — what motivates him, what drives him — because he provides a window on the cultural and political place of taiko in Asian America, but he eludes me. Rev. Tom says that his thinking is 75% that of a Sansei, but he didn't explain what the other 25% is. He is my teacher and I have spent considerable time with him over the past two and a half years but, as I have written elsewhere in this book, knowing people and understanding them isn't a simple business. Writing about Asian America has meant writing about people who I sometimes know very well indeed, and this has pushed my ethnographic envelope in useful ways even as it has complicated my personal ethical sense of where friendship leaves off and objectification begins. I write here with a strong sense of allegiance, knowing that other taiko players will read these pages and disagree with some of the things I assert. I am located within this tradition in very specific ways — through Rev. Tom, through my personal sense of Asian American political mission, through my still-limited exposure to taiko, etc. I know that taiko players of non-Asian descent may have particular problems with what I write, but I have no intention of vacating their experiences of meaning even as I insist that they acknowledge the particular meanings taiko has for Asian Americans. In short, I am keenly aware that I am writing from certain positions as well as for certain audiences, some of them no doubt critical — and I find myself most concerned with what Rev. Tom will think when he reads this, which should convince you that I write as a student.

Taiko Material Culture

Taiko means "large drum" in Japanese (*tai,* "large," and *ko,* "drum"), but a beginning taiko student's first lessons rarely involve the drums to any great extent. You are first handed a pair of *bachi,* wooden sticks about sixteen inches long and three-quarters of an inch in diameter. The first pair that you handle is probably from a big box full of beat-up mismatched *bachi* used only in beginning classes; they are probably made of cheap pine, are dinged up, and you usually find out the hard way that they'll give you splinters if you handle them wrong. You stand in front of an old car tire propped up on a chair and you learn how to hold the *bachi,* gripping them an inch or two above the end and then extending your arms horizontally in front of you, arms outstretched so that the *bachi* are a straight continuation of the line of your arms; the far end of the *bachi* should rest on top of the tire, almost but not quite touching, so that your arms-plus-*bachi* form a V-shape. Your elbows should be straight but not locked. You face the tire, feet about three feet apart, left foot slightly forward, left knee bent, right leg straight but not locked, torso straight, butt and gut pulled in, shoulders back. This is *kamaete* position, "ready" position: whenever your teacher calls out, "*Kamaete!*," you get into this stance as quickly as you can.

You buy a pair of pine *bachi* from your teacher for $5, or you go to the hardware store and make your own; you scout out the garages in your neighborhood and find an old car tire that's being thrown out; you cover it with an old tee-shirt so your *bachi* won't get black rubber marks all over them, and you keep the tire somewhere at home where you can practice.

In class, for many weeks, you pound on tires. If you're lucky, your teacher may bring a drum or two and everyone rotates frequently so you eventually get to actually play on a drum for a few brief moments. The emphasis, though, isn't on the drums but on *kata* — form, style, stance, shape, i.e., the way you hold your body while you play. You spend weeks playing simple quarter-note and eighth-note patterns, learning how to bring your right arm across your body, leading with the elbow, snapping the wrist at the just the right moment so that your *ki,* your energy, is propelled through the *bachi* as you strike the tire with its tip. You learn warm-up exercises that focus on the shoulders, the thighs, the wrists, the forearms, but you end up hurting all over anyway; the day after class means limping around because your left thigh isn't used to supporting most of your weight, and your forearms protest because they weren't meant to be a high-impact zone. You might even have some bruises from whacking yourself on the hands or arms by accident, because you spend most of your time flailing around trying to get it all coordinated — there's so much to think about, you never knew that you had so many body parts or that they could be organized in these particular ways. You feel clumsy, awkward, inept. But you're getting used to certain things, such as moving into *kamaete* position and following the *kane,* the small brass hand gong (more formally called the *atarigane*) that your teacher strikes with a small wooden beater — its sound cuts through everything and it quickly becomes the sound of authority for you, the sound that you follow in a sea of uncoordinated drum beats and tire thuds, the sound that you hold onto with your ears and perhaps with your eyes as well.

You are learning to shout, too. *Ho! Yo! Sore!* This is one of the hardest things, as if managing the body wasn't already complicated enough. You aren't used to being loud, especially if you're Asian American. Your teacher explains that *kakegoe* is part of the music: some shouts are literally part of particular patterns and others are fit in more spontaneously, but they are all sonic realizations of *ki,* the energy/spirit focused in your solar plexus that drives your physical movement and which is realized in taiko more generally. You understand this intellectually but can't bring yourself to *do* it: you aren't yet strong in that way, really, you feel terribly shy and self-conscious about shouting from the gut, especially when you're busy flailing around. When you force yourself to try, you sound pathetic — lame, half-hearted, like the beginner you know you are.

Meanwhile, you have actually started to learn a piece, "Renshu," by Seiichi Tanaka, the legendary master who founded San Francisco Taiko Dojo. *Renshu* means "to practice," and it takes some weeks to learn the five lines of the piece and their choreography. In between classes, you forget a lot of the details that make all the difference. *Don* (bring your right arm back up)! *Don* (bring your left arm back up)! *Don* (leave your right arm down)! *Don* (now leave your left arm down)! Every class involves relearning what you forgot, but certain things are beginning to accumulate almost without your being aware of it. You and your classmates are starting to become friends — the vulnerability of being clumsy together speeds up the whole process — and as you look around the classroom, you can see each of them doing certain things that help make you more aware of what you're doing right or wrong.

The months go by, and you've learned how to stagger the patterns of "Renshu," with the class split into two groups that start out together, then overlap certain patterns, and finally come back together. You have your first performance together: after a group of more advanced students plays, you and your classmates trot out and play "Renshu" (the only piece you know), and although it has moments of chaos (someone leaves out a beat somewhere and doesn't realize it for awhile, or several people lose track of which round we're in and end early, looking foolish), it flies, and we're all giddy with our accomplishment. You buy your first nice *bachi:* $10 for a pair of white birch beaters that are the same size as your practice *bachi* but heavier and more attractive. You carry them to class haphazardly stuck into your purse or bag until you realize that *bachi* aren't just sticks, they're instruments as much as the drums are, and you start treating them with more care and respect, carrying them in a special bag and sanding them down every so often as they get dinged up and grimy. You're learning to pace yourself in class so that you don't get exhausted halfway through. You've discovered that it's easier to play on an empty stomach. You resolve to lift weights. As you drive to class, you speak through the (now) two pieces that you know, having found that class goes better if your head is ready before you walk in the door. You're still a beginner but you're driven by a particular kind of longing to be *better*, to be *stronger*, to be more focused. You have your first dream about playing, and in that dream, you experience what it's like to *really* play. The memory of that vicarious experience feeds the longing. You're obsessed before you even know it.

The Taiko "Group"

North American Taiko groups come and go, though some have had great longevity. New ones appear and old ones are remembered. At this point (the late 1990s), there are more than one hundred and fifty taiko groups in the U.S. and Canada, based in Buddhist temples, community centers, and universities (mainly as student clubs, often called "collegiate groups"). The ideological, spiritual, and ethnic bases for different taiko groups open up important issues of identity construction.

Taiko is unquestionably ancient but until recently was generally played as a solo instrument to accompany festivals or Buddhist ritual. *Matsuri*, seasonal festivals with numerous regional forms, often feature a small ensemble of musicians (*hayashi*) featuring an *odaiko* (large drum), a flute (*take-bue* or *shino-bue*), and several other drums that generally accompany dance (Malm 1959: 48–50). Taiko also accompanies the recitation of Buddhist *wasan* (prayer chanted to a steady beat on an *odaiko*) (Malm 1959: 69) and has a central role in O-bon festivals, held in August to honor the souls of the dead.[3] In this context, taiko accompanies the *bon-odori* dance, and it is in this role especially that taiko was carried abroad via the Japanese diaspora during the early part of the twentieth century and remains central to Japanese American O-bon festivals (Yano 1985). North American taiko players consider the traditional taiko pieces for *bon-odori* particularly difficult; they have become part of a specialized repertoire known only to players who make a point of learning it.[4] *Kumi-daiko*, or "group" taiko, was created in Japan in the 1950s, changing taiko from a solo instrument used to accompany dance, drama, and prayer to a lead instrument; massed ensembles of taiko are thus a very recent development in the history of the instrument (Tusler 1995: 20–21). Some North American groups have maintained taiko specifically as a Buddhist art form (*horaku*), but many have not (Asai 1985); in some ways, taiko has been secularized as the *kumi-daiko* tradition has become more established, though the way in which taiko teaches Buddhist values is often subtle.

Oedo Sukeroku Daiko in Tokyo has probably had the most far-reaching influence on North American taiko groups. Its history is complicated, involving several founding members who each eventually formed their own groups which all share certain stylistic hallmarks including a characteristic *kata* (stance) with the left leg bent and the right leg straight and the diagonal Sukeroku stand for *chudaiko* which is widely used by North American groups. Their style blended *hogaku* (classical music), *budo* (martial arts) and *buyo* (dance), and — as David Leong notes (1999) — their influence is so wide-spread that it is now too often unacknowledged, having been absorbed into North American taiko "tradition." Furthermore, Oedo Sukeroku Daiko was the first professional taiko group in Japan: although numerous *kumi-daiko* clubs sprang up in Japan during the 1950s–60s, Sukeroku was, and continues to be, a professional troupe with an extensive schedule of touring and concerts.

Oedo Sukeroku Daiko's style and repertoire was brought to the U.S. by Seiichi Tanaka, the founder of San Francisco Taiko Dojo. Tanaka-sensei, as he is known in the U.S. (*sensei*, "teacher"), studied and performed with Sukeroku and received the group's permission to teach their material abroad; Tanaka-sensei remains Sukeroku's official representative in the U.S. David Leong's extended history of Sukeroku and his diplomatic effort to make sense of their recent attempts to exert copyright control over their repertoire and drum stands (addressed in more detail below) makes for fascinating reading (1999). After interviewing Sukeroku members, Leong (1999) noted that, "Following Japanese style, all introductions and visits to the group should be arranged through Tanaka-sensei. Groups have been able to successfully contact Oedo Sukeroku directly, but usually are scolded for breach of protocol."

I will return to the matter of control over repertoire and the questions it raises about authority and authenticity in the *kumi-daiko* tradition, but should first outline the early years of taiko in the U.S. Tanaka-sensei and the San Francisco Taiko Dojo (founded in 1969) have been hugely influential. Many American groups were founded by Tanaka-sensei's students who absorbed the Sukeroku style through him. As Leong writes, "It would not be a far reach to say that most groups in North America owe a stylistic debt to Oedo Sukeroku. In fact, many groups play Oedo Sukeroku's repertoire, often improperly, without permission, and without realizing where the material originated from." Unlike Sukeroku, the San Francisco Taiko Dojo is a school rather than a professional troupe and its focus is on the spiritual and martial arts basis of taiko. Tanaka-sensei's teaching style is considered particularly rigorous, and American taiko players regard any training with him (either through classes or workshops) as a mark of authority. Although he is not regarded as the *only* source of "authentic" taiko in North America, his lineage carries a particular weight even though it is not always explicitly recognized as a link to Sukeroku. I will address the ideology of authenticity and authority that underlies performers' attitudes around these matters, and its link to lineage and genealogy, in much greater detail below.

In the 1970s, numerous other taiko groups were formed in the U.S. and in Canada, and *kumi-daiko* took off in Japan with the spectacular success of the professional group Kodo. The chronology of some of the more well-known groups, all still extant, is as follows:

Taiko Group	Year founded
Yushima Tenjin Sukeroku Daiko (later reformed as Oedo Sukeroku Daiko) (Tokyo)	1959
San Francisco Taiko Dojo	1968
Kinnara Taiko (Los Angeles)	1969
San Jose Taiko	1973
Soh Daiko (New York, NY)	1979
Kodo (Japan)	1981

All of these early American groups were formed by Japanese or by Japanese Americans and had primarily Japanese American student bases; most of the Japanese American groups were originally based at Buddhist temples.

Rev. Tom has been in quite a few groups since he got involved with taiko in the 1970s, and his personal history is a fascinating window on differences within the Southern California taiko scene. He was an early member of Kinnara Taiko (1976–78) and describes their style as free-wheeling, involving lots of improvisation and open jamming during rehearsals; he notes that Kenny Endo joined Kinnara at the about the same time and that, coming from Chicano-influenced East Los Angeles backgrounds, they both found Kinnara's West LA character (located in and around historically African American neighborhoods) strikingly different from what they knew. Rev. Tom found himself wanting to reach the next generation of Japanese Americans, and in 1978, he became director of Sozenji Taiko, which at that point was entirely Japanese American in its membership and connected to him through his father's temple. While in Japan from 1980–83, he was a member of the Japan Folkloric Dance Study Group (Nihon Minzoku Buyu Kenkyukai) in Tokyo and studied *hayashi* and taiko. After Rev. Tom returned from Japan in 1983, he joined Los Angeles Matsuri Daiko Aiko Kai; he says that those years with L.A. Matsuri were a good training ground in technique. He reestablished Sozenji Taiko in 1983 and was Zenshuji Zendeko's (then called Zen Daiko) first instructor from 1985-86 at Zenshuji Soto Mission (his father's former temple). In 1986, Rev. Tom's father died and he took over his father's duties as minister at Sozenji Buddhist Temple.

In 1993, West Covina Taiko (established in 1981) reformed as Kishin Daiko and Rev. Tom, already their teacher, became Kishin's artistic director; Kishin's home base, East San Gabriel Japanese Community Center, dictated that the group was not Buddhist-focused and was primarily but not entirely Japanese American in its membership. Indeed, Kishin's mission statement describes the group as explicitly multicultural and multigenerational,[5] and this broadening of its community base has had important implications for Rev. Tom's motivations in teaching taiko. In other words, after 1993 he was no longer entirely directed toward Japanese Americans or Buddhist-based instruction but rather moved toward a more inclusive model of taiko instruction without losing its foundation in Asian American political and spiritual dimensions. From 1995–99, he also served as instructor and advisor for Kodama Taiko, which started out as Jishin Daiko at California State University, Northridge. To summarize, between 1976 and the time of this writing (1999–2000), he has been connected to no fewer than seven taiko groups as a member or as a teacher, and several of those groups underwent metamorphoses during that time (changing names and/or affiliations).

Rev. Tom formed the Taiko Center of Los Angeles in 1997 as a way to coordinate the classes that he was already teaching over a seventy-mile radius. By then, he had on-going classes at the Pacific Asia Museum in Pasadena, at the Japanese American National Museum in Little Tokyo, in Monterey Park, in Redondo Beach, etc. Although the Taiko Center of Los Angeles didn't exist in any single space, it was essentially a way to link his widely dispersed student base, and I would say that it worked. When I started taking classes with him at the Pacific Asia Museum in Pasadena in October 1997, I quickly got to know the students in the classes before and after mine, and when my classmates and I started performing publicly (on a limited basis) in the summer of 1998, we were often combined with students from his other classes, as we all knew the same repertoire. His student base was made up of approximately sixty students ranging in age from six to sixty, mostly Japanese Americans but also including other Asian American ethnicities, quite a few White Americans, and a few Latino/as; women outnumbered men about 4:1. In 1999, Rev. Tom parted ways (through mutual agreement) with Kishin and Kodama, and within a month, he formed Satori Daiko from his student base in the Taiko Center of Los Angeles. Satori is only the second group he formed himself: like Sozenji Taiko, it is made up of his students, but it is apparently more select.

Our first meeting was on a Wednesday night in mid-November 1999, at Sozenji. The group was made up of twelve people: seven women and five men, nine Japanese Americans, one White American, four Asian Americans of mixed ethnicity, four young people under twenty, one man in his twenties, and seven middle-aged members in their 40s–50s:

Bev	Japanese American	50s	Woman
Elaine	Japanese American	40s	Woman
Brady (Elaine's son)	Japanese American	teenager	Man
Todd	Japanese American	14	Man
Audrey	Japanese American	40s	Woman
Lani (Audrey's daughter)	Asian American, mixed ethnicity	12	Woman
Gary	Japanese American/White American (hapa)[6]	50s	Man
Harriet	Japanese American	40s	Woman
Taylor (Harriet's daughter)	Japanese American/White American (hapa)	10	Woman
Ryan	White American	20s	Man
me	Chinese American/White American (hapa)	40s	Woman
Rev. Tom	Japanese American	50s	Man

Bev had known Rev. Tom as a member of Sozenji Taiko and then as a member of Kodama; Audrey had worked with him for six years through Kishin Daiko; the rest of us had come to him within the last two or three years through the Taiko Center of Los Angeles. We hauled drums around, setting them up in rows so that we could start learning a rather flashy piece in which each player uses two drums, reaching to the left with their right hand to strike the drum beside them. I think we were all feeling both shy and excited even though we mostly knew each other, some better than others; beginnings are important, and few of us were entirely sure what we were getting into. Rev. Tom drew us into a circle and said, Let's talk for a bit before we start playing. Within a few sentences, I realized that he was laying things out in as direct a way as I might hear for a long time, and I listened with growing excitement, as a student and as an ethnographer. I remember wishing that I had a tape recorder running and then thinking, Well, it probably wouldn't be the same if he knew I was documenting it, and then thinking, Oh, but I must try to hold onto this!

He said that working with Kishin and Kodama had been rewarding but that he hadn't really had control over who he was working with as they weren't "his" groups. And now he *could* choose who he worked with, so he was going to establish a TCLA performance group. He would pare back on the amount of performance that his TCLA students were doing — that having them perform as much as they have been is actually very unusual, but he did it because those were the performers he'd had at his disposal until now. But he didn't want anyone to feel left out, and he wasn't sure how to approach the whole matter. He said, I want people who have the right attitude as much as anything else — people who work well together — it's not a matter of skill in itself. He said,

> I want to explain why I've created this group. Performing should be a privilege. This group will perform, and will take over the lion's share of TCLA's performances. We will work toward a concert perfor-mance, probably next July or August, and we need to be very focused, very disciplined, because that's not very long from now — once we get past the holidays, we will only have five or six months to prepare, not long at all. I already have a name for the group: Satori Daiko. *Satori* means "enlightenment," so this is a name that we can't possibly live up to, but we must try to do so. We aren't yet that group, we haven't earned that name. We have to start working together and see where we end up. We're going to have to work hard, but it will be rewarding — we will become a group, a unit, and I haven't had that yet with TCLA. It will be fun! Taiko is a way to improve your life — I believe that quite strongly — but taiko is just taiko, and I understand that you will approach this with different levels of commitment.

In short, Rev. Tom's career to date has included taiko groups with an explicit base in Buddhist instruction; groups that were/are primarily Japanese American but not exclusively so; groups that were/are multiethnic; groups that emphasized improvisation and others that emphasized rigorous training. In forming Satori Daiko, he brings together most of these possibilities, all at once. This group looks as if it will emulate certain Buddhist values even though some of its members are Buddhist and some aren't; its members are primarily Japanese American but are not exclusively so; and it will have a base in traditional playing styles though it will also emphasize new compositions and cross-cultural collaborations. In some ways, it sums up Rev. Tom's personal history to date.

Identity politics are acknowledged by some taiko groups and ignored by others. Some groups, especially those formed at Japanese American Buddhist temples, are explicitly formed to support members' relationship to their ethnic and spiritual heritage. Non-Buddhist groups represent an astonishing range of stances. Paul Yoon has written at length about Soh Daiko's hands-on approach to matters of identity work; he feels that the group has evolved into an Asian American identification via its efforts to accommodate members of Asian but not Japanese descent as well as in response to audience's orientalizing gestures. He writes (1999):

> A number of forces work to re-inscribe Soh Daiko and Taiko in general into a hegemonic category of the Oriental Other. One example which does this to Taiko in general is a group I will call Taiko Y. Taiko Y's membership is entirely non-Asian, and predominantly white, middle class men. However, this group strives to speak to each other in Japanese and introduces all of their pieces in Japanese. They address each other as _____ San and incorporate sempai-kohai, a Japanese hierarchical ordering method. One member of Taiko Y even chastised a Chinese American member of Soh Daiko for not knowing Japanese, her supposed heritage. This group's actions re-exotifies and essentializes Taiko as something Other, an Oriental object.

Taiko Y's attempts to be "Japanese" contrast markedly with other group's unabashed attempts to redefine taiko according to specific needs and interests. In Vancouver, for instance, Sawagi Taiko is a feminist/lesbian group; in Santa Monica, Soka Gakkai International is a Black women's Buddhist taiko group. At some point, virtually every taiko group seems to go through a process of self-examination and self-definition when its purpose and identity becomes a matter for focused reflection.

Although any taiko group is primarily concerned with its own activities, two emergent venues for inter-group contact have begun to create a broader sense of taiko "community" both in North America and linking North America to Japan. The first is the Rolling Thunder Resource, an award-winning website maintained by David Leung and devoted to taiko; this comprehensive site was created in 1996 and contains everything from an extended database of taiko groups (organized by continent) to a catalog of taiko equipment and supplies as well as extensive historical and cultural information about the tradition. Its electronic discussion list, taiko-l, also allows aficionados to stay in touch through the Internet. The semiannual summer Taiko Conference, inaugurated in 1997 and held once more since then at the Japanese American Community Cultural Center in Los Angeles' Little Tokyo,[7] has established a second way for taiko groups to interact and to exchange repertoire; groups attend from all over North America to spend three intensive days attending workshops and performances, which of course results in a widened dissemination of material.

In sum, the taiko "group" exists in dynamic relation to the broader taiko "community," which crosses geographic lines into the virtual world. Understandings of "group" and "community" emerge out of direct contact as well as through Internet discussions and are anything but fixed. As I will address below, a recent conflict brought these matters into sharp relief, but I first need to consider questions of gender, representation, and racialization.

The Asian/American Body: Drums, Rising Sun and the Question of Gender

The potential in taiko for slippage between the Asian and the Asian American body is staggering. Paul Yoon has written about the ways that American audiences map the Asian (and more specifically the Japanese) onto the bodies that perform taiko, documenting White Americans who come up to Japanese American and Asian American taiko players assuming that they are Japanese, sometimes even trying to speak to them in classroom Japanese (1999). Taiko excites an expectation of the foreign in the White American spectator, and I have played in altogether too many performances where this was precisely what was counted upon.

San Francisco Taiko Dojo appears in the fourth scene of *Rising Sun*[8] (about six minutes into the film) playing their signature piece, "Tsunami."[9] The physical and sonic presence of the taiko players creates a stage for xenophobic anxiety over Japanese corporate conspiracy; their ominous strength completely pervades this key scene. The sound of the drums is a sonic path that draws the viewer into the party and into the entire framework of the film, wherein Japanese businessmen adroitly "manage" their American counterparts with bicultural acumen even as they remain deeply, unknowably foreign, strange and ruthless.

We have just seen Eddie Sakamura and Cheryl, the high-class White call girl, in her apartment; she's nude, sitting at her makeup table and watching the news on television. He's just stepped out of the shower and wears only a towel. She says, "I don't get you, Eddie," and, deadpan, he says, "So what." With the camera still on his face, faint taiko drumming suddenly wells up on the soundtrack for about two seconds and *bam*, we're into the next scene: three members of San Francisco Taiko Dojo on stage, filling the screen. They're playing furiously: two young men wearing Japanese workers' aprons (*harakake*) without shirts underneath, and Tanaka-sensei, bare-chested. Cut away to White guests in black tie and evening gowns outside — two couples — climbing the steps outside a skyscraper in Little Tokyo; they're talking among themselves, reminding each other to "bow when you're bowed to." The camera pans up the front of the dark skyscraper, which is festooned with a banner reading "Nakamoto Towers Grand Dedication." Inside, the elevator doors open and when two geisha bow to us, we realize that we're seeing the scene from the perspective of the White guests. Again, they remind each other, "bow when you're bowed to," and they bow back to the geisha. They move into the crowd, which includes lots of Japanese men and lots of White American women. The camera lingers for a second on a group posing for a snapshot: three small elderly Japanese men in tuxedos with five beautiful White women standing behind them and towering over them. In the soundtrack, we suddenly hear a loud *kakegoe,* "Uhhhhhhh!" One of the new arrivals says to his friend, "Taiko drums!" His friend says, "Eh?" He leans over to explain, "Taiko drums! Long ago, they were used to drive away evil spirits." His friend says, "Oh," and the camera cuts back to the taiko group. Tanaka-sensei is now pounding on a metal bar, creating a fusillade of brilliant sound.[10] The camera cuts to Eddie Sakamura looking at his watch with an *odaiko* player who looks tremendously powerful in profile behind him. Eddie slips up the stairs. The sound of taiko continues, but a *shakuhachi* trill is laid on top of it, and the effect is suspenseful and a bit foreboding.

We're now in the boardroom, which is dark except for a few isolated floodlights. Cheryl is there; she says, "Come here," and a man (who we see from behind) grabs her, lifts her, and she wraps her legs around him. The sound of taiko continues beneath increasingly foreboding *shakuhachi* and synthesizer sounds. Cheryl says, "No, here," and gestures for the man to carry her over to the huge table that fills the room. From above, we see him plunge his face into her groin, but we still can't see who he is; we assume it's Eddie Sakamura. She's moaning.

The taiko is suddenly loud and we're back downstairs at the party: the face of a cocktail waitress fills the screen, staring at us, her geisha-like makeup making her seem all the more impassive. She pivots and the camera pans to the face of one of the White businessmen we followed into the party: he gazes at her and then looks aside in distaste.

The camera cuts full-screen to San Francisco Taiko Dojo on stage. The huge *odaiko* at center stage is now being played by a muscular young man. Cut to the Nakamoto CEO's assistant, who is listening to something coming in on his earphone, hand cupped to ear, looking worried; ominous *shakuhachi* again, and he exchanges a significant look with the White assistant. Back to a full-screen view of the taiko group, and Tanaka-sensei is now on the huge *odaiko*: he stands in a frozen *kata* and then strikes, DON!

(pause) DON! (pause) DON! Cut to a close-up of Cheryl's crotch, and we see a flash of her pubic hair as the man rips off her underwear. She sinks back onto the table and he tears open her black dress; her breasts spill out and he begins to pump at her with her legs over his shoulders. "Come on," she says. Full-screen, the taiko ensemble, to a closeup of Tanaka-sensei on the *odaiko*. We see him from the back. *Don don don don don don don don, doko doko doko doko.* Back to the Cheryl's face under the spotlight, then a shot of the man from behind and her legs wrapped around him. "Yes," she says, and he folds his hands around her neck. She's moaning. Cut to a close-up of Tanaka-sensei from the back. Cut to the man's hands around Cheryl's neck as she gasps, "Yes, oh yes, oh yes, oh yes." A phone ringing carries us sonically into the next scene as the camera cuts to Wesley Snipes answering the phone, and the sequence is over.

Tanaka-sensei is unstoppable — well, *we* know who he is, though to "the viewer," he is just a generic taiko player. We never see the face of the man with Cheryl but the camera and the soundtrack have made it utterly clear that he is Japanese. The huge round face of the *odaiko* is visually analogous to the round spotlight on the boardroom table, and Tanaka-sensei's spectacularly strong work on the drum amplifies (visually and aurally) the man's work on Cheryl. It's not terribly subtle: we see Tanaka-sensei from behind, we see the man from behind. The militarism, volume, and masculine strength of taiko equals the man's sexual conquest of the beautiful White woman. We get it. Tanaka-sensei's muscled back and arms is the perfect eye candy for the trope of the martial: he is beautiful, invincible, and deeply threatening in his strength and perfection. The entire scene "works" because of its reversal of a coupling more familiar to the American gaze, i.e., the White American man and the Japanese woman, popularized and romanticized in the 1950s through such films and novels as *Sayonara* (1957). As Traise Yamamoto has written, that interracial relationship was constructed as "somewhat acceptable — or at least safely titillating" (1999: 27) because it acted out Japan's defeat in World War II in specifically gendered and ethnicized ways; the Japanese woman had at that point undergone at least a century's worth of Western construction as a "metonymic representation of Japan itself" (23) in need of rescue by Western men. In *Rising Sun*, the gaze figures the sexually aggressive and perverse man as Japanese via taiko (both its sound and its visual militarism). The White American woman receives the decidedly unsafe titillation of sexual congress with a Japanese man and more; he overcomes her in ways that could not be more menacing. We know, at some level, that this is an inversion of a relationship that we would find satisfying if the ethnicities were reversed. In the film's denouement, we discover that we were mistaken: the White woman's lover was a White American senator. But we are also tricked, as it turns out that he didn't kill her — he was engaging in a consensual act of sexual asphyxiation meant to heighten her pleasure. In a clumsy and confusing scene meant to tie up the loose ends, we learn that a *second* man came in and finished her off — by strangulation — as she lay alone on the table recovering from her pleasure. He was Japanese! No, he was White American! But by then we are so wholly convinced that the Japanese assistant to the CEO has acted out of perverse, knee-jerk loyalty to the company that we hardly care when the White American assistant is thrown out of a skyscraper by *yakuza* into a pool of wet cement. We know who really killed her. Crichton has "proven" that he's not a xenophobe by playing with ethnicity and nationality, but we've still gotten the point.[11]

And it was taiko that got us there. Rev. Tom says that that key scene in *Rising Sun* is a completely inappropriate representation of taiko despite San Francisco Taiko Dojo's fine performance; how could they know what would happen in the editing room? Taiko is constructed as both masculine and sinister; this particular confluence of gender and race presented through taiko is built up out of older tropes that "work" because they are so terribly familiar. The (White) viewer of *Rising Sun* is clearly meant to understand taiko as a mimetic stand-in for Japan, and a masculinist, dangerous Japan at that. I am asking an old and difficult question: how can a single cultural form — taiko — be read in such completely different ways by different groups of people?

Taiko players tend to have opinions about that scene in *Rising Sun* and, as far as I can tell, Japanese American and Asian American taiko enthusiasts aren't alone in identifying the film's problems: taiko players generally (whether of Asian descent or not) focus on the taiko scene as a microcosm of the film's xenophobic narrative. As one taiko musician, Martha Durham of Austin Taiko, wrote to me,[12]

> I saw the taiko scenes in the previews 7 or 8 times before the movie was released. So the racy encounter mix wasn't part of my first experience with the taiko scenes. When the movie was released and I saw the racy scenes mixed in, I was uncomfortable with those scenes, I thought the storyline was dark and negative.

Durham went on to say that the excitement of seeing San Francisco Taiko Dojo play in the film led her to take a taiko class and that she and her husband have been involved in taiko ever since:

> Since many people have seen the movie, when I tell someone that I play taiko, and they get a blank look on their face, I ask them if they have seen *Rising Sun*. Many have, and they all remember the drumming more than the racy scenes that were mixed in with it. I have to think we can't be the only ones who were introduced to taiko by that movie, and even though the storyline scenes were violent, seeing taiko played was worth the viewing, and, in my opinion, a boost to awareness of taiko in this country.

Whereas Durham felt that taiko basically transcended the film's narrative devices, Tiffany Tamaribuchi, the director of Sacramento Taiko Dan, questioned the juxtapositions created in the editing room:

> From what I understand SFTD was not aware that the footage was going to be intercut that way and [Tanaka] Sensei wasn't too happy about it when he found out.
>
> Personally, I was disappointed with the movie and disappointed with the way in which the scene was presented. I think the scene with Kodo in "The Hunted" played much better, but in both of the movies Taiko seemed kind of forced in to the story line. Understanding that Taiko is very powerful and primal, I can see why the director might choose to intermix it with a sexually themed "murder" scene, but to me it seemed in poor taste and really kind of disrespectful to intercut the footage the way they did from the drumming to the sex to Tanaka-sensei's face to the sex, etc. I think this is in part due to the fact that I studied under Tanaka-sensei, but even still, just as a fan of Taiko it was just disappointing to see. Taiko has always been a very uplifting and spiritually moving thing for me. The scene didn't match my image of what Taiko is or what its potential as an art form is.

Kenny Endo (Director, Taiko Center of the Pacific) took a pragmatic approach to the matter, suggesting that intervention sometimes involves compromising:[13]

> All of us in the music, performing arts, or entertainment business rely on getting gigs to survive. I talked to Tanaka-sensei during the filming of that movie and he was torn between the context that his drumming was used and the exposure that a major motion picture would give to the art of taiko. If he didn't do it, they would have asked someone else. I supported his decision and would have probably done the same had I been asked.

Roy Hirabayashi, managing director of San Jose Taiko, asked some very pointed questions:

> [The film] was a very controversial issue when it was being filmed. The movie came out at a time when Japan bashing was at its peak. We were asked if we wanted to work on the film, but we turned the project down.
>
> Did the movie help the "taiko movement?" It is hard to say.
> Did the movie project taiko in the best light and image? No.
> Did the movie continue to project a negative stereotype? Yes.

In short, taiko players' responses to the scene offer a range of indictments ranging from mild complaints that the framing narrative was "dark and negative" to more focused accusations of racist stereotyping. Loyalty to Tanaka-sensei is also quite evident in two of the four responses. All four perspectives suggest that taiko players have a strong sense for how representational practices can reframe and redirect meaning in in/appropriate ways, even with a figure as iconic as Seiichi Tanaka. How far they are willing to critique or to assert control is another matter. As bell hooks writes (1992b: 128), "While every black woman I talked to was aware of racism, that awareness did not automatically correspond with politicization, the development of an oppositional gaze." hooks suggests that interventionist response can take a wide range of forms, from critical spectatorship to the creation of alternative texts to the maintenance of counter-memories, and that politicization may lie anywhere along the way. For taiko players, any politicized discussion of *Rising Sun* is too closely situated near Seiichi Tanaka, entangling matters of authority with questions of representation and thus creating a conundrum.

I now need to carry this matter of heterosexist stereotyping into a broader consideration of taiko's intersection with the construction of Asian/American gender and its reading by audiences. The performance costumes worn by members of the Taiko Center of Los Angeles are specifically and authentically Japanese: *hachimaki* (headbands), *tabi* (sock-like shoes), bright Japanese shirts, and the kind of apron worn by Japanese craftspersons (*harakake*). I have moments of confusion, wondering why I have to become so Japanese in order to feel Asian American,[14] and why the identity politics of our performances are so easily and consistently misread by audiences. Paul Yoon has addressed these issues through his experiences as a Korean American member of Soh Daiko in New York City, arguing that Soh Daiko (and any taiko group) presents all too many possibilities to audiences every time they perform (1999):

> Within the context of the United States, Soh Daiko, and the music they play, Taiko, can be variously constructed (construed) as Japanese, Japanese American, or just Asian (Oriental), rather than or over and above being Asian American. Without complete control over perception, the members of Soh Daiko must contend with, work with, and/or manipulate numerous identities and assumptions, some favorable, others less desirable. For various audiences the music of Soh Daiko creates spaces that are conceived of as Japanese, Japanese American, Asian American, or Asian (Oriental) and in some of these cases these situations are directly counter to either their intentions or desires.

Yoon suggests that Soh Daiko relies on certain kinds of strategic essentialism (*à la* Spivak) to slip out from under the orientalist gaze, and part of me wishes this were as simple as it sounds. Reception is consistently undertheorized as a space filled with both risk and potential — the risk of misunderstanding, and the potential for activist response (i.e., intervention). Given the susceptibility of American audiences to orientalist pleasure — their willingness to give themselves over to it — I must ask what happens when performers think they are saying one thing and audiences hear something else entirely, and whose responsibility it is to redirect the reading. bell hooks argues for a performative recuperation of the gaze (1992b), but I am not only interested in witnessing Asian American empowerment through spectatorship — I am fairly certain that that happens routinely through taiko, though I think its specific linkage to "the Japanese" bears scrutiny.

How a single expressive practice can bear the weight of completely different interpretations is the puzzle: Asian American audiences willingly place themselves in the loop of the performative (they see empowered performers, therefore they feel empowered, therefore they *are* empowered), and meanwhile, non-Asian spectators shift easily into the orientalist gaze. Kondo addresses the ways that Michael Crichton used her monograph *Crafting Selves* to create a bounded, racist picture of Japanese culture in his novel and screenplay, and she reflects on how her stint as dramaturge for Anna Deavere Smith's *Twilight: Los Angeles 1992* helped her address the "problem" of reception and its uncontrollability (1997: 250):

> *Twilight* foregrounded for me the salience of the intentional fallacy, for authorial/dramaturgical intention could never guarantee meaning. In the case of Crichton's reading of my book, the intentional fallacy seems all the more fallacious, for authorial intention not only failed to guarantee meaning, but the text generated meanings antithetical to authorial intent. Once released in language, the subject-positions, histories, and (structurally overdetermined) interpretive schemas of readers and audiences shape reception. We can but do our best to anticipate certain overdetermined readings and preempt them, taking seriously authorial responsibility and attempting to do battle with the misappropriations of our work.

In short, authorial responsibility doesn't stop at the end of the book or the foot of the stage, but the key problem of how, then, to work against the uncontrollable and the overdetermined is the question. Two incidents come to mind. Student members of the newly-formed University of California, Riverside taiko club sought me out the day after a gig in which they had found themselves showcased, they felt, as "cute little Orientals," and they wanted to know what they could have done to anticipate or to intercept the organizers' intent. Another moment, just last week: I was sitting with fellow Satori Daiko members, resting between two sets at a large convention, and a White woman came up to us and asked one of our younger members, "What are you?," i.e., what's your race/ethnicity? Japanese, she said shyly. The woman then proceeded to the next taiko player — What are you? and you?, tracing the question down the line. When she got to me, I quickly, desperately turned the question back to her without answering it: "What are *you*?," I asked. But by then she was already satisfied with the answers she had gotten ("Japanese." "Chinese.") and was all too happy to provide me with the details of her Polish-German-Russian-English background, relieving me of the burden of redirecting her reading of us but also leaving it intact.

Why are the majority of taiko players in North America women? In a cross-cultural context, it is extremely unusual for women to play drums, let alone to specialize in them, and it is even more unusual in the Asian traditional arts (with the notable exception of Korea). A significant number of Japanese American women (and Asian American women generally) are drawn to taiko for empowerment, and I don't think they do so in an attempt to map the masculine/menacing onto themselves. Rev. Tom frequently notes that the majority of his students are women — as many as three out of four, and this is true for many taiko groups in North America. Two of the leading professional Japanese groups, Kodo and Sukeroku, have a majority of men, but amateur taiko groups in Japan also contain large numbers of women, though not as significantly as in the U.S. and Canada. As Mark Tusler notes (1999: 6):

> Since the establishment of taiko ensembles in the late 1950s in Japan, women have become increasingly active as taiko players. Kijima Taiko of Japan is all women. In North America it appears that more women play taiko than men; only 6 out of 25 performing members in the San Jose Taiko are men; approximately two-thirds are women in the Sacramento Taiko Dan, a group founded and led by a woman; the LAMT [Los Angeles Matsuri Taiko] is about even; Soh Daiko in New York City is approximately three-quarters women; the San Francisco Taiko Dojo, a group with around 30 to 40 members, appears almost even; and so on. The involvement of women in North American taiko drumming has played an important role in the development of identity for Japanese American women; gender has therefore been an important articulating factor for the continued success of taiko groups.

I would venture to guess that the qualities made threatening in *Rising Sun* are particularly attractive to — and transformed by — Asian American women: strength, control, loudness. Certainly these qualities speak to Asian American men in similar ways: given historical tropes that have consistently feminized Asian men (e.g., as addressed in David Henry Hwang's *M. Butterfly*), the strength and power expressed through taiko holds a particular performative appeal for Asian American men. Nevertheless, the overwhelming presence of Asian American women in North American taiko speaks to a certain reconfiguration of the Asian American woman's body and to a claim made on sonic and social space. As Mary Baba, one of my Japanese American classmates, suggested,[15]

> The taiko is a very powerful instrument, it gives a feel of strength and command. In this day and age, even with opportunities for equality, women need outlets to feel power. Playing the taiko fulfills a need.

Baba's emphasis on "strength and command" is notable, as the transformation of the Asian/Asian American woman from a delicate, submissive stereotype to a figure capable of moving with power and authority is clearly the appeal. The struggle with silence is also addressed head-on through taiko, whether through the sound of the drum itself or through the realization of *ki* as *kakegoe*. Mitsuye Yamada (1983: 36-37) has written at length about the link between Asian American women's silence and invisibility, suggesting that stereotyping and reinscription are deeply entangled:

> [W]e Asian American women have not admitted to ourselves that we *were* oppressed. We, the visible minority that is invisible. ... I had supposed I was practicing passive resistance while being stereotyped, but it was so passive no one noticed I was resisting; it was so much my expected role that it ultimately rendered me invisible. ... When the Asian American woman is lulled into believing that people perceive her as being different from other Asian women (the submissive, subservient, ready-to-please, easy-to-get-along-with Asian woman), she is kept comfortably content with the state of things. She becomes ineffectual in the milieu in which she moves. The seemingly apolitical middle class woman and the apolitical Asian woman constituted a double invisibility.

Similarly, Sonia Shah has written that Asian American women searching for forms of expression were continually brought short by first-wave feminist models that located Asian American feminist responses as "American" (i.e., White) rather than Asian; instead, Shah calls for a "bicultural feminism" or a "pan-Asian feminist agenda" that would work against the Black/White paradigms driving American feminism and engage with "our own form of cultural schizophrenia, from the mixed and often contradictory signals about priorities, values, duty, and meaning our families and greater communities convey" (1994: 154).

I would argue too that part of taiko's appeal lies in its redefinition of the Asian American woman's body and its dialogic relationship to "women's work" — i.e., the nimble fingers behind the clothing and computer industries.[16] The contained movement of women's fingers vs. the woman's body filling space with large gestures; the closed doors of the sweatshop vs. the stage; women taking orders vs. the woman stepping forward, in "leisure," into furious movement. Taiko opens up the body: the legs are wide apart and the movement of the arms commands a large personal space. How many of us were taught to keep our knees together and to speak softly? Taiko provides alternative ways of moving through physical and sonic space that are passionately appealing to Asian American women for real reasons, but it does so while creating ties of cooperation and collaboration. I am reminded of the only time in a taiko class when I found myself intensely irritated, angry beyond reason. Rev. Tom was absent and one of the advanced students in the class, Elaine (a Sansei in her forties), was leading us on *shime*. We were having trouble staying together during a particular phrase in a piece and Antoine, a Swiss man in his twenties, suddenly said, I'll play *kane*. The *kane* is only played by the person in charge, usually Rev. Tom. We tried it again, with Elaine still on *shime* but Antoine now playing *kane*. He slouched against one of the pews, looking down at the *kane* as he played fast and loud, driving all of us. In fact, it was too fast, though he certainly played more "authoritatively" than Elaine, so we were even more ragged. We stopped and people made various cautious comments ("That wasn't much better, was it?"); of course, no one was going to do or say anything confrontational, though I felt that Antoine's decision to seize the *kane* was inexcusably so. After waiting a moment to see if the situation would resolve itself, I said to him, Maybe it's better with just Elaine. He paused, and just when I thought he was going to argue with me, he shrugged and put down the *kane*. Thinking about it later and trying to sort out my own irritation, I recognized the racialized and gendered shape of the encounter: Asian American woman, White (European) man. He challenged her authority despite her greater experience and in fact her twenty years' seniority; he didn't maintain *kata* or eye contact with her *or* the rest of us when he played; he disregarded — challenged — both the social construction of authority in the class and the group dynamic that we have all grown to depend upon. And it left me completely unsettled.

The women I know who play taiko do not necessarily self-identify as feminists, but I do think that taiko is a sounded bodily channel for addressing the ongoing gendered dialectic of the Asian vs. the Asian American. I don't know how taiko speaks to Japanese women or to gendered social practices in Japan; this in itself would make a fascinating study. In a sense, I only have half the picture of taiko as a transnational gendered phenomenon, but it is impossible to write about Asian American taiko without addressing its elisions and distinctions from the Asian body, and the specific spin that all this has for Asian American women. As the anthropologist Aihwa Ong has written, emancipation-in-diaspora is not a given, nor does feminist ethnography offer a denationalized set of critical practices unless we insist that it do so. Instead, Ong suggests that we develop a "dialectic of disowning and reowning, of critical agency shifting between transnational sites of power," which can result in "a deliberate cultivation of a mobile consciousness" (1995: 367–8). Taiko is not a matter of Asian American women "rediscovering" a certain kind of Asian body but is rather an intricate process of exploring a Japanese bodily aesthetic and refashioning/re-embodying its potential for Asian American women. In this sense, I am locating an erotics of taiko that reclaims the territory mapped out by *Rising Sun*. How "deliberately" any of us do this isn't really the question: the passionate involvement that taiko can instill is simply an example of how belief, understanding and the body come together in ways that are different from abstracted, objectified thought. In this case, thought and bodily action join in ways that are in fact theorized in the Buddhist martial arts, though few of us explore that route through books. For Asian American women, taiko is a true performative act, one so profoundly understood through the body that it is rarely channeled into other media like words.

Which brings me back to experience and its liveness, though this time with a gendered twist. The ephemerality of performance is no less a mode of cultural production than those institutions (i.e., government, religious life, the law, the workplace) often taken more seriously as spheres of determination and influence. Taiko is a complex site that highlights the meeting ground of transnational movement, gender and the insistence on being seen and heard. Lisa Lowe has encouraged a closer examination of "those institutions, spaces, borders and processes that are the interstitial sites of the social formation in which the national intersects with the international" (1996: 172), and taiko is one such location that opens up an Asian American space in conversation with the Asian. Its liveness is fundamentally part of its power, and (I believe) part of its power for Asian American women. Dorinne Kondo has tried to write about the place of liveness in her own excitement about Asian American theater and her understanding of its link to empowerment; she relates how seeing Hwang's *M. Butterfly* on Broadway made her feel that she *had* to write about it, "as though my life depended on it" (1995: 50). Describing the liveness of theater as "another register," she notes that turning her research toward Asian American theater represented "a kind of paradigm shift away from the purely textual toward the performative, the evanescent, the nondiscursive, the collaborative" (1995: 51). As an anthropologist, Kondo articulates something that I think many Asian American woman taiko players know intuitively: that those moments of choreographed sound and movement speak in many different ways at once, channeling power and pleasure through the body and redefining that body through pounding heart and shouted presence.

Learning a Piece

It's our third class as Satori Daiko, and once again, we put all the drums in a long row to continue learning the new piece, "Ayako Mai." We're now using vertical stands for the *chudaiko* due to the Sukeroku copyright controversy, so we arrange a long row of some five *chudaiko* with an *odaiko* at either end plus a few tires so that everyone has a place. Audrey and Rev. Tom write the entire piece on the white board.

I missed the previous class so I'm feeling anxious about being behind, and the piece looks complicated; I've never played on two drums and I have no idea how it works. Several of my classmates start reviewing what they had learned in the last class and it's every bit as complicated as I thought. I start trying to do air taiko behind them (that is, I go through the motions in the air, without striking anything) and when Audrey sees me struggling, she comes over, grabs my hands, and puts me through the motions of the piece — like a puppeteer, with me as the puppet — and I give myself over to it, still with no idea how it all works. They're all playing faster and faster and I finally stop and just watch. Rev. Tom reappears, goes *ten-ten-ten!* on his *kane,* and everyone stops playing. He says, "Yoro-shiku one-gai shi-masu," bows, and we all answer, "Yoro-shiku one-gai shi-masu," bowing in return. He says, "OK, let's review the first line of the new piece — air taiko, call and answer," and he picks up his *shime bachi.* While playing in the air, he calls out, "Ten! Ten-Ten! Ho! Teke Ten-Ten!" and we respond in kind. He moves over to the *shime* and plays the pattern without saying anything. We all move forward to the drums, get into *kamaete* position, and when he finishes the pattern, we play it back to him, returning to *kamaete* position when we finish. He plays it again, we respond. And again. We concentrate on raising our left hands as our right hands come down on "Ten, Ten-Ten." And again. And again. He picks up the tempo a bit. And again.

My anxiety has evaporated. I should have known that he would start at the beginning — he always does when teaching a new piece. I'm between Gary and Taylor. To my right, Gary: tall, with a mop of dark graying hair, a big mustache, and a terrific sense of rhythm; he teaches music in the San Bernardino public school system and is an amazing drummer. He is always ready with a joke and laughs at the least excuse. To my left, Taylor: diminutive, only ten years old and all bones and sinew, long gangly arms and legs — she's exquisite, has a virtually perfect *kata,* and is utterly unaware of how lovely she is. We play the pattern over and over until finally Rev. Tom stops us and says, "OK, second line." He plays it in the air while speaking it. I suddenly "get" it: "Don" means a stroke with the right hand but reaching over to the next drum on the left. You leave your left hand in place, above the drum in front of you, and you trust the person on your right to whack your drum without hitting your arm, and you try to do the same to the person on your left. We do antiphonal air taiko several times and then move to the drums. Call and answer, Rev. Tom on *shime* and then we respond. Again, he eventually picks up the tempo. Soon we're playing line B really fast. He says, "OK, let's connect it to the first line, call and answer," and he plays lines A and B through at a slower pace. We play the two lines back to him and all of our eyes are glued to the whiteboard, reading as we play. After we go back and forth several times, Audrey calls out, "Shouldn't there be a crescendo on the first line?" We all wait as she runs up to the whiteboard and puts in a big crescendo mark under "Teke Ten-Ten." We try it and agree that that's more interesting; we try the two lines together again, with the crescendo. Again. Again. Again. After a while, Rev. Tom goes and stands in front of the whiteboard so we can't see the notation; everyone laughs and groans but keeps playing, now from memory.

On to line C, which has a neat little syncopated lift — "Don-Don Tsu Don," with the right arm crossed over the body for the *don* strokes and "Tsu," an upbeat tap on the *chudaiko* in front of you with your left hand before striking the drum on your left again — and we play that line over and over. This line is fun, jazzier and less four-square than lines A and B. We're all warmed up now — more than warm, sweating, in fact, but time has started to move in a different way as we concentrate and repeat and repeat. Rev. Tom backs us up and has us play lines B and C, and then lines A through C. He adds on line D, eventually B, explains that the piece ends by returning to line A. We've now been playing for more than an hour, and we try to play the whole piece through even though we're all completely glued to the whiteboard. It's a bit ragged, but we go around and around several times until Rev. Tom stops us and says, "If you could see your-selves!" We stand there panting, thinking, Oh — it probably looks pretty neat, all that right-hand-on-the-next-drum-over movement. "Again," he says, and we do it again, around and around, the entire piece; he picks up the tempo and then drives it even faster until we're flying, and one by one, we start to mess up, it's so fast, and we still don't really know the piece, we're reading it rather than playing by heart. We're all laughing, and finally only Gary and Rev. Tom are playing, and then Gary breaks out of the piece and goes into a wild, exuberant riff on his *chudaiko* and mine, pure jazz, and stops, laughing. It's after 9:30 p.m. and we have to stop so that the neighbors who live around the temple aren't kept awake by the sound of our pounding.

Philosophy, Ownership, Authenticity

While there is no fixed agreement on how one should approach learning taiko, there is great overlap in attitudes; I would go so far as to say that this overlap amounts to a Japanese American/Asian American aesthetics and poetics of taiko that its practitioners can and do talk about, though with no particular emphasis on formalizing it. Some groups link these values to Buddhism and some don't. The San Jose Taiko page states that, "Indeed, the practice and performance of taiko requires selfless dedication, physical endurance, harmony, and a collective spirit."[17] Tanaka-sensei's philosophy of taiko is quite explicit and is codified, among other ways, on the San Francisco Taiko Dojo website as follows:[18]

Karada: Discipline of body strength, power, and stamina
Kokoro: Discipline of mind, self control, and spirit
Waza: Musical skills, physical expressions, and rhythm expression, and rhythm
Rei: Communication, manners, courtesy, respect, harmony, language, and unity of spirit

Drawn from Zen Buddhism, these elements are considered interrelated: Tanaka-sensei (1999) writes, "These are all the basic elements of Taiko and cannot stand separately. They must come together as one unit."

Rev. Tom didn't decide to become a Zen priest until he was in his early thirties. Despite the long line of ministers in his family, his parents didn't expect him to enter the priesthood — indeed, they knew from experience that it was a hard life, and they let him choose his own career. Nonetheless, when Rev. Tom was in Japan, he decided to study Buddhism toward the end of his stay and he describes this decision as "10–15% obligation" and the rest his own interest. He says he never took any courses in Buddhism and doesn't even particularly like to read about Buddhism; rather, "it was always there, in my surroundings." His interest in ethnic identity politics led him to taiko, and taiko led him to refocus on spirituality. He says that the whole process was gradual:

TK: Taiko is rooted in Buddhism, and Buddhism is rooted in Japanese culture. I began to see all that as connected. Rev. Masao Kodani was a great influence on me. ... He started this organization called Kinnara which is not only taiko but is an organization promoting Buddhism through Buddhist-related music. It incorporated the ancient court music, *gagaku,* and the ancient court dance, *bugaku.* There were three components in Kinnara: *gagaku, bugaku,* and taiko, and taiko was the most popular. Here was this very unconventional priest — I had this image of what a Buddhist minister should be like, and he totally did not fit the mold! Even though my father never talked to me about becoming a minister, my mother was more or less against me becoming one.

DW: Why?

TK: Well, it's a hard life — financially, and if you have a family, it's very hard. ... My father only made $700 a month — when he passed away in 1986, that's all he was making, $700 a month. And my mother had to work all her life. So it was hard. I mean, she wasn't dead set against it, but my father never forced me to look into it. In fact, he never even talked about it. But it was something that I thought I would try. I thought to myself, What is the most important thing? And the most important thing is my family, my parents. Going to the monastery was 10 to 15% out of obligation, but the rest I really wanted to do, so at the end of my three-year stay in Japan, I spent three months in a monastery, and trained as a monk.

Zen principles are implicit rather explicit in his teaching despite the centrality of Buddhism to his life and his involvement with the Japanese American community. You have to look long and hard through his written materials to find any straightforward statement of what he thinks students should get out of taiko study. In a one-page description of the TCLA (part of a publicity package), the last two sentences read, "As a performing artist with the Los Angeles Music Center Education Division, Rev. Kurai conducts taiko classes and workshops for students as well as for teachers in public and private schools. The emphasis in these presentations is to introduce Japanese-American culture and to reinforce concepts such as respect, cooperation, teamwork and self-esteem." Audrey Nakasone echoes this, saying that she thinks taiko is an ideal educational tool because it "teaches things like respect and discipline, but indirectly."[19]

Within the far-flung taiko community, there is general agreement that the spirit of taiko involves discipline, humility, and a willingness to put the group before self, but this generalized philosophy recently came head to head with issues of repertoire and ownership in very specific ways. Group identity is linked to awareness of lineage, among other things, but it is also related to repertoire. There are three kinds of "pieces" in the world of taiko: (1) traditional works with no specific author or owner, (2) works composed by individuals, and (3) works that are group composed. Group-composed works often become signature pieces that are rarely played by anyone else except the group that created it, as the identification of the work becomes part and parcel of that group's personality. "Traditional" works are rarely just that, as particular arrangements of such pieces become well known in their own right and (it is generally agreed) should be acknowledged as the work of a specific arranger. Works composed by individuals are rarely guarded in any jealous or exclusive way, though there is general agreement that a piece's composer should be named on concert programs.

The movement of repertoire between groups was a matter of informal courtesy until the summer of 1999. Ideally, a group would ask permission of a piece's composer before learning it, especially if they meant to learn it from a recording or secondhand, from a composer's student, but that was essentially the extent to which repertoire was considered ownable. In August 1999, this changed when Seido Kobayashi, artistic director of Oedo Sukeroku Daiko, sent a letter to the North American taiko community by asking Sukeroku's representative, Seiichi Tanaka, to formally present it at the 1999 Taiko Conference in Los Angeles (held July 30-August 21).[20] Kobayashi asked that groups playing Oedo Sukeroku Daiko's repertoire without permission stop doing so. Given the fact that virtually all North American taiko groups play Sukeroku pieces and generally owe a tremendous stylistic debt to that group (whether directly or, more often, indirectly), this sent shock waves through the taiko community and excited a storm of discussion. Kobayashi-sensei then wrote a second letter that provided specific guidelines for how Sukeroku's repertoire and distinctive *chudaiko* stand were now to be used.[21] He argued that the pieces, the stand, and the *kata* used in playing drums on such a stand were inseparable and the unique creations of the group Sukeroku — and their property. He used the term *dageikyoku* to describe the interlinked nature of repertoire, stand, and *kata*:

> *Dageikyoku:** All the music by O-Edo Sukeroku Daiko which is played with the "Folding Tilted Stand©," the "Assembling Odaiko Stand©," and performed with "diagonal beating and choreography." It also includes the compositions (Shiraume, Matsuri, Nidan-Uchi, Yodan-Uchi, etc.) created by the artistic director, Seido and other original members. All these compositions are played with the specific style of Taiko, the Sukeroku style. Therefore, it is impossible to play this music unless the players have mastered the basics of the Sukeroku method.

The letter outlines the permission process as follows:

How to Get Permission

If you wish to use the Dageikyoku of O-Edo Sukeroku Daiko in Japan, please study with O-Edo Sukeroku Daiko and obtain permission from the artistic director of O-Edo Sukeroku Daiko.

If you wish to use the Dageikyoku of O-Edo Sukeroku Daiko in North America, please study with Grand Master Seiichi Tanaka of San Francisco Taiko Dojo and obtain permission from the artistic director of O-Edo Sukeroku Daiko.

If you are in any other area, please contact us in either Japanese or English at "Sukeroku-ryu Kai."

In the process of obtaining permission, the "Sukeroku Method Mastering Club" may help you. As requested, we plan to have workshops and exhibition performances. For detailed information, please contact the O-Edo Sukeroku Daiko general office.

Also, everybody must be registered with "Sukeroku-ryu Kai" in order to use the Dageikyoku of O-Edo Sukeroku Daiko.

Registration fee: $1,200 per year (per group or per person)

Royalty: 7% of the proceeds per performance

If you are in North America, please ask for the application and the management of obtaining permission from Grand Master Seiichi Tanaka of San Francisco Taiko Dojo.

Please compete the process stated above before you use any of the Dageikyoku of O-Edo Sukeroku Daiko.

This pronouncement hit the North American taiko community like a bomb, and led to weeks of heated online discussion. Kobayashi's radical move to assert control over several central aspects of taiko (*kata,* stands, and repertoire) had serious ramifications for virtually every North American taiko group in existence; discussion ranged from how/whether he was justified in taking these measures to expressions of sheer anxiety, as most groups couldn't afford the new "registration fee" and royalty. Ideologically, the predicament forced a widespread assessment of the relationship between North American and Japanese taiko, and this geocultural imaginary was brought into sharp (and sometimes uncomfortable) focus.

John Ko, a former member of Soh Daiko, has written about the controversy and the issues raised by it. As he summarized it (1999: 31):

> This whole copyright issue has opened up a can of worms and brought into the spotlight certain issues within the taiko community that have always lurked and festered in dark corners. These issues include respect for musical/cultural traditions; public acknowledgment of influences; the idea of artistic lineage; appropriate use of a style or a particular piece; who is qualified to teach others and to pass on or publicly represent certain styles and pieces; getting permission to play certain pieces; innovation, altering pieces/styles; the art of taiko (which involves "kata" or the form, movement, etc.) vs. percussion with taiko drums.

Ko boils the business down to two contending approaches: the "old school or Asian mode" vs. the "new world American or Western mode," though he immediately disavows any tidy distinctions between the two; rather, he argues that "much of the discussion is arising out of this *perceived* dichotomy" (1999: 31, emphasis mine) — a discerning take on the ideological shape of the debate. He basically observes that members of the taiko community theorize their own praxis in ideal terms — and thus essentialize the cultural dynamics of ownership and practice because they don't/can't/ won't acknowledge the difference between theory and practice.

In this regard, Rev. Tom and Kenny Endo represent useful similarities and contrasts. They are close in age, started studying taiko at practically the same time, were both in Kinnara Taiko for several years, and both went to Japan for further study during the same period (the late 1970s-early 1980s). Both compose new works as well as perform traditional works, and both have experimented with fusions of taiko and other world music traditions. Their career paths, however, suggest different priorities that are worth considering in terms of taiko as a North American/Japanese American/Asian American tradition. Endo is much more tradition-based than Rev. Tom, and I mean this in terms of his ideological base rather than knowledge in and of itself. Their respective journeys to Japan took place along different axes. Whereas Rev. Tom went to Japan and discovered that he was Japanese American, Endo regards the traditional Japanese base of taiko as an authentic source of information and spirit; in going to Japan, he felt he put himself into contact with that source. Traise Yamamoto has explored the literary narratives of Japanese Americans who travel to Japan, arguing that "Going back to Japan" … is not, however, a sentimental journey to recover "roots" or an authentic Japanese self. It is a necessary journey in the process of disentangling Japanese American identity and subjectivity from racist configurations that elide the differences between Japanese Americans and Japanese" (1999: 82).[22] If there is a Western *and* a Japanese American tendency to construct "the Japanese" as more authentic than the Japanese American, these gestures are not necessarily equivalent. Rev. Tom's and Endo's attempts to locate "Japan" were significantly different from the orientalizing gaze of non-Asian American audiences that finds Japan in every taiko player. That is, the pilgrimage to Japan involved no reorientalizing, no reinscribed enfolding of race and identity, but rather two entirely different answers to the same question of location.

Endo does not, however, regard himself as making Asian American music when he plays taiko, despite the deeply innovative nature of much of his work. I asked him whether he thinks of his work as particularly Japanese American or Asian American and he answered:[23]

> **KE**: It's not anything I consciously think about or that I do. For myself, when that term "Asian American music" started to be used, there was so much that could be considered Asian American music. To me, a lot of times, it was Asian American musicians playing Western instruments, almost copying African American form or style, and simply because of their race, it was labeled Asian American music. Maybe if I could do that well, I would do that too. To me, what was missing in Asian American music was the Asian component. For myself, and I don't think it's true for everybody, it was necessary to go to Japan and learn some of those traditions. Especially playing an instrument like taiko, you have to go to the source. [*pause*] What my concept is — and actually I did a workshop at the national taiko conference a couple of years ago, called "Tradition as a Basis for Innovation" — because some of my teach-

ers once told me in Japan, you enter a tradition, you learn the basics, you become a practitioner of that tradition, if you become good enough, you become a bearer of that tradition, and then you get recognition and you do that for many years. And they say only at that point can you actually break the tradition and really create something new. And the idea behind that is if you have no foundation, no basics, and you start creating something new from there, it's going to lack authenticity as well as quality. It's just a different aesthetic. … The label "Asian American music …." Well, I'm pretty uncomfortable with it, no matter what kind of music it is, whether it's good, bad, or whatever.

Endo thus situates himself as both a traditionalist and as an innovator, linking the two at a processual level. Both he and Rev. Tom made similar ideological decisions in Japan to immerse themselves in praxis (language, music study, etc.) and both came away from that experience (ten years long, in Endo's case) with impressive foundations in traditional knowledge, but their attitudes are markedly different. Politically, they ended up in radically different places though both teach taiko. Rev. Tom says that his political awakening as a Japanese American led him to explore Japanese culture, and that this in turn led him to Buddhist spirituality *as a Japanese American*; he explains the progression in precisely these terms and then notes that a political sensibility necessarily underlies all these things for him. Endo's rejection of an Asian American identity that might emerge out of interaction, difference and performance is thus a fundamentally different arrival from Rev. Tom's, though both men are successful and effective teachers.

While Endo is very sure that traditional Japanese culture is the font for any meaningful taiko experience, others — like myself — come to taiko in search of a specifically Asian American experience, though this too can raise more questions than it answers. Carolyn Okazaki and I started taking taiko classes together in the fall of 1997 and have become good friends. Carolyn, a Sansei from Hawaii, is about fifty years old and works as a counselor and psychologist at California State University, Northridge, specializing in issues of multiculturalism. Over the two and a half years we have known each other, we have had many post-class lunch-time conversations about taiko and its importance to us as Asian Americans. When I finally asked her if I could interview her for this chapter, she was surprised but agreeable and we had a long taped conversation about the place of taiko in creating a new kind of Asian American confidence. We also moved into a new area — new for us, that is: the peculiar dynamics of being Asian American in a group of other (mostly) Asian Americans learning a Japanese tradition. Our class has about sixteen people in it: it is about two-thirds Japanese American, and the other five students are one White American, one Swiss, one multiethnic Latina, and one multiethnic Chinese American (me).[24] We agreed that our group had an unspoken but nonetheless strong social aesthetic that could be described as "Asian," with each of us trying hard to efface ourselves in ways that we can't in our daily lives. Carolyn said that she moved into this kind of behavior easily and without much thought, and that it has been central to her experience of taiko class even though it is so markedly different from her professional life. Still, she wasn't sure how or why we all slid into habits of deference and non-confrontation as quickly and easily as we did, and the ways that our non-Asian American classmates sometimes *don't* comply with these behaviors is (similarly) a matter that is never openly addressed or acknowledged. We agreed that our apparent propensity for code-switching was puzzling to us: were we trying to be "Asian" or Asian American? The day after we talked, Carolyn sent me the following e-mail note:[25]

> I was thinking about your question as to "Why taiko?" And I recognize that there was more to it than I related. I believe at the time I was looking for an activity that was physical, but also Asian American. While I've always had Asian American friends, almost all of my work life was spent with non-Asians, primarily Euro Americans, and to some degree that was somewhat true of my private life. At work, for example, I was usually the only minority or one of only a couple people of color. And while I learned to adapt to the different cultural expectations of the majority group, I had to in order to survive, I was also tired of feeling "different." I was tired of dealing with majority expectations of how I relate. I was tired of the competitiveness, looking out for and promoting "number one." I was looking for other people to relate to that were more like me and could relate to my experiences, including the issues related to diversity.
>
> Inadvertently, of course, in my struggle to survive in the majority culture I had become less traditionally "Asian" and found myself in another process of adjustment in terms of fitting in to the taiko group. I believe there is always a process of adjustment in getting to know anyone, as we're all different from each other, but it was a curious process. Whereas with the majority culture, I had to learn to jump into discussions or get left out, with the taiko group I found myself feeling that I had to restrain myself so as not to take too much attention. What I observed is that others responded as if they did not want the attention, or felt uncomfortable with it, although I do not believe that to be the case in reality.

In short, after further reflection, Carolyn decided she sought out taiko as an Asian American, but then found that she had gone through two processes of relearning: first, it highlighted how she had taught herself to be less "Asian" in her mainstream American workaday world (putting herself forward, speaking up, etc.) and then she had to unlearn those behaviors in the context of taiko class. Her last sentence alludes to the fact that virtually none of us spend the rest of our time in Asian American environments, so (presumably) we've all had to learn how to be less "Asian" or suffer the consequences of being overlooked and unheard. How then did we all manage to slide right into Asian behaviors of modesty and self-effacement in taiko class? "The Asian" becomes a vexed self, a more authentic shadow self that we didn't know we had, that we're not sure we *want* to have, yet it serves as a vector for how we come together in this vital, comfortable, unspoken way even as it leaves us more unsure than ever about the in/authenticity of the Asian/American.

The politics of ethnicity in taiko are thus bottomless, yet I remain sure that I learn something about Asian America when I play. Certainly taiko remodulates every category it touches — the Japanese, the Japanese American, the Asian, the Asian American — and the sensual sounded body passes through these noisy historical constructions and emerges asserting yet new presences. The complications and the risks are so fundamentally part of it all that I must end by arguing they are intrinsically part of the pleasure — the pleasure of listening to taiko, of learning it, of performing it, of teaching it. Perhaps that is what I take away from it, most of all — that the impossibility of containing the meaning of such a clamorous practice sets up a performative too boisterous to be denied, too loud to be any one thing.

Endnotes

1. From *Eastern Definitions*, by Edward Rice (Garden City, New York: Doubleday Anchor Books, 1980), 316-17.
2. "Shuyu" was Rev. Tom's father's Buddhist or Dharma name, given to him when he was ordained as a Zen priest. His birth name was Hideo.
3. In Japan, O-bon is held in mid-August, but Japanese Americans celebrate it at different dates between June and August, depending on their temple. In the U.S., O-bon has developed into a festival and fund-raising event held in conjunction with Buddhist ritual, and in Hawaii and Southern California, the concentration of Japanese temples has led congregations to stagger their O-bon festivals to avoid competition and to allow attendance across congregations, as the event is an opportunity for the broader Japanese American Buddhist community to come together. See Yano 1985 for more.
4. The *bon-odori* repertoire is largely traditional in North America, but certain contemporary works with a self-consciously Japanese American sensibility have appeared, such as Nobuko Miyamoto's "Yuiyo Bon Odori" and "Tampopo" (Asai 1997: 268–72).
5. See Kishin Daiko's website at http://www3.pair.com/mccarthy/kishin/index.html.
6. The term *hapa* is Hawaiian pidgin meaning "half," and was first used by Asian Americans to refer to anyone of mixed Asian/European descent. It has more broadly come to mean anyone who is multi-ethnic and part Asian.
7. The third taiko conference was held at the JACCC in summer 2001.

8. *Rising Sun* (1993), starring Sean Connery, Wesley Snipes, Harvey Keitel, Cary-Hiroyuki Tagawa, and Kevin Anderson. Directed and produced by Philip Kaufman. Screenplay by Philip Kaufman, Michael Crichton, and Michael Backes, based on the novel by Michael Crichton. Music by Toru Takemitsu. Released by Twentieth Century Fox.
9. San Francisco Taiko Dojo also played on the soundtracks for *Apocalypse Now, Return of the Jedi,* and *The Right Stuff.*
10. This instrument is called the "cannon" by members of San Francisco Taiko Dojo because of its physical appearance. It consists of three pieces of metal pipe welded together and mounted on a stand so that it stands horizontally at waist height. It takes the place of three *kane* with different pitches (Tusler 1995: 14). Rev. Tom refers to it as a "muffler," again due to its appearance.
11. Dorinne Kondo's indictment of the film along these lines (1997: 240–51) is both thoughtful and sweeping.
12. I posted a query to the Rolling Thunder taiko discussion list, asking for responses to the taiko scene in *Rising Sun,* and I received several responses from list participants between January 14–30, 2000.
13. E-mail note, 30 January 2000.
14. Paul Yoon (1999) notes a similar response from a member of Soh Daiko:
    Another member, who is Chinese American, recounted her grandmother's reaction to the uniform. "It's been an issue for us "colonized" groups. We've all gone through our processes with our parents. You know, my grandmother, who lived through the war, hates Japanese with a passion, in the abstract. She saw a picture of me in my happi, she said to my mom, "Can't they make it look just a little less Japanese?" She wasn't denying that it was a Japanese art form, I think she was just freaked, as I was when I first saw myself in a happi. It's no-kiddin' around, it's Japanese." These instances, and others, reveal an alienation on the part of the members when confronted with Soh Daiko's Japanese appearance in contradistinction to their own perceived identity or their sense of what is Asian American. This ultimately requires the reevaluation or shifting of their understanding of Asian American identity in order to reposition themselves within the context of this identity or rather to reconstruct and broaden the boundaries of their definition.
15. E-mail note, 16 February 2000.
16. Lisa Lowe has written at length about the historical processes linking Asian and Asian American women's labor in the global economy, and she posits deep connections between capitalism and racialization (1996: 158):
    [T]he focus on women's work with the global economy as a material site in which several axes of domination intersect provides the means for linking Asian immigrant and Asian American women with other immigrant and racialized women. Asian immigrant and Asian American women are not simply the most recent formation within the genealogy of Asian American racialization; they, along with women working in the "third world," are the "new" workforce with the global reorganization of capitalism. ... They are linked to an emergent political formation, organizing across race, class, and national boundaries, that includes other racialized and immigrant groups as well as women working in, and immigrating from, the neocolonized world.
17. See the San Jose Taiko website at http://www.taiko.org.
18. See the San Francisco Taiko Dojo website at http://www.taikodojo.org/zen.html.
19. Personal communication, 10 December 1999.
20. The letter can be seen in translation at http://www.taiko.com/history/oedo_letter.html.
21. The letter can be seen in translation at http://www.taiko.com/history/oedo_letter2.html.
22. Yamamoto examines Dorinne Kondo's *Crafting Selves: Power, Gender, and Discourses of Identity in a Japanese Workplace* (1990), David Mura's *Turning Japanese: Memoirs of a Sansei* (1991), and Lydia Minatoya's *Talking to High Monks in the Snow: An Asian American Odyssey* (1992), all Sansei autobiographical narratives that address the experience of going to Japan.
23. Interview with Kenny Endo on 6 March 1999.

24. Specifically:

Elaine	Japanese American	40s	Woman
Irene	Japanese American	40s	Woman
Gladys	Japanese American	50s	Woman
Joanne	Japanese American	30s	Woman
Penny	Japanese American	40s	Woman
Susan	Japanese American	40s	Woman
Mary	Japanese American	40s	Woman
Lily	Japanese American	40s	Woman
Carolyn	Japanese American	50s	Woman
Janet	Japanese American/ White American (*hapa*)	40s	Woman
Kisha	White American	40s	Woman
Lucia	Latina/mixed ethnicity	30s	Woman
me	Chinese American/ White American (*hapa*)	40s	Woman
Chester	Japanese American	40s	Man
Tom	White American	50s	Man
Antoine	White European	20s	Man

25. 28 December 1999.

10
Just Being There:
Making Asian American Space
in the Recording Industry

MA RAINEY: *Wanna take my voice and trap it in them fancy boxes with all them buttons and dials… They don't care nothing about me. All they want is my voice. … As soon as they get my voice down on them recording machines, then it's just like if I'd be some whore and they roll over and put their pants on. Ain't got no use for me then. I know what I'm talking about. You watch.*

—From August Wilson's *Ma Rainey's Black Bottom*[1]

Our whole thinking is, if we don't do it, who else will? That's what it boils down to. If you want it done, you have to do it yourself. I'm saying the same thing I say to Asian American film makers who always complain that there just don't seem to be very good Asian American role models in film or TV: Well, you need to become a producer, in one of those positions of power where you can make those decisions.

—Nelson Wong, co-founder and -director of AARising Records Corporation[2]

There is a moment in August Wilson's play *Ma Rainey's Black Bottom* when several African American musicians argue among themselves whether to play the version of a song requested by the Black blues singer or by the White manager. It's Chicago, 1927; the entire play takes place in a recording studio run by a White producer. The trumpet player says (Wilson 1981: 37):

LEVEE: Hell, the man's the one putting out the record! He's gonna put out what he wanna put out!

And the piano player answers,

TOLEDO: See, now … I'll tell you something. As long as the colored man look to white folks to put the crown on what he say … as long as he looks to white folks for approval … then he ain't never going to find out who he is and what he's about. He's just gonna be about what white folks want him to be about. That's one sure thing.

Levee and Toledo outline an old but nonetheless complex argument. "The man" — a gendered, racialized stand-in for corporate America — will maintain complete socioeconomic control over the music industry unless American Others can opt out and achieve some measure of cultural self-determination. This, in a nutshell, is the dilemma of cooption — becoming what the system requires you to be and acknowledging its might even when resisting. In other words, opting out isn't easily accomplished: trying to step outside the system in order to regain some kind of cultural authority is another kind of reinscription. As Peter McLaren has argued, "When people of color attack white ground rules for handling disputes, or bureaucratic procedures, or specific policies of institutionalized racism, these are necessary oppositional acts, but insufficient for bringing about structural change" because they assume the dominance of white culture (1994: 61). The postcolonial, postnationalist subject — the subject who inhabits border cultures — does not live through "an inverted Eurocentrism," but rather asserts "an identity that is anticapitalist and counterhegemonic but is also critically utopian. It is an identity that transforms the burden of knowledge into a scandal of hope" (ibid., 65–66).

The Mountain Brothers are a three-man Asian American hip-hop group based in Philadelphia (introduced in Chapter 8). I have admired their music for some time, and I want to do several things in this chapter. I want to create an ethnographic portrait of the group as an up-and-coming hip-hop crew, and I quite deliberately hope to play a part in the capitalist system that creates or denies success — that is, by writing about them, I want to give the Mountain Brothers some public airplay, and I do so with no qualms whatsoever. As Cornel West has reminded us, race matters in America, and I write with a vested interest in seeing more Asian American performers make it in a system that's often stacked against their presence. In short, this chapter is about a particular hip-hop group as well as identity politics and the racialized hegemonies of the transnational music industry.

Not the Mountain Boys

The Mountain Brothers came together in 1991. Chops (Scott Jung), Peril-L (Chris Wang), and Styles (Steve Wei) attended high school in various suburbs of Philadelphia and were later brought together at Penn State University through friends and common interests. At the time of this writing (summer 1996), Styles had just graduated from Penn State, Peril-L was starting his second year as a graduate student in biology at the University of Pennsylvania, and Chops had dropped out of graduate school at Michigan State University to produce the Mountain Brothers full-time. All three are Chinese American. One of the Brothers' pet peeves is the frequency with which they become "the Mountain Boys/ Boyz" when outsiders handle their publicity. They suspect that the slip is part of a broader American history of infantilizing people of color, and Asians in particular. As a group, the Brothers are keenly aware of their image as Asian American men — both positive and potentially negative — and they try to control the ways in which this image is produced and received.[3]

The group has been trying to break into the business for some years now. They assiduously attend industry conventions and have gone through the long process of sending out demos and getting callbacks. They have pursued protracted negotiations with several different independent record companies. They represent a principled attempt to enter the mainstream music industry on their own terms. Their allegiances are to the Asian American as well as to the hip-hop communities, and this bifocality lends them a special depth and texture. As one of the Brothers, Scott Jung, explained to me:[4]

> We like to think of ourselves as hip-hoppers first — and not necessarily before we're Asian, because we're Asian no matter what we do — but especially how we're going to be marketed and stuff, as somebody who's serious about their music, trying to be as good as we can be about it, as someone who loves the music. You know, we bring up certain issues because they're relevant to us, just like any other hip-hop artist would do, and in doing that, we have to bring up Asian American issues.

Unlike some Asian American musicians, though, the Mountain Brothers have chosen not to sign with an Asian American label. The Asian American recording company AARising (for "Asian Americans Rising," discussed below) provides them with a space on its homepage (including the text of a long and detailed interview), but the Mountain Brothers are openly after mainstream success and recognition. Such recognition would, to their minds, serve its own purpose, above and beyond their personal hopes: as they see it, their mere presence as an Asian American group is significant in its own right. They are keenly aware of their self-presentation as Asian Americans. As Chris Wang/Peril-L, one of the Brothers, put it, "I think just us *being* there is a big step. I mean, we could talk about nothing, and we'd still make a big statement."[5]

Working toward "being there" has involved strategic choices. The group performs for Asian American community events with some frequency.[6] Still, they're constantly on the lookout for opportunities to reach audiences beyond the Asian American community, believing that this will eventually lead to their getting signed. One of their bottom-line conditions for any recording company is to maintain control over their own "beats," that is, the tracks over which they rap. Scott Jung has taken music courses (theory, sightsinging and sightreading, and basic instruction in several instruments) since grade school. He has spent years creating a particular sound for the Mountain Brothers: he took courses in electronic music as an undergrad at Penn State and funnels the group's performance fees back into sound equipment. In fact, the increasing sophistication and accessibility of sound hardware and software gives composers/performers considerable control over their own production, and Jung is determined to maintain that control even after the group is signed. During much of 1996, the Mountain Brothers negotiated a contract with a major independent hip-hop label, so this issue was at the front of his mind. As he explained it:

> **Scott Jung:** That's going to be an issue once we get down to negotiations. One point that we made early on was that, as far as presenting ourselves, we need to have a big say, because if we don't have a big say — if not final say — it could really hurt, not just us, but other Asian groups that might come along in the future. So that's really important to us. And in terms of artistic control, they're pretty much giving it to us.

> **Chris Wang:** [The company] seems pretty cool about that.

> **Scott Jung:** Some of the other labels we were talking to were suggesting we have other producers make the beats, the music, for us, for half the songs, or a certain number of songs on the album. Which [could be] good, because it [would] lend some credibility — would lend a name producer who would make the music and we'd rhyme over it, and it would help us get in quicker. But that's not something we were really particularly interested in, because we think we have our own sound. And that's one thing [this present company] agrees with, so we're happy.

> **Chris Wang:** You look at a lot of new groups coming out — a lot of them use other producers — use them to try to get in, to try to attract more people.

> **Scott Jung:** So they end up sounding like the other groups the producer does, a lot of times. ... That's something we're trying to avoid.

As an ethnomusicologist, I have inherited a century's worth of keen interest and keener *angst* over recording technology. Ethnomusicology was made possible by such technologies — witness the thousands of wax cylinder recordings of Native American and other "ethnic" musics in countless archives. Who's recording whom is a matter of central importance; *for* whom is another. Audio technologies and the traditions that they fix on tape, vinyl, or plastic disks are often connected in problematic ways. Recording a performance can enable a tradition's continued existence, but it can also provide the means for its appropriation or expropriation. Their relationships usually represent asymmetrical political realities.

What does an Asian American presence mean in the racial politics of the music industry? I suggest that Asian American performers and recording companies are sites of cultural as well as commercial production — indeed, I question the distinctions between politics, ideology, aesthetics, and the commercial, and suggest that the very existence of Asian American sounds, produced musically *and* commercially by Asian Americans, offers a kind of critical pedagogy for listening. Much has been written about the power of representation in the media, yet a critique of listening practices has yet to take shape. I haven't yet met an Asian American musician or producer who is interested in creating something aurally recognizable as an Asian American sound; rather, almost all such cultural workers are interested in the political and artistic potential of Asian Americans who could change social land- and soundscapes with their mere presence. I'd like to explore the possibility of such interventions by considering the dialogic relationship between "indie" labels, "the industry," and Asian Americans who make music.

The important historical point is that smaller people's musics have almost always been recorded by bigger peoples. Ethnomusicologists going off to the pueblos with their Edison wax cylinder recorders at the turn of the century and Mickey Hart going into the rainforest with the latest DAT recorder in the 1990s enact, reflect, maintain, and construct power differentials.[7] I don't mean to suggest that smaller, i.e., non- or less-dominant peoples haven't generated mass-mediated music industries of their own. They have and they do.[8] Multinational recording companies' interest in World Beat, however, has created new possibilities for capitalist use of the Third World. If a history of music and imperialism is worth writing, then it is worth noting that small people's musics have long existed in the United States, recorded and disseminated for over a century.[9] The question is, by whom, for whom, and how? And what are those musics? They're easily defined by what they're not: not Tin Pan Alley, not Hollywood, not Top 40, not MTV or VH-1. These are the musics of immigrants and people of color.

In fact, the musics of ethnic enclaves in America have often been recorded by and for their own communities. The great European immigrations of the first half of this century led to lively community-based, entrepreneurial recording industries of Yiddish musics in New York City (Slobin 1982), Polish musics in Chicago and Detroit, and so forth. These industries were similar to community-based newspapers, that is, directed inward or at most to similar ethnic communities in other cities. More recently, Asian immigrations have prompted the growth of local entertainment industries directly tied to large-scale transnational flows of goods and peoples. Cassettes and CDs of Chinese, Korean, and South Asian Bollywood pop sold in your local Asian supermarket were probably produced in Hong Kong, Taiwan, Seoul, Bombay, and Calcutta — not in LA or New York City. In other words, the very nature of immigrant communities and the flow of capital that sustains them has changed.[10]

Looking at the recording industry as a particular site of political struggle is an exercise in uncovering historical inequities. From the beginning (i.e., the 1890s, when the phonograph, invented by Thomas Edison in 1877, became commercially available), "the recording industry" has been dominated by a few major companies which, in the 1990s, have become international conglomerates. Only six international "megacorporations" — BMG, MCA, Polygram, Sony, ThornEMI, and WEA — control approximately eighty-five percent of the record market (Schreiber 1992: xiii).[11] Nevertheless, the phenomenon of independent labels, now called "indies," has always been central to the music industry. In other words, the creative and economic tension between large-scale, corporate recording companies and smaller-scale independent companies has been part and parcel of musicians' hopes and realities for over a century.[12]

Indies tend to come and go. They can be as small as one person and a garage recording studio, or may be companies that grow over time and have staying power. Norman Schreiber, in his guide to indie labels (1992), outlines several characteristics of independent recording companies. As he puts it, "so much happens" first and last on indies (1992: xiv) — that is, indies often discover and record musics that only later become widely popular (e.g., Cajun, New Orleans R&B), and often maintain historically significant musics long after their initial popularity has come and gone. Furthermore, indie labels tend to "stand for something" — they're often brought into existence because someone believes that a band, a genre, or a heritage should be preserved. Schreiber (who is openly partisan) describes the "indie virtues" as "passion, spirit, hope, dedication, individualism, education, and respect for other cultures" (ibid., 195). In fact, indies' producers often have a renegade attitude because the might of the multinational recording companies simply can't be denied; there's more than a little Don Quixote in most of them (ibid., xvi).

The relationship of any recording company, whether indie or corporate, to American peoples of color is fraught with cultural politics. It does matter who's recording whom and how a market is conceived, defined, and targeted. The phenomenon of race records is a case in point: between 1922 and 1949, records of African American musics (jazz, blues, etc.) were generically referred to as "race music" by the industry, and were an attempt to tap the African American market (Oliver 1984: 8, Eastman 1989: 30). Only later, as the possibility of a so-called crossover market into White audiences became evident, were other names coined for African American popular musics. Since American popular music basically *is* African American music, these histories provide a very interesting window on the racial politics of the American recording industry.

I am concerned with the intersection of factors that may seem unrelated but are in fact intimately connected. When aesthetics, racialized bodies, and ideas of capitalist profit are brought into close configuration, you get the twentieth-century recording industry. Though the deceptively transcendent language of modernist aesthetics suggests that matters of artistic quality are somehow divorced from the messiness of the marketplace and the shove and push of racial politics, the global flow of capital and the language of aesthetic quality come from older discourses of imperialism and colonialism that established the political vocabularies of us/Other, here/Elsewhere. It's no coincidence that musical sounds (like labor and natural resources) have become part of the transnational movement of capital, i.e., that the dominant recording companies are international conglomerates based in particular parts of the First World. Nor is it coincidence that these spatial and racial geographies are reproduced within the confines of the U.S.

Asian Americans Recording and Getting Recorded

Asian Americans have never had a significant — or even a defined — place in the American recording industry as either performers, producers, or as a market.[13] Whites, African Americans, and Latino/as have long been targeted by recording companies as markets for particular kinds of music; Asian Americans, however, have been nearly absent from these socioeconomic geographies, whether real, imagined, or created. Between 1902 and 1937, several recording companies (including Victor, Edison, and Columbia) recorded Chinese, Japanese, and South Asian musicians in New York City, San Francisco, Hollywood, and Camden, New Jersey (Spottswood 1990: Vol. 5, 2535-52). Most if not all of these records were intended for the Asian/Asian American market: most were of traditional ensembles, though a few featured intercultural performances, e.g., a Chinese tenor singing hymns in Mandarin (ibid., 2537) and two Japanese American sopranos singing Verdi, Stephen Foster, and Schubert in Japanese (ibid., 2547-48). For the first half of the twentieth century, no documentation exists for any Asian American recording companies.[14]

Since 1987, at least three recording companies that are owned and managed by Asian Americans and largely feature Asian American musicians have appeared in the Bay Area. Asian Improv, a non-profit label, was founded in 1987; AARising and Classified Records, both commercial, were founded in 1990 and 1993. These three companies represent different purposes, different ambitions, different audiences, and different conceptions of Asian American music. In other words, they help constitute Asian American *musics*, decidedly plural, impossible to essentialize.

Like many indies, Asian Improv had several predecessors. The group of Bay Area jazz musicians who collaborate on Asian Improv met in the late 1970s, brought together through jazz and the Asian American movement. Mark Izu, Jon Jang, Anthony Brown, and Francis Wong formed the group United Front and began to record in the early 1980s on their own label, called RPM (Revolutions Per Minute), putting out the album *Are You Chinese or Charlie Chan?*, among others.

By 1987, United Front and RPM were moribund. As Francis Wong put it (Jang, Newton, Zhang, *et al.*: 4):

> I guess we were sitting around in Jon's living room, … and he said why don't we have a label so we can have some identification out there in the industry or in the field? So Jon came up with the term "Asian Improv," and I think that pretty much says what we're about, trying to bring the African American tradition of improvised music and jazz together with our Asian roots.

Wong further notes that "RPM was not functioning anymore, so there was almost no choice. We didn't have a longterm plan; [Asian Improv] was mainly seen as a vehicle to promote Asian American creative music and document our compositions" (Yanow 1994: 31). Asian Improv aRts is now a nonprofit arts organization, supporting a newsletter, symposia, performances, and the recording label Asian Improv.[15] As their mission statement puts it, Asian Improv was formed:

> … to work for cultural empowerment, self-respect and artistic excellence. This is achieved through creating, recording, and presenting adventurous, cross-cultural work of Asian American creative musicians; producing art that is born out of the Asian American experience; and bridging artists and community.

To date, they have put out fifty-two albums featuring over thirty musicians, mostly Asian American. Asian Improv's style might be called new music with a strong base in African American jazz; the musicians themselves shy away from categorization, preferring to simply call it "creative music."

For all the Asian American musicians closely associated with Asian Improv, the organization has served as a safe place from which to make music as Asian Americans, but it may not be the only place they choose to record. Asian Improv's distribution is limited outside the Bay Area and is dependent on online marketing. While the label provides a principled

Fig. 10.1 Album cover, *Never Give Up!* (1989): Jon Jang and the Pan Asian Arkestra. (Reproduced with the permission of Asian Improv aRts and Jon Jang.)

Asian American place in the industry (in the way that only an indie probably can), professional success beyond Asian American audiences may require recording elsewhere. Jon Jang, for instance, issued his cassette album (Figure 10.1) *Never Give Up!* (1989) on Asian Improv but has since has ventured out to Soul Note, a major jazz label. Jang thus released three early albums on Asian Improv,[16] but released (Figure 10.2) *Self Defense!* (1992) and *Tiananmen!* (1993) on Soul Note. Similarly, Glenn Horiuchi has released seven albums on Asian Improv[17] and one[18] on Soul Note. He told me that a number of considerations go into such decisions: he put out his first three albums on Asian Improv after Soul Note rejected them (including *Oxnard Beet*, Figure 10.3) but he's subsequently chosen to release two other albums on Asian Improv because Soul Note can take up to three years to get a CD onto the market, and won't release more tha-

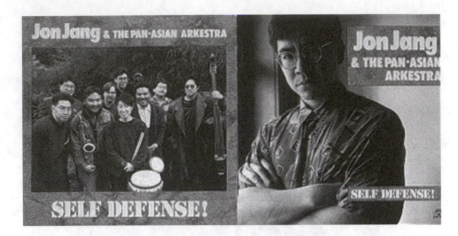

Fig. 10.2 Album cover and liner note photograph for *Self Defense!* (SoulNote, 1992). Left to right: Jon Jang, Francis Wong, Melecio Magdaluyo, John Worley, Jr., Jeff Cressman, Susan Hayase, Anthony Brown, Jim Norton, and Mark Izu. (Reproduced with the permission of Flavio Bonandrini and Soul Note.)

Fig. 10.3 Album cover, Glenn Horiuchi's *Oxnard Beet.* (Reproduced with the permission of Asian Improv aRts.)

none of his albums per year. On the other hand, their advance pay and their distribution is "much better" than Asian Improv's.[19]

AARising — that is, Asian Americans Rising — is self-consciously different from Asian Improv. Formed in 1990 by two Asian American DJs, Nelson Wong and Andy Kawanami, AARising is everything that Asian Improv is not: commercial and explicitly focused on popular musics. I asked Nelson Wong how he'd compare AARising to Asian Improv, and he said:[20]

> I would hate to use these terms, but this is pretty much what Jon [Jang] and I have defined it as. I guess [AARising is] more quote-unquote commercial, and it goes back to the fact that [we at AARising] are trying to sell our stuff to as many people as we can, because that's the way we make money. [At Asian Improv], they're doing it more for an artistic, political sort of means. And they're using Asian Improv as a vehicle to promote their beliefs, their art. Which is different from what we're doing — at least, we're not doing it as overtly as they are. Ours is a little more subtle. Neither is right or wrong — it's just a different approach. Like I said, I've talked with Jon about this many times. We just have a different way of doing things. We're on friendly terms. We both have similar goals, as far as the end goal, which is to get more visibility for Asian Americans in art, in music — but the approaches are different. ... And they have a different target market, anyway.

Moreover, AARising is self-consciously eclectic and solicits Asian American performers' and composers' work; their "concept" is simply Asian Americans performing popular music — of nearly any sort. Their target market is, first, "everyone," then Asian Americans, and particularly (pragmatically) young women between the ages of twelve and twenty-nine, who (studies have shown) represent 60% of the album-buying market.

AARising's webpage (Figure 10.4) reveals something less obvious about the company, though: it features links to five other groups on its primary page, but only one is actually signed to them. The others — The 18 Mighty Mountain Warriors, the Mountain Brothers, etc. — have no professional connection to the company but are Asian American performance groups admired by Wong and Kawanami. Talking with Nelson Wong, it's obvious that he's as much in the business of promoting Asian American performers in general as he is in signing them to his own label. In 1996, AARising had only one group signed to them, One Vision, an Asian American pop group whose first single (a ballad) came out that summer.

Nelson Wong freely acknowledged that AARising's main competitor wasn't Asian Improv but rather a third label called Classified Records. Classified Records (1993–2000) was formed by Kormann Roque, a Filipino American Bay Area DJ and songwriter whose first experiences in the industry included seeing a song he'd written hit the Top 40 after he'd lost rights to it.[21] He decided to get smart and to form his own company, and Classified had three staff members who ran the office by day while Roque and his partner held down other fulltime jobs. Classified had one of the snazziest web sites around until it closed in 2000, not least because the label had twelve groups signed. Most but not all of its groups were Filipino

Have you ever wondered why you don't see Asian Pacific Americans (APAs) in mainstream popular music in America? Well, two native San Franciscan DJs wondered the same thing. Andy Kawanami and Nelson Wong decided that they would take it upon themselves to do something about it and as a result **AArising Records** was born.

Being in the Bay Area, many of the clientele that Wong and Kawanami catered to were APAs, a question arose: why are there very few APAs performing the music so many APAs were listening to? The answer was not so clear.

To provide an answer, **AArising Records** was born as an idea in January 1990. Changing the status quo was the goal for Wong and Kawanami. "Our goal is to diversify the APA images out there," says Wong. "The more images you have out there the less chance that someone will be able to stereotype Asian Pacific Americans as being a certain way."

Response to **AArising Records** has been tremendous from within the APA pool of talent. "We've received tapes from people singing everything from Frank Sinatra songs to folk music," says Wong. Background isn't important -- **AArising** is looking for talent. "We don't want a pretty face and no voice," he says. "We want to first establish that Asian Americans do have talent."

AArising isn't looking to necessarily push a political agenda or to produce records only for APAs. The goal is to release records that happen to be by APAs. "If the music is good, it will cross all boundaries," says Wong. "Obviously our label cannot avoid getting political, but we want our messages to be subtle yet effective. We want people to hear the song on the radio, go to the record store to buy it, and then see the picture on the album cover and be surprised to see an Asian American on it."

It shouldn't be a surprise that the name **AArising** stands for Asian Americans Rising. The two capital A's represent Asian American, according to Wong. "We believe that Asian Americans can and will make a difference in the popular music industry in the near future and from this point forward. Asian Americans can keep rising to the top."

With all of this ground breaking working going on, where do the people behind

Fig. 10.4 AARising homepage (from the World Wide Web).

American; for instance, one group, Heaven, was a female trio (Latina, Latina, and Eurasian, respectively). Their up-and-coming group was the Pinay Divas, four Filipina Americans whose *a capella* numbers in English and Tagalog have attracted much attention in the Bay Area; their first album was released in the summer of 1996.

Classified Records' major artist was Jocelyn Enriquez, formerly of the Pinay Divas but now a solo artist. Her first full-length album, *Lovely,* was released in 1994, and her second, *Jocelyn,* came out in 1997. When she first began to attract attention, some fans assumed she was Latina, and neither she nor Classified initially did anything to suggest otherwise; several musicians have told me that some Latino listeners were then distressed when Enriquez was "outed" as a Filipina. Her section of the Classified Records website included the statement that "Jocelyn Enriquez is 100% Filipina, is proud of it, and has never claimed otherwise."[22] The politics of ethnic "passing" in the California music scene are complex, to say the least, but all this suggests that Enriquez doesn't sound Filipina or Asian American and indeed, Classified Records had no interest in developing anything that might be called an Asian American sound. Most of Enriquez's album *Lovely* is straight-ahead dance music, not unlike early Madonna but with occasional brief breaks into Latin riffs and scratching.

Kormann Roque, president of Classified Records and one of two founding partners, was careful to characterize his label as neither Filipino American nor Asian American. He insisted that they're just after "talent and good music, of any sort," and he readily asserted that his goal is for one of their artists to break into the Top 40.[23] Whereas Asian Improv and AARising self-identify as Asian American, with explicit ideological links to the Asian American movement and activism, Classified Records downplays ethnicity and has no explicit stake in identity politics. When I asked Roque why most of his artists and almost his entire staff are Filipino American, he explained that he wanted to support "Asians" in the industry and to get them out into "the mainstream" so he emphasized his artists' talents rather than their ethnicities. Several other Asian American producers I've spoken with (who will remain anonymous) expressed some resentment over Classified Records' coyness around its Asian American character; one even suggested that he thinks the label's management has played up ethnicity (when it has) simply to reach a potential market. Self-identifying as Asian American and expressly connecting oneself to the Asian American movement are two different things, however, and there is quite a bit of room for how ethnicity is displayed electronically, e.g., on the Web. Classified Records' "Loud Shouts" page provided a long list of "our favorite links," with hotlinks to over forty musicians and a few Asian American resources, including *Yolk Magazine* and AARising Records. In other words, choosing to self-present as Asian American in the music industry can be done in a number of ways, openly or subtly, or even both at once.

Breaking into the Biz

Some Asian American performers have a slightly different perspective on the challenges of the industry. Most are keenly interested in having their work recorded and commercially distributed. Some also think about their ethnicity and its impact on how they are heard or packaged. Commercial success and control over one's own image don't necessarily go hand in hand; getting ahead in the industry usually requires considerable resourcefulness — for any performer, certainly, but especially for musicians of color and most particularly for Asian American musicians, whose niche in the music industry is largely undefined or even unconsidered.

Unlike Asian Improv and AARising, the Mountain Brothers have sometimes aimed for explicitly mainstream networks for advertising, and in

April 1996 they had a big break: they won a national competition for a Sprite commercial, called the "Rhymes from the Mind" contest. Working out of Jung's home studio, they produced a spot that won first the regional and then the national contest. They were flown out to Los Angeles to receive the prize at the SoulTrain music awards ceremony. Three versions of the spot (30, 40, and 60 seconds long) were broadcast nationally on urban radio stations during 1996–97 (Audio Example 10.1). Here's the Mountain Brothers' suggestion that we all drink Sprite:

Chops:
sippin a sprite, ya know it's me, flippin the tight poetry,
upon the mic, obey ya thirst and come check the flavor,
verse one:
mountain brothers gonna need another one-liter
because we're done with the first.
image is nothin but bluffin in the city of brotherly love
we're takin charge right from the west side

Peril-L:
yes i'd like a large sprite with extra ice it might affect my life yo
this beverage gives leverage, see i'm the man next to mice
check the cipher up the street, ock, kids rhymin over beatbox,
time to show my stee rocks the crowd, the texture's nice
cool & bubbly, gulpin sprite, i'm provin lovely, spoken bright poetics
at ease knowin one day, we'll be chokin mics for grands

Styles:
it's mad hot my man chops got a jam up at his spot
he said to drop by and since it's sticky it'd be nice
to pack a six of sprite if it's alright, no problem,
got em in my fridgerator, then later tear the tab
and engineer the thirst cure
waitin for the subway train i say hey, talking to a lovely jawn
sharin sprites on the platform…
arrivin late at this fellas house, mellow taste in my mouth,
chops & peril give out pounds
mountain brothers downin sprites all around

I want to examine this brief moment of hip-hop from a number of different angles because it encapsulates so many salient issues around Asian America, the recording industry, and strategies for participation in cultural production. In deciding to feature the Mountain Brothers in this chapter, I was torn between focusing on the Sprite ad or discussing any of their longer works, which might be seen as free from the tight grip of the corporate world (for what could be more overtly commercial than marketing soft drinks?). But the idea of utter creative freedom, exempt from the constraints of a market, is a romantic notion sustained by the objectified values of Western art ideologies; I suggest instead that the relationship between creativity and the market is dynamic and open to manipulations and interventions. Such issues crystallize in the Mountain Brothers' Sprite ad. While I will focus my interpretive energies on these sixty seconds, I urge you as reader to seek out the Mountain Brothers' other work.[24]

The advertisement heard over the airwaves was produced not in an industry studio but in a West Philadelphia basement. Scott Jung has singlehandedly produced all the Mountain Brothers' demos to date in his home studio (Figure 10.5). Such studios, usually crammed into a corner of a musician's living room or (in this case) basement, are important sites of cultural production — simultaneously local but hoping for more, commercial but shaped by a shrewd sense of identity politics. Identity politics aren't the special purview of ethnic Americans, of course, but it does matter who's speaking to whom (and on whose terms) in a postindustrial context like this. In this way, distinctions between literal production (getting particular sounds onto audiotape) and cultural production (making culture, enacting or disrupting ideologies) are less than clear. Consider the startlingly simple movement from basement to national airwaves: that the sounds of this hip-hop site could bridge such disparate levels of production points to what might be called the democratizing aspects of certain technologies. Jung's studio reflects increasingly affordable sound equipment as well as a great deal of resourcefulness. His first experiences in a sound studio were during high school in a professional recording facility, sponsored by an internship program; he later took an introductory electronic music class at Pennsylvania State University in which he "got A pluses for fooling around."[25] In 1996, his studio contained a digital sampler, a MIDI keyboard, an ancient synthesizer, a double-deck cassette tape-deck, a DAT recorder, a four-track tape recorder, a synch box, a sound module with reverb, delay, compressor, de-esser, equalizer, etc., a mixer, a patch bank, two microphones with homemade pop filters constructed out of pantyhose and coathanger wire (to soften explosive consonants), two studio monitor speakers, and two DJ turntables for practicing scratching. Some of the Mountain Brothers' concert proceeds are consistently funnelled into new equipment, as technology is central to hip-hop; in the late spring of 1996, a new keyboard and a digital recorder with at least eight tracks were at the top of Jung's wish list.

The Sprite ad used four tracks and took the Mountain Brothers six or seven hours to produce, from start to finish. Their compositional process is collaborative yet highlights each individual's personal style. When I asked Chops[26] about the process of creating the Sprite spots, he said:[27]

Fig. 10.5 Photograph of Scott Jung (*aka* Chops) in his basement studio in Philadelphia, 1996. (Photograph by Deborah Wong.)

> we write separately, usually. [but] we did that in one day, together. yeah. as soon as we heard the ad on the radio about the contest, i was already writing ideas down (i'm sure steve and chris were too)

No one member is ever more prominently featured in the Brothers' pieces; instead, the three take turns (in this case, each Brother had one verse) and each writes his own poetry though revisions may occur during the recording process, in response to one another. Chops explained that recording the Sprite entry went like this:

> …it took us maybe 2 hours to actually record [it].

> laying down the vocals took maybe an hour or so, max. we generally can record pretty quick these days, since we're used to the recording process. we each laid one track, and then each of us laid a background track for one of the others' vocals. this was all on an old-ass 4-track machine (we have 8 track digital now, thanks to a loan from a good friend)

> then doing things like dropping the beat out at certain points, dropping the bass out, around the vocals took me another hour or 2

> mixing down, adding reverb and eq, etc. took me another few hours

considering the equipment we had, it sounds pretty good. i wish we could have done a little more sound-wise though. over the radio, it's good enough. can't wait until we have some better studio gear though.

The lyrics for the Sprite ad reflect a canny sense for advertising necessities interspersed with references to Philadelphia (i.e., localizing phrases) and hip-hop braggadocio of the best sort. Later, I asked the Brothers to explain the lyrics to me, and although they graciously provided the elaborations provided below, they were also a bit reluctant to have their explanations appear here. As Chops noted:[28]

the slang one uses is something picked up (or made up, if you're creative) over time, and not something to really give away at the drop of a hat. in a way, explaining the meaning of a slang term can deaden [its] impact...

Given this uneasiness over exegesis, I must emphasize that I here include the Brothers' explanations of their lyrics with the purpose not of commandeering their meaning or deadening their originality but rather to unpack that originality for those not as immersed in hip-hop culture and aesthetics. In "understanding" the Sprite lyrics, it is also important to realize that the power of these poetics lies in their ownership and their placement in particular performers' creative arsenals.

Chops opens by, well, sippin a Sprite, but then immediately moves into the reflexive oratory of hip-hop, referring to himself, to the well-knit quality of his verse, and to the microphone — the technologically and socially empowering vehicle of the rap artist — before circling back to the soft drink. As he explained to me, *flippin* is "execution with flair," and *tight poetry* "is well-constructed, seamless, gapless." His next phrase, too, adroitly combines advertising with a classic African American performative: he "places" himself as a performer by declaring that it's the Mountain Brothers who will "need another one-liter," i.e., he inserts a signature into the spot virtually at the outset so that there can be no question about who has the mic. Chops provided this exegesis of the phrase *image is nothin but bluffin:*

sprite's catchphrases are "obey your thirst" and "image is nothing"

so i used the phrases they had, and extended it some.

to basically just say, around here, image is just a bluff, exterior nonsense, whereas we get to the heart of the matter.

"The city of brotherly love" is of course Philadelphia, but he's specifically referring to "the west side," a predominantly African American part of the city where Chops and Peril-L both live. Furthermore, the Mountain Brothers are assertively *takin charge* as only rappers can.

Peril-L too gets Sprite in at the beginning of his verse and invests it with power, using it to point to his own skill and ability. As he explained to me:[29]

> in the line "this beverage gives leverage" i was saying that drinking sprite gives me an edge over other mc's.

> "i'm the man next to mice" refers to that book "of mice and men" (which i've never actually read). basically, it means i'm a man (or i'm THE MAN) and you're just a tiny little mouse.

Having established his skill, he moves back to the street (*the* symbolic landscape of hip-hop), where he encounters a *cipher,* a central hip-hop street performative. As Peril-L explained:

> a "cipher" is a group of mc's (usually standing in a circle, on the street) rhyming. either freestyles or written rhymes. and the rhymes may be done a capella, with someone beat-boxing, or over an instrumental track. one person starts it off and the next person jumps in whenever he/she feels the urge. usually a certain order is maintained in the cipher (but not necessarily clockwise or counter-clockwise), and if someone rhymes out of turn, he/she is said to be "f*ckin' up the cipher." but order of rhyming is not always strictly enforced. often times people just jump in and out whenever they feel. … they usually attract large crowds on the street.

Again, the reflexivity of embedding a description of an actual performance into the body of a performed text is classic rap rhetoric. Peril-L explained that "'ock" is a slang word referring to any individual; e.g., "what's up, ock?'" Note his reference to *kids rhymin over beatbox*: hip-hoppers refer constantly to the technologies employed in their compositional process, e.g., beatboxes and mics, but in this case "beatbox" means rhyming out loud over a human beatbox, or mouth percussion accompaniment — a performative history that reabsorbs the acoustic percussion → electronic beatbox process back into oral performance. *Stee* is short for *stee-lo,* a slang word for "style." Peril-L decides it's time, in the street narrative he's established, to join the cipher and to show his stuff — and when he does, he *rocks the crowd.* Indeed, *the texture's nice,* but does he mean his poetry or the Sprite? The two are elided. The ease of his poetry shifts seamlessly into his own confidence that *one day* the Mountain Brothers *will be chokin mics for grands* — that their commercial success is assured. This clever reference to the industry, to the group's aspirations, and to their unquestioned skill closes his verse.

In the third and final verse, Styles continues to join references to Philadelphia, the urban landscape, the Mountain Brothers, and Sprite in slippery metaphorical ways. As Chops noted later:[30]

> unlike chops's and peril's, styles's verse is in narrative story form, starting from his place and ending at chops's. we think that's pretty cool.

The scene shifts to Chops' apartment, where a *jam,* a music session of some sort, is taking place; Sprite of course helps out. Sharing Sprites with the Mountain Brothers shifts to Styles sharing a Sprite with a young woman, a *jawn,* on a Philadelphia subway platform. Not only the subway but *jawn* localizes the scene:

> jawn means woman or girl… as a term it doesn't have any implications about the type of woman it refers to… however, the same word is used to mean "thing' (like "could you hand me that jawn over there?") in other cities (and Philly as well)… maybe you could read something into the creation of the word from that (i.e. thing = woman) but it's not intentional. the word jawn is mostly used in the philly area and a little in new york (the use of jawn to mean girl however is exclusively a Philly thing).[31]

His verse, and the sixty-second spot, end with the Mountain Brothers together, greeting each other by *giving out pounds* (like shaking hands only striking right fists together) and, naturally, drinking Sprites.

Textually, this brief moment of hip-hop establishes the Mountain Brothers as adept in any number of ways — as orators, as street smart, as objects of admiration by other hip-hoppers. At another level, the Brothers are proud of their craftsmanship, noting[32] that

> just for your own fun info purposes, notice that unlike many rappers, we often have polysyllabic rhymes, for instance "rhymin over beatbox" and "time to show my stee rocks" in peril's verse makes a pair of 6-syllable strings that rhyme with each other. we think this is pretty cool too, but … anyway it's more cool for listeners to figure that out on their own…

Their collaborative composition created another kind of authenticity, too. When the Mountain Brothers mailed their cassette and press kit to Sprite for the contest, none of their materials referred to their Asian American identities: no photographs were included (no giveaway Asian faces), and they referred to themselves only by their handles (no giveaway Asian surnames). Unlike some of their other raps, the Sprite spot obviously contains no textual references to their Asian American identities. In short, they passed as *African* American hip-hoppers, and this careful presentation of self was a matter of strategy. The Mountain Brothers have learned that they are most quickly accepted by the hip-hop community if their music precedes any knowledge of their ethnicity. In other words, they have found that listeners hear them differently depending on whether they're already known to be Asian American. Indeed, they have found repeatedly that listeners who know they are Asian American beforehand take them much less seriously than when given no racial clues at all, so the Mountain Brothers have become more and more careful to control listeners' initial reception to their sound. After reading a draft of this paragraph, the Brothers noted[33] that:

> we avoid initially making explicit references to ethnicity so that we can be given a fair unbiased listen based on the merits of our music, lyrics and style, as opposed to avoiding making explicit references to ethnicity so that we can pass for Black.

Over the years, they have created two separate sets of promotional material, one directed toward Asian American audiences that includes explicit references to their ethnicity (including photographs) and another in which their Asianness is methodically concealed.

Sprite is owned by The Coca-Cola Company. The Sprite contest was developed and executed by Burrell Communications Group, one of the oldest and largest African American-owned advertising agencies in the U.S., which has overseen The Coca-Cola Company's advertisements for the African American consumer market since 1973. When the Mountain Brothers won first place in the contest, Coca-Cola's and Burrell's executives didn't realize that the group wasn't African American. William Colvard, the Burrell account executive in charge of the Coca-Cola business, openly acknowledged that the Brothers' Asian American identities came as a complete surprise. I asked him if this was a problem or an issue at any point since, after all, Burrell Communications Group is in the business of marketing Coca-Cola products to African Americans. But Colvard said:[34]

> Not at all. Coca-Cola's goal was to reach urban teens, and the Mountain Brothers are part of that audience. The music was real. It was authentic, the best — it was good hip-hop.

Authenticity is a curious measuring rod in American hip-hop, based but not based in constructions of racial, ethnic, and bodily experience, and its merciless standards can as easily condemn as approbate. The Mountain Brothers passed that ultimate test, but they "passed" (in at least two ways) because they knew the rules of hip-hop authenticity and were savvy enough to abide by them — on their own terms.

This meeting of the local and the transnational — of the 'hood and the global corporate — in music production is no longer unusual. I'm not suggesting that the Mountain Brothers have sold out — far from it. Rather, I think that they have adroitly, wisely, and cleverly used all the means at their disposal to create a space for themselves in the industry. That particular space can be talked about in a number of different ways. It is a performative alliance with African American expressive culture — rather than American popular culture more generally — that hearkens back to other Asian American musicians participating in African American expressive forms, and indeed to the birth of the Asian American movement as an expression of coalition as well as specifically Asian American empowerment. This social space is racialized in particular ways: as Chris Wang said, it's Asian American because *they* are. Yet of course it is, and isn't, that simple. This aural space is defined by Asian American voices making musical sounds that they are careful to claim as their own, through performance. When the Mountain Brothers urge us to drink Sprite, they become part of the global image factory — that is, they could be seen as coopted — but on the other hand, they are quite openly using it as a step up, as a way to get into the industry, where they will surely rap about far more than Sprite. They are both pragmatic and determined to become part of that bigger system — to reap its rewards — but to remain who they are.

The Recording Industry, "the Mainstream" and Leaky Dikes

The three companies I have described, and the Mountain Brothers as one example of an Asian American performance group, have participated in the hegemonies of "the industry" yet, at different junctures, have withdrawn from and resisted it too. What *is* "the industry?" Or rather, what does it represent for different Asian American performer-producers? How is it imagined, and how is it both used and resisted? "The industry" and "the mainstream" delimit a phantasmatic late capitalist framework that effectively defines and maintains an Elsewhere much as race records did during the first half of this century. It is the marked category against which — through which — Asian American indies and performers define themselves, in much the same way that Asian Americans in general necessarily see themselves as outside the mainstream, yet often aspire to become part of it since success very clearly lies within, not outside, that social geography.

The popular musics created and disseminated by the performers and companies I have described are at once sites of Asian American empowerment as well as an interface with cultural technologies located outside Asian American communities. Asian Americans claim rights to particular sounds and technologies through different strategies. I suggest that cultural (re)production, as channeled through music, creates a complex landscape of hearing and speaking — in other words, Asian American musics empower in many ways, not least through the painstaking, mundane creation of explicitly Asian American niches in the late-industrial realities of a transnational music industry. Speaking, listening, consuming and producing may not be disparate processes; audiences and performers may have overlapping roles in creating new ways of listening, and new ways of becoming entitled to hear — not to mention new ways of consuming products shaped (to varying degrees) by identity politics.

How do these cultural workers deal with the slippage between community and mainstream, and commercial success as assimilation? These producer/performers are manipulating the capitalist framework of the mass media in ways that are both mindful and conflicted. Asian Improv has (to some extent) deliberately placed itself outside that framework by remaining a non-profit organization. AARising aspires to succeed within that framework, though the jury's still out on whether they'll succeed or not. Classified Records perhaps relocated itself as Asian American rather than Filipino American in an attempt to cash in on what they see as an emergent market. The Mountain Brothers try to penetrate the mainstream while maintaining control over their own production from the fiercely local site of their West Philadelphia basement studio.

Every year, the NAACP Image Awards are broadcast on television, honoring positive portrayals of African Americans in television, film, literature, and the recording industry. Lurking behind this annual event is the question of control, i.e., the straight-forward proposal that more African American producers, directors, writers, and composers are likely to make a difference in the free play of ethnic representation in the media. The Quincy Joneses, Bill Cosbys, Nelson Wongs, and Mark Izus of the world no doubt make a difference, though this is not to say that the problems of reinscription don't wait under every rock, or perhaps I should say in every inch of celluloid and in every laser track. Cultural theorist John Fiske tells us that a culture of power is a culture of representation (1993: 147). Asian American efforts to reclaim self-representation are necessarily projects of reflexive self-empowerment. Asian Americans in the music biz are thus insurgents of a very special sort, walking a line between capitalist assimilation and the creation of new cultural industries that will allow for different ways of listening.

Acknowledgments

This chapter was originally presented at the annual meeting of the Association for Asian American Studies in Washington, DC, May 31–June 2, 1996, and I'm grateful for audience members' responses as well as suggestions from my fellow panelists, Casey Man Kong Lum and Cynthia Po-Man Wong, and from the panel chair, John Kuo Wei Tchen. Nelson Wong and Kormann Roque were generous with their time and thoughts. All the members of Asian Improv, and especially Francis Wong and Mark Izu, have gone out of their way to answer my questions and to include me in their events. Finally, the Mountain Brothers have been exemplary post-structuralist subjects, patiently sharing their work and their hopes, and helping me to incorporate their responses into this essay.

Endnotes

1. Wilson 1981: 79.
2. From a telephone interview, 29 April 1996.
3. See their website, www.mountainbrothers.com, for self-representation.
4. From an interview with Scott Jung and Chris Wang in Philadelphia, 29 February 1996.
5. Ibid.
6. In 1995-96, for instance, they performed at the University of Pennsylvania's Asian Pacific American Heritage Week, at Asian Americans United (a Philadelphia community group), for the 17th Annual Asian Pacific American Heritage Festival in New York City, for the 2nd Annual Kensington Cultural Festival in Philadelphia (in an Asian neighborhood), etc.
7. Mickey Hart represents a recent twist in the history of recording other musics. He is fascinated by this history in its own right and has published a book about audio documentation (Hart 2003). Best known for his work with the Grateful Dead, he began making his own recordings of non-western musics in the 1970s (often while on tour with the band) and then moved into producing tours and albums focused on non-western musicians as well as a series of notable cross-cultural percussion collaborations as a performer. His friendship with ethnomusicologists Steve Feld and Anthony Seeger has led to other involvements with audio documentation, including a seat on the board of directors for Smithsonian Folkways, a stint as a trustee for the American Folklife Center, and a seat on the National Recorded Sound Preservation Board at the Library of Congress (Hardin 2003: 15). One could see this as the involvement of a high-profile dedicated amateur drawn into the sphere of government-sponsored folklore programs, or as a new alignment of commercial/market and scholarly trajectories. Certainly Hart has blurred the line between 'preservation' and the creation of new intercultural musics. Whichever the case, Hart is a major figure and has redefined the market for audio documentation in certain ways by making Third World sounds commercially viable. See also Taylor 1997: 28 for reflections on Hart's role as both 'curator' and producer.
8. The major Third World music recording industries have been based on cassette technology, which carries with it the democratizing possibility of allowing consumers to be producers as well: cassette recording technology can be part of the same equipment that plays sound back, and this simple fact points to the tremendous proletarian potential of cassettes, which essentially took over the Third World in the 1970s (Manuel 1993: 21-35, Wallis and Malm 1984: 5-7). Other recording technologies have also been described as democratizing, e.g., Daniel J. Boorstin writes that "The phonograph asserted itself in American life largely because it was a democratic instrument. It was a machine which not only repeated experience but democratized it. [...] [W]ithin a decade or two it was one of the primary resources for reaching everybody with music..." (American Folklife Center 1982: xii). Any technology thus begs the question of how and why it reaches particular groups, communities, and nations—or not.
9. Ethnic recordings in the U.S. are discussed in a number of chapters in Lornell and Rasmussen 1997, where this chapter originally appeared.
10. The important exception, now changing, is the communities of Vietnamese, Cambodians, Lao, and Hmong in the U.S., who have had to generate their own mass media for over twenty years. The Vietnamese American music and film industry in Southern California has been especially lively, as described in Chapters 4 and 5.
11. Timothy Taylor (Taylor 1997: 198–201) suggests that the market share of sales of recordings controlled by the multinational conglomerates may be as high as 93%. He points out that only one of the multinationals (Time-Warner) is now based in the U.S., suggesting that we may need to rethink older ideas of economic cores and peripheries.
12. See Wallis and Malm 1984: 85–119 for a good discussion of independent recording companies in international context in the 1980s. They propose a dynamic view of the relationship between what was (then) the five international conglomerates and independents in smaller countries—a relationship obviously open to exploitation, but also of vital support to emergent local musics. They refer to "the elusive concept of 'independence'" (109):

    ... [I]ndependents are normally *dependent* on someone else. Some authors use the term solely to refer to a company which has the resources to bring a phonogram to the point of release, but which does not have the facilities to manufacture, fully promote and rapidly distribute records to the users. ...

Another definition links the concept of independence to the introduction of simpler technology, cutting the cost of entry into the market. Thus the advent of cheaper tape recorders and retail sales of reel-to-reel tape recoders in the Fifties led to the 'creation of numerous small independent companies'. A similar upsurge could be observed twenty years later with the widespread introduction of cassette technology. This link with cheaper technology tells us little about the activities or the raison d'être of the independents. Other factors have to be introduced to understand their cultural role.

13. On the other hand, Asians have long been the subject of stereotyped and (usually) racist representation in American popular and art musics, as documented by Judy Tsou (1996), John Kuo Wei Tchen, Ellie Hisama (1993), Dennis Park and Dina Shek (1996), Rob Lancefield (forthcoming), etc. One might say that the primary place of Asians and Asian Americans in the music industry has been as representations, not as agents.

14. Cohen and Wells (1982: 219) report that they found no evidence for commercial recordings of "Far Eastern Asian-American cultural traditions," and suggest that available recordings were recorded and imported from abroad. The absence of evidence does not, however, prove that there were no Asian American recording companies.

Su Zheng (personal communication, 1996) notes that almost all the recorded materials she encountered while doing research on Chinese American musics in the metropolitan New York area during the early 1990s were imported from the PRC, Hong Kong, and Taiwan; she was told by a number of Chinese/Chinese American musicians that it is still less expensive for them to get recorded in any of those countries and then to import the results into the U.S., suggesting a diasporic economic circuit. A section of her dissertation, "Media Products in the Musical Life of Chinese Americans," examines the roles of cassettes, videotapes, LPs, and CDs in the lives of Chinese immigrants (Zheng 1993: 200–43).

15. The newsletter is called *ImprovisAsians;* Asian Improv is also a primary organizer (with the Kearny Street Workshop) for the annual Asian American jazz festival, begun in 1981.

16. *The Ballad or the Bullet?* (1987), *Jangle Bells* (1988), and *Never Give Up!* (1989).

17. *Kenzo's Vision, Live in Berlin, Little Tokyo Suite, Poston Sonata, Manzanar Voices, Issei Spirit,* and *Next Step.*

18. *Oxnard Beet,* Soul Note, 1992.

19. From an e-mail conversation, 20 May 1996. Horiuchi noted that he was about to release a new album, *Hilltop View,* on yet another label, Music and Arts, because its release time was shorter than Soul Note's (though its advance was smaller).

20. From a telephone interview, 29 April 1996.

21. From a telephone interview, 22 May 1996.

22. Located at http://www.crworld.com/music/je_lovel.html.

23. From a telephone interview, 22 May 1996.

24. The Mountain Brothers' work can be ordered on their Web site at www.mountainbrothers.com.

25. From an interview with Scott Jung on February 29, 1996 in Philadelphia.

26. From this point on, I refer to the Mountain Brothers by their handles as I regard their explanations of their art as another kind of performance.

27. All of Chops' textual explanations are from two e-mail notes sent on September 5, 1996.

28. From an e-mail note sent by all three of the Mountain Brothers, 11 September 1996.

29. All of Peril-L's textual explanations are from an e-mail note sent on September 4, 1996.

30. From an e-mail note sent on 11 September 1996.

31. All of Styles' textual explanations are from an e-mail note sent on September 4, 1996.

32. From an e-mail note sent by all three of the Mountain Brothers on 11 September 1996.

33. From an e-mail note sent by all three of the Mountain Brothers on 11 September 1996.

34. From a telephone conversation with William Colvard on September 2, 1996.

11

Finding an Asian American Audience:
The Problem of Listening

To deny what audience produces in performance is to disavow its capacity to produce its own associations, in favor of an imperative to manage its desires with respect to a world of products run wild.

Randy Martin (1995: 114)

We were having dinner at an Italian restaurant in Riverside, California on a rainy night in February, just the four of us. Writer David Mura was in an expansive mood, having just given the second of two public presentations at the University of California, Riverside; two of my colleagues, Ruth Chao from Psychology and Rodney Ogawa from Education, rounded out the table — so we were four Asian Americans, that is, two *Sansei* men and two Chinese American *hapa* women, and the conversation turned to the kinds of topics that they do when the people around the table self-identify as Asian American, toward the conversations we (often) don't have when we socialize with our (often) Anglo partners or colleagues.

David asked us where we had grown up and whether we had had much contact with other Asian Americans during childhood, and we began reminiscing about our families and our neighborhoods. David and I grew up in White suburban enclaves, but Ruth and Rod had grown up in Southern California and had had friendships with Latino/as, African Americans, and Asian Americans. Describing his childhood in Pasadena in the 1950s, Rod suddenly stopped, looked at me, and said, "You know, I listened to African American music all through elementary school and high school, but I remember that that changed when I went to college at UCLA — within a year, I was listening almost entirely to White music." We started

257

talking about the place of different allegiances in our lives and how these identifications have changed over time, and I asked Rod if I could interview him at more length about his listening habits.

This chapter is based on that interview, which we had several weeks later.[1] I am doing two slightly unusual things here: I focus on listening and consumption — rather than production, e.g., composers — as a way into Asian American cultural production, and I dwell on an in-depth conversation with a friend. The latter move is deliberately particular: part of my commitment to ethnography is a commitment to particularities, and I thus focus on one person to get at the dynamics of his life and choices rather than attempting a broad, totalizing look at Asian American listening practices. Writing about someone who was a friend before he became my subject is new to me, though I have certainly pursued many Asian American musicians who have subsequently become my friends. Working back in the other direction forces me into an accountability that can only be useful.

Reception, consumption, and audience remain under-theorized in ethnomusicology and performance studies. Most work on Asian American music-making (my own included) has focused on composers and performers, but this essay addresses the listening practices of a Japanese American friend. In talking at length with Asians of several generations, I am inspired by the study *My Music* (1993) and its main point: that people are able to reflect on how they use and value music in their lives, and the ways they choose to articulate this are well worth listening to.[2] In an effort to listen, I am led to ethnography as an essential inroad to the politics of everyday life — in this case, the politics of Asian American listening habits.

Listening practices are a crucial interstice for commodity capitalism and subject formation. At once intimate, individual, and inflected by global capitalist systems, listening is a site where considerable slippage occurs between agency and coercion. Neither producers nor consumers lie outside the sphere of commodity capitalism, but some of the most challenging work in cultural studies considers where and how intervention can matter. Listening can be treated as a site "where social transformation appears in material form" (Kondo 1997), not least because any close look at consumption begins to look a lot like cultural production once agency and choice are taken seriously. De Certeau suggests that walking through a city constitutes the city — a rather extreme take on agency — and I similarly argue that listening at once constitutes the product and listener, though neither can be placed beyond the reach of commodity capitalism; rather, one must negotiate its flow through one's life.

Asking what music an Asian American listens to is a way to consider how and why Asian Americans make choices about identity, pleasure, and location, not least because very little public culture is Asian American. In other words, I think it's worth considering how Asian Americans choose to partake in what *is* out there, whether it is "mainstream" (i.e., White)

Fig. 11.1 Rodney Ogawa in his office at University of California, Riverside in 1999. (Photograph by Deborah Wong.)

American popular culture or anything else. The uneasy Asian American location between Blackness and Whiteness is right at the center of these matters, and I consider it at length in other chapters. I am not arguing that some musics are African American and others are White American: the ethnicity of music isn't any less complicated than the ethnicity of people, which (just like music) moves dialogically between self-identification and coercive categorization. I think most of us would locate many musics in those ways even while allowing for multiple, interethnic audiences.

Dance theorist Randy Martin — one of few critical writers to consider the dynamics of the audience — reflects on the ways that audiences experience "moments of common focus" that a choreographer controls through design, but he also acknowledges that audiences constantly shift between heterogeneous and homogeneous response to what they witness. Listening to the sounds of an audience at a dance event, Martin takes in the creaking of chairs, clearing of throats, laughter, etc., and suggests that "… part of what the audience was trying for was the assertion of its capacity for evaluation. The audience was listening to itself" (1995: 107–8). If we move beyond the material presence of "an" audience sharing social space in a darkened theater, Martin's conception of the audience opens up what happens when anyone listens to a music — they listen to themselves, but this act of choice and perception is no solipsistic mirror but rather a critical moment of representation. Martin argues that the audience is always unstable, as it is only constituted through performance, and that this audience "suggests a mobilized critical presence" with "the potential to extend an understanding of the political" (ibid., 110). In Rodney Ogawa's case, the construction of an Asian American listener took place through his consumption of African American and White American musics: one could say that he was trying in both cases to "hear" himself, but through a politicized and ethnicized process of subject formation vis-à-vis musical sound.

This listening history is therefore a particular window on Asian American strategies for identity construction: listening practices (along with lots of other things) are constitutive sites for Asian American subject formation. Somewhere between Asian American music being made for an Asian American audience is... everything else, including my friend Rod sitting in his office at UCR with a poster of Miles Davis on the wall (Figure 11.1). Rod, a Japanese American university professor and administrator in his fifties, reflected at length on his preference for African American popular musics during his childhood/young adulthood and his subsequent shift to mainstream White American musics during college. I am fascinated by Rod's account of his own history and habits precisely because he reflects on himself through the lens of education and Asian American Studies. Work in postcolonialism has most notably addressed the question of the impact of domination through education. Fanon particularly addressed the role of class and education in the experience of colonialism, arguing that the class with the privilege of education feels most keenly the impact of its own subjugation because it has closer contact with the agents of colonial domination than the poor. Similarly, one of the longest-standing conflicts within Asian American Studies is the relationship between its placement in the academy and its role(s) in the community; the ways that this troubled link begs the question of class has generated untold amounts of writing that is alternately anguished and utopian. Part of my interest in writing about Rod lies in his willingness to reflect critically on his own location as an educator, a listener, a consumer of culture. Rod isn't more interesting than any other Asian American listener: rather, he provides an extended window — and one articulated in specific ways — on race relations through music. Indeed, we both proceeded from the assumption that the two are linked, and I acknowledge that part of my interest in Rod's account is the way he addresses the politics of listening pleasure through critical frameworks drawn from Ethnic Studies and the social history of education.

Rod moved from Boyle Heights in East Los Angeles to Pasadena when he was four years old, in 1952. In Boyle Heights, his family rented an apartment from a Mexican family and he says, "I remember walking with my dad, you could smell the tortilla shops... We'd go down and buy fresh tortillas." When Rod's father helped his brother-in-law move to Pasadena, Rod remembers that he said, "'This is really a nice place!' You know, a far cry from — it's very much unlike East Los Angeles." Indeed, the neighborhood in northwest Pasadena to which the Ogawas then moved was mostly White and residential, and Rod says that that was part of its attraction for his father:

> Yeah, it was much quieter, and it seemed — even though it was just down the freeway fifteen or twenty minutes from where we were previously — it seemed like a world apart. It really did seem like a world apart. Anyway, that's what attracted him.

Rod and his family settled into a quiet suburban life. Bear in mind that their move to Pasadena was only seven years after the Japanese American resettlement following the closing of the internment camps, so many Japanese American families were still in the process of reestablishing their communities, creating new ones, and generally trying to recover. Rod's father was a gardener, like so many Nisei men at that time, and Rod's mother took in ironing and later worked in the school cafeteria. Rod joined the all-Japanese American Boy Scout troupe.

Nevertheless, their new neighborhood changed dramatically about four years after they moved in, and their presence probably had something to do with it. As Rod tells it:

> … when we moved in, you know, the little area that we lived in was still largely white. And then I started school. My best friend, from kindergarten/first grade/second grade, was a white kid — Bobby Cimeral. You know, we were just devoted friends. Then, between the second and third grade, white flight occurred in that section of Pasadena at a rate that was absolutely breathtaking. (**DW**: Really?) Yeah, I mean whole neighborhoods would go from majority white to at least half-black, just over a summer. (**DW**: Wow!) Yeah, I must have been eight, so it would've been 1956. FOR SALE signs would go up. The way my dad explains it, as we [the Japanese Americans] started moving into these areas, we began to destabilize the ethnic solidarity, or the racial unity, of the community. Many of the white families started getting nervous. A black family would move in and BANG! — it would just turn overnight.

DW: You all were the beginning of the end. (laughs)

RO: Yeah, that was sort of the sense — that we were the beginning of the end, right! And so, very quickly the area, and hence the schools, became largely African American, at least in that neighborhood. I went from hanging out with a handful of Japanese American kids and a large number of white kids, to a handful of Japanese Americans — which was a growing handful at that point — and, suddenly, all of these African American kids. Now in hindsight, I was aware of the fact that there was something racial going on — that suddenly all these white kids were replaced by all these black kids… (**DW:** You did notice this.) Yeah, I did notice that, but it really didn't matter. You know, instead of Bobby Cimeral there was Buzzy Jones. And so, my best friends were Japanese American — I think for lots of reasons — mainly because of the strong ties in that community between church, they had sports leagues like they do now, they had the Boy Scout troupe. So, everywhere you would turn, outside of school, almost all of my contacts were with Japanese American kids. The only place where I socialized with non-Japanese Americans would be at school — and there it shifted from white to black. Maybe it wasn't as dramatic as I remember it, but that's how it felt. Between second and third grade, that summer, [it was] like the whole neighborhood just turned over.

So the Ogawa family's brief attempt at White American suburban life was in fact part of the catalyst for White flight out of their neighborhood, and over the next few years, Rod's social life moved between the Japanese American and the African American:

And then, starting in the seventh grade, I started attending a junior high school which sits right in the middle of the traditionally African American community in Pasadena — Washington Junior High. It had this horrible reputation — people get in fights, get picked on, all this kind of stuff. I remember I was starting to get a little nervous the summer before because of all this talk about what a tough school it was. It was maybe about a mile and a half from our house — maybe two miles from our house. We would walk everyday, up this gradual hill to the junior high school, and we would walk right through what was largely, about 80%, an African American community. I never had a moment's trouble in the three years that I attended that school. That only time I got jumped was by another Japanese American kid who was mad at me for something or other — and that amounted to nothing.

The junior high school was 70–80% African American, and Rod says that this new environment had everything to do with his teenaged musical tastes:

So [all this happened] right at that time when [I was] an early adolescent, twelve, thirteen, and starting to be aware of music and beginning to cultivate [my] own musical taste separate from what [my] parents listened to. You know, almost all of my non-Japanese American classmates were African American, so my tastes, all of my close friends' tastes — it wasn't just shaped, I mean we simply *adopted* [my African American friends' tastes]. ... As a twelve–thirteen year old, as Motown was flowering, I was just becoming aware of this music. I had a group of three cousins who, when I was eight or nine, were already teenagers, on my mom's side. My mom's family is very close, and we would see each other socially all the time. The three of them — Julie, Susan, and Naomi — would be doing their teenage thing together. They would be playing records, 45s and what not, and so we were exposed to that. And what they listened to was early rock and roll, a lot of which had very strong black roots.

By the time we hit junior high school, while we did listen to other sorts of pop musicians of the time — like a lot of the young Italian American singers out of Philadelphia, that was all in the mix — but, by the time I was in the eighth grade, it was clear to me that the real music was rhythm and blues — specifically the Motown version of it. Through junior high school into high school, the Temptations were my favorite musical group, Smokey Robinson was my favorite singer (he fronted a group, The Miracles), and, you know, the Four Tops, the Supremes. We saw the Temptations, we saw the Tops, we saw the Supremes, Martha Reeves and the Vandellas...

At that point, Rod's listening was eclectic but he knew what his favorite music was. Motown was urban African American music, in fact the first mass-marketed African American music produced by an African American studio; it was also part of a broader phenomenon through which the White American market encountered and consumed African American musical sounds. Drawing on smoothed-out R&B, gospel, jazz, and pop, Motown almost immediately appealed to a crossover market (Fitzgerald 1995), which included the teenaged Rod in Pasadena; although some scholarly work has begun to examine the ethnic politics of Motown's appeal, none of it accounts for Rod or indeed for any Japanese American teenagers in the 1960s, as "crossover" continues to mean White to Black or Black to White in the industry. Indeed, the identification of Motown as a "Black" music raises useful questions: it was regarded by Rod and his friends as an African American music, but Motown's place in the racialized imaginary of American popular music looks more complicated if one considers arguments by African American critics who suggest that Motown provided a model of assimilation for Americans — a means for making the Black body palatable for White/non-Black audiences even while clearly not quite, not-White (Bhabha 1987). Historian Suzanne Smith writes impatiently that Motown is now too often portrayed as a Black business that sought both Black and White consumers (1999: 55). She thinks it better to "shift attention away from Motown's crossover success with white audiences" toward a consideration of "the false promise of black capitalism"; she has no faith that "capitalism can be enlisted to remedy racial inequality" (1999: 8, 255). Post-internment Japanese American anxieties over the nature of "the American" put yet another spin on this: Motown appealed to Japanese American teenagers as *American* in particularly troubled ways that bring together the trope of the not-quite-White with emergent identifications across communities of color. Yet Motown was unequivocally "the real music" for Rod, and its identification as African American was part of its realness:

> Of course, at the same time, there was the Beach Boys in California. (**DW:** That's true, they were getting going.) Yeah, they were getting going, and were very popular. We would listen to them, but when we bought records, we bought Motown records. And we dressed in what, at that point, was sort of African American urban style — (**DW:** Really!) — black pointy shoes that you polished up, and I can't remember what kind of pants they called them, but they didn't have belts, they just had this band that came across and clipped. And we learned to speak our version of black dialect.

Ethnomusicologist Ingrid Monson has questioned White American appropriations of African American speech patterns, clothing, and music during the emergence of bebop in the 1940s, pushing at the limits of White hipness as incursion (1995). I write elsewhere in this book about the parallels and differences between White American and Asian American forays into African American culture, and here as in other cases they are not analogous. Rod was making choices for particular reasons, aware of other possibilities but puzzled by them. He said,

> When the Beatles came along in '64, it was like a non-event. I mean, we understood it was important — it was on *Ed Sullivan*, right? I couldn't figure out what all the deal was about, you know.

Japanese Americans and White Americans were not alone in their cross-identification with Motown. With his characteristic combination of hilarity, pathos, and anger, Chicano writer and performance artist Luis Alfaro writes about his discovery of Motown in the seventh grade and how deeply he and his brother identified with its "American" sounds and the window they provided on a certain kind of sensuous emotionality. "We got too many Marvin Gaye albums inside us," he says. "We've started talking *Soul Train* dialects ..." (Alfaro 2001: 14). He remembers a passionate summer full of "*Superfly, Shaft,* and a diet of Bruce Lee movies" (op. cit), reiterating the additional link between African Americans and *kung fu* cinema, here refracted through the experience of a young Chicano. Tellingly, he says that listening to Motown at the noon dances in the school gym was "the only time of day when I got lost in the magic of being American" (15). Yet this magic was of course a complicated construction, involving Alfaro's innocent discovery of a sensuousness that was undeniably life saving. He listens to Minnie Riperton sing "Come inside my love" and learns how the yearning for love and home is something he already understands though he is still only beginning to realize that he doesn't yet have "experience" (15):

> How come I know that feeling and I ain't even lived yet? I mean really lived. Fallen in love or kissed someone on the lips or gotten dumped or had the government repossess something of mine.

He joins a record club and gets to know one Motown artist after another, and as he listens, "I feel like I know who I am, more and more" (16). The self he discovers through the Motown Other is a self of potentiality, but as much as it is transmitted through the racialized authority of the Black voice (in all of its sensuous glory), Alfaro connects it directly to his Chicano family and roots, making a bold and essential connection between himself and the "authentic" effect of the Black voice — without simply giving himself over to ventriloquism. He sits in a Black bar in South Central Los Angeles, listening to a soul singer, and he is transported (18):

> I was taken someplace beyond Vermont Boulevard. I was back in the Central Valley with my Grandma picking grapes off the vine. I was in Tijuana feeding the pigs in the backyard. I was watching my dad play soccer. I was watching my mom curl her hair like Elizabeth Taylor in *Butterfield 8*. I was in the world of my people. A world of simple pleasure, of being poor, of downtown streetcorners. Buying pizza slices from the counter at Woolworth's on Broadway. I was sitting in the last row of the twenty-six bus running down Pico. I was free. I was a queer Mexican boy from the barrio, but I was also one of the *Soul Train* dancers.

Certainly this rhapsodic discovery of self still relies on the trope of the saving Black presence more commonly deployed in White narratives, in which Blacks become sidekicks who selflessly further the (White) protagonist's goals. Brian Currid similarly argues that house music relies on a spectacularized consumption of the Black diva, where her "natural" femininity and sexuality is used as a kind of "sonic drag" for the White queer boy or drag queen to play with embodiment and desire (Currid 1995: 186–91). Alfaro experiences all this and more: the fantasy allows him to "be" who he "is," even as he discovers the performative power of simultaneous phantasmatic identifications. Minnie Riperton's voice helps him locate a place where race, class, and sexual orientation share an interconstitutive site of emergence without forcing him to let go of the performative means of enablement. As Alfaro puts it, "Minnie Riperton saved my life" (2001: 18).

Rod was not yet identifying with his African American classmates as a person of color relating to other people of color — those locations were not consciously part of his personal landscape at that point. In his part of Pasadena, ethnicity and class intersected in provocative ways: his family's presence tipped the balance of their formerly White neighborhood and their tentative social mobility from working- to middle-class was arrested by White flight. Rod's parents, however, were still aware of their in-betweenness and their placement as non-Black; their home was *not* the place for experimentation with African American dialect, for instance. As Rod said,

> Now, when we got home, of course, that went out the window. Mom would allow us to listen to the music, but the other stuff went out the window. You know, "When you talk at home, you speak properly!"

The differences perceived by his parents were not so evident to Rod. He explains his and his Japanese American friends' adoption of African American urban style as a choice between limited options, but a choice that still felt "comfortable." His high school was about 55% white, 35% black and 10% everything else, including about 5% Asian (mainly Japanese American), but when he was channeled into the college-prep track, his classmates were suddenly far more White than Black; he remembers that he was "surrounded by White kids" in his classes but that his musical preferences, his clothing, and his speaking style were another matter, and he notes that part of his choice recognized a certain absence:

> I mean, while I was at school, I was probably shoulder to shoulder as much with Ronnie Butler and Bernard Clark as I was with Wayne Omakawa and Kenny Oda. It was just that kind of thing. And they had a version of American culture — it was Black American culture. With us, we [i.e., he and his Japanese American friends] didn't have that identifiable "something" indigenous to us that was still American. So we took what was there, I think. And it was very comfortable, and it was kind of cool, you know. I don't know. Yeah, it was a really comfortable place and time.

Indigeneity is of course one of the more vexed tropes of "the American," and Rod was clearly aware of a certain cultural production of Blackness as American — whereas Asians have been constructed as "foreign" over and over again through legislation, the construction of Blackness as peculiarly and indigenously American already cross-hatched his and his friends' experimentation with identity work.

Much later in our conversation, it came out that Rod had in fact played the clarinet all through junior high and high school, but it was clear that he didn't think of himself as a musician, nor did he consider all those years of band and orchestra as central to his musical tastes.

> I took piano lessons and I played clarinet in high school and all of that — yeah, a good Japanese American kid always took music lessons. I could play, I was in the All-City band and stuff, but I was never into it. I was *mechanically* okay, but I just ... I never felt like a player. You know, someone who could just play an instrument. (**DW:** What do you mean, just play?) I could read notes and I could mechanically reproduce the notes said I was supposed to reproduce, but I never felt — I've always been so envious of musicians who seemed to have this *thing* ... It's true I never really worked at it, because it was a duty thing — your parents make you take piano lessons. And then in school, you gotta play something, and I remember I said I wanted to play whatever, and they said, "No, you gotta play clarinet," because all these Japanese American families decided clarinet was the right thing, I don't know *why*. There were, like, eight of us who all played clarinet! in the same junior high school band! And then in orchestra too. I had one Japanese American friend who was a year older than us who played trumpet, and the rest of us played clarinet. I'm trying to think of anyone else ... I had a Filipino friend who played alto sax — Ruben could play, now that boy could play. Kenny on trumpet was pretty decent and then there was this *army* of Japanese Americans all playing clarinet, all these little black sticks, you know. And I never liked the sound of it. I would trade Kenny for his trumpet and we would play at his house, and I found it much more interesting but, "No, we bought you a clarinet, you stick with what you start with, okay?" So we played the clarinet. Like I said, I got good enough to play in the All-City band, but — I don't know — it never *took*. It was kind of fun. It was more fun kind of hanging out with the people, being a part of the group and making the music, but I never felt like a musician ... as I imagined a musician to be, and I don't know what that would be like, but I never had the opportunity to think that that was even a possibility, even as an avocation. It was what you *did*, like you did homework. It was like, you did your chemistry homework, okay, you're done with that, now you go practice your clarinet. I *hated* it.

Music-making was thus a duty, a chore, whereas Motown was a passion, pursued through the transistor radio in his room, through 45-rpm records, and concerts whenever possible.

In 1966, Rod entered UCLA and moved from Pasadena to a dormitory in Westwood, and his environment changed again. He continued to have many Japanese American friends, but he had more White classmates than African American. He got involved with the emergent Asian American Studies program, and although many of his Asian American classmates are now well known figures, his growing intellectual and political involvement didn't change his listening habits — for one thing, the Asian American music scene hadn't yet come together. Within months, his listening began to change:

> [During] my freshman year, I was still listening to a lot of Motown, especially when I went home, but at school … well, things were changing. White music was starting to sound a lot more interesting. American pop music was taking a turn. Buffalo Springfield, youthful rebellion — I started identifying more with that world. … I was with different people, and they were listening to different music.

Sitting in his office in 1999 and reflecting on these changes in his music preferences, Rod said he thought it was a combination of his environment and the nature of the music itself — he feels that the rock scene went through substantive changes in the mid to late 60s that simply made it more compelling:

> It wasn't that I wasn't listening to rhythm and blues at all, but the balance shifted: in high school, it was 70–80% R&B, 20–30% this other stuff, and it just completely reversed within four years. It wasn't as if Black musicians had gone away, but I wasn't listening to Earth, Wind, and Fire — I was listening to Cream, or to The Doors. … Part of it was company, but part of it was that the nature of the music began changing.

As an ethnomusicologist, I don't think it is ever "the music itself" that attracts or compels — music has no agency of its own, people do, and they make choices about what they like or hate; indeed, I would venture a guess that all Americans go through changes in taste during their lives, reasons that are always already politicized. Thinking about his own changes, Rod theorized taste as the interstice between a listener, a social environment, and available musics.

While immersed in the rock scene, Rod was also aware of the politics of race in music. He listened to Hendrix but knew that there were questions around the "Blackness" of his music, and he participated in his own way in the racialized discourse of roots and origins that appeared in the late 60s and early 70s:

> After they had made it, some of the [White] musicians became a lot more explicit about their connections to blues and to African

American music ... Like, Clapton would say, "I'm really a blues artist, and if I had my druthers, that's what I would always play." When I was in the masters program at Occidental College in 1971, 72, there was a station in Pasadena that broadcast out of the basement of a church and they had a program called "Blue Monday," and they played blues, and I remember sitting in my apartment studying and listening, and that's when I discovered Robert Johnson and more contemporary folks like John Lee Hooker and Daddy Oak. I went out and bought some John Lee Hooker — he had an album called *Steamed Heat* or something — and brought it home, and it was this revelation — like, "Oh my GOD, this is REALLY music!" Yeah. But what took me there wasn't rhythm and blues, it was rock n' roll! So Motown seemed *really* silly by then.

I am drawn to Rod's discovery of the blues because of its tangled identifications and the way it provides yet another perspective on how race is literally played out through music. While explaining his return to African American music but his increased distance from Motown, Rod acknowledged its route through the White American rock musicians he had grown to love. Of course, Rod is not the only American to have discovered the blues in this way in the early 1970s, but I would argue that a Japanese American's engagement with these related sounds suggests something nicely complicated about cultural ownership and appropriation. George Lipsitz has written pointedly about Eric Clapton's self-identification with Robert Johnson, suggesting that:

> Eric Clapton's construction of Robert Johnson has less to do with the blues itself than with the traditions of romanticism in Western cultures that date back to the late eighteenth century. ... While claiming a mystical connection with Robert Johnson as an individual, Clapton ignores the economic and social structures that enable him rather than an African American to make a fortune playing African American music (1998: 121–22).

Whether Rod came to and heard the blues in the "same" way that White Americans (or the British Clapton) did closes down the more interesting question of Japanese American positionality within the discourse of racial authenticity in music. The relationships between yellow, Black, and White in the U.S. have been critically examined by a few scholars (Okihiro 1994, Lipsitz 1998,Omi and Winant 1994), with general agreement that, when the chips are down, yellow can be "a shade" of Black but not of White (Okihiro 1994: 34).

As time went on, Rod became increasingly interested in jazz, first through Miles Davis's work and then in bop and fusion. He says he was drawn to its complexity, saying that a lot of it was "opaque" to him but still attractive; he remembers going to the Wherehouse with a friend, coming upon an LP of *Bitches Brew* in one of the record bins, and both of them agreeing that they'd heard it but didn't understand it. Rod connects his liking for jazz with his deepening scholarly career: as he went on to doctoral work, jazz struck him as "more interesting and challenging. By then, I was an academic, and I guess I started taking my head more seriously, thinking, "I've gotta deal with this more complex shit." " His younger brother turned him on to Chick Corea's fusion jazz, and Rod remembers his surprise in discovering that his mother liked Corea's music too:

> One time I came home and I walk into the house and I hear Chick Corea. I say, "Hi, Mom. Is Ernie home?' She says, "Nah." I said, "I didn't think so. Who's playing the music?' She said, "Oh, I am." And she looks at me, like, you numskull — "That's good music!" I thought, maybe there's a genetic thing going on here, because I never knew my mom *liked* that kind of music.

Since then, his tastes have remained much the same, though he continues to explore within jazz. Summing up his changing tastes over time, he said, "there was that shift from the time I was a kid, to the time I was an older kid, to the time I was almost an adult, to the time I was a young adult. I guess I stayed there for a long time." He still tends to return to the rock of the 70s when listening to the radio:

> But then there are days I just want to relax and not listen to music real hard. I won't listen to The Wave [laughs], which is real easy listening, but there are certain stations that play the kind of rock that I grew up with when I was a kid. There are days when I just don't want to be challenged and I just want to listen, I just want to tap my toe, so I'll listen to KLOS, to that old stuff. It's sort of comfort music. The Motown stuff I grew up with is real *nostalgic*, but ... it seems really silly. I can't relate to it much at all.

Most of us in Southern California spend a lot of time in our cars, and what you listen to on the radio as you drive is deeply personal, especially since most of us drive alone. In 1998, Rod became the associate dean of the School of Education at UCR, and his new administrative duties have been quite demanding. I asked him what radio stations he's programmed into his car radio, and it turned out that he doesn't listen to anything at all when he's in his car:

> My car radio doesn't work. My car has a radio, but it hasn't worked for several months. I don't drive long distances very often, but when I do without the radio ... Maybe it's coincidental with my work responsibilities — I have less time to think about my own

work, my own scholarship, so it's suffering. I had a two-hour drive back from LA a few weeks ago, and I thought about this one paper that I'm trying to work on the whole time and it was *wonderful* because I had two hours where no one could call me (I don't carry a cell phone or anything) and I had two hours where I could just think about this paper. [My wife] Chris says, "Well, why don't you just go have a new radio put in?' I even went down to price them … but I haven't brought myself to do it. (**DW:** Sounds like the silence is working for you right now.) Right. So when we drive to Pasadena in Chris's car, which does have a radio… Her station is always 105.1 — she's always on classical music. She's very clear in her tastes, she'll listen to jazz but her tastes are classical. But she lets me choose [when we're together in her car]. Often on weekends I'll turn on KLON — it's a jazz station out of Long Beach, 88.1, it's hard to get out here. They play jazz-blues. … That's a sweet station. Sometimes I'll listen to the University of Redlands station [which features a lot of jazz]. But if my radio were working and I was driving home and I just didn't want to think, I'd probably have it on something like KLOS, which hasn't changed since the time I was nineteen or twenty. They'll play an old Neil Young song or something, and I won't need to think.

In short, Motown is the only music that Rod has really left behind: classic rock and jazz remain his preferences, though they have different places in his life. His need for silence is evidently new and is related to his changing career, as is his occasional preference for music that won't require him to think.

Over the course of some fifty years, Rod has moved easily and fluently between African American and White American musics, and he himself identified his preferences in that way, i.e., in racialized terms. The late capitalist mass mediation of American musics has created enormous tensions between intended/imagined markets — often defined in terms of race, age, class, and gender — and the complex realities of consumption. In the 1990s, different forms of Asian American popular culture have proliferated: magazines, films, theater, dance, and music made by Asian Americans for Asian American audiences are out there, though they are far from mainstream. Obviously, Asian Americans don't *only* watch or listen to things Asian American — by any means — and what we do choose to consume opens up Randy Martin's observation that the audience listens to itself. The extent to which we find ourselves, or don't, in particular forms of popular culture, and why, is partly the question, as it just isn't an Asian American world out there, but the dialogical nature of performance works against an audience that simply seeks out mirrors of itself, i.e., a performance that either is or isn't "like" itself. Josephine Lee's arguments for Asian American spectatorship are well taken; she writes (1997: 57) that the utopian ideal "of Asian American theaters full of Asian American audiences recognizing their common authenticity and reality has never been achievable." Interrogating feminist theories of spectatorship including Jill Dolan, Laura Mulvey, and Judith Roof, Lee is ultimately dissatisfied with their fixed placement of gendered action and passivity, in which watching is necessarily incriminated as voyeurism and control; she argues that some Asian American drama actively forces "a reexamination of our own conditions of spectatorship" (51). She outlines the problematic ways that identification with an authentic Asian American experience is linked to realism, working against the differences that actually constitute Asian America. Ultimately, she calls such impulses "wishful thinking," finding that they reveal efforts "to find solidarity in shared experience and at the same time expose the tensions and contradictions in these perspectives" (60).

Listening pleasure and political placement are ultimately interconstitutive. The musical sounds that we find pleasing or rousing or relaxing are positioned within the same material and political dimensions that shape the rest of our lives, and Asian American subject formation emerges from those choices as well as from many others. I know many Asian American jazz musicians and hip-hop artists who self-consciously align themselves with those traditions as statements of solidarity with African American political concerns, but an identification with those sounds can speak to less conscious alliances, affective and beyond. Economist Jacques Attali treats all music as "noise," suggesting that music is merely social noise that has been channeled, controlled, or organized in particular ways, and always in the service of a given political economy. He writes that listening thus has strong implications — in fact, the first chapter of his book *Noise* (1985: 6) is titled "Listening." "Listening to music," he writes, "is listening to all noise, realizing that its appropriation and control is a reflection of power, that it is essentially political." Arguing that noise/music links a power center to its subjects (8), he presents the radically optimistic view that music is ultimately prophetic, that "it makes audible the new world that will gradually become visible" (11), and that musicians are thus "even when officially recognized, are dangerous, disturbing, and subversive" (ibid.). Listening therefore carries with it the potential for violence, freedom, and knowledge.

I believe that Rod's movement between musics racialized in different ways speaks to the uneasy position that Asian Americans negotiate between Blackness and Whiteness. Rod now recognizes that negotiation as political, though he didn't have that perspective as a young adult. His return to certain African American musics (e.g., the blues) as more "real" than other musics is not analogous to Eric Clapton's search for authentic African American aesthetics (cf. Lipsitz 1998) but rather tells us something more complicated about the ways that Japanese American and African American class and social mobility were outlined in Pasadena in the

1950s–60s, and the ways that this shaped Rod's political consciousness and identifications. Gary Okihiro (1994: 33) quotes Harry Kitano saying, "Scratch a Japanese American and you find a Wasp," but the upward social mobility hoped for by Rod's parents and attained by Rod through education did not assert a Wasp but rather worked in tandem with a progressive political sensibility that led him to explore Asian American Studies and, ultimately, education as a career. This particular formation of Asian American subjectivity is not split or fragmented between Whiteness and Blackness — the usual poststructuralist language — but instead was placed relationally, through listening to the sounds of Blackness and Whiteness. After all, Rod didn't have the option of resorting to authentic Asian American listening practices. I dwell instead on that moment of realization and understanding, when he reflexively thought about his listening in racialized terms and saw himself as subject to, and responding to, the conditions of his environment.

Finally, it is worth theorizing the place of friendship in this ethnography of listening. I place myself within contemporary poststructuralist ethnographic practice, where questions of subject formation have dislodged Elsewheres and Others. I could say that I "know" Rod pretty well — we have been acquainted for some three years, socializing and going to meetings together — but of course "knowing" is a tricky business. On the other hand, we know each other for particular reasons, as Asian American faculty members involved in Asian American activities on our campus: our friendship is based in certain political commitments, and the exchange discussed here is less "interview" than conversation; it grew out of previous conversations and assumes continued talk in the future.

Feminist anthropologist Ruth Behar has repositioned the "life history," consciously working against its traditional location as a genre that was not-autobiography but rather the recuperation and representation of marginalized voices — those-who-don't-write, those who must rely on someone else's pen, those "lacking access to the means of production and often even the ideological constructs necessary to turn talk into an autobiography in the first place" (1993: 272). In her book *Translated Woman,* she makes two arguments that help me situate writing about Rod. First, Behar notes that most life histories are based on a commitment to decenter expectations of whose lives are most worth knowing; second, she describes the life history as "a hybrid form that inscribes the doubled voices of a native speaker and a translator" (op. cit.). Her emphasis on translation grows out of her subject, her *comadre* Esperanza, a working-class Mexican Indian woman whose life story is the core of the book; moving *across* nation, language, class, and ethnicity is the genesis for Behar's thoughts about life histories. Sameness retreats once looked for, but the conversation between Rod and myself emerged out of things shared, in addition to differences of gender, academic status, ethnicity, and age. Elsewhere, Behar argues passionately for "vulnerable anthropology," that is, for ethnographic work that grapples with the emotional and empathetic engagements central to "knowing" people and places (1996). If I have become a bit weary of readers' easy insistence that we always "locate" ourselves within our work, and of the too-frequent practice of dispensing with this in a sentence or two, then I am also aware that my conversation with Rod could seem overly located, too enclosed. Instead, I hope it moves out from a glimpse of one man's listening practices to the continued construction of Asian American sensibilities, including the cultural work done between Asian American intellectuals. In focusing on quotidian experience through the intimate pleasures of musical sound, I hear Asian Americans doing serious identity work while getting down and rocking out.

Acknowledgments

The lion's share of thanks goes, of course, to Rodney Ogawa for his friendship and generosity in allowing me to make him into a subject. This essay was first presented at the annual meeting of the Association for Asian American Studies in Philadelphia on April 2, 1999, and I would like to thank Josephine Lee, George Uba, Neil Gotanda, and Garrett Hongo for their comments, which moved me forward. Comments from audience members in the Department of Music at the University of California, Berkeley were also a great help; I am especially grateful to Jocelyne Guilbault and Oliver Wang for their responses to my colloquium presentation there. At the University of California, Riverside, my colleagues at the Center for Ideas and Society — Hershini Bhana, Mary Gauvain, Paul Green, and Jacqueline Shea Murphy — provided spirited critique and suggestions at a late stage of writing, when such camaraderie made all the difference.

Endnotes

1. Held on February 18, 1999 in his office at UCR in the School of Education.
2. One study that stands out for its focus on fandom is Daniel Cavicchi's *Tramps Like Us: Music and Meaning Among Springsteen Fans* (1998).

12

ImprovisAsians:
Free Improvisation
as Asian American Resistance

*I mean, of course we confirm certain things by coming together and
playing, but we've been together already.*

Francis Wong

Why "Asian American Music?"

I was talking with improviser George Lewis on the telephone about his
work with the Asian American musician Miya Masaoka.[1] He said:

> I have a certain way that I know I'm going to be working with the
> material — I can just make up the material and work with it in that
> way, because I know what the processes are going to be, or I have an
> idea of certain processes that I'm interested in and that I'm going to
> work with. Part of our process was to create the material which then I
> could subject to further reflection. So that was a negotiation point,
> really, because we have these very different ways of thinking about
> structure. These kinds of negotiations go on *before* the music, but
> really they also go on *during* the music. And really, if you're trying to
> get people to learn how to listen, that's one of the things you want
> them to listen for — this negotiational thing that happens.

It is precisely "this negotiational thing" that I aim to explore here: the
overwriting of musical process and interethnic political coalition that takes
place in the free improvisation of certain Asian American and African
American performers.

This chapter explores the salient terms in my title. What Asian Americans are, or what they might be, is far from clear in the American imagination, and Asian Americans are rarely imagined as resisting. Resistance is valorized by cultural studies and is sometimes discussed as though it were the same thing everywhere, happening under the same conditions. And it is through learning about free improvisation — its terms and its conditions — that I come to a particular understanding of a particular kind of Asian American resistance. This understanding arises from my conversations with a number of Asian American improvisers as well as with two leading African American improvisers, George Lewis and Joseph Jarman. In other words, this Asian American musical response to racialized inequities emerges out of an African American/Asian American encounter, and I will ask several musicians to speak at length in this essay because it is their terms that guide me.

Locating the political in music is an ongoing problem in both music scholarship and cultural studies. Scholars in cultural studies tend to regard expressive culture as a reflection or extension of agency. As Robin Ballinger writes (1995: 21), "Part of the problem is one that habitually plagues the Left: a desire to find explicit political agendas and intellectual complexity in the art it wants to claim …" Earlier studies confined the political to protest musics or sought it only in song lyrics.[2] With consistent sophistication, Robert Walser has discussed popular musics as social practices, paying close attention to the production of musical sound and looking (as he says) "beyond the vocals" to timbre, rhythm, mode and harmony, etc., as sites where opposition and cooption are constructed (Walser 1993, 1995). Gage Averill's book, *A Day for the Hunter, A Day for the Prey,* is one of the best recent attempts to get at power relationships through music: Averill painstakingly establishes vocabulary and metaphors in such a way that he never discusses "the political" but rather Haitian epistemologies of the political, and this difference allows him to move out from what he calls a "grounded Haitian politics" to music (1997: 3). Hearing power relations in music is thus an exercise in learning how to listen, and the musicians themselves often have a lot to say about this.

Free Improvisation As Coalition Politics

Henry Louis Gates, Jr. has complained, "This is how we've been taught to do cultural politics. You find the body; then you find the culprit" (1992: 184). Taking his hint that there might be better ways to go about this, I aim to examine the politics of coalition-building in free improvisation by Asian Americans with African Americans.

Anthropologist Virginia Dominguez points out that specific cultural forms are often unproblematically identified as resistant without recourse to critique. As she puts it (1992: 25):

Many non-European countries, especially those long-subjected to direct colonial domination by colonial powers, indeed make concerted efforts to establish cultural politics that highlight and celebrate forms of creative expression thought to have been developed before the establishment of European hegemony. This is typically perceived to be a form of resistance. Yet it is arguably more a continuation of a form of European ideological hegemony more than an example of resistance.

When Asian Americans participate in African American musics, they do not simply inscribe African American histories onto Asian American bodies. Improvisational music and its performers are situated in a particular tradition of politicized music-making, and this music will say more and, indeed, mean more if its social context is understood. I return to the loosely knit circle of about eight Asian American improvisers in San Francisco's Bay Area who have produced music since the early 1980s that they identify as Asian American (introduced in Chapters 8 and 10). They founded Asian Improv aRts, a nonprofit recording label, in 1987 and produce a newsletter, *ImprovisAsians* (which I borrow for my title), that covers their activities. All of them have backgrounds in social activism and the Asian American movement, and all create music that they describe (among other things) as political. All have a base in jazz and most have moved into free improvisation, openly drawing on the model of the Association for the Advancement of Creative Musicians in Chicago. Ronald Radano has vividly described the "spirit of radicalism" that led to the formation of this Black nationalist institution in the 1960s and 70s and its members' shift from jazz to (often) atonal free improvisation. Rejecting established categories, musicians like Muhal Richard Abrams and Roscoe Mitchell referred to their work as "creative music" (Radano 1993: 104), a term consequently adopted by the Asian Improv musicians in conscious reference to the ideological model of the AACM.

Unlike the musicians of the AACM — who were dedicated to the creation of a Black nationalist aesthetic — the musicians associated with Asian Improv are not trying to create a bounded Asian American music. They are clearly committed to the idea of Asian American music, but in the end, this music always emerges relationally — either between musicians in performance, or in terms of ethnic and racial bridge building, i.e., the histories behind the bodies that produce it. Moreover, it is not so much that bridges are built but that coalitions form. Bridges and coalitions are not at all synonymous. As the historian Gary Okihiro puts it, "yellow is neither black nor white," but then again, African Americans and Asian Americans "have both been relegated to the margins of American racial politics as 'non-whites'" (1994: xi). Okihiro ultimately argues that "insofar as Asians occupy the racial margins of 'non-white' with blacks, yellow is a shade of black, and black, of yellow" (op. cit., xii). The politics of African

American/Asian American collaboration are particularly fraught in music. In his book *Global Pop,* Tim Taylor writes, "I'm not arguing for separatism or authenticity, but rather for new modes of production in collaboration" (1997: 174) that work by acknowledging power relations, not ignoring or "transcending" them. Similarly, Asian American musician Fred Ho has characterized his work as explicitly inter-ethnic in genesis and character (1995: 140):

> Up until 1986 I characterized my music as "jazz" with Asian Amer-
> ican thematic and musical references ... During many years of
> committed cultural work within the "movement," I was struggling
> with the question: what makes Chinese American music Chinese
> American? What would make for an Asian American musical con-
> tent and form that would be transformative of American music as
> well, and not simply be subsumed in one or another American
> musical genre such as "jazz." I began to embark upon a course
> which I now articulate as creating "an Afro-Asian new American
> multicultural music."

Talking about Free Improvisation: Miya Masaoka and George Lewis

The encounter between the AACM and Asian Improv is sometimes acted out quite literally: in 1996 and 1997, Asian Improv improvisers collabo-rated with two members of the AACM, George Lewis and Joseph Jarman. I would like to address the "inside" of the free improvisational process by drawing on Miya Masaoka's and George Lewis's work together and their explanations for how they interacted musically.

Miya Masaoka is a composer, performer and performance artist at the center of the Asian American creative music scene in San Francisco. Born in 1958, she came of age during the ferment of the 1970s, when her politi-cal sensibility was shaped. Trained on the Japanese *koto* (a zither), she has extended the instrument's possibilities not only through her base in jazz and new music but also through the innovative application of computer electronics. George Lewis is a composer, renowned trombone player and computer music specialist. A professor of improvisation and critical stud-ies at the University of California, San Diego, he supports a full schedule of teaching in addition to his frequent concert tours. A member of the AACM since 1971, his personal philosophies, like Masaoka's, are rooted in explicitly activist models for social change. Lewis and Masaoka have col-laborated on several projects. Lewis played in Masaoka's work, *24,000 Years is Forever, for Improvising Orchestra and Tape,* and Masaoka has performed in two versions of Lewis's *Voyager,* a "nonhierarchical, interactive musical environment featuring improvised interaction between music-generating computer programs and music-generating people" (Lewis n.d.). Their mutual interest in the interface of technology and improvisation has

The Usual Turmoil and Other Duets with
George Lewis trombone & Miya Masaoka koto

Fig. 12.1 Cover of *The Usual Turmoil and Other Duets with George Lewis (trombone) and Miya Masaoka (koto)* (Music and Arts, 1998) (CD 1023). (Reproduced with the permission of Fred Maroth and Music and Arts.)

consistently opened up new musical possibilities, and finalizing their album, *The Usual Turmoil and Other Duets with George Lewis (trombone) and Miya Masaoka (koto)* (1998) (Figure 12.1) gave me the chance to talk with them about their musical processes.

Lewis emphasizes not the sound of the music but the performers' identity, pointing to the social and political contexts that form an improviser's sensibility (n.d.):

> Working as an improviser in the field of improvised music emphasizes not only form and technique, but individual life choices, as well as cultural, ethnic and personal location. Improvisers reference a transcultural establishment of techniques, styles, aesthetic attitudes, narratives, historical antecedents and networks of cultural

Fig. 12.2 Miya Masaoka's album, *Compositions/Improvisations* (Asian Improv, 1993) (AIR 00014). (Reproduced with the permission of Asian Improv aRts.)

and social practice. ... The notion of improvised music as I have defined it recognizes personal agency and narrative, seeing social necessity and difference as crucial to music-making.

Looking for a definition of his work and Masaoka's based on musical style alone thus misses the boat.

Masaoka's solo album *Compositions/Improvisations* (Figure 12.2) was produced by Asian Improv in 1993 (AIR 00014); its title points to the creative tension between the improvisational process and Western ideas of "composition." George Lewis devotes much of his teaching, writing, and thought to this tension — indeed, he questions the entire ideology of composers and composition, proposing instead what he calls "real-time music." He suggests that the improvised music generated by some performers in real-time self-consciously reflects "Afrological" aesthetics and values whereas the tradition of composers writing music *out* of real-time is central to "Eurological" values. Lewis doesn't racialize either aesthetic sphere in a straightforward manner; he notes that not all real-time music is Afrological in framework nor do all African American composers and improvisers work strictly within Afrological frameworks. Yet many traditions of pre-composed music are, he points out, Eurological in basis (often devaluing real-time practices), whereas improvisers create works that are "performer-supplied" rather than "composer-specified" (Lewis 1996: 91). Lewis sees improvisation and composition as antithetical: valuing composition over performance (whether scripted or spontaneous) has created a social hierarchy that he regards as a recent Western construct, and he thus chooses not to subsume "improvisation" under "composition":

> You know, I had this conversation with a certain composer: he had the perfectly reasonable view that any kind of thing where you're generating music is a kind of composing, and therefore improvisation is a kind of composing. [But] the problem is not just taxonomical. When you do this, you bump up against the vernacular definition of composition, and you also bump up against the social role of composers, which has been pretty carefully put together over a really long time. So what you're doing is placing yourself under the hegemony of composers, or people who call themselves composers. And then you become this step-child — that's the way improvisation has been treated in that world. I think there's also a problem because there are issues improvisers face that composers do not face. Once you decide you don't *need* to be accepted as a composer, then you should be accepted as doing what *you* do. You should be accepted as an improviser. If I wanted to go to some artists' colony somewhere, they have lists of disciplines that are accepted, like art, composition — but they don't have 'improvisation' listed. If you want to go there as an improviser, you have to go as a composer in drag: you've got to come with scores, and you know, I think that's a waste of my time. I don't want to do this. There are processes for articulating improvisative sensibility and practice that have nothing to do with this, so I don't feel creative artists — particularly ones who have established their track record as improvisers — should have to go there through these fixed doors.

Masaoka too has addressed the challenges of improvisation, made more complicated for her by questions of intercultural musical experimentation. She has traditional training on the Japanese *koto* and in the ancient Japanese court music called *gagaku* but chooses — mindfully — to play the *koto* in nontraditional ways. This places her in a potentially difficult position *vis-à-vis* her Japanese *koto* and *gagaku* teachers as well as Western scholars who argue that imperialist gestures lie behind intercultural borrowing. Masaoka suggests that her own position as a Sansei (third-generation Japanese American) artist must be taken into central consideration and that her commitment to improvisation is not coincidental (1996):

> But for me, being of Japanese heritage and born in America, biculturalism and transcultural identity has always been a part of my existence; it is this hybridity that engenders and perhaps necessitates a new cultural expression for me.
>
> As a composer concerned with new sounds, contexts, structures and realities, I have no choice but to construct my own musical reality. In traditional Japanese music the emphasis is on refinement rather than creativity, emulation of one's teacher rather than developing a personal style. As such, traditional music represents a culture, a way of life of a collective people emanating from a particular location in history and geography. A contemporary composer, however, is required to grapple with both tradition and innovation, Western or otherwise, and the finished oeuvre is primarily that of an individual. Musical configurations using collective improvisation by the individual performers, such as I have experienced in the Cecil Taylor Orchestra and performing works of Pauline Oliveros, Christian Wolfe, and George Lewis, reduces the singular control of the composer, and relegates more responsibility — and hence individuality — to the performer.

How do improvisational musicians decide what to play from moment to moment, and how exactly do they interact with one another musically? What is spontaneous and what is prearranged? These very questions highlight how Western ideas of composition as a process *preceding* performance has shaped our very ideas of what constitutes music. Masaoka suggests that she shifts between playing "with" or "against" an improvisational partner. She says:

> Sometimes we'll start playing together and other times one person will start before the other person, and it's almost like a conversation. Like, do you want to start talking at the same time, what do you want to say, how do want to say it. You start playing and you see what comes out of the instrument, and often it's a process that's not entirely on a conscious level. You can start playing with a note, thinking about pitch, or thinking about tone, or maybe the feeling of giving something to one note, or maybe a melody that pops into your head, or motives, and developing that. Working within a particular scale or mode and developing that. Or with different timbres, and then responding to what you're hearing.

Lewis agreed with this description and takes it further:

> One of the plans is always to create a contrast. One of my princi-
> ples is that I want to have a choice between (as she says) playing
> "with" and "against." I blend in with what Miya's doing, but then
> I might pose a contrast. Inexperienced people think that structure
> in improvisation consists of call and response. In other words,
> you follow what the other person is doing. The thing is, you need
> to be able to establish a link without following totally. So you
> investigate a potential link point — a point of commonality. And
> then you investigate points of difference; then you make *that* be
> the thing that you put out into space. Once you find that, you
> have a more orchestrationally rich situation than what you would
> ordinarily have. That's what I'm trying to do — make sure that
> there's enough complexity in what you might call a vertical sense.
> That's going on pretty much all the time. Because Miya *does* that
> — I mean, she's not following you around. [*laughs*] She's very
> much establishing her own presence, which is what the really
> good people do. For the trombone there's a tradition for this kind
> of thing, but for *koto,* there isn't. She's out there in space of her
> own making. This is really what's most exciting about the whole
> thing. And of course there's no precedent for a trombone-*koto*
> duo at all.

Masaoka is indeed creating her own space through the *koto,* and she does it
by extending the very capabilities of the instrument. Whether playing the *koto*
acoustically or electronically, Masaoka constantly pushes its possibilities:

> One thing I think about when improvising is the physicality of the
> production of sound. So not only am I working on creating new
> vocabulary, often while I'm playing I'm developing a personal
> vocabulary and I'm also reinterpreting it in different ways in
> response to who I'm playing with. And that either means going
> with them or going against them, or it can create juxtapositions. So
> when I say the physicality of the production of sound, I mean
> searching for new ways that my instrument can make a sound. So
> at different times I might put a cymbal between the strings so when
> I pluck the string, it sounds the cymbal. That becomes part of the
> improvisational process.

Masaoka has had several residencies at STEIM (Studio for Electro
Instrumental Music), an electronic music studio in Holland dedicated to
live performance. Working closely with technicians, she has developed a
unique technology for her *koto* that dramatically extends its vocabulary.
The SensorLab, an analog to Midi converter made at STEIM, is a small,

custom microcomputer that converts incoming analog electrical information into a standard digital code which is then interpreted by a personal computer or by Midi devices. Masaoka also employs a sensor system combining pick-ups for the *koto* bridges, foot pedals, and ultrasound sound-rings for her hands that capture gestures of movement, transforming them into gestures of sound. She calls this new instrument "KOTO-monster," playfully and ironically acknowledging its new possibilities as well as its challenges. Masaoka notes that she doesn't think of electronic extension as a categorically different vocabulary: its production is obviously different from acoustic techniques but she prefers to move seamlessly between the two possibilities. Her aesthetic sensibilities pointed her toward a particular kind of interaction with Lewis, who plays acoustic trombone:

> I'm all plugged in, but if the other person is not using electronics, then I don't necessarily want to be *the one* with the electronics, thus setting up a really obvious dichotomy. I prefer to have things more woven in. … A lot of times I don't necessarily want to make it real obvious. There might be just an accent in electronics, and then back to acoustics. And then other times, it's all electronic.

Good improvisation is not necessarily the product of musicians in total accord. Indeed, as Derek Bailey has suggested (1980: 152), good improvisers are focused "more on means than ends." While improvisers need to have certain agreements, it is clear that the creative tensions arising from differences are just as important. Questions of vocabulary and even the length of an improvisation may point as much to differences as to agreements, and these differences can result in interesting music or in frustration for both improvisers. Learning how to play off differences is part of a good improviser's skill. Consider Masaoka's distinction between playing "with" or "against" an improvisational partner: playing "against" a partner's expression may lead to something new and interesting that then furthers the performance as a whole. Lewis and Masaoka agreed that they have different internal senses for when to end an improvisation: Masaoka tends toward shorter sessions whereas Lewis has a instinct for longer interactions. As Lewis put it:

> Miya likes to have things kind of short and really aphoristic — I think she has kind of an aphoristic style. Whereas I often like to spin the tale out for a while. One of our differences is that when she thinks that something is over, I think it's not quite over yet. That's one of the sources of creative tension — there's a real difference [between us] in what constitutes a unit of structure, if you will. My tendency is to say, Let's see, maybe we'll just turn this unit into something else, instead of just leaving it and moving on.

They agreed that this creative difference furthered their collective process. Lewis also emphasizes how an improviser's musical "vocabulary" is dynamic, emerging in relation to particular improvisational partners:

> The premise is that other people have interesting things to say, and if you listen, you'll learn a lot. That's what I like to hear in an improvisation — I want to put myself in the position of learning about other people through sound. That's more important than getting my point of view. In fact, that's the basis of the whole thing. The analytic part of the improviser is really the critical part. Like, jazz books spend most of their time telling you what licks to play. If you practice a whole bunch of licks, you get a personal vocabulary. Now, that's important — you got to have that — but you also have to have a kind of listening vocabulary. That's not just a generative vocabulary in reverse: that also involves how am I going to shape these things that I know to fit the situation — well, I've got to know what kind of situation I'm *in*. You're going to hear what people think about their environment by what they *play*. You've got to be sensitive to that. So if all that's happening, then I tend to enjoy it.

Finally, it is worth noting that free improvisers may be pleased with their performances, but such performances are essentially a by-product of process — and this is really the heart of the matter. As Derek Bailey writes (1980: 150),

> [W]hether a finished piece can on examination be considered a good piece of music in any terms is not the prime aim of free improvisation. It is, of course, a consideration, but more important as an objective is the promotion of the improvisation, the raising of the improvisation to a level where all the players are involved equally and inextricably in the music-making act. And the achievement of this experience is always seen as a liberation.

The process of free improvisation thus joins the political and the personal. I spoke at length with Glenn Horiuchi, Francis Wong, and Joseph Jarman (Figure 12.3) about an improvised performance that they released as an album,[3] asking each of them to talk about their encounter. Horiuchi and Wong have played together extensively, but performing with AACM member Jarman in 1996 at the Asian American Jazz Festival in San Francisco was an important experience for both, as their improvisative sensibility was formed by their understanding of the AACM's ideology and years of listening to the music of the Art Ensemble of Chicago and other AACM members. Horiuchi and Wong had much to say about how this influence is manifested in their music and in their musical politics. In a conversation, Francis Wong explained it like this:

Fig. 12.3 Cover of *Pachinko Dream Track 10.* Album of free improvisation by Glenn Horiuchi, Francis Wong, and Joseph Jarman (Music and Arts, 1999) (CD 1040). (Reproduced with the permission of Fred Maroth and Music and Arts.)

[T]he whole thing about self-determination, and creating your own organization, has been really important to me. The members of the AACM had their thing about great black music, ancient to the future, you know. That allowed us a way to look at our heritage and see the continuum. So [the members of the AACM] had a very important influence [on us] in aesthetic as well as political ideas in terms of what we need to do to realize our vision and not necessarily to rely on others to make it happen for us — we can make it happen ourselves. Their ability to navigate through a lot of the modernist and postmodernist terrain of the last period and to be able to do that while maintaining a sense of identity… Well, that became a role model because that's what we're trying to do. We're trying to follow in their footsteps in terms of navigating through that whole postmodern thing.

I also wanted to know what Jarman thought, so I asked him about the experience of improvising with Horiuchi and Wong. His involvement with Buddhism is quite evident in his response:[4]

> **DW**: Can you say anything about the actual musical interaction between [the three of] you? I know this is something that's really hard to talk about but, you know — the actual give and take in the improvisational process. I gather that it's very different with different people.

> **Joseph Jarman**: Yeah. But when it just becomes one mind, it's like a collective, you know? If you give up your egotistical booboo and allow your energies to merge into the pool of the collective, that's how it works. I mean, it's just a "giving-up." And you know from your own experience — if you have something going with someone, then some little misunderstanding comes up and you try to resolve it, and if you can't it just gets more and more painful, and then you figure out how to resolve it and everybody's happy. So with the music it's the same way: in case something *does* come up, you still have to be able to give instead of demanding, you know? You have to give — you have to give up. [The Asian Improv musicians] all practiced humility and compassion. And that's how the music works. They're not interested in fighting. Nor am I. And a lot of people are. You can just walk down the street and you can see 'em. You can feel that in their aura and in their tempers.

> **DW**: Well, I'm sure you've played with lots of musicians who are not thinking about collaboration and humility and all that good stuff.

> **JJ**: Oh yes.

> **DW**: So is it different, or even challenging, to play with folks who are like-minded?

> **JJ**: Yeah, it's challenging in different ways in that you have to really, really do the whole thing, because they're really, really doing the whole thing. With people who aren't doing the whole thing then you can cheat and not do the whole thing.

> **DW**: What's the whole thing?

JJ: That's the undescribable thing. [*sic*]

DW: Oh, goodness.

JJ: That's the thing that I mean about giving up completely — you must become them and they must become you. Psychically. So that the vibrations and the energy of the sound can merge without conflict.

My argument — based on the musicians' — is that this music is a model for social process. Considering cross-cultural collaborations in world music, Tim Taylor suggests (1997: 204),

> Just as subordinate groups in U.S. culture have always done more than the dominant groups to make radical positions available through new sounds, new forms, new styles, it looks as though it is the subordinate groups around the world who are doing the same, perhaps even showing us how to get along on this planet.

To that end, I would now like to turn to a discussion of a particular improvisation performed on February 13th, 1998, by Glenn Horiuchi and Francis Wong.

We're All Waiting for the Resolution

Glenn Horiuchi (1955-2000) was a Sansei pianist and, in the latter years of his life, a *shamisen* player (Figure 12.4 and Figure 12.5). He and other members of his family were very active in the reparations movement, as nearly all his relatives in his parents' generation were interned during World War II. Horiuchi recorded extensively; in the last years of his life, he turned away from the piano and composition and devoted himself to learning the traditional *shamisen,* which he used in free improvisation. Francis Wong is a second-generation Chinese American saxophone, flute, and *erhu* player; he cites Coltrane as a major influence on his playing. He has recorded extensively as a sideman and has two albums out as a leader. The two were close in age and worked together for over ten years. I asked them to give a lecture-demonstration on Asian American music in one of the large undergraduate world music courses at UC Riverside, and I would like to turn here to one of several improvisations they performed during that class.

Turning to their five-minute improvisation is a problematic move, for improvisation inherently defies traditional analytical methods. Its real-time nature denies the very possibility of music analysis despite the fact that any improvised performance can be pinned down and fixed through recording technology. Unlike ethnomusicology or (more lately) musicology, music theory and analysis as a field is not generally marked by reflexivity or a

Fig. 12.4 Glenn Horiuchi playing *shamisen*, 1996. (Photograph by Deborah Wong.)

Fig. 12.5 Glenn Horiuchi with his *shamisen* teacher, his aunt Lillian Nakano, during a *nagauta* lesson at her home in Gardena, California, 1996. (Photograph by Deborah Wong.)

questioning of its own terms. Indeed, this is a move that I rarely make in my own work — to turn exclusively to the examination and explication of a "piece" of music. I have never worked in a musical tradition that objectifies "the music" in any way and have avoided the problem of analysis by relying on emic explanations and casting myself as the interpreter of *that* rather than "the music." As Kofi Agawu has outlined in an article titled "Analyzing Music under the New Musicological Regime," formalism — and with it music analysis — came under attack by relativists in the 1980s and has never quite gotten out from under it. He points out that the new musicology is profoundly anti-formalist (1997: 301):

> Since analysis is associated with formalism, and since the new musicology is, among other things, an anti-formalist movement, and since the discipline of theory is constituted in large measure by practicing analysts, it would seem that the aims of theory and the new musicology are fundamentally incompatible. Is there any way in which music theory can embrace the positive tenets of the new musicology and still give due attention to what Adorno called the "technical structure" of musical works, not as an end but as a means to an end?

Agawu ends up doing little more than lambasting new musicologists' attempts to rework analysis, noting that they "often fall back on conventional methods" (302). He further argues that "To object to theory-based analysis as a self-fulfilling and self-referential exercise is to pretend that tautology and circularity are ever avoidable in the criticism of art — they are not" (304). Although I am not sure which aspects of criticism he finds tautological, I would recast his argument and suggest that the "circularity" of any interpretive system was better described by Clifford Geertz in his famous observation that "Art and the equipment to grasp it are made in the same shop" (1983: 118). In other words, the point is to see how epistemologies are played out at any number of different levels and to see on what terms they are complete or incomplete. One can only do this in terms of particular subjectivities, not through generalized analysis. I offer a reading of an improvisation by Wong and Horiuchi as heard through my experience and admiration; I don't describe "the improvisation" but rather put forward what I heard and — importantly — what I understood the sounds to mean.[5] The first person is very much behind this reading: as Philip Brett has written, "All this can only be done when one has learned to say 'I' rather than 'we' or 'it'" (1997).

In class, Francis had been talking for a few minutes about how improvisation is a way for musicians to "tell their stories" when he nodded Glenn toward the piano. As Glenn got up and went over to it, Francis said, "Because it's not just about playing these melodies or these instruments. We're contributing to the society right now. We have an *opinion* about the society right now, and what the society stands for, where we're going, and how we're going to participate." As he uttered the last few words, Glenn began to noodle around on the keyboard as if he was just getting a feel for the instrument's touch (Audio Example 12.1). At the time, I didn't notice that a broken phrase — the beginning of "The Star Spangled Banner" — emerged but was cut off by a brusque phrase; I only noticed this later, watching a videotape of the class. Francis started playing "The Star Spangled Banner" rather loudly. The high note at the end of the first phrase was rude, overblown — a first indication that something besides patriotism was being expressed. The timbral effect of the saxophone's high register *in extremis* was the first hint of critique. Francis continued into the next phrase while Glenn rumbled around in the lower register of the piano, and Francis then broke off into chromatic runs that tumbled straight into, once again, the opening phrase of "The Star Spangled Banner," but even more rudely than before. Glenn started to alternate aggressive left and right hand chords on the piano, so assertively that he was driven to his feet for a moment. "O'er the ramparts we sailed" emerged out of this forest of jagged, furious chords but was quickly absorbed into something else. On top of this, Francis spun into ascending and descending runs; at the bottom of one run, he slipped up a step and then stayed there. The sustained pitch was a sudden surprise after so much movement, and the surprise shifted into a different surprise as I suddenly realized that he was starting to play another piece, "Lift Every

Voice and Sing." This was the first moment of doubled-up listening: you thought you were hearing one thing but then it became something else, and for a split second you were in both places at once, and you knew it. And it felt good; it was pleasurable.

Francis played the first few lines of "Lift Every Voice" fairly straight as Glenn continued to dash around on the keyboard. By the time Francis was into the fourth line, Glenn had joined him, playing beautiful gospel tremolos underneath. But instead of playing the cadence, Francis began to play the Chinese national anthem. After the 6/8 of "Lift Every Voice," the anthem sounded a bit ponderous and four-square, and Francis emphasized this heavy-footed quality. The first phrase ended lugubriously, but Francis immediately dashed off into emphatic licks that eventually became the Chinese national anthem again — which, again, he pushed into chromatic runs that become increasingly strangled and punctuated with high-register squawks. Francis then began to play the anthem softly and lyrically; after a line, Glenn once again joined him with big octave tremolos and they ended together, with Francis holding the last note just long enough to create anticipation ... and then swung into "Great Wall" with a sassy little bounce. Glenn kept up the tremolos but gave them a rhythmic little punch and his left foot began to pump, keeping time. Just at the point where I was caught up in the pulse, the beat, the groove, Francis sank back into rubato and pulled them both down to a halt. Glenn stopped playing. Out of nowhere, Francis carefully, deliberately played a rising fourth and sustained the second, higher pitch, strikingly exposed without the piano. He went on and suddenly the melody was recognizable as "Amazing Grace." After five long seconds, Glenn came in with thoughtful running passages parallel to Francis's line. By the time they got to "That saved a wretch like me," Glenn was into his tremolo gospel accompaniment again, striding through the sustained notes. It was a straight rendition yet still moving. When Francis played through "I once was lost," he was overcome: he squeezed out the high note at the top of the line and unexpectedly landed a 5th higher than it should have been, head thrown back and sax pointed at the ceiling. As he came down again, had it now become "The Star Spangled Banner?" I wasn't sure. He sat on a long unresolved pitch and slowly faded out on it.

A heartbeat. Then Glenn started throwing little pointillist chromatic phrases around the keyboard and after a moment, Francis started playing a blues with lots of scooping up into each note: "God Bless the Child." He played it rather straight, though Glenn didn't — Glenn was all over the place, and the difference between the two parts was a little disturbing. But then Billie Holiday suddenly slid into "Oh, say does that star-spangled banner ..." Just as I realized it had changed again, Francis started to belt: each note seemed to come from his gut, each more emphatic and more distressed. Or was the distress located in Glenn's pounded tone clusters? Francis stomped into "O'er the land of ..." but he slapped "of" down into the bottom range of the sax, stayed there growling for a moment, and then ascended into "and the home of the …." And stopped. Glenn pounded out chromatic scales all the way up the keyboard and then all the way back down. And stopped. An infinitesimal pause, and then they both relaxed, off-hand. Glenn stood up and Francis slouched. The students laughed and then applauded.

Francis refers to this improvisation as "an anthem" even though not all of the chosen songs are technically anthems. At the very least, it is an ongoing improvisatory attempt to suggest that the Emperor isn't wearing any clothes. As Francis says, "We're all waiting for the final cadence," for resolution. Playing "Lift Every Voice and Sing" pays tribute to African American activism even as it becomes a gesture of solidarity. "God Bless the Child" makes a point about self-determination: God bless the child that's got his own. The Chinese national anthem is as much about the fact that Francis isn't Chinese as "Great Wall" is about being Chinese American: many Chinese Americans learn "Great Wall" in Saturday morning Chinese school as children.

Francis told me that he has been experimenting with improvised anthems since 1994, and his chosen repertoire has changed. He first played with the idea in the context of Glenn's work, *Poston Sonata*, a four-movement composition/improvisation about the Japanese American internment camp in Arizona. Francis's solo at the end of the second movement was completely open, and he began to juxtapose "The Star Spangled Banner" with "Take Me Out to the Ball Game," pointing to the irony of baseball's popularity in the internment camps. In later performances, he began to throw in "America the Beautiful" and the big band tune, "Don't Fence Me In," which was played by some Japanese American swing bands in the camps as protest. Later still, he added Malcolm X's favorite song, "You Don't Know What Love Is," as a tribute to African American self-determination. Finding that some audiences didn't make the connection, he began substituting "Lift Every Voice and Sing"; he felt that "You Don't Know What Love Is" was "more human," but that "Lift Every Voice and Sing" was more certain to be "read" correctly by multiethnic audiences. Both songs, as he puts it, are "a reverence and reference to African American leadership."[6] He said that the point is "an identification with those struggles, and then trying to bring that identification to audiences." He explained that any improvisation on these anthems is:

> an interpretation of America. … It's like trying to understand America: there are different histories of change and struggle, and we're making a music that expresses and mediates it at the same time. … Any anthem is about having a mission, about bringing people together.

But of course it is not enough to only consider what the performers feel they are doing. *How* they are heard and by whom is equally important and much harder to get at; reception is still one of the black holes of scholarship on performance. To get at how Glenn and Francis are heard, we would need to look at everyone who ever attended one of their concerts or public appearances as well as at everyone who has bought or listened to one of their albums. In other words, their audiences are far-flung, and the fact that they record on independent labels means that their sales aren't "tracked." Still, it matters how they are heard, so I distributed a questionnaire to the undergraduates in the music class at UCR with four questions, none particularly original:

1. Describe your ethnic background.
2. Did you like the music performed by Francis Wong and Glenn Horiuchi? (yes/no)
3. If yes, why? If no, why not?
4. Think back to the anthem that Francis and Glenn improvised, drawing on "The Star Spangled Banner," "God Bless the Child," the Chinese national anthem, etc. How did this piece make you feel? (Just list some words.)

I got back thirty-nine questionnaires from 14 Asian and Asian American students, eight students of European descent who were mostly ethnic mixtures ("Scottish, English, Welch [sic], French, Dutch, German," "Caucasian American," "German-Scot," "European-American), six Latino/Hispanic students ("Mexican/Brazilian," "Mexican-American," "Latin American"), five multiracial students ("Spanish and Irish," "African-West Indian," "Filipino/White," etc.),[7] three students of African descent ("African American," "Jamaican," and "Black"), one Native American, one Iranian (Persian), and one self-identified "Human."

Their responses deserve a paper in itself, but I was especially struck by the small number of "no" answers to my question asking whether they liked Wong's and Horiuchi's music. Only six students wrote that they didn't like it: two students of European descent, the self-professed "Human," one "Jamaican," the single Native American student, and one multiracial student, who transgressively created a third box (beyond "yes" and "no") labeled "some of it," which s/he checked off. The Native American student honestly wrote that s/he didn't like "New York jazz," only Dixieland, but then went on to write that it made him/her feel "upset, pissed off, as if they were disrespectful, yet [I] understood very well where they were coming from." A student of German-Scot descent wrote, "It was too PC — it was not made for the sake of the music." A European-American student went so far as to write on the back of the questionnaire, complaining, "People tend to assume that because they write, etc., about events of great significance that their works are consequently of great significance as well." The "Human" wrote that it "sounded like a woodpecker mating call" and that s/he "liked the parts I recognized, which was about 3 seconds out of the piece," raising questions about the aesthetics of non-recognition:

this student apparently felt irritated and possibly shut out, leading me to wonder which came first, the primary identification as Human or the inability to understand?

I am particularly interested in how the students of Asian descent said they heard this music. All fourteen of them checked off "yes" and had a lot to say about how and why the music spoke to them. Many of them noted that the music confused yet also moved them. A Filipino student said that the music made him/her feel "uneasy at times, but [I] was amused by the bringing together of all the anthems." Three other Filipino students said, respectively, that s/he liked it but "their improvisational piece was very confusing and sounded more like disorganized noise than music," that it was "intense, makes you want to cringe," and that it made him/her feel "lost, jumbled." A student of Japanese descent wrote, "At first, I felt they were messing around, but after I heard their philosophy, I totally understood what they did and why they did it that way." A Japanese American student said, "My family lived in an internment camp, so I related to a lot of Horiuchi's ideas for songs," and indicated that the music made him feel "energized, confused, unresolved, I loved it!"

Students from very different ethnic backgrounds experienced confusion while listening and they were honest about it: words like "tense," "overwhelmed," "frustrated," and "disturbed" appeared more than once, and "confused" many times. I would venture to say that this confusion was felt and experienced differently by different students. For the Asian and Asian American students who answered my questions, this confusion was stirring; for some students from non-Asian backgrounds, it was irritating. In many ways, I suspect this is a microcosmic glimpse of identity politics at the undergraduate ground level.

Conclusions

Kofi Agawu closes his essay by "demanding" that new musicologists fashion a "new and improved approach to analysis" that solves all the problems they have identified (1997: 307). I would argue that my description and analysis don't solve *all* those problems but is a step in that direction, prompted by the nature of the musical product itself. By moving away from prescriptive records (i.e., scores), improvisers create extended real-time moments that probably shouldn't be subjected to the kinds of analysis dependent on fixed objects that can be examined and re-examined. My attempt to do a blow-by-blow reading and to work out from it to social considerations is thus hopelessly synchronic at one level and inappropriate on another — i.e., according to the terms of real-time music production. On the other hand, my analysis is "about" more than the sounds: I am trying to locate the production of a listenership. I consider the generated sounds and their relationships, plus what the improvisers said about all that, plus how some members of their audience said they reacted, and all this, together, begins to construct the kind of analysis that Agawu contends has not yet happened. Nor do I think my "analysis" — or rather, what I would call interpretation — is utterly new. Any number of ethnomusicologists and new musicologists do this kind of interpretive work. It only suggests that we need to let go of the idea of music analysis itself as it begs the very question of the music object in isolation. Notice, for instance, that I couldn't talk about "the piano part" in the description above: Glenn's playing and the piano part were inseparable, and I *had* to locate the sounds as *Glenn*, not as "the piano."

Nor can we simply assume that "Lift Every Voice" is "political": we cannot essentialize the formation of the political in songs any more than we can in people. What matters is how Francis and Glenn conceive of it as political and whether any listeners hear it in a similar way. Their rendition of "The Star Spangled Banner" is not equivalent to Jimi Hendrix's (though it may be homage) any more than it is to Roseanne's rendition with crotch-grabbing. (Francis himself alludes to the song's cultural transformations in pointing out its origins as a British drinking song.) Resistance is not the same thing everywhere: Hendrix's incursions into rock carry a family resemblance to Asian American incursions into jazz and free improvisation, but crossing musical color lines is always closely situated in time and place. And we have to take Francis's final point seriously:[8]

> In a lot of ways, Glenn and I don't play music anymore. In a sense. We're just telling our stories, you know. It's not like playing pieces. We play ourselves.

This chapter is an attempt to take the materiality of improvisational sound production seriously and to consider not "the politics of music" but rather music *as* politics — and to thus carry forward the ethnomusicological project of showing how the music is always more than just the notes. Henry Louis Gates, Jr. has criticized "the cunning trap that practically guarantees that the marginalized cultures [glorified by the left] will remain marginalized" (1992: 184). The free improvisations by these musicians are one response to that cunning trap. The politics of ethnic minority coalition building are never simple and always emerge from specific need; they are constructive at a basic level. As Yen Le Espiritu has written, "This task of bridging reminds us that ethnicization — the process of boundary construction — is not only reactive, a response to pressures from the external environment, but also creative, a product of internally generated dynamics" (1992: 176). The improvised sounds by these Asian American and African American musicians are doing cultural work of the most difficult sort; they are as confusing and as full of promise as we are able to hear them.

Acknowledgments

Versions of this chapter were presented in colloquium series at UCLA, Brown University, SUNY Stony Brook and Rutgers University during March and April 1998. My thanks to all the students and faculty members who offered comments and suggestions, and especially to Susan McClary and Rob Walser for their suggestion that I explore the idea of doing a "reading" of Wong's and Horiuchi's improvisation. I am especially grateful to George Lewis, Francis Wong, Glenn Horiuchi, Miya Masaoka, and Joseph Jarman for their time and trouble in helping me to understand their work.

Endnotes

1. Telephone interview with George Lewis, 17 December 1997 about *The Usual Turmoil and Other Duets with George Lewis (trombone) and Miya Masaoka (koto)*, an album of free improvisation. Music and Arts CD 1023 (1998).
2. Cf. Sheila Whiteley (1992: 2), who considers that "the *meaning* in [rock] music ... was not simply tied to the lyrics, but spilled over into the sound itself" in progressive or counter-cultural rock in the 1960s–70s.
3. *Pachinko Dream Track 10*, an album of free improvisation by Glenn Horiuchi, Francis Wong, and Joseph Jarman. Music and Arts CD 1040 (1999).
4. Telephone interview with Joseph Jarman, January 8, 1998.
5. My thanks to Susan McClary for articulating this and encouraging me to move away from a "description" of the improvisation.
6. Telephone interview, 21 March 1998.
7. The attention to ethnic/national affiliation by this group of students as well as by the large number of self-identified multiracial students may have been partly the result of my lecture in this class, in which I addressed my multiracial background and my self-identification as Asian American.
8. Telephone interview, 21 March 1998.

13
Ethnography, Ethnomusicology, and Post-White Theory

For in America, cultural radicalism is not so much a question of the controversial content expressed in art forms, as it is a question of what methods of social change are necessary to achieve freedom of expression within a national culture whose aesthetic has been cultivated by a single, dominant, ethnic group.

— Harold Cruse (1967: 464)

What we need are perspectives that situate an isolated speech or performance by a black public intellectual within a larger context: progressive black figures' lack of access to mainstream media and political institutions — and, ultimately, the relative inability of these intellectuals to effect political change.

— Michael Hanchard (1996b)

Cultural Politics and Theory: Locating Public Intellectuals

As Philip Brett has pointed out, music has always been political — it is only particular scholarly practices that separate music from culture and politics (Brett 2000: 421). "Cultural" politics are different from politics plain and simple: the politics of culture point to fundamental matters of values and belief, and — importantly — to issues of control over the expression and formation of culture itself. I hold that some theoretical approaches are far more useful than others if we want to take a serious look at how particular musicians *wield* cultural politics in mindful and constructive ways. In other words, cultural politics surround, shape, and

299

emerge from musicians' activities, but that's not all of it. I am especially concerned with the intersection of theory and the politics of race. Post-modernist and poststructuralist theory may help locate cultural politics and cultural critique, but I am not convinced that they enable social change or provide tools for social action. Certain constructs have consistently emphasized the connection between theory and social *praxis* while others haven't. Accordingly, I consider "high" theory a social construct. I don't argue that all high theory is White and apolitical, but I believe there is a color line in twentieth-century high theory that isn't difficult to identify. Its foundation lies in different models of social responsibility, and locating its reality for certain musicians has essentially changed how I am able to think of them.

Indeed, ethnomusicologists still don't quite know how to position the people whose musical experiences they address. While we tend to avoid the overtly positivist frame of the "informant," the colonial history of the fieldwork paradigm still weighs heavy. Whether we insist there is no they there by recasting these musicians as teachers, colleagues, partners, or friends,[1] the nature of the knowledge gained and the manner of its getting remains largely unaddressed, though more and more ethnomusicologists wrestle with the possibility of dialectical relationships with their informants (Feld 1990; Rice 1997). Questions of knowledge and knowing loom large, but the micro- (let alone macro-) politics of the role of the musicianly expert in an ethnographer's experience remains uncomfortably untheorized. We celebrate our informants' knowledge, we thank them in our acknowledgments, we protect their identities when necessary, we pay them for their time and efforts. William Noll speaks disparagingly of "the culture member formula," i.e., the belief that authoritative understanding can only emerge from the lifetime experience of a culture member (1997: 164). He argues (ibid.) that:

> At its worst, the "culture member formula" is a search for an ultimate answer, a final fieldwork choice in the form of special partners who are above critical consideration, an attempt to find people whose backgrounds ostensibly make them suitable candidates for producing a magic formula that everyone else can plug into with impunity.

Noll's efforts to literally level the field thus allows him to consider a wider array of informants, including other ethnographers (past and present) as well as performers. In his effort not to valorize certain cultural experts, he invests the ethnographer anew with the interpretive authority to range freely between sources of cultural knowledge.[2] Where this leaves musicians and musicians' knowledge is another question. For many musicians, "knowing" music is not an end in itself but is rather the lens through which cultural politics impacts their lives and worldview. In other words, the play of power and control not only moves through their daily lives but through their musical activities as well.

Whether postmodernist theory disables the possibility of political mobilization has disturbed many writers, including Christopher Norris. A literary critic at the University of Wales, Norris almost certainly wrote *Uncritical Theory* in a state of high indignation. Composed in response to Baudrillard's essay on the Gulf War, the book is an impassioned argument against the unmoored realities he sees proposed by postmodernist thought. Norris argues that postmodernist theory is little more than apolitical skepticism "pushed to the point where it becomes just a pretext for strategies of moral and political evasion" (Norris 1992: 86). According to Norris, Baudrillard's essay, published in *The Guardian* in 1991, focused on the Gulf War as a "mass-media simulation" (ibid., 11), is an extreme example of a war of words. Norris consistently oversimplifies Baudrillard's argument into a ridiculous denial of real war and real death in order to make his main point, that postmodernist thought is "the giddy extreme of a fashionable *doxa*" — "a position that negates the difference between truth and the currency of consensus belief" (ibid., 184). Norris insists that "theory has *consequences* in the strong sense of the term" (ibid.), that is, real-world consequences handled irresponsibly, as he sees it, by Baudrillard and other "disciples of French intellectual fashion" (ibid., 11).

Norris's polemic is an admittedly extreme stance toward postmodernist theory, but his position that theory has a responsibility toward material politics has points of contact with less dismissive scholars. Some African American intellectuals have also questioned the implications of postmodernist theory. African American commentator Adolph Reed has, like Norris, wondered whether the assumption that discourse is all may deflect sustained analysis away from matters of institutional power. Similarly, Lewis Gordon complains that "The collapse of theorizing practice into *theory as practice* has provided some contemporary intellectuals with an imaginary access to political achievement" (James 1997: xv).

Considering the cultural and economic politics of the world music industry, Timothy Taylor questions why certain musicians are characterized as hybrid postmodern agents whereas western musicians who collaborate with musics from other parts of the world are simply described as rock musicians. Taylor describes a "voracious aesthetic" that permits authentic borrowings in some directions but not others. He suggests that "postmodernism-as-style" is a problematic political construct that assumes the ability of a professional-managerial class to consume Third World sounds. Taylor is especially critical of the effects of postmodern theory on political change, objecting to the postmodern removal of agency from subalterns and the negation of "metanarratives of progressive political change" (Taylor 1997: 204).

Cornel West focuses like Taylor on the postmodern restructuring of the international capitalist order. He suggests that Black intellectuals face the particular crisis of trying to "keep the notion of being a political intellectual alive in a world of shrinking options and alternatives for leftists" (1992: 689), options narrowed by a global capitalism that creates (and is maintained by) an expanding professional managerial strata which includes the academy and thus threatens to engulf Black academic public intellectuals (ibid., 690). West looks at the compromised circumstances that the academy presents to African American intellectuals and questions the political conditions of its placement in a postmodern economy.

"Public intellectuals," "popular intellectuals," "praxis intellectuals," and so-called "political intellectuals" are (in some ways) all the same person. Not simply "intellectuals," they are literally marked categories that set them off from the unmarked category. As is true of all marked categories, "intellectuals" *without* a qualifying adjective speak from a position of power, privilege, and influence, whereas all others speak contestatory languages. I suggest that the presence of adjectival intellectuals tells us something interesting about the politics of knowledge. They point to its racialization and control as well as to the Whiteness of the high theories that shape nearly everything we are able to talk about in the academy, including music and performance. Certainly there are intellectuals of color who write high theory, but I am concerned with the implications of racialized theory for musicology and ethnomusicology.

I come to a consideration of intellectuals in an attempt to reframe how I might write about the Asian American jazz musicians in the San Francisco bay area. How I address their work (and my interactions with them) is challenging because these musicians are sophisticated self-producers: they are keenly aware that self-representation is crucial for any Asian American, so my attempts to write about them necessitates a kind of double awareness. If I write about them, I must acknowledge and indeed employ their chosen self-representations, and this in turn shapes their place in my writing as subjects *and* informants. Yet a basic shift in thinking has kept me from losing myself in considerations of *how* to write about what I want to write about. By regarding these Asian American musicians as public intellectuals, I am able to join in their conversations, of which this essay is then a part.

Henry Giroux has written that "While there has been a great deal of work published recently about public intellectuals, there has been very little work focusing on how public intellectuals themselves engage in a dialogue about their own social formation, pedagogical practices, and self-critical writing"' (1995: 196). I am fortunate to have been able to listen in on the Asian Improv musicians' dialogues about their own activities. Some of these conversations have been informal, between them and myself. Others have been more public, as they are acutely aware of the importance of public discussion as well as public performance. I believe that their *very* public argument with the organizers of the San Francisco Jazz Festival illuminates cultural politics at the level of making — in a moment of exchange which, though contentious, led to other possibilities. As Edward Said has written, not enough attention has been paid to "the image, the signature, the actual intervention and performance" of the intellectual (1994: 13). As an ethnographer, I think it best to focus on particular people at particular moments,[3] and I therefore consider one event that took place on Sunday afternoon, October 20, 1996 in Oakland, California's Chinatown.

The huge literature on intellectuals emphasizes two issues: the relationship of intellectuals to a public, and the relationship between intellectual activity and practice — that is, to social action. Long-standing African American traditions of intellectualism have two consistent characteristics. First, it is generally agreed that cultural work, whether creative, religious, or political, should somehow help the African American community in its long-term project to gain equal access to cultural resources. Second, it is generally recognized that writing is not the only site of intellectual work, i.e., *praxis* (whether music-making, preaching, or community organizing) is inherently intellectual.[4]

The nature of the public intellectual is worth exploring in some detail. Edward Said writes, "The central fact for me is, I think, that the intellectual is an individual endowed with a faculty for representing, embodying, articulating a message, a view, an attitude, philosophy or opinion to, as well as for, a public" (1994: 11). He asserts that "There is no such thing as a private intellectual, since the moment you set down words and publish them you have entered the public world. Nor is there *only* a public intellectual, someone who exists just as a figurehead or spokesperson or symbol of a cause, movement, or position" (1994: 12). I must take issue with one of Said's assumptions, as they are fundamentally different from those of many public intellectuals of color. Said believes that the intellectual automatically enters the realm of the public at the moment of reception. To Said's mind, publication = accessing the public, and this movement is described as unidirectional, i.e., the intellectual brings his/her "words" to "the public."

Traditions of intellectualism with a basis in social responsibility are culturally constructed: American public intellectuals have frequently come from ethnic minority groups, notably Jewish Americans and African Americans. During the past decade, African American public intellectuals have attracted quite a bit of attention, not least because certain academic superstars like Henry Louis Gates, Jr. and Cornel West have helped change the shape of American education. The African American tradition of the public intellectual has a much longer history than many realize, yet it has consistently emphasized agendas for social change through action and responsibility. The fundamental connection between a public intellectual and a community is the nexus that generates thought-as-action.

Still, a certain cynicism has greeted the phenomenon of the African American academic "star." Michael Hanchard suggests that the very ways in which we are *able* to talk about Black public intellectuals are "impoverished" (1996b). He notes that White leftist analysis of Black intellectualism has often treated "racial oppression as mere flotsam on capitalism's undulating surface" (ibid.) without recognizing the structural relationship between political action, social responsibility, and intellectual thought in Black traditions. Black public intellectuals walk a delicate line between being seen as "atomized 'sell-outs'" by members of their communities and as "spokespersons for the race" who interpret their communities for White audiences (ibid.).[5] If African American intellectuals are held in somewhat clumsy regard by some White liberal intellectuals, their reception in African American communities is even more complex. Joy James refers to the "precarious rootedness" of African American intellectuals in their communities (1997: 191). The entire question of who their "public" *is* looms large. African American public intellectuals who choose the academy as their environment can face suspicion and skepticism from their own communities. Again, Michael Hanchard puts it well (1996a: 101):

> [I]ntellectuals belonging to marginalized ethnic or racial groups must travel some distance from them to make their concerns "public." This, in turn, may place them at a distance from the people they claim to represent or at least identify themselves with.

Parallel to questions of audience and reception, the systemic disempowerment of Black public intellectuals is an on-going issue. Thirty years ago, in his now-classic *The Crisis of the Negro Intellectual,* Harold Cruse wrote (1967: 475),

> Even at this advanced stage in Negro history, the Negro intellectual is a retarded child whose thinking processes are still geared to piddling intellectual civil writism and racial integrationism. This is all he knows. In the meantime, he plays second and third fiddle to white intellectuals in all the establishments — Left, Center, and Right. The white intellectuals in these establishments do not recognize the Negro intellectual as a man who can speak both for himself and for the best interests of the nation, but only as someone who must be spoken for and on behalf of.

Looking even more broadly at the social location of African American intellectuals, Michael Hanchard points out that the most significant figures (e.g., Malcolm X, Muhammad Ali, and Martin Luther King, Jr.) never held elected public office, i.e., they spoke from "the interstices of civic life" (1996a: 95). Not only socially marginalized, African American intellectuals were politically marginalized as well; as Hanchard says, "The sanctions imposed on these figures pinpoint the coordinates at which public discourse and state power meet" (ibid.).

Many intellectuals of color are mindful of the Whiteness of high theory, but I know of only a few sources addressing theory in relation to race. bell hooks' and Cornel West's remarkable published dialogue, *Breaking Bread: Insurgent Black Intellectual Life,* covers a range of topics related to the challenges of joining intellectual activity and social responsibility. Characteristically, hooks poses the question in a manner down-to-earth yet far-reaching (1991: 35):

> [W]hat place does the theorizing of White, Euro-centric intellectuals have for Black people? I read Terry Eagleton's book, *The Significance of Theory,* and what I liked very much about his particular essay on theory was that he tried to talk about how everyone uses theory in their practical daily life, which is certainly what I've tried to stress in my work, particularly when speaking to Black students who are questioning the significance of theory. What do you think about the fact that many of us are influenced these days by European theorists Michel Foucault, Julia Kristeva, Derrida, Lacan, and Third World, non-Black theorists like Edward Said, Gayatri Spivak, and Homi Bhabha? What do those intellectuals outside Black experience have to teach us, say to us, that can in some way illuminate and enhance that struggle?

In her classic essay, "Can the Subaltern Speak?," Gayatri Chakravorty Spivak pushes more strongly at the histories and epistemologies behind the high theory of the West, pointing out that "Western intellectual production is, in many ways, complicit with Western international economic interests" (1988: 271). She insists on marking the "positionality" of Western theory and the manner in which it creates "investigating subjects" that are central to the constitution and maintenance of "Other as the Self's shadow" (296, 280). Indeed, she goes so far as to describe the effects of applied theory as a kind of "epistemic violence" that constitutes and erases simultaneously, and she links it to the imperialist project as expanded in the twentieth century. But even after extended consideration of how theory constructs a subaltern that cannot speak, Spivak notes that the question itself — can the subaltern speak? — opens up "interventionist possibilities" (299).

Though seldom addressed in writing, the gap between high theory and the racialized experience of cultural workers is old news to those committed to *praxis.* Indeed, when I shared the abstract for this essay with Jon Jang, he responded that his theoretical models lay elsewhere, particularly in African American writers and musicians (Jang 1997b):

> You cited some intellectuals in your [abstract]. Although I respect and admire the contributions of many of those intellectuals and writers, I think it is important to include thinkers/writers/scholars

who have helped shape our philosophy. The first important writer
is Amiri Baraka. I also think philosophies from the AACM [the
Association for the Advancement of Creative Musicians] are
important. There is a strong link between the Pan African New
Music movement in Chicago and the Pan Asian New Music movement in San Francisco. The frame of reference must be based on
those intellectuals who have influenced us. Otherwise, it is going to
feel funny. Frank Kofsky's book on Black Nationalism in Jazz feels
funny. Although he has important interviews with artists such as
John Coltrane, his Trotskyite ideology dominates the discussion to
the extent that you feel disconnected from John Coltrane's perspective. I say to myself: "The cat is trippin." Between Francis [Wong],
Glenn [Horiuchi], and myself, Amiri Baraka has been one of the
most influential writers.

I certainly do not suggest that all American ethnic minority intellectuals
look to one another for models and ideas — by no means. African American ideological differences with Jewish American intellectuals, for
instance, have been addressed with great candor by Harold Cruse.[6] Given
this, the extent to which Jang and his Asian Improv colleagues draw on
African American models stands out as extraordinarily promising for ethnic coalition politics. Moreover, they emphasize points of ideological contact (indeed, indebtedness) in a mindful, performative manner enacted
through music itself (their interests in particular kinds of improvisation
and multi-ethnic ensembles) and through talk.

Musicians As Public Intellectuals

African American musicians have long been regarded as public intellectuals by their communities. Many forms of music and religious discourse
share performative qualities of orality that have carried immense cultural
capital at different historical moments.[7] Joy James examines the work of
Bernice Johnson Reagon, who argues that "Those who articulate in their
own voice, with their personal style or signature, are highly respected
within African-American culture." Reagon refers to 'original sound' as signature," that is, music or oratory presents a kind of primary evidence that
is authoritative in the context of African American culture (James 1997:
149). Musicians are thus taken seriously as cultural workers, and the Asian
Improv musicians have absorbed this epistemology through the music of
Coltrane and the writings of Baraka, among others. Their models thus
encourage them to act — to make music and to speak as cultural workers.

In October 1996 I watched leading Asian American jazz composer Jon
Jang take the organizers of the San Francisco Jazz Festival to task for their
cultural politics. I had been warned that Jon and his Asian American
musician colleagues weren't entirely satisfied with their relationship to the

festival administrators, but I didn't realize that a public argument was in the making. Trying to write about these musicians, I have struggled with modes of presentation because as Asian Americans focused on perfor- mance, my politics and theirs overlap considerably. Given the problemat- ics of ethnography, there are no satisfactory ways to represent them as colleagues, despite Jody Diamond's rather naive suggestion that it is high time we start doing so (1990). Despite my commitment to feminist anthropology and other poststructuralist methods, locating the agency of these Asian American activist musicians as cultural workers is a method- ological contradiction. Agency is what ethnographic writing wrests away from its subjects, yet it is precisely this dynamic that interests me — indeed, draws me — to want to write about these musicians. They are self- consciously engaged in culture-making, and I want to reflect critically on their strategies as well as pay homage to their cultural work.

I was moderating their symposium in the Oakland Asian Cultural Cen- ter, sitting at the end of a table lined with some of the best Asian American jazz musicians in the U.S., all from the Bay Area: Miya Masaoka, Mark Izu, Francis Wong, Anthony Brown, and Jon Jang. All have recorded with the nonprofit Asian Improv label, dedicated to Asian American new music; most have performed together extensively since the late 1970s. Mark Izu, a Sansei composer and jazz bass player, had organized the symposium at the invitation of the San Francisco Jazz Festival; in a few days, he and several of the other panelists were scheduled to present an evening of Asian Amer- ican jazz as part of the festival, and the symposium was meant to pave the way as one in a series of "Jazz Dialogues" sponsored by the Festival (Figure 13.1). Izu invited me along as the panel moderator, so I introduced each of the panelists and generally kept things moving. Each of the panelists spoke and presented some of their work, e.g., Anthony Brown played a recording of his work, "E.O. 9066." Izu and Francis Wong performed a free improvi- sation on double bass and sax. Wong spoke generally about influences on his work and the necessity of creating new "sound vocabularies," and then stood up, pulled the mouthpiece out of his sax, and played an extraordi- narily lyrical free improvisation on the mouthpiece alone (Audio Example 13.1).

Izu had warned me that the panelists had long-standing issues with the organizers of the festival over matters of ethnic representation, so after several audience members had asked questions, I tried to move things toward their concerns by asking for comments on the politics of multicul- turalism in the Bay Area.[8] What followed was remarkable: one by one, the panelists spoke — first generally, then more and more specifically — to their long-time frustrations as Asian American jazz musicians in the racial politics of the Bay Area arts scene. They were articulate, reasoned, irritated and patient; they took turns but carefully played off one another's com- ments. In the end, two staff members from the San Francisco Jazz Festival — both women of color — were angry and defensive enough to

Fig. 13.1 Mark Izu performing at the Asian Pacific American Heritage Festival in New York City, 1996. Notice that he is playing his double bass with a chopstick. (Photograph by Deborah Wong.)

step forward and speak, but the testimony of several audience members eventually made it clear that they were outnumbered. In the end, the cultural politiks (as Jon Jang would call it) enabling the San Francisco Jazz Festival had been interrogated by panelists and audience members alike, and the five Asian American musicians had done it through straight talk with a long history in American intellectualism. I now realize that Mark Izu and his colleagues had a very explicit agenda in organizing the symposium discussion. When Izu invited me to moderate, he alluded to old differences with the San Francisco Jazz Festival organizers; in fact, the five musicians had long-standing issues with the Festival organizers over their exclusion and the Festival's use of their names (i.e., their ethnicities) in applications for federal funding. I imagine that the musicians strategized with one another more than they did with me, but I also suspect that they were simply willing to see what would happen once everyone was talking.

The symposium was one of eight "Jazz Dialogues" sponsored by the Festival during October and November 1996. The dialogues were meant to be "A series of discussions and musical demonstrations led by some of jazz's foremost musicians and scholars examining the history of jazz culture and the ideas behind the music."[9] The October 20th symposium was advertised as "Asian Concepts in Jazz," and the blurb stated that:

> Asian American jazz is one of music's most exciting currents, and it was born right here in the Bay Area. In this panel discussion with music, the founders of Asian American jazz explore the roots of their music and look to the future.

The audience that Sunday afternoon was diverse. A majority of the fifty-odd people were Asian or Asian American but Anglo and African Americans also attended and the age range was broad. Each of the panelists spoke at some length about their music, influences and current projects; some performed short live pieces while others played recordings of their compositions. We were into our third hour when I opened the floor for discussion with my question about multiculturalism and the music scene in the Bay Area.

Anthony Brown was the first to respond. Looking at the transcript from the event, I can see that the panelists approached my question — in fact, their agenda — in an extremely methodical and pedagogical manner. They were careful to set up their terms before becoming confrontational, and they took turns, each deploying their personal strengths. Brown — then a doctoral candidate in ethnomusicology at Berkeley, half Japanese and half African American, a composer and a jazz percussionist — "answered" me with an exploration of multiculturalism, its earlier manifestations, and the current political climate:

> **Anthony Brown:** [Multiculturalism] is a catchword… First it was 'melting pot,' and everyone was going to melt together and become unicultural — … we were all going to melt into the pot and come out with a unified concept that was based on the European model. That didn't work too well, so then there was cultural pluralism. Well, even in that design, there still wasn't what one would consider mutual respect for what was being brought to the table culturally, so the catchword of pluralism really didn't include accepting other cultures at that time — non-European cultures. But they didn't come with the same kind of parity, the same kind of importance, and primarily the same kind of *power* — economic power. So multiculturalism is a new word that we have, and it seemed to be working, because there is now a concept of acceptance of difference. But, as you are probably all aware, Proposition 209[10] is trying to reverse that. We in the art world, as represented here, have come together

to engage in dialogue, not only musical but social and cultural. In the population at large, we can see that there's a reversal of that trend — there's an effort to minimize or to curtail that kind of acceptance of difference. And so, if nothing else, let's hope we keep that foremost in our minds come the election — that we are looking toward the future, those of us who are parents, and those of you who have children or grandchildren, we've got to make the world a better place. The world is getting smaller through technology — we're becoming a global community. And that's best represented in the Bay Area, by what you see before you, by what you see around you, by who *you* [the audience] are. I think it's paramount we keep that consciousness above all others — that we are different, but that we can live together. Efforts like 209 are trying to stop that consciousness.

Brown thus spoke to the cultural politics of the moment by broadly addressing multiculturalism as an idea with a history. Mark Izu spoke after a pause and gently pulled the conversation toward the issue on all the panelists' minds — the programming and funding for the Festival — without naming names:

> **Mark Izu:** I think a lot of this basically boils down to money, the economy. There are many groups that suddenly became fundable [as] multicultural programming. And it's very interesting, in these times when a lot of these sources of funding are starting to dry up — the NEA, and other arts funding sources — some of these groups are not doing that kind of programming anymore, because basically it wasn't coming from their mission, or who they are and what they believe, but it was coming from a pocketbook. It's a very sobering view — if there wasn't funding for this, you may not see it as much. But then I think the flip side of it is that people who are really trying to do work like this, that comes from a different source besides European or American culture, are doing it because they really *believe* in it. And it's not because they're getting funded for it. And other people who may be doing it because there's funding will not be doing it anymore, so the artists who are really trying to create these genres are going to keep doing it, and we just hope we'll have your support.

Francis Wong then spoke up, pointing out that partnerships between "grassroots" artists and funding organizations are crucial:

> I think it still comes down to: what are we going to do? There was a saying in the Civil Rights movement: 'it's going to be, it's up to me.'

A lot of it has to with creative partnership: we're putting our lives, our families, our livelihood on the line to do our work. In some ways — to put a positive spin on it — it's like a challenge, a challenge to the funding world, a challenge to those who have resources, for us to work together and do this. I think part of what's great about this afternoon is, OK, this is what we're trying to do. Can we meet together and try to do something, whether it's at the grassroots level or folks in institutions trying to do something.

With the play of politics and economic support for the arts now established, Brown began to zero in on the central problem — whether all artists have access to the "pots" of money and resources that sustain creative activity:

Anthony Brown: The analogy of the various pots is all good, but finding the money to keep those pots full, or alive with culture — that's really the issue. The concept that we can all sit at the table — you come sit at the table, various other people sit at the table — and we share the resources — rather than somebody says, OK, you're sitting at that table, I'll give you *this*, and *you*, we're going to give you all *this*, because you represent something that we can relate to, or something that we're more comfortable with. Again, it's an acceptance of difference, and acceptance on an equal basis, a sharing of the resources …

At this point, Jon Jang burst in, clearly itching to get specific. One of the founders of Asian Improv and a second-generation Chinese American, Jang is a composer, pianist, and leader of multi-ethnic ensembles assembled to perform his large, ambitious works. Intensely verbal, Jang was eager to get down to brass tacks. The San Francisco Jazz Festival organizers had used his name and Mark Izu's — without asking either of them — in a grant application to the NEA in a somewhat transparent attempt to demonstrate a commitment to multiculturalism. Jang didn't take long to circle in:

Jon Jang: … I'm not sure if in this discussion of multiculturalism people understand what we're talking about … I'll preface this by saying that what we're trying to do is to achieve a meaningful solution and a meaningful strategy towards building Asian American arts which benefits all of us, because I think the other thing about affirmative action — if we're talking about Proposition 209 — [is] that when Asian Americans benefit (at least in my ensembles), European American and African American musicians benefit. There's more work, and there's a development of those musicians' artistry as well …

I'm going to focus on some of the problems. Let's talk mainly about Asian Americans in San Francisco. First of all, you should know that this Thursday's concert in the Herbst Theater — the 'Asian Concepts in Rhythm,' Mark Izu is the artistic director — this is the first time that Asian Americans are featured in a concert. The last time was 1988, my ensemble, Jon Jang and the Pan-Asian Arkestra — we were sharing a concert with Peter Appelbaum, so it wasn't a full evening. Anthony Brown [also] had an ensemble in 1992, but that was in a hotel … So those are [the only] two examples of our participation in the San Francisco Jazz Festival. Now, over fifteen years, we've made valuable contributions to San Francisco — we've made what San Francisco *is* … The San Francisco music presenters have not made a serious commitment — actually, a serious effort — towards nurturing our work as leaders, composers, and artists. You talk about affirmative action: for those of you who are Asian American and are familiar with the issues, it exposes the myth of meritocracy or artistic excellence and also illustrates the insidious role of social circles and cliques of the White arts establishment.

At this point, the audience was listening pretty closely and I was wondering where this was going to end up. Without yielding the floor, Jang asked for audience participation — a basic pedagogical move, as it enabled and encouraged listeners to take their own stand. Proposing a call-and-response exercise, Jang offered the audience several case studies and asked them to choose between two responses, "Jazz in the city" and "Jazz insidious." For his first "call," Jang outlined this scenario:

> Here's one presenter who decided they wanted to write a grant using Mark Izu's name, Jon Jang's name, and they wrote it to the NEA and they requested some funding and [got it, and then] said, Well, we didn't get enough money, so we can't present you *this* year, and then, we kept waiting and wondering, Well, are they sincere about really presenting us? Or are they padding that grant so they can get that quote-unquote multicultural money? What is that?

Either shy about participating or startled by the shift from general discussion to specific grievances, the audience was silent. After a moment, one man called out, "Jazz insidious!" Jang answered:

> Jazz insidious! It's an example of cultural appropriation or cultural colonialism where you're using people of color as a *commodity*, not really embracing the music.

> OK, here's another example. An African American cultural organization meets with a music presenter about doing a project that's

three years long, about trying to [consider that] in the Bay Area and also at an international level, there are Asian audiences that can support the arts, and yet have not been encouraged — whether through the educational system or through the art scene — to participate on all levels, from audiences, to staff, to boards of directors, to artists. And [this African American organization has] a comprehensive, long-term view about that particular audience ... Anyway, these presenters have met with us for three or four years to try to have dialogue with artists like myself... So what is that example?

Several audience members cried, "Jazz in the city!," and Jang confirmed that this was the "correct" answer. Mark Izu broke in to make a joke about Jang's ability to talk at length once he gets going, but then suggested that any real changes in ethnic minority participation in the arts would only take place if long-term structural commitments are made:

Mark Izu: I think Jon's point is really well taken, and I want to address some of these issues. I've been working with the Asian American Jazz Festival for fifteen years and I've been Artistic Director for ten, and we've been doing it at the Asian Art Museum, which is definitely one of those institutions that, when you say you work with them, people kind of look at you funny [i.e., it is a conservative institution]. The way I've done this is — like Jon's talking about — to propose a multi-year plan. It takes more than one year to develop a program. I think anyone in a business field would know if you do a one-shot deal, it's not going to succeed: you have to say, this is going to succeed after so many years, and it's going to become something important. There they were willing to talk like that: yes, we want this to be an important event — what are we going to do, where do we want to be three years from now?

This is the kind of conversation I've been having with the San Francisco Jazz Festival too, saying, this is the way I'd like to work: we have to think, where do we want to be three years from now? Do we want to have a partnership, do we want to have a relationship, and what is that going to be? If that kind of conversation isn't entertained, there's no point in even doing something at all, period ... Let's talk like that. If someone's willing to talk in those terms, then you know you have someone who is a partner.

Jang reconfirmed Izu's point:

I don't want to paint it in black and white, where you [only] have 'Jazz in the city' and 'Jazz insidious.' I did that to point out what the problems are. When we deal with solutions for the United States, we're really dealing long-term with *investing* in the United States — that's what Jesse Jackson said … And Asians are a part of that, especially in California, where in the year 2020, Asian Americans and Latinos are going to become the majority.

By then it was almost time to end, so I asked if there were any questions from the audience. Instead, an Asian American woman got up and walked to the microphone at the front of the room. Anthony Brown introduced her to the audience as Villy Wong from the San Francisco Jazz Festival. Wong said that she felt compelled to try to respond as she was the director of business and operations for the Festival. She said that executive director, Randall Kline, was responsible for programming decisions though he also received input from an artistic advisory committee composed of musicians and knowledgeable community members. She noted that Kline "sincerely welcomes" feedback and suggestions, and then she began to get defensive:

> This is my fourth festival, and I'm personally really proud to be part of the festival, even though it's a White presenting organization. I am a person of color, as you can see, and to me, it's important to have as diverse a representation as possible. The world is not perfect, and I wish there were many more presenters who [could] showcase these musicians as we have in the past. I wish the funding weren't going away, but that's what makes my job very challenging — to try to make the business ends meet. If anything, I hope everybody walks away [today] with a very positive feeling that we have incredible musicians here who are a part of this very community, that we're able to have at our back door. (H)aving you here today at this Jazz Dialogues is a very important part of our public programming — having free public symposiums, public forums, for you to voice your opinion. It's something that's a very important part of the San Francisco Jazz Festival as well. This is the kind of way that you can make a difference — to show that you care and that you have opinions, and that you want to support the music.

An audience member asked whether the Festival staff had pursued any Asian community support for the Festival and Wong said no even as she insisted that the Festival was mindful of different communities:

> As far as individual vendors [go], there are specific individuals who are very interested in jazz and would support us in one way or another, whether it's through contributions or even just being regular patrons. But there's no active Asian vendor that consistently might come back and say, 'We're going to be a sponsor' — and that's a very good point, because when we do our solicitations for

donations and sponsorships, we really go across all the different communities, and I think what you find is it's not just Asian money supporting Asian causes, but that there's a pot of money, and it's the general public, it's the jazz lovers, who are really supporting us as a whole, because this [Asian American] form of music is just as much jazz to us as anything else — as Betty Carter is. So we do sell targeting, but at the same time we really hope that the causes are being filled by the community as a whole.

Jang became visibly impatient and began to ask pointed questions about the artistic advisory committee and its ethnic composition. Wong said that she wasn't familiar with the members of the committee — her responsibilities didn't bring her into contact with them — but Jang kept asking questions until it came out that the advisory committee had approximately twenty members and only one was Asian American. The spectacle of an Asian American musician taking an Asian American arts administrator to task was an uncomfortable but illuminating moment, made more complicated when Festival staff member Isabel Yrigoyen stood up in the back of the room and began speaking, eventually working herself into angry tears. She too argued that her presence as a person of color (in this case, Cuban) meant something, and she was infuriated by the accusation of structural racism (and her implication in it), recasting the argument as a matter of "objective" and "subjective" decision-making:

Anything that we do is blind and subjective, so to say that decisions can be made in a way that's objective is, I think, would be unrealistic and not true. I think we always make choices, and the Jazz Festival, I can say for myself, represents one aspect of the jazz world, and I don't think it's going to represent *everything* that everyone thinks of as jazz. I think it's always going to be subjective — …. What is the point of having an artistic director? I don't think we should base [the membership of the advisory committee] on whether there's a certain number of people: we should base it on consciousness, we should base it on personal experience, we should base it on integrity, we should base it on what the community at large is looking for, and we should also base it on reality — business reality. One of the things I think has not been stressed enough here is the foundation world. The government in the United States does not support the arts … For the First World, for the richest country in the world, we are doing a terrible job — our government is doing a terrible job. What do we depend on foundations, and we depend on individuals who help us do our work. Now, *we've* got to change the foundation world. We need to let those foundation people know what we want. And a lot of these foundations don't know what we want, and they take their subjective

> reality and they give their money to what they think is important, and what I think we should do as minority people of color — I'm Cuban — we should go to these people and educate them. Because that's where the money is …
>
> So I feel we need to come together as a community — frankly, I took it very wrong, I feel very upset that you call [the San Francisco Jazz Festival] a "White presenter." I and Villy and other people of color with the San Francisco Jazz Festival — what are we? I think there's a lack of consciousness, maybe, on *your* part, as to what we're about. You come to the organization, you look at the organization work.

Yrigoyen abruptly sat down, fighting tears, and Anthony Brown filled in the charged pause that followed with a conciliatory comment, noting that her presence and Villy Wong's on the staff of the San Francisco Jazz Festival represented a significant change in how jazz was presented in San Francisco. But some members of the audience had a lot to say, and a lively exchange about marginalization and tokenization began. An African American man said,

> The reason why we have White presenters at every single one of these festivals, the reason why every community can't get together or won't get together, doesn't have anything to do with 'subjectivity' or 'objectivity.' It has something to do with power relations … And that is of course the *problem* — right? Because that's what tokenism is, and that's what happens when people are *not* honest about how that kind of manipulation goes on, and who's responsible for it. Because we're not talking about individuals, we're talking about power relations. And I think *that's* the context in which we need to address the real question of how programming is going to be resolved for the entire community in the Bay Area.

In the end, we went almost an hour over time and I finally had to close the session, but by then the audience had taken over the conversation and was actively wrestling with the issues. Wong's and Yrigoyen's resort to arguments of inclusion based on their presence on the Festival staff reflected a blindness to the mechanics of representation that wasn't lost on many of the audience members. Following the panelists' lead, they took it upon themselves to consider how a cultural institution might create a relationship with its urban communities.

Ethnomusicology and Post-White Theory

I use the term "post-White" both seriously and playfully.[11] If post-ness is the condition of the late twentieth century, then perhaps we can also consider a moment of shifting racialization: after all, the demographics of the United States are about to swing irrevocably away from Whiteness as a majority proposition. Considering post-Whiteness, I explore a different relationship between fieldworker and informant, a relationship mindful of colonial histories and racialized class formations yet able to look beyond them to other explanatory systems.

And explanatory systems — that is, theory — is what it's all about. By accepting the conditions of poststructuralism, the necessity of critical theory becomes all the more evident. Different kinds of theory provide different equipment for living, for knowing. In other words, particular theories provide particular ways of knowing, and the worlds each puts forward represent different histories. Theory is made by people thinking through the valences of their moment. Regarding theory as part of culture makes visible the conditions of its construction — i.e., the fact that theory, like any part of culture, will be inflected with the power play of race, ethnicity, gender, sexual orientation, class, etc.

I should note that the conversation didn't end that afternoon. About a week later, I received a copy of a letter written by Jon Jang, addressed to Isabel Yrigoyen, Villy Wong, and Mark Izu and copied to me. In it, Jang thanked them all for organizing the event. "Although the ... discussion on issues pertaining specifically to Asian American music artists ended in a heated debate, it is important ... that problems be identified for the purpose of achieving meaningful solutions and strategies," he wrote. He noted his own involvement in a number of San Francisco arts organizations and artists' of color efforts to move toward cultural equity. "The bottom line," he said:

> is that we feel used by the 'white presenter' and not respected as human beings. I am familiar with the formula: after we are used, there is no commitment toward nurturing our work and audience development. Unfortunately, ... the SF Jazz Festival has contributed to the problem of cultural colonialism and institutionalized racism. It is too bad that partnerships can't be built because everybody loses.

In closing, Jang expressed his disappointment and reservations about future prospects:

> I no longer wish to meet and discuss these issues because there is a lack of recognition of the problem and no effort to come to a solution and strategy. The SF Jazz Festival collaboration with Mark Izu was a positive first step and I hope it will continue. If it doesn't, then the SF Jazz Festival will sing that old familiar song of cultural colonialism and tokenism.

I was inspired to look at this event because it struck me as a successful moment of *doing* theory and cultural politics. I have never heard Mark Izu or Jon Jang self-identify as public intellectuals, yet as Henry Giroux points out, the very attempt to link personal interventions to a broader consideration of cultural politics is the identifying mark (1995: 195).[12] Looking at what the Asian Improv musicians say, and to whom, is part of my broader project of exploring how cultural politics and identity politics might meet within the framework of ethnographic inquiry. Theory focused on social action has a dangerously marginal relationship to "high" theory. I put forward the idea of the post-White both to defamiliarize how we think about theory (i.e., as floating above culture) and to illuminate this moment of American multiculturated identity politics, which presents us with conversations that can help us hear why some theorizing propels us into social action and some doesn't. Of course, the traditions of public intellectualism that I describe as post-White have long histories that parallel the development of high theory. Whether it is appropriate for identity politics to make an appearance in an ethnography, or indeed in any scholarship, is a question that looms.[13] Respecting one's subjects and even sharing their beliefs is nothing new. Finding ways to critique and to interrogate those beliefs is the challenge, especially when the ethnographic eye is itself implicated. Conceiving of the Asian Improv musicians as public intellectuals has been a way to open the field for inclusion — not, as is commonly argued, for their inclusion as my colleagues (which they already are), but rather for me to become a partner in their conversations in a manner that closes the apparent distance between us.

Identity politics are central to my desire to write about Asian American musics. I was keenly conscious of my chosen self-identity as an Asian American scholar as I wrote this book, and I regard "identity politics" as a handy moniker to talk about social actors (including scholars) who own up to their cultural politics. I was therefore surprised when a close friend and colleague responded to my request for advice on how to frame this book by saying that he hoped I *wouldn't* "do" identity politics. An acceptance of identity politics thus sets up an uncomfortable meeting between warring ideologies: by accepting the terms of the ethnic politics proposed by my subjects, it may seem at some crucial level that I give over a critical stance — that is, if I fully accept the terms of my subjects' agency as cultural workers, I may seem to have relinquished my critical edge as a scholar. I don't think this need be true, and I have focused here on a particular model for cultural workers that has helped me reconsider my relationship, both ethnographic and political, to these Asian American musicians. By focusing on *their* strategies, I am able to shift frames and see them in terms of their relationship to particular American histories of activism — which in my case must have implications for the writing of ethnography. In short, an ethnography can enact cultural politics: engaging with one's subjects can occur at the point where strategies for social change are shared. These musicians argue against their inaudibility in ways that theorize jazz (and indeed music generally) as always already directed toward power relationships. The Asian Improv musicians' attempt to engage in public discussion reflects a theoretical position based in the expectation of action. Indeed, who has the right to say (or perform) what about the social world?

Acknowledgments

I would like to thank Philip Brett, Jocelyne Guilbault, Traise Yamamoto, and Eric Usner for comments and suggestions.

Endnotes

1. This is a reference to Diamond 1990.
2. Noll does not suggest that any single interpretation can stand alone, either (1997: 164): "I do not regard anyone's interpretation of culture as inviolate, final, or best, and that includes any single native ethnographer. It includes my own work as well."
3. One of the best arguments for "ethnographies of the particular" is put forth by Lila Abu-Lughod (1991).
4. Michael Hanchard writes that (1996a: 106) "Grassroots organizers, academics, journalists, nurses, lawyers, and grandmothers in communities across this country who engage in sustained collective action against the burning of books, antiabortion guerrillas, teenage violence, and the Contract with America are also public intellectuals."
5. Hanchard writes (1996a: 101), "[W]hether anointed with the title of public intellectual or not, *all* black intellectuals are placed in an ambiguous position when they write for white newspapers and journals on issues of racial politics."
6. Two chapters in *The Crisis of the Negro Intellectual* (1967) address these issues: "Jews and Negroes in the Communist Party" and "Negroes and Jews—The Two Nationalisms and the Bloc(ked) Plurality."
7. See Dyson 1993 for extended discussions of these issues.
8. All comments from the symposium are transcribed from tapes generously provided by Mark Izu. My rather muddled question was:
   ... I'd like to seize the moment and to ask some questions about, more broadly, what's going on here today. We all know that there's a current push toward multiculturalism in the arts, and I'd like us to pause for a few moments and to think about what that means, what it *might* mean, what we can *do* with that. We're here together today because these musicians are going to participate in the San Francisco Jazz Festival, and as I understand it, this is a fairly new thing—for them to participate in this long-standing Bay Area institution. What does that mean? I'd like to hear more generally, beyond the context of just the jazz festival, in what ways you all feel you've been made an integral part of arts institutions in general—you know, not necessarily just in this area. In what ways do you feel you've been used, and what can we do with the dynamics of that enforced power play of all of that?
9. From the *1996 San Francisco Jazz Festival Official Program Book*. The Jazz Dialogues were all free and open to the public, held in different venues in San Francisco and Oakland (including a jazz club, a performing arts center, and the San Francisco Jazz Festival Store). They were funded by the James Irvine Foundation, The California Council for the Humanities, and Transamerica.
10. Proposition 209, the "California Civil Rights Initiative," was on the November 5, 1996 ballot in California and was voted into state law two weeks after the symposium. Its primary directive held that, "The state shall not discriminate against, or grant preferential treatment to, any individual or group on the basis of race, sex, color, ethnicity, or national origin in the operation of public employment, public education, or public contracting." It effectively ended affirmative action practices.
11. I am indebted to James Moy for the phrase and for the idea.

12. In his afterword to *Women Writing Culture*, Giroux notes (1995: 195), "[The writers in this volume] do not define themselves self-consciously as public intellectuals. And yet, what is so remarkable about the interviews and narrations they provide is how these various theorists link their feminist and other political interventions to broader considerations of cultural struggle, whether it focuses on race, national identity, writing, or teaching."

13. My thanks to Tim Taylor for ongoing conversations around these issues.

14
My Father's Life in Music

I close this book with a conversation at home. I have been careful through-out not to write about "Asian American music" and not to focus solely on the "makers" of music. Trying to blur distinctions between production and consumption, I have cast back and forth between performers, composers, improvisers, listeners, producers, audience members and so forth. If we're going to move away from great-man theories of history, then there's sud-denly a lot to attend to, and this is especially true as we open up ideas of music history and music cultures to, well, everyone else — all those others, including women and people of color. I have suggested that the space between creating music, distributing it, and consuming it is rife with com-peting expectations and that Asian Americans haven't often figured into the phantasmatic configurations driving these patterns.

Having listened to what Rodney Ogawa had to say about racialized changes in his listening tastes over time, I turn to my own home and my own family. *My Music* (Crafts, Cavicchi, Keil, et al. 1993) is one of my favorite books about music because it teaches us to listen to what people say about their pleasures and epiphanies when listening to music. I regard listening as a kind of making: I want to call into question the most basic assumptions around music production. This book is subtitled *Asian Amer-icans Making Music* for that reason. Our vocabulary for talking about the participation of ordinary people in music is paltry. Ordinary people "con-sume" music, or dance to it, or take lessons for a few years, or sing in the church choir, or listen to the radio, or buy CDs. Ordinary people are understood to "listen" to music, yet I believe that the act of listening is at once richer and more complex than we have yet theorized. Crafts, Cavic-chi, Keil, et al. offer abundant evidence of this; Christopher Small (1998), R. Murray Schafer (1994), and Jacques Attali (1985) have perhaps come the closest to theorizing listening as central to the place of music in culture. I constantly ask my students to talk and write about what they listen to and why, and this exercise is always full of discoveries as well as disappointments, because ordinary people aren't taught to value their own opinions about music or to express them in particularly searching ways. Asian Americans tend to devalue their own musical experiences twice over (at least) because they're both ordinary people (those of us who aren't Yo-Yo Ma, anyway) as well as a group of Americans who are rarely encouraged to pursue "the arts."

So I turn to my own home and the sounds that I heard in it while growing up. How did I get here, anyway? These ideas that I have about music (as an ethnomusicologist, as an Asian American) come from somewhere, surely.

I could go on and on about how my parents are unusual people, but the point here is that I grew up in a progressive political and social environment under the purview of two adults who had made it through the 1950s after making some difficult personal choices that allowed them to explore the changes of the 1960s. My father was from a working-class family and my mother from a newly white-collar one; they seized the upward mobility of hard-won college educations and new opportunities. They liked music. Growing up in the (mostly White American) suburbs of New Jersey, I remember that the radio was almost always on at home, tuned to a classical station broadcast out of New York City some fifty miles away. My parents had stacks of LPs including lots and lots of Broadway (*The King and I, My Fair Lady, Man of La Mancha,* etc.), Pete Seeger, and soft jazz (those racy Herb Albert covers!). They arranged for me to take flute lessons. They loved the collegiate glee club tradition: my father was the Dean of Students at Rutgers University, and when its glee club went on a tour of Europe, my parents went along as chaperones. My thirteenth birthday present was a trip to Lincoln Center to see *La Traviata* at the New York City Opera. They took my brother and me to see dress rehearsals of a student production of *Hair* at the Rutgers Student Center (complete with full frontal nudity and great songs). They loved to watch Mitch Miller on TV.

So this Asian American knew the Grand March from *Aïda* and Pete Seeger's rendition of "We Shall Overcome" before I got to middle school. I was also sent off to Saturday morning Chinese school, where my brother and I learned traditional Chinese songs (as taught by nationalistic Taiwanese immigrants who no doubt had their own ideas about what it meant to be "Chinese"). I liked music because my parents liked music, and I liked a lot of different sounds because that's what they listened to.

It's therefore appropriate to turn now to a conversation — all right, an interview — I had with my father about listening to music, making music, and liking music. My parents spent the winter holiday with me in Riverside not too long ago, and I taped this conversation with my father, then seventy years old, on January 4, 1997. John Wong (1927–2000) was born in Buffalo, New York to immigrant Chinese parents. His mother, his father, and his father's father emigrated to Buffalo from the Toishan region of Guangdong province, so he was both second- and third-generation Chinese American and he grew up in a working-class household surrounded by Chinese immigrants; he didn't learn English until he went to kindergarten. I knew that his musical tastes and experience ran from playing the accordion to singing with his fraternity at the University of Buffalo, so I decided to ask him about it and to try to sort out what it all might mean in the context of Asian Americans and music. Of course I'm not after a "typical" Asian American musical profile, not least because there isn't such a thing, and also because the very construction of the "Chinese" and the "American" were joined in my father's experience. I'm fascinated by the ways that he was framed by music and used it to explore other ways of being American. He wasn't very engaged with the "Asian American," but it's all in the mix — it's all part of his musical idioculture, his personal soundscape, and at some level, it's at work in this book. So let me try to sort it out here.

He had five siblings. Betty was the oldest, then Frank, then Jim, then him, Fred, and Jean. Like most kids with lots of brothers and sisters, they learned a lot about music and popular culture from each other. I asked him about his earliest memories of music, and he answered:

> All of our musical interests, we gained from each other. We heard music in the big-band era — and that was American music, Western music. We were introduced to classical music because our sister Betty, the oldest, was first introduced to classical music — operas, as well as what used to be the Red Label Victor records, and the old shellac records — she'd bring them home from school and she'd introduce all of us to them — that kind of music.
>
> What Chinese music we heard was usually heard during the holidays on festive occasions — the moon festival, New Year's, banquets and dinners — and if we were real lucky we'd have someone in the Chinese community who could play the Chinese version of the dulcimer — the two-hammer dulcimer. Occasionally we'd have the performance of a lion dance if somebody was coming in from out of town, and we'd have people who would know how to play the percussion instruments — the drums and the gongs and everything else. And I think what gave us kids the biggest charge was that some of these people would teach us how to use or play the percussion instruments, and they'd cue us, when we were to play what. And of course, much of it was repetitious, so we picked it up very quickly, but all of us were fighting for the chance to play the different instruments…
>
> **Me:** What were they called, some of those, in Chinese?

My father: They did it almost phonetically, or descriptively. They say the gong was the *cha-gong* — so that the rhythm, there's 1-2-3 1-2-3 *Cha-gong! Cha-gong! Cha-gong-gong! CHA-gong!* you know? And that's the way we learned. That was great fun and I think one of the saddest things was that these instruments, all stored up in the Chinese Benevolent Association meeting room, started to fall apart when the Chinese community started to die — we no longer had a Chinatown in Buffalo — and one of the families took these instruments and stored them in the garage. It took years for Mom [i.e., his mother] and me to trace it down and find out where it was — and then we found out that Mr. Lee, who had taken all these instruments, later threw a lot of them away because he didn't know they were any good or something like that; I can't remember. He got rid of a lot of them. And Mom and I were looking for these because we were hoping to get 'em to give 'em to you.

Me: Me!

My father: To the musicologist in our family. That was the Chinese music we had and that's all I can really recall.

He had vague memories of the occasional Chinese opera troupe coming through, but traditional Chinese music was the least of what he remembered. The music he recalled most vividly was American big band — Glenn Miller, Jimmy Dorsey — and his older brother Jim was considered the family expert, the connoisseur of jazz.

My father: We listened to *Hit Parade* on the radio, sure, we listened to that. We were familiar with all of the songs, and I think all or most of us can probably sing and remember all the lyrics from all the old songs of the time. We were fortunate in that we had a real ear for music. We loved singing, we loved all kinds of music — the whole family did — and as for my mother, she liked the music and she knew much of the popular music that was being played. She'd recognize the popular music. And of course, you gotta remember that at that time we were kids, and I'm talking about my early teen years, yeah, early teen years, twelve, thirteen, fourteen. The big bands at that time were coming through the cities and playing the theaters.

Oh yeah. Yeah. The big bands would come through and play at the beach resort areas — we used to go to Crystal Beach, which was in Canada across from Buffalo. Yeah. Stan Kenton, Jimmy Dorsey, they all played there, and they had a big ballroom. So you'd have dancing; and all of us younger kids always envied the older ones because we couldn't get in. You had to be sixteen to get into most of these places. Yeah, it's the big-band music that I can remember and which I still have in my ears now.

He played the accordion. As long as I can remember, there was this big suitcase of an instrument in some corner of the house, and he would open it up and play wheezy, cheesy tunes once or twice a year, singing along with his own playing. He bought it in 1950, when he was twenty-three or so. The Wurlitzer School of Music was five or six blocks from their house; first his older brother Frank took guitar lessons there and then he got interested in the accordion. They sold him a used Hohner for $400 — an astounding sum of money at that time. He said, "I had to pay for a long time. I said 'I'll work for it, I'll pay for it, and I'll get it.' But I enjoyed it so much." He fell for the accordion because he and his brothers went to "roadhouses," that is, social centers where people played pinochle, had Friday night fish fries and danced:

> **Me:** Buffalo was this big polka town, right? So, I mean, accordions? Buffalo?
>
> **My father:** Yes; that's the Lawrence Welk accordion. Buffalo was Polish Buffalo; Buffalo was Italian Buffalo; Buffalo was Irish Buffalo…
>
> **My mother:** They must have been playing accordions for those polkas. Sure they were.
>
> **My father:** Sure. Always. They always were. That was your main instrument for polkas. That's why Lawrence Welk played the accordion.

(Years after this conversation, I find myself poring through *Polka Happiness* [Keil, Keil, and Blau 1992], looking for evidence of all this. Polkas and Buffalo are like ham and cheese. I love all those photographs of burly White people having a great time dancing. The photos are from the 1970s, twenty years after my father was going to the roadhouses. Can I picture him amidst all those hefty Polish Americans?)

Hoping for some sign of interethnic contact and interracial sensibilities, I suddenly thought of Jon Jang's longtime interest in Paul Robeson and the large piece he has been working on with African American flutist James Newton, titled *When Sorrow Turns to Joy,* which draws on Robeson's interest in China and his historic recordings of Chinese songs. I asked my father about those recordings, which I have never heard:

> **Me:** Do you remember as a kid being aware of Paul Robeson singing Chinese stuff, by any chance?

My father: Oh sure. Yeah.

Me: Really?

My father: Yeah, I remember that. You know why I remember? 'cause I can remember people who were saying in Chinese, "How does that nigger know our music?"

My mother: How's that for a historical comment?

My father: But, you know, so many of us — and it almost sounds like a cliché — but so many of our friends, really close friends, were black in Buffalo, 'cause we lived in the heart of the ghetto. But most of the Chinese business people — particularly the restaurateurs — were afraid of blacks because they would see the blacks at their very, very worst. They opened the restaurants in black neighborhoods and they're open — on weekends especially — they're open till two or three o'clock in the morning, sometimes later. So you'd get a lot of the really mean, mean black drunks. I don't think you've ever seen anything that can scare you as much as a mean-eyed drunk black. And I saw it 'cause I used to work in restaurants on weekends when I was going through college and everything else — and I can remember my cousin being stabbed with a long knife by guys holding up one right into his head and sticking in his head. It didn't go through the bone, it kind of glanced off and was going sideways, but the knife was stuck in his head. He was getting his cleaver, and he was going to fight it out, and they stabbed him in the head. But, you know, it was that kind of thing … So, they have a Chinese term which means the same thing as "nigger" — but it's the *way* it's said … But they generalized and that was wrong. Because they also knew that there very good, nice black families came into these restaurants — or, most of them came for takeout. But, you know, it was like that sparerib dish that I made the other night: that was one of the most popular dishes in Chinese restaurants for the blacks. And it used to cost eighty-five cents. Eighty-five cents, you'd get a bowl that was bigger than your cereal bowl there like that with the gravy and the spareribs, and then you get an order of rice almost the same size, for eighty-five cents — plus hot tea. That was a very popular dish and they used to come in … The meanest drunk could come in on a Saturday night at two o'clock in the morning or something like that — they might really give my cousin a hard time — who was the owner, the cook, and everything else. They always treated me well — I was the waiter and the busboy, and that sort of thing. The guy who would give my cousins a hard time would not ever treat me the same way. 'Cause I think they identified with me as a worker, or something. And it's funny, 'cause very often in working situations like that I was also exposed to Chinese music, because they'd play records, and background music — and you could hear it now. Same restaurants, same music.

These encounters move me. Identifications, cross-identifications; beauty, hostility. Working in a Chinese restaurant, smitten by the accordion, dealing with racialized crossroads while Chinese tunes played on the turntable. I've seen our family photos from those years and my young Chinese American aunts and uncles all look terrifically wholesome and clean-cut, but I wonder how they appeared to others in Buffalo: they look so American to me but I doubt they did to the (presumably) White American crowd at Crystal Beach or to the working-class African Americans who frequented their restaurants.

Surprisingly, my father attributed his interest in music directly to his immersion in the Chinese language. Somehow, this is related to oblique family comments I've heard over the years that he was the one who was perhaps a little too eager to assimilate, a little too enthusiastic about mainstream American culture. This was his only effort to connect his enjoyment of (mostly mainstream American) music to his ethnicity:

> I think — I've thought about this — a lot of the singing interest that all of us had may well be related to the fact that we were taking Chinese lessons, because the Chinese language is such that you've got to have an ear for pitch; you've got to know what each of these words mean. Take the word G-E-E. Well, in Chinese you can give it five different pitches of intonation and it can mean five different things. So you have to learn to speak correctly and you develop an ear for music. And all of us sang a lot when we were growing up … which is the kind of thing that led to my own interest, continued interest, in singing all through my life, whether it's barbershop quartet, or glee club, or choral work, or whatever.

He learned Gilbert and Sullivan from his fifth-grade music teacher. But it was Miss Fairbanks who had the biggest impact, and it was through her efforts that my father and his brothers and sisters became part of the play of orientalist representation in Buffalo. My father remembers the whole business fondly. I hear the stories and the memories and wonder. A lot of different understandings came together around Miss Fairbanks and her creation of a Chinese children's choir. How to explain this? It came out piecemeal. Miss Fairbanks was a White Baptist woman who wanted to save the local Chinese children by bringing them into the church and who tried to raise money for the Chinese Nationalist troops — U.S. allies at the time — along the way. At least, I *think* that's what she was up to. What it comes down to is that she recruited a bunch of local Chinese and Chinese

American children in Buffalo, had them dress up in "Chinese" clothes, arranged for them to learn "Chinese" songs, and had them perform at fundraisers. She got a Chinese American teenager to teach the songs, which the children learned phonetically. Unbeknownst to her, the songs were a decidedly odd hodgepodge of things, including the Chinese Communist anthem, drinking songs, and lots of hymns. My father already knew "Bringing in the Sheaves," "Rock of Ages," and "Gather by the River," and he already liked to sing them.

Memory is a funny thing. Sitting in my dining room in 1997 and thinking about singing in Miss Fairbanks' choir led my father right into thinking about the songs, which made him want to sing them (so he did), which made him remember singing them in the past, which made him remember singing them specifically in the early 1950s as a student at the University of Buffalo, where he taught one of the songs to his fraternity brothers. I was so busy trying to understand what he was singing, for whom, how and why that I didn't start to think about the bizarre triangulation of these songs and his experiences of them until later. Listen to Track 11 on the enclosed compact disc. Take in his pleasure in remembering, and the grain of his hoarse voice and the eagerness with which he tells us what happened.

Transcription of Track 11: Interview with my father about his memories of music in Buffalo.

> **My father**: Yeah. But unlike so many of the other people who thought it was their mission to convert us heathens, Miss Fairbanks did. She was sincere. She loved us kids — I don't know if it was because we were Chinese or what. But she loved us and she just kind of took us all in hand. She was the one who pulled all of us together, and then, coincident with the war, the Chinese-Japanese War, she had this nucleus already, so that when it came time to raise funds for the China war relief and everything else, here was a ready-made group. And we went around and entertained in churches and schools and sang. And most of us, well, *my* family spoke some Chinese 'cause we were all taught Chinese in growing up, but the other Chinese families, that had mothers, fathers, and children, they really didn't know any. Like, especially the Lees, who were close friends of ours, didn't know any Chinese. So all of the Chinese songs that we sang as part of this thing to raise monies had to be taught phonetically.

> **Me**: Oh, wait a minute. So Miss Fairbanks was not Chinese, right?

> **My father**: No, she was Caucasian. Baptist. But she pulled us all together, because we were all the Chinese, the Sunday School nucleus group. But she — I can't remember that Miss Fairbanks

was part of First Baptist Church even. But she was Baptist. And she took us in hand; and it was through Miss Fairbanks that some of us began to take piano lessons from her friend, Miss Maine — yeah, Miss Maine — Miss Maine was our piano teacher. She taught all of us piano at one time or another.

My mother: How did you practice in between lessons?

My father: On her piano. And Miss Fairbanks had a piano, and the church had a piano. So we always had a piano that we could practice with — but we had to *go* to the piano; the piano was not at our home. It wasn't until we moved to Tioga Street — I think that we finally got a piano at home, that we got from somebody — I can't remember who. But we were taught these Chinese songs —

Me: Miss Fairbanks was teaching you all Chinese songs?

My father: No. Anything that had to be done to facilitate our learning of Chinese language and to sing would be through her efforts. She got Peter Chin, who was a person who really got so actively involved 'cause he liked my sister Betty, who didn't want to give him the time of day — but she remained friends with Peter Chin for life; they're still friends. He wrote everything out phonetically so that those who did not know Chinese could learn the words; and then, of course, somebody else would teach us the music. And to this day, I'm sure that at least in *my* family — I don't know about the other kids that we grew up with, our contemporaries — we know what is the Communist national anthem of China. We were taught that phonetically. Never knew what it was. All we knew was that it was a national anthem.

Me: Oh my god. You didn't know it was Communist, you just knew it was …

My father: Yeah, we knew it was a national anthem; we didn't know that it was the *Communist* national anthem. It was years later, I think I was seeing one of the old movies that — I don't know if it was Pearl Buck, or whatever — but I heard the singing and I said "*We* know that! 'cause I *sing* it!" And somebody said, "That's the Communist Chinese Anthem. How do you know it?" The chorus'd go (sings) "Chi lai, chi lai (etc.)" One of the other songs we were taught as part of that repertoire of Chinese music to raise money for China was a song that I later taught to my fraternity brothers in college as part of our — we were competing in the interfraternity sing. Every year there was a competition. And we were gonna do the songs of the world, which fits in with yours and René's class.[1]

My mother: University songs.

My father: University songs. And of course, that was synonymous with drinking songs, right?

My mother: Yes.

My father: (Laughs.) So I taught my fraternity chorus in the same way that we were taught in growing up, writing everything out phonetically for them. So our repertoire, or contribution included the "Main Sein" song, "The Halls of Ivy," we sang, and then there was this Chinese song, and we all sang it in Chinese. We won. We won hands down.

Me: Were you were the only Chinese boy in this group of frat guys?

My father: Yeah. I was practically the only Chinese boy in the school; I think my brother Frank and I were the only Chinese in the University of Buffalo at that time. But we sang that, and …

Me: What song was it that —

My mother: "Peking Drinking Song."

My father: It was called "The Peking Drinking Song."

Me: (to my mother) You were there?

My mother: I was there!

My father: She was at all the rehearsals! (Sings song.)

My mother (as he sings and sings): They were a smash.

Me: (laughs) Now, Miss Fairbanks did not teach you that.

My father: No. Generally it was Peter Chin, or George Boleyn, you know these people that Betty talks about that she still keeps in touch with; and George Boleyn is married to a second wife and he's in Houston now.

My mother: Oh, George! Oh, wow! —

My father: George Boleyn.

My mother: — They just kinda "pulled it out." It was a surefire winner. They knew they were gonna win before they ever stood up.

Me: What do the words mean?

My father: (Sings line.) It means "Each one will raise our glasses and will all sing. (Sings.) Wei-Guo[2] [his Chinese-born brother-in-law] would know this one.

My mother: Oh, I'm sure.

My father: We didn't learn it *together*; we didn't know 'em then, the three kids. But we used to sing these songs, and, as kids, sing all this repertoire, and, like I was saying, most of us didn't know what it meant. But we went around and raised money; and here we were, raising money, singing the Communist Chinese national anthem. And we were raising money for the Nationalists. You know, the United States was always allied with the Nationalists, the Kuo Min Tang, certainly not the Communists. Well, I thought there was a splendid kind of irony in that.

Me: So, how many little kids were in this group that —

My father: Let's see ... Six Lees, six Wongs, and then the other three Lees ...

My mother: Oh, the other three Lees. Right.

My father: And then the Wongs: Billy — William, Helen, and George Wong, 3. So, how many is that? 6 ... 12 ... 15 ... 18 ... and I think there might have been one or two more. We've got a picture of them somewhere —

My mother: Betty?

My father: No, we have the picture that was taken at the First Baptist Church; we were all standing there ... Oh, we have a picture of it somewhere. Yeah. We all had a picture of it (Figure 14.1).

Me: What kind of places did you sing at?

My father: Well, churches first of course, all the churches around Buffalo; it didn't have to be a Baptist church.

Me: Unless there's a Chinese audience —

My father: Oh no; no. The whole idea was to go and raise money.

My mother: From the greater community.

Fig. 14.1 The Chinese children's choir in Buffalo, New York, ca. 1935–36. Front row, seated: Fred Wong, John Wong. Second row: (far right) Jean Wong, (sixth from right) Betty Wong. Third row: (right) Jim Wong. Back row: (left) Frank Wong, (second from left) Miss Fairbanks. (Wong family photograph.)

My father: And I can recall vividly one thing that really impressed the dickens out of us. Mr. Marlon — or Marron — Young. He was the chairman of the board of the Humboldt Museum. So, very wealthy. He had a *big* estate across from St. Joseph's Cathedral, on Delaware and Utah — on Utica I mean. And it was a huge estate, and he had gardens, and had a pool. So, we were going to have a fund-raiser at his house — he was inviting all of his rich friends — and we were there, and they took movies of us and everything else for that 'cause they were going to send a movie around the country; and I can remember that one of the cutest shots in that was my sister Jean who was about this big. Jean must have been, what, in kindergarten, if that, and she had that haircut, the bangs right across her forehead, her Chinese high-neck gown, and she'd duck behind the rose bushes; then she'd stand up and she'd wave, and she'd duck down, and she'd giggle. And I can remember Jean doing this, and singing this poem. But we sang for all of these people. Whenever we sang we were always in costume; the girls wore the *cheong sam* and the boys wore kind of pajama suits, and that sort of thing, which my older brothers hated; they refused, they were going to boycott once 'cause they thought it was kind of —

Me: Where did these clothes come from? Did Grandma have to make them?

My father: A lot of mothers made them; yeah. The girls' dresses were especially nice. But, again, we learned all these songs — we sang a number of Western songs as well and church-like songs — but we were always a hit when we sang in Chinese. And I don't think the people realized that most of the kids who were singing didn't know what they were singing 'cause they never spoke Chinese. Ours was the only family that really *studied* Chinese, learned it at home. So we learned the geography, history, mythology, and reading and writing. The other Lees — the family of three Lees — could speak Chinese, but they never took any classes; they couldn't read or anything else. But we all did learn to sing. I don't know how good we really sounded but...

My mother: Little kids always sound good.

Me: Little kids sound like little kids. Sure.

My father: But, yeah, it's funny 'cause we talked about it and these things come out. When you first said you wanted to talk to me about this, I thought, "How am I going to remember what we did?" But in *talking* about it — this is how it all comes back.

Me: Sounds like you all were pretty busy.

My father: Well, we grew up with the war and it was part of our war effort and we were made to understand and appreciate the fact that we were Chinese. We were Chinese — and that was the motherland, you know? That it was up to us to do our part to help China win the war. And I don't know how much you remember of the history of that war over there, but there was the Rape of Nanking which is where they were showing a baby's being thrown up in the air and caught on the Japanese soldiers' bayonets. Well, it was at that time all of this was going on that we were singing. So it really didn't take much to make people dig deep, and we met all the people in the greater Buffalo area that had the deep pockets. I mean, people who came to these parties were people like Larry Bell who was the head of Bell Aircraft, who made the Air Cobras that helped to win the war over in China. And Curtis Wright Aircraft was part of Buffalo and the president of that was part of this deep pockets group that gave 'em the money. And they were the ones that built the B-40s that John Wayne flew in *Flying Tigers*, you know, in the China-Burma-India theater. So these were the people that were all part of our growing up, and the people we were entertaining and getting money from — and the reason we learned these songs. I think there were a number of us who probably gained a better appreciation for Chinese music, Chinese culture, because of these songs that we had to learn. As I recall, we learned very, very fast, very quickly. So there must have been real motivation there. Part of it I think was that we were helping to raise money to win the war.

Me: So you didn't feel, you know, forced into it?

My father: Oh no, no, we didn't feel that we were being exploited or anything. I don't think Miss Fairbanks ever really gave us a chance — she was very protective of us. She was like a mother hen. I mean, if she felt that we were exploited she would be like a mother.

My mother: Was that around 1937?

My father: Was what?

My mother: 1937? That you were doing the singing? 1938?

My father: This would have been even earlier, maybe '35,' 36, '37. The war, the Chinese-Japanese War, didn't start till '37. And that same year my grandfather died. So we remember that quite clear — but, before that, we were already singing.

I'd like to unpack this in my own way, though I'm pretty sure it's not the way my father thought about it. I would guess that Miss Fairbanks figured that she could accomplish two things by assembling this children's choir, and it's likely that the two things — religious commitment and patriotic effort — were intertwined in her mind. She wanted the children to learn to be Baptists, and she wanted to support what we now can recognize as the early American war effort even though it was several years before Pearl Harbor and the entry of the U.S. into World War II. Her cause was the Chinese Nationalist resistance to the rise of Communism. What better vehicle for all this than Chinese American child Baptists? But they couldn't be too American. Indeed, the whole point was that they embodied a better kind of "Chinese," a Chineseness indebted and committed to certain American core values (Christianity, democracy). She put her effort into casting them as "Chinese" in specific ways and trusting context to do the rest. The children learned Chinese songs in Chinese, and they wore "Chinese" clothes. Never mind that most of the kids (beyond my father and his siblings) weren't particularly fluent in Cantonese and had to learn the words phonetically. They intersected with the monied elite of Buffalo, because the end goal was fundraising, so their charming, controlled Chineseness was spectacularized in very specific ways. As my father put it, "We were made to understand and appreciate the fact that we were Chinese." There is so much going on in that statement.

Cut fifteen years forward, to my father in college in the early 1950s. He had breached the walls: he, his brother Frank and the Lees were, to his memory, the only Chinese Americans at the University of Buffalo, and he was right in the thick of it. He was a veteran and a fraternity brother. He joined Sigma Alpha Nu, a frat formed by veterans, who were all a bit older than the usual undergraduate. But he knew he was different, and he was adept at framing his Chineseness in ways that rendered it charming and interesting rather than foreign and threatening. He taught his frat brothers the Peking drinking song in the same way that it had been taught to him and his Chinese American friends: phonetically, as sounds to be memorized — and now as part of a universalized cross-cultural brotherhood of beer. What did his fraternity brothers think of it? My mother remembers that they loved it. She was already there, albeit on the sidelines — an eighteen-year-old White girl who was the first in her family to go to college, and who was busily breaching the walls in more ways than one (including falling for a Chinese American man). What was going on there? Was my father a kind of harmless mascot for the otherwise White fraternity? Certainly those young men were experimenting with new kinds of tolerance, ready to regard him as their brother, genuinely supporting the interracial marriage-in-the-making unfolding before their eyes. My mother remembers that they were all thrilled to know the song: to them, it signified open-mindedness and acceptance, and they knew it set their group apart as special at the interfraternity sing. They all stood up and sang the Peking drinking song, and they knew it was good, and they knew they would win, and my parents recalled it in 1997 with pleasure and triumph (Figure

14.2). In other ways, that moment at the University of Buffalo reenacted a century of yellowface and yellowvoice.[3] A group of (mostly) White fraternity brothers singing a "Chinese" song taught to them by a Chinese American who had learned it from another Chinese American directed by the inimitable Miss Fairbanks. And yet I suspect that that's not really it, though the ease of such a reading is tempting. For one thing, those young men were outlining new social realities: Italians, Poles, and Irish in Buffalo weren't yet White in the ways that WASPs were, and social mobility had been resituated by the G.I. Bill. How many of those young veterans would have gone to college without it? My father remembered Miss Fairbanks with respect and affection, all bound up with his feelings for music.

> I think one of my strongest memories living on Allen Street — and this of course would have been after the war — I can remember lying on the couch listening to that same radio — because it had a good sound, it had a good bass and everything else — you got just bass and treble — and hearing the first recordings that some disc jockey was playing from *South Pacific*. They played "Some Enchanted Evening." And I lay on that couch and I was absolutely enthralled. There were tears in my eyes; and I thought, "Wow, that's beautiful!" And then from that point I was learning, hearing all the different music. But, you know, beginning interest, when we were kids, leads into this kind of thing. I don't know if anybody else in my family, my brothers and sisters, is as affected emotionally as I am. When I hear good music, I have tears ... 'cause it'll reach me. When we talk about it now, we were so lucky to have Miss Fairbanks, Miss Maine ... I miss 'em. If all of us hated Uncle Korn [his father's brother and their Chinese language teacher] for being such a strict person with us — a disciplinarian — and forcing us to learn Chinese, we loved Miss Fairbanks for exactly the same reasons! I mean, she rode herd on us, and she was a strict disciplinarian; she didn't let us horse around and play — there's a time for play, and there's a time for learning. And if we were going to do our jobs to help China, this is the time for learning. But we realized how serious and how sincere she was; we loved her for it. We all did. We did a lot of laughing about it.

I wonder too about the nature of that laughter. I understand the respect that he and his brothers and sisters had for her, but I'm also trying to listen to their laughter. They all ended up going to college, and they were proud of their Chinese heritage as well as attuned to the vagaries of American racism. That laughter may have a subtext to it, an awareness that Miss Fairbanks wasn't exactly innocent and that they had been part of something that could be understood in more than one way. Indeed, Asian American involvement in music can always be understood in more than one way.

Fig. 14.2 The Sigma Alpha Nu fraternity at the interfraternity sing at the University of Buffalo in Buffalo, New York, ca. 1953. Front row, left to right: Ed Eisenheimer, Dan Palmer, Paul Rizzo, Chuck Barressi, John Wong, Peter Donatelli. Middle row: Jim Massora, Jim Woods, Chuck Schwindler, Ron McMahon, Phil Klass. Back row: Peter Martina, Ron Toffalo, Bill Sugnet, Dan Meyers, Burt Lapp, Bob Mooney. (Wong family photograph.)

I offer this story about the Peking drinking song and its (re)circulation as emblematic of Asian American involvement in music not because it was an "Asian" song but because its movement was defined through specific ideas of race, nationality and belonging that delineated American Chineseness at two rather different historical moments. I see the movement of the song as exemplary, not problematic. Surely this book has made it clear that authenticity isn't the point. Surely it is equally clear that my considerations of Asian Americans making music call the very idea of American music and Americanness into question. This final chapter resonates with earlier parts of the book. My father's encounters with Blackness are in counterpoint to Rodney Ogawa's pleasure in Motown and the Mountain Brothers' efforts to make good beats. His experiences in the Chinese children's choir have points of contact with the Cambodian immigrants' and Miya Masaoka's move into a fraught public sphere. The ways that he was framed from without, the ways that he participated in troubling forms of reinscribed and expropriated orientalia, and the ways that he chose to participate in interethnic musical encounter (polka, big band) are typical of the choices that Asian Americans make constantly in their daily lives. He listened to *South Pacific* on the radio and was enthralled: he was an Asian American listening to a Broadway fantasy of the romance of the South Seas, a musical that celebrates the orientalist and imperial effort to control remote parts of the globe, whose plot hinges on the promise and threat of the interracial encounter. He married a White woman. He found "Some Enchanted Evening" beautiful, no doubt in the sensual, untheorized yet mindful ways through which most of us experience music and performance. We know it moves us; we know that that's important.

I focus here, at the very end of this book, on the moment when my father turned it around and taught what he was taught, on the eve of the Civil Rights movement, as a new kind of Asian American. Go back a few pages and cast back and forth between the two photographs. They are mirror images of each other. Their formal portraiture transforms the moment of sound into an architecture of arranged bodies. Look at the pride shining out of each photo and think about the parameters of that pride. Each photo asks you to find who's different. Who's the odd one out? In each case, it was the other who offered up a new choreography of sound and racialized body: Miss Fairbanks grimly overseeing her flock of Chinese children in 1936, my father beaming, triumphant, in 1953.

He's singing — listen to it again on Track 11. He loved to sing.

Endnotes

1. He is referring to the world music courses that René T.A. Lysloff and I teach at the University of California, Riverside.
2. "Wei-Guo" was my uncle, Wu-Wei Li, married to my father's oldest sister, Betty.
3. I owe the term "yellowvoice" to Rob Lancefield (forthcoming), whose dissertation will be centrally concerned with the history of mimetic orientalist performance in the U.S.

Appendix

"Thinking About the Old Village"
(*Khit haut baan kao*)

Written and performed by Khamvong Insixiengmai. Transcribed and translated by Deborah Wong. (Audio Example 2.1)

Although this poetic text was composed by Khamvong, he used (as is customary among singers of *maulam*) certain formulaic expressions. The opening stanza of salutation is expected, in which a singer addresses his or her audience. After that, s/he addresses the song to a beloved, either present or (in this case) absent. Khamvong refers throughout to the woman as *naung* or "younger sibling" as is usual in Lao; no blood relationship is implied but only the intimacy of the relationship. He frequently refers to her beauty by evoking her cheeks and her eyebrows, both common phrases in the *maulam* tradition, and he often closes an extended set of lines with a single long line of impressionistic references to her cheeks or her black eyebrows, replete with sighs of "oh!" (*oey*). Notice the constant references to Buddhist belief, e.g., to the couple's past lives (true lovers meet again and again through reincarnation), to making merit and to *karma* (fate and the implications of actions carried across reincarnations).

This song is and isn't a linear narrative. Khamvong is essentially reminiscing and he jumps back and forth between different events and memories. There is no "story" and no closure to the narrative; rather, the overall effect is of the combined emotions of love, longing, loss, poignancy and sadness.

aun aun sii kaem caw aun aun	Your cheeks are so soft
müa nii phom kau yau muu kaun	Now I would like to raise my hands in respect
hay khun phra thang laay	To all of you here
thang phra yaa caw naay	To all you respected ones
phuu maa laum maa niaw	To all you who circle me
hay fang oey	Please listen
Ohhhhhhhhhhh… oey	
fang yoe	Listen
fang siang taek tüng	Listen to the sound of the thunder
niam phay akhanee nii khun yoe naang oey	There is danger everywhere, dear woman
phom ngaaw naa faa maung	I am lonely, the sky is dark
meek chuan si tam taung	The clouds hang low
dang khanaung yuu bon faa	Loud thunder is in the sky
siang thom thom nam fon lang	The sound of rain falling
khit haut khraaw lang lang	I think back to the past
yaam naa maa haut laew	The season for planting rice has arrived
phay si phaa caw sang	Who will help work?
an waa tham hua pluuk maak taeng	Who will plant betel nut?
man haak lüa haeng aay	There is no one to help but myself
an waa nau hak naung ka taung huang khanüng haa	Since I love you, I have to worry and think of you
cit wang wee wong thüng	I miss you and think of you
un manoo nam taa yauy	My heart is at ease but my tears flow
mii tae khauy thaang klam	There is only waiting
sawankham baan kao	To return to Sawankham, the old village
khit haut han la luuk taw	I think of the village and its children
an muun khaw kaw lang	And its origins in the past
bat nii khit haut yaat phi naung	At this time I think of my relatives
an phau mae lae aaw aa	Of my parents, my father's relatives
thaang pay naa maa suan	Of the paths to the ricefields and gardens
an bung thaam baun khoey saang	Of the earthen dikes that cut through the fields
khit hen thiang thaang nauy	I think of the shelter along the small path
an san caun khrang kaun kaun	That I traveled in the past
khit hen naa bang aun	I think of my sweetheart's face
khraaw pay bun khrang nan	Of that time we went to make merit
haw khoey waw tau kan	We used to talk together
saung haw day phuuk man	We two promised
waa bau haangkan nii	That we wouldn't separate
bung bang fay pracam pii	At the annual rocket festival
an thii mau talaew nauy	At Mau Talaew Nauy
naang yang khauy cay dan	Please wait for me
an khan doen pay haut thii	When I returned to that place
aay laut lat lau paa may	I took a short cut through the forest
lauy khuan ta fang see	I swam across the See River to the other bank
uk cay dee khiw koong khon oey hang taa dam oey	Her eyebrows, oh, her black eyebrows

bat nii aay cüng pay phop phau naung	I therefore went to meet you
day nang aen prüksaa kan	We sat and talked together
khaat khanee saung saam pii	We thought that in two or three years
cüng taeng ngaan kan nau naung	We would marry
saung khon haw dauk khoey phau	We two used to meet
an nay ngaan caw baan thuat	At the Baan Thuat festival
saaban kan bau hang	We swore we wouldn't separate
bau waang thim haang saung	Wouldn't be far apart
yaam müa aay lae naung	When you and I
khong day yuu nay phi phop	Were in the world
chiiwit saung khon haw	Our two lives
haak waa khong cop long	If they ended
haak waa nau bau long lüüm	If you were unable to forget
aat daawray lüüm day	If an unlucky star allowed you to forget
phay phuu tham laay laang	The people who destroy
satcatham khan huam	[?]
thaat ing hang nan naa baun haw khoey nop way	We used to worship at the Ing-Hang shrine
saaban taung tau kan	We must promise each other
khüü waa hak thae thae	To truly love each other
phuak haw huam athithaan	We prayed together
saaban long nay wat	We promised in the temple
kheet aaram wong kwaang	In its spacious area
paang müa chaat paang kaun	In our previous lives
khraung müang thük tok lom	We ruled the city of Thük Tok Lom
aay day kom kraap way	I knelt down in obeisance
saung haw day hak kan	We two loved each other
an dii bau nuan kham oey	Oh, good, not soft words
khraaw nan lam cüng khau sang naung	At that time, I wanted to sing for you
phra can caem sut thii hak	The light of the moon, most beloved
aay haak naew naam chaay	If I go the way of men [i.e., become a soldier]
lüat thahaan haan suu	Full of a soldier's blood, bravely fighting
aay sii khauy cay dan	I will wait, impervious
asay bun nam naung un	I will be secure in your merit
pay pok khlum pha phi aay	You will protect me
phuu naun som yuu paa naa	We who sleep in the dense forest
aay ak suu phüa naung	If I fight for you
an wong muu chaaw waan	For the people
plot plauy khaum muun nii	To expel the communists
auk caak laaw hay suun sia	Out of Laos, to make them disappear
thüng hok pii aay naun son	For six years I have slept lying in ambush
thüng hok pii aay naun son	For six years I have slept lying in ambush
an khaem law khook bung	At the edge of Law Khook Bung
aw bay kung naep nüa	I take leaves and cover my body
an taang phaa homnaaw	As a blanket in the cold
thüng yaam naun aay huang naung	When I go to sleep, I worry about you
nam taa lang ram phuang	My tears flow constantly
ngaem saung düan thüng weehaa	I look up at the sky
raung ham nam thuklaeng chaaw	I weep morning and night

bat nii khit haut yaam hiw khaaw	Now I think back to the times I was hungry
aay doen thaang haun heng	I hurry along
leng plaay püün lan naaw	I aim my gun and shoot
weelaa aay phop muu maan	Whenever I meet up with the evil beings [i.e., the communists]
suan waa ton aay nii	As for me
mii tae kiaw khwaamhak	There is only love
praatthanaa cay maay	I want to love you [?]
tau phra naang nong naung	You, dear woman
cüng day lam dauk pen rüang	Therefore I sing our story
an kham klaun at song	And tape record and send this poem to you
law khwaamlang thii hak naung	I tell of the past when I loved you
day maay man tau kan	And we made promises to each other
sawaan müang khon oey khiwkoong khon ngsaam hang taa dam oey	You heavenly one, oh! your eyebrows, you beautiful one, your black eyebrows, oh!
bat nii suan waa khraaw khrang nan	Now at that time
sanyaa tau duangdüan	We swore under the moon
sanyaa kan klaang wan	We swore to each other by day
tau phra in yuu thüng faa	And to Lord Indra in the sky
haw bau yaum dauk wang haang	That we wouldn't allow anything to separate us
an waang kan day pa plauy	We freed one another, we abandoned each other [?]
khwaamhak khauy lae caw	My love and yours
day wang hua chua chiiwang	We hoped we would be together our whole lives
khrang nüng dayyin khaaw	One time I heard
saaw phanaang naat naung waa caw plauy khwaamkhit	That you, dear woman, were unconscious
phayaathi khlum khaa nüa	Were ill
aay day müa yaam yüü	I left the army
thüü khaung kin pay taun un	I brought you food
thüü yuk yay pay biip khan	I brought you medicine and prepared it
an pua naung ming manii	So that you, precious one, would recover
aay… naung cüng dii luk day	I… Soon you were well enough to get up
an khay paak waacaa	We said that
thuk chaat maay khwaamhak	In every one of our lives
tau kan saung kam	We would love each other
khon mot müang maen khaw waw	Everyone in Maen said
waa uan chaay kap naung nii	That you and I
maay kaut naep kiaw man	Would marry
wang saun ruam sanee	And hoped we would live together happily
phau müa thüng düan haa	When the fifth month came
sangkhaan pen pi may	We had the New Year's festival
hok düan cet nan day	The sixth month, the seventh month
khan waa faa ham haung phansaa khaw laung thüng	Was the time that the sky thundered and Buddhist Lent arrived

suan waa aay lae naung	And you and I
day yüan tau düan sip saung	And waited for the twelfth month
haa ngoen thaung phau khrop	And looked for enough money
cüng taeng daung nau naung	So we could marry
maat waa müang laaw bin	When Laos was controlled
an fuung khaum khaw naw nang	By the communists
aay mot wang hang naung	I lost all hope and left you
caun dan caak phanaang	And went away from you
aay… aay mii tae yüün caung	I… I could only keep watch
taam baan thaang khaung baan un	Over the paths to your house
khran mii tae caung haa naang thuk	When I could only stand and keep
chaaw kham	watch, looking for you every morning
	and night
thuk kham laeng lae chaaw	Every evening and morning
khanüng oo aaw nam	I thought about you all the time
naem saung pay thaang kam	I look back
nay khong kheet müang laaw	At Laos
hen tae waayoo phat	I see only the wind
waunwon yuu thüng faa	Blowing in circles in the sky
bang faung hen nan naa taam tae wayoo	Sometimes I see the wind blowing
faay	
müang song phuu wa naat	Like the wind on Mt. Vanath
nam taa aay yaat yauy	My tears fall
khanüng oo aaw nam kaam oey ween dee	I think always of our bad karma, oh!
bak huacay khon oey	
bat nii wang waa kaew kaen na naung	Now I hope that you
khong khit ham phra uan faay	Still think of me
aay cüng baay aw sau	Therefore I take up pencil
paak ba kaa kap cia	Pen and paper
taeng pen klaun lam laew	I have written this poem
an at siang say theep song	Recorded it on tape and sent it to you
khamwong day haang naung	Khamvong sings about being far from
	you
tok yuu khon la thiip klam bau khraung	[?]
day cuak phra naang	
khit waa naung yuu phun	You are back there
mii cayhaang waang chaay	Maybe you are unfaithful
ba hay law lamoe haa	I talk to you in my sleep
an suu yaam khanüng naung	I think of you all the time
sanyaa haw dauk maay way	The promises we said we would keep
an nam kan khrang kaun kaun	When we went together [to the shrine]
	in times past
nuan bang aun khong cüü day	You have not forgotten
khwaamhawwaw tau kan	The matter we discussed
khan waa phay haak hang	If we are separated
day yaek haang hoen kan	And are estranged from each other
saay samphan khwaamhak	The line of our love
phuuk maytrii sanyaa tang	We promised to be friends
phay phuu wang tham laay laang	Our hopes were destroyed [?]
an khraung sin hay maung mon	And we observed the religious precepts
	in sadness [?]
tok sau long say ngiang day	When he hears the bad news [?]

pen sian siap pha thay	It pierced my heart
a dee day naang oey khiwkoong khon oey	Really, woman, oh! your eyebrows, oh!
saeng taa dam naa	the light of your black eyes
bauk waa ween sanaung song hay	It is said that bad karma will come back [?]
day taam klaaw sanyaa waa nii dee naang oey	I kept the promises we made — did you? [?]
pen tay dii rüü raay	Whether we die well or through evil
bau long lüüm kham klaw	Don't forget our words
satruu maan phaa maang	Evil ones separate us
pa khauy suu bau waang	But we fight and don't give up
phay phuu day phaa maang	Whoever breaks
an ton kaun hay pen saung	[The promise] first
hua hap haung khwaamphit	Whoever is wronged
suu taay bau lüüm day	Will never be forgotten
nay hok pii klaay maa laew	When six years passed
bua thaung naung haak naay	You became tired [of waiting]
klaay sanyaa phaa maang	You broke our promise
loey suun siang suu khwaam	Your words meant nothing
naung haak nii caak aay	If you fled from me
aay nii caak naung	I fled from you
khauy khaum phuak muu maan	From the communists, the evil ones
an din daan daen laaw	From Laos
tat khaat saay samphan	And broke off the relationship
rawaang wong kap naung	Between you and I
[?]	
som sanuk lam theen	Enjoy the *lamtheen* trees
thin satüüm khaung aay	At Satüüm, my village
kap thang suy naung nam	And Suy Pond
kut maak khaen baun khoey thiaw	And Kut Maak Khaen, where we used to go
naa ray liaw baan thuat nüa	And the rice paddies around the village of Thuat
an waa nüa lae tay	To the north and south
khamwong aay sang laa khwan taa khon oey chuu phoen phuu ngaam oey	I, Khamvong, say farewell to you, to your soul, oh! to you, beautiful one, oh!
müa nii laan si laa caw phuak paa	Now I bid farewell to you, my aunts
naung phüü kaw thang saung khaw	To the village of Naung Phüü Kaw
daun khayaeng taan sum	To the villages of Daun Khayaeng and Taan Sum
lanaat din daun khaw	To my place of birth, now disturbed
thaa haak bun khamwong lon	If I make lots of merit
sii khüün khaup kheehang	I will return home
cau tau kun si khong hen	I will probably return in the Year of the Dog or the Pig
praap muu maan hay suun	And will completely subjugate the evildoers [i.e., the communists]
khap muu kaew phuak khon raay	I will drive the evil Khmers out
an kray saun phuak maa paa	And Kaisone, the wolf

saung haw cüng khauy waw	We two must wait before we speak together again
sanee saun may chom	Before we can love each other again [?]
saathu in phrom faa	I salute Indra and Brahma in the sky
theewadaa phuu ling lam	And all the deities, the most respected ones
in phrom daen yuu kam	To Indra and Brahma in the realm above
sawaan faa thii suung	In the heavens high above
khau hay bun dauk lam day	I would like to have enough merit to be able to sing
an somdang manoo maay	It is my heartfelt desire
khap lay maan fuung khwaang	To drive out the evildoers
luang klaay auk klay ban	To drive them far from our home
khwaamlam khaan maen si thuk	I will know such sorrow
an waa nau thuam faa	That it will rise to the sky [i.e., like a flood]
khrüang nung hom thüü	My sarong
naun taam din fon ham	I sleep on the ground in the light rain
thuk kham khüün khauy suu	Waiting every night to fight
khau aasay paa law an waa dee khaem som	I live cooped up in the forest, hiding on its edges
yung yang müat hae	With mosquitoes and ticks
kap ton tua kam lae	[?]
an maung mua kaw sii	Which is old and stained
tem thii laew naang oey chuu phoen ween oey saay lom nuan oey	It's terrible, woman, oh! to flirt with others is bad karma, oh! the soft wind, oh!
bat nii khwaamthuk nay khrang nii	These are sorrowful times
an saen weetthanaa nak	They are pitiful in the extreme
prawat laaw phaay lang	The past history of Laos
bau khauy mii maa phau	Was not like what has come to pass
khwaamsau phau maa pun	Lies and falsehood have come together
kuan laaw hay thuk maak	And have caused much trouble and sorrow
khwaamlambaak tang tae dee	There have been difficulties since that time
an waa nau kaun kii day maay maang muu maan	And I wanted to destroy the evil ones even before they came
thuk chaat hay phaan phon	For every life beyond this
ton tua hang khwaamsaam	May we be far from misfortune
yaa day pay dauk phaan phop	Don't go [?]
huam thaang phaan phau	[?]
wit caak lookaa kwaang	When we leave this wide world
sawaan phrom phop cuap	We will meet in Brahma's heaven
praatthanaa liik ween	I deny my desires
an sin haa hay haang kan	The Five Precepts[1] are distant now
ii lii day kham oey bak huacay khon oey	Really, these words, oh! this is a person's heart, oh!
bat nii saung khon haw cüng khauy tang	At this time we therefore wait
maa pen khuu phua mia	To become husband and wife
naun huam hiang khiang maun	To sleep together in bed, our pillows side by side

baun sawaan müang faa	In the heavenly city
aay khau laa caw nuan naung	I would like to bid you farewell
hong thaung kaem pa klin	You beautiful one, with the fragrant cheeks
chiiwit haw bau sin	Our lives are without end
khong ca day huam sanee	Hopefully we will be together, dearest
müa dayyin khwaam waa saang	When you hear this
khamwong klaaw kaanthalaeng	My account of this
top tarng plaeng waunkhay	Composed to show you
dot klaaw maa waun naung	To tell and implore you
khau hay nong naung naang naung	Please, dear woman
dot trük traung caw khit aan	Consider this carefully when you read it
manut nay songsaan	Humankind is in pitiful shape
man haak yaak kradau	It's so difficult
man saen plüüm tae phra thay aay dee naang oey	It pleases my heart so, you and I together, oh!
bat nii nii si dauk klay phoeng	Now flee far from here, my flower far from the bees
an paa thüng si klay thung	Go into the forest, far from the fields
süa khrong klay paa may	The tiger is far from the forest
paan si haung nam siang	Go, call to it
aay caak naung müü nii	I am far from you now
khüü faa sang laa fon	That is, the sky sends down rain like a farewell
kop khiat puu plaa hauy	The frogs, the crabs, the fish, the clams
yaa sang laa naung nam	Don't bid farewell to the marsh!
sang phüa thay hong kwaang	We build so that people everywhere can be free
phayaa luang auk suu paa	The royal family has gone out into the forest
naa paa kap ngaun don	They live bravely in the forest [?]
dot pan müü bau cuap kan	[?]
man haak pen thii aay	If this is the time
cit aay waa saban	That my thoughts are scattered
yaam si caak caun nii yaam si klay	At this time I wander, I have fled far
saeng sii hang kan hoen laew	We are farther and farther from one another already
laa duk doe naang kaew	I bid farewell to you, dearest
siithandaun long kaun	My Lam Siithandaun[2] is ending now
khau yok klaun thau nii	I would like to raise the poem like this
an long way chua si long	I have reached the end now
oey sinaawaa khan plauy way saakaun thau nii laew	This is enough, I'll end like this

Endnotes

1. The Five Buddhist Precepts proscribe killing, stealing, wrongful sexual behavior, lying and consuming alcohol.
2. The name of the specific poetic form he has been singing in, i.e., his song.

Bibliography

Abu-Lughod, Lila
  1986 *Veiled Sentiments: Honor and Poetry in a Bedouin Society.* Berkeley: University of California Press.
  1991 "Writing Against Culture." In *Recapturing Anthropology: Working in the Present,* Ed. Richard G. Fox. Santa Fe, New Mexico: School of American Research Press.
  1993 *Writing Women's Worlds: Bedouin Stories.* Berkeley: University of California Press.

Acosta-Belén, Edna
  1993 "Defining a Common Ground: The Theoretical Meeting of Women's, Ethnic, and Area Studies." In *Researching Women in Latin America and the Caribbean,* Eds. Edna Acosta-Belén and Christine E. Bose. Boulder, Colorado: Westview Press.

Agawu, Kofi
  1997 "Analyzing Music under the New Musicological Regime." *The Journal of Musicology* 15 (3): 297–307.

Akinnaso, F. Niyi
  1981 "The Consequences of Literacy in Pragmatic and Theoretical Perspectives." *Anthropology and Education Quarterly* 12 (3):163–200.

Alfaro, Luis
  2001 "Minnie Riperton Saved My Life." In *Another City: Writing from Los Angeles,* Ed. David L. Ulin, 13–18. San Francisco: City Lights Books.

Altman, Irwin and Martin Chemers
   1980 *Culture and Environment.* Cambridge: Cambridge University
   Press.

American Folklife Center
   1982 *Ethnic Recordings in America: A Neglected Heritage.* Washington: American Folklife Center, Library of Congress.

Ames, David W. and Anthony V. King
   1971 *Glossary of Hausa Music and its Contexts.* Evanston: Northwest-
   ern University Press.

Anderson, Elijah
   1990 *Streetwise: Race, Class, and Change in an Urban Community.*
   Chicago and London: University of Chicago Press.

Arana, Miranda
   1994 "Modernized Vietnamese Music and Its Impact on Musical
   Sensibilities." *The Journal of Vietnamese Music* 3 (1 and 2):
   91–110.

Armstrong, Larry
   1992 "What's that Noise in Aisle 5? 'Karaoke' May Be Coming Soon
   to a Supermarket or Mall Near You." *Business Week,* June 8, 1992,
   n. 3269, p. 38.

Asai, Susan Miyo
   1985 "Horaku: A Buddhist Tradition of Performing Arts and the
   Development of Taiko Drumming in the United States." *Selected
   Reports in Ethnomusicology* 6: 163–72.
   1995 "Transformations of Tradition: Three Generations of Japanese
   American Music Making." *The Musical Quarterly* 79 (3): 429–453.
   1997 "Sansei Voices in the Community." In *Musics of Multicultural
   America: A Study of Twelve Musical Communities,* Eds. Kip Lornell
   and Anne K. Rasmussen, 257–85. New York: Schirmer Books.

Attali, Jacques
   1985 *Noise: The Political Economy of Music.* Minneapolis: University
   of Minnesota Press.

Augé, Marc
   1995 *Non-Places: Introduction to an Anthropology of Supermodernity.*
   Trans. John Howe. London and New York: Verso.

Austin, J.L.
   1962 *How to Do Things with Words.* Cambridge: Harvard University Press.

Averill, Gage
   1997 *A Day for the Hunter, A Day for the Prey: Popular Music and Power in Haiti.* Chicago and London: University of Chicago Press.

Bailey, Derek
   1980 *Improvisation: Its Nature and Practice in Music.* Ashbourne: Moorland Publishing.

Ballinger, Robin
   1995 "Sounds of Resistance." In *Sounding Off! Music as Subversion/Resistance/Revolution,* Eds. Ron Sakolsky and Fred Wei-Han Ho. Brooklyn: Autonomedia.
Barz, Gregory F. and Timothy J. Cooley, Eds.
   1997. Shadows in the Field: New Perspectives for Fieldwork in Ethnomusicology. Oxford and New York: Oxford University Press.

Basso, Keith
   1984 "Stalking with Stories": Names, Places, and Moral Narratives among the Western Apache." In *Text, Play, and Story,* Ed. Edward M. Bruner.

Bauman, Richard
   1977 *Verbal Art as Performance.* Prospect Heights, IL: Waveland Press.

Beck, Nora
   1992 "The Silent Voice: Lip-synching and the Performance of Popular Music." Paper presented at the annual meeting of the International Association for the Study of Popular Music, November 2, 1992, Denton, TX.

Becker, A.L.
   1979 "Text-building, Epistemology, and Aesthetics in Javanese Shadow Theater," in *The Imagination of Reality: Essays in Southeast Asian Coherence Systems,* Eds. A.L. Becker and Aram Yengoyan. Norwood, NJ: Ablex.
   1982 "The Poetics and Noetics of a Javanese Poem," in *Spoken and Written Language,* Ed. Deborah Tannen. Norwood, NJ.: Ablex.
   1987 "An Essay on Translating the Art of Music," in *Karawitan: Source Readings in Javanese Gamelan and Vocal Music,* Vol. 2, Ed. Judith Becker, ix–xx. Michigan Papers on South and Southeast

Asia, No. 30. Ann Arbor: Center for South and Southeast Asian Studies, University of Michigan.

Becker, Judith
1979 "Time and Tune," in *The Imagination of Reality: Essays in Southeast Asian Coherence Systems*, Eds. A. L. Becker and Aram Yengoyan. Norwood, NJ: Ablex.
1981 "Hindu-Buddhist Time in Javanese Gamelan Music," in *The Study of Time IV*, Ed. J.F. Fraser. New York, Heidelberg, Berlin: Springer-Verlag.

Behar, Ruth
1993 *Translated Woman: Crossing the Border with Esperanza's Story*. Boston: Beacon Press.
1996 *The Vulnerable Observer: Anthropology that Breaks Your Heart*. Boston: Beacon Press.

Ben-Amos, Dan
1983 "Introduction." *Research in African Literatures* 14 (3): 277–82.

Berland, Jody
1992 "Angels Dancing: Cultural Technologies and the Production of Space." In *Cultural Studies*, Eds. Lawrence Grossberg, Cary Nelson, and Paula Treichler, 38–55. New York: Routledge.

Bérubé, Michael
1995 "Public Academy." *The New Yorker*, 9 January 1995, 73–80.

Bhabha, Homi
1987 "Of Mimicry and Man." In *October: An Anthology*. Cambridge: MIT Press.

Blau, Herbert
1990 *The Audience*. Baltimore and London: Johns Hopkins University Press.

Bohlman, Philip V.
1997 "Fieldwork in the Ethnomusicological Past." In *Shadows in the Field: New Perspectives for Fieldwork in Ethnomusicology*, Eds. Gregory E. Barz and Timothy J. Cooley, 139–62. New York: Oxford University Press.
2002 "World Music at the 'End of History.'" *Ethnomusicology* 46 (1): 1–32.

Bonus, Enrique
1997 "Marking and Marketing 'Difference': Filipino Oriental Stores in Southern California." *positions: east asia critique* 5 (2): 643–69.

Bourdieu, Pierre
1977 [1972] *Outline of a Theory of Practice.* Trans. Richard Nice. Cambridge: Cambridge University Press.

Brett, Philip
1994 "Music, Essentialism, and the Closet." In *Queering the Pitch: the New Gay and Lesbian Musicology,* Eds. Philip Brett, Elizabeth Wood, and Gary C. Thomas, 9–26. New York and London: Routledge.
1997 "Musicology and Cultural Politics." Position paper written for the panel *Musicology and Cultural Politics,* International Musicology Society, 16th Annual Congress, London, Royal College of Music, 14–20 August 1997. (Published in shortened form as Brett 2000.)
1998 "The Personal Politics of Scholarship." Unpublished keynote address at the annual meeting of the Society for Ethnomusicology Southern California Chapter, UCLA, February 28th.
2000 "Musicology and Sexuality: The Example of Edward J. Dent." In *Musicology and Sister Disciplines: Past, Present, Future,* Ed. David Greer, 418–427. Oxford: Oxford University Press.

Brown, Kimasi L.
2000 "Ritual, Music, and Class on the Northern Soul Scene." Unpublished paper presented at the annual meeting of the Southern California Chapter of the Society for Ethnomusicology. February 26–27, 2000, University of San Diego.

Butler, Judith
1990 *Gender Trouble: Feminism and the Subversion of Identity.* New York and London: Routledge.
1993 *Bodies That Matter: On the Discursive Limits of "Sex."* New York and London: Routledge.
1997 *Excitable Speech: A Politics of the Performative.* New York and London: Routledge.

Castelo-Branco, Salwa el-Shawan
1987 "Some Aspects of the Cassette Industry in Egypt." *The World of Music* 29 (2): 32–45.

Case, Sue-Ellen, Philip Brett, and Susan Leigh Foster, Eds.
    1995 *Cruising the Performative: Interventions into the Representation of Ethnicity, Nationality, and Sexuality.* Bloomington: Indiana University Press.
    2000 *Decomposition: Post-Disciplinary Performance.* Bloomington: Indiana University Press.

Catlin, Amy
    1985a Review of "Khamvong Insixiengmai, Thinking about the Old Village: Traditional Lao Music." *Ethnomusicology* 29 (1): 133–34.
    1985b "Harmonizing the Generations of Hmong Musical Performance." *Selected Reports in Ethnomusicology* 7: 83–97.
    1987a "Apsaras and Other Goddesses in Khmer Music, Dance, and Ritual." In *Apsara: The Feminine in Cambodian Art* (Exhibition Catalog), Ed. Amy Catlin. Los Angeles: Woman's Building, 28–35.
    1987b "Songs of Hmong Women: Virgins, Orphans, Widows and Bards." In *Textiles as Texts: Arts of Hmong Women from Laos* (Exhibition Catalog), Eds. Amy Catlin and Dixie Swift. Los Angeles: Woman's Building.
    1992 "*Homo Cantens:* Why Hmong Sing during Interactive Courtship Rituals." In *Text, Context, and Performance in Cambodia, Laos, and Vietnam,* Ed. Amy Catlin. *Selected Reports in Ethnomusicology* IX: 43–60. Los Angeles: Department of Ethnomusicology, UCLA.

Cavicchi, Daniel
    1998 *Tramps Like Us: Music and Meaning Among Springsteen Fans.* New York and Oxford: Oxford University Press.

Chan, Sucheng
    1991 *Asian Americans: An Interpretive History.* Boston: Twayne.

Chang, Jeff
    1994 "Race, Class, Conflict and Empowerment: On Ice Cube's 'Black Korea'." In *Los Angeles — Struggles toward Multiethnic Community: Asian American, African American, and Latino Perspectives,* Eds. Edward T. Chang and Russell C. Leong, 87–107. Seattle and London: University of Washington Press.

Chow, Rey
    1993 *Writing Diaspora: Tactics of Intervention in Contemporary Cultural Studies.* Bloomington: Indiana University Press.

Clifford, James
　　1986 "On Ethnographic Allegory." In *Writing Culture: The Poetics and Politics of Culture*, Eds. James Clifford and George E. Marcus, 98–121. Berkeley, Los Angeles, London: University of California Press.
　　1992 "Traveling Cultures." In *Cultural Studies*, Eds. Lawrence Grossberg, Cary Nelson, and Paula Treichler, 96–116. New York: Routledge.
　　1997 *Routes: Travel and Translation in the Late Twentieth Century*. Cambridge and London: Harvard University Press.

Cohen, Norm and Paul Wells
　　1982 "Recorded Ethnic Music: A Guide to Resources." In *Ethnic Recordings in America: A Neglected Heritage*, 175–250. Washington: American Folklife Center, Library of Congress.

Collins, Patricia Hill
　　1998 *Fighting Words: Black Women and the Search for Justice*. Minneapolis: University of Minnesota Press.

Compton, Carol
　　1975 "Lam Khon Savan: A Traditional Form and a Contemporary Theme," in *A Tai Festschrift for William J. Gedney*, Ed. Thomas W. Gething, 55–82. Southeast Asian Studies Working Paper No. 8. Honolulu: University of Hawaii.
　　1977 "Linguistic and Cultural Aspects of Lam: The Song of the Lao Mohlam." Ph.D. dissertation, University of Michigan.
　　1979 *Courting Poetry in Laos: A Textual and Linguistic Analysis*. Special report No. 18. Dekalb: Center for Southeast Asian Studies, Northern Illinois University.

Cowan, Jane K.
　　1990 *Dance and the Body Politic in Northern Greece*. Princeton: Princeton University Press.

Crafts, Susan D., Daniel Cavicchi, Charles Keil, et al.
　　1993 *My Music*. Wesleyan University Press.

Cross, Brian
　　1993 *It's Not About a Salary ... Rap, Race and Resistance in Los Angeles*. London, New York: Verso.

Cruse, Harold
　　1967 *The Crisis of the Negro Intellectual*. New York: William Morrow & Co., Inc.

Csordas, Thomas J.
1996 "Imaginal Performance and Memory in Ritual Healing." In *The Performance of Healing*, Eds. Carol Laderman and Marina Roseman, 91–113. New York and London: Routledge.

Currid, Brian
1995 "'We Are Family': House Music and Queer Performativity." In *Cruising the Performative: Interventions into the Representation of Ethnicity, Nationality, and Sexuality*, Eds. Sue-Ellen Case, Philip Brett, and Susan Leigh Foster, 165–96. Bloomington: Indiana University Press.

Davis, Mike
1990 *City of Quartz*. New York: Vintage Books.

Davis, Susan Gray
1988 *Parades and Power: Street Theatre in Nineteenth-Century Philadelphia*. Berkeley: University of California Press.

Della Cava, Marco R.
1996 "DJ's Voice Cuts Across Colour Lines." *The Nation*, February 8, 1996, C6.

Desjarlais, Robert R.
1996 "Presence." In *The Performance of Healing*, Eds. Carol Laderman and Marina Roseman, 143–64. New York and London: Routledge.

Diamond, Jody
1990 "There is No They There." *MusicWorks* 47: 12–23. Also at http://www.gamelan.org/jd/theythere.html

Dobson, William J.
1998 "Dissidence in Cyberspace Worries Beijing." *San Jose Mercury News*, Sunday, June 28, 1998.

Dominguez, Virginia R.
1992 "Invoking Culture: The Messy Side of 'Cultural Politics'." *South Atlantic Quarterly* 91 (1): 19–42.

Drew, Rob
2001 *Karaoke Nights: An Ethnographic Rhapsody*. Altamira Press.

Dyson, Michael Eric
  1993 *Reflecting Black: African-American Cultural Criticism*. Minneapolis and London: University of Minnesota Press.

Eastman, Ralph
  1989 "Central Avenue Blues: The Making of Los Angeles Rhythm and Blues, 1942–1947." *Black Music Research Journal* 9 (1): 19–33.

Ellsworth, Elizabeth
  1992 "Why Doesn't this Feel Empowering? Working Through the Repressive Myths of Critical Pedagogy." In *Feminisms and Critical Pedagogy*, Eds. Carmen Luke and Jennifer Gore. New York and London: Routledge.

Espiritu, Yen Le
  1992 *Asian American Panethnicity: Bridging Institutions and Identities*. Philadelphia: Temple University Press.

Falassi, Alessandro
  1987 "Festival: Definition and Morphology." In *Time Out of Time: Essays on the Festival*, Ed. Alessandro Falassi, 1–10. Albuquerque: University of New Mexico Press.

Fanon, Frantz
  1968 *Black Skin, White Masks*. Translated by Charles Lam Markmann. New York: Grove Press.

Faruqi, Lois Ibsen
  1981 *An Annotated Glossary of Arabic Musical Terms*. Westport, CT: Greenwood Press.

Feld, Steven
  1990 [1982] *Sound and Sentiment: Birds, Weeping, Poetics, and Song in Kaluli Expression*. 2nd edition. Philadelphia: University of Pennsylvania Press.

Finnegan, Ruth
  1976 "What is Oral Literature Anyway? Comments in the Light of Some African and Other Comparative Material." in *Oral Literature and the Formula*, Eds. Benjamin Stolz and Richard S. Shannon, III, 127–76. Ann Arbor: University of Michigan.

Fishman, Joshua A.
  1982 "Whorfianism of the Third Kind: Ethnolinguistic Diversity as a Worldwide Societal Asset (The Whorfian Hypothesis: Varieties of

Validation, Confirmation, and Disconfirmation II)." *Language and Society* 12:1–14.

Fiske, John
1989 *Reading the Popular*. Boston: Unwin Hyman.
1993 *Power Plays, Power Works*. London, New York: Verso.

Fitzgerald, Jon
1995 "Black or White? Stylistic Analysis of Early Motown Crossover Hits, 1963–1966." *Popular Music: Style and Identity*, 95–98. Montreal, Quebec: Centre for Research on Canadian Cultural Industries and Institutions.

Foley, John Miles
1988 *The Theory of Oral Composition: History and Methodology*. Bloomington and Indianapolis: Indiana University Press.

Foster, Susan Leigh
1995 "Choreographing History." In *Choreographing History*, Ed. Susan Leigh Foster, 3–21. Bloomington: Indiana University Press.
2000 "Introducing Unnatural Acts, 1997," in *Decomposition: Post-Disciplinary Performance*, 3–9. Bloomington: Indiana University Press.

Foucault, Michel
1977 *Discipline and Punish*. New York: Vintage Books.

Freer, Regina
1994 "Black–Korean Conflict." In *The Los Angeles Riots*, Ed. Mark Baldassare, 175–203. Boulder, Colorado: Westview Press.

Friedrich, Paul
1979 "Poetic Language and the Imagination: A Reformulation of the Sapir Hypothesis." In *Language, Context, and the Imagination*, Ed. Paul Friedrich. Stanford: Stanford University Press.
1986 *The Language Parallax: Linguistic Relativism and Poetic Indeterminacy*. Austin: University of Texas Press.

Frith, Simon, Andrew Goodwin, and Lawrence Grossberg, eds.
1993 *Sound and Vision: The Music Video Reader*. London and New York: Routledge.

Gabbard, Krin
    1995a "Introduction: Writing the Other History." In *Representing Jazz*, Ed. Krin Gabbard, 1–8. Durham and London: Duke University Press.
    1995b "Introduction: The Jazz Canon and Its Consequences." In *Jazz Among the Discourses*, Ed. Krin Gabbard, 1–28. Durham and London: Duke University Press.

Gallagher, Winifred
    1993 *The Power of Place: How Our Surroundings Shape Our Thoughts, Emotions, and Actions.* New York: Poseidon Press.

Gates, Jr., Henry Louis
    1992 *Loose Canons: Notes on the Culture Wars.* Oxford and New York: Oxford University Press.

Geertz, Clifford
    1983 "Art as a Cultural System." In *Local Knowledge: Further Essays in Interpretive Anthropology*, 94–120. New York: Basic Books.

Gibbs, Jason
    1997 "Reform and Tradition in Early Vietnamese Popular Song." *Nhac Viet: The Journal of Vietnamese Music* 6: 5–33.
    1998 "Nhac Tien Chien: The Origins of Vietnamese Popular Song," *Destination Vietnam*, http://www.destinationvietnam.com/dv/dv23/dv23e.htm

Gilroy, Paul
    1991 "Sounds Authentic: Black Music, Ethnicity, and the Challenge of a *Changing* Same." *Black Music Research Journal* 11 (2): 111–36.

Giroux, Henry
    1992 *Border Crossings: Cultural Workers and the Politics of Education.* New York: Routledge.
    1995 "Writing the Space of the Public Intellectual: Afterword to *Women Writing Culture*." In *Women Writing Culture*, Eds. Gary A. Olson and Elizabeth Hirsh. Albany: State University of New York Press.

Goldberg, David Theo, Ed.
    1994 *Multiculturalism: A Critical Reader.* Oxford, UK and Cambridge, USA: Blackwell.

Gooding-Williams, Robert, Ed.
  1993 *Reading Rodney King/Reading Urban Uprising.* New York and London: Routledge.

Goody, Jack
  1968 *Literacy in Traditional Societies.* Cambridge: Cambridge University Press.
  1987 *The Interface between the Written and the Oral.* Cambridge, London, and New York: Cambridge University Press.

Gotanda, Philip Kan
  1991 *Yankee Dawg You Die.* New York: Dramatists Play Service.

Graff, Harvey
  "Reflections on the History of Literacy: Overview, Critique, and Proposals." *Humanities in Society* 303–33.

Greene, Paul
  1995 "Cassettes in Culture: Emotion, Politics, and Performance in Rural Tamil Nadu." Ph.D. dissertation, University of Pennsylvania.
  1999 "Sound Engineering in a Tamil Village: Playing Audio Cassettes as Devotional Performance." *Ethnomusicology* 43 (3): 459–89.

Gronow, Pekka
  1981a "The Record Industry Comes to the Orient." *Ethnomusicology* 25 (2): 251–84.
  1981b *Statistics in the Field of Sound Recordings.* Paris: Unesco.

Grossberg, Lawrence
  1992 *We Gotta Get Out of This Place: Popular Conservatism and Postmodern Culture.* New York and London: Routledge.

Grossberg, Lawrence, Cary Nelson, and Paula Treichler
  1992 "Cultural Studies: An Introduction." In *Cultural Studies,* 1–22. New York: Routledge.

Haas, Mary R.
  1964 *Thai–English Student's Dictionary.* Stanford: Stanford University Press.

Hamamoto, Darrell Y.
  1994 *Monitored Peril: Asian Americans and the Politics of TV Representation.* Minneapolis: University of Minnesota Press.

Hanchard, Michael
1996a "Cultural Politics and Black Public Intellectuals." *Social Text* 14 (3): 95–108.
1996b "Intellectual Pursuit: By Ignoring Our Social and Political History, We Have Impoverished Debate about 'Black Public Intellectuals.'" *Nation* 262 (7): 22–24.

Hanna, Thomas
1970 *Bodies in Revolt: A Primer in Somatic Thinking.* New York: Holt, Rinehart and Winston.

Harada, Wayne
1992 "DeLima, Kapena, Cecilio — Sing Along with Them All." *Honolulu Advisor,* November 4, 1992, B7.

Hardin, James
2003 "Mickey Hart in Search of the World's Music." *Folklife Center News* 25 (2): 14–15.

Harris, Scott
1995 "Leno's O.J. Jokes, Dancing Itos Keep Reality at a Safe Distance." *Los Angeles Times* v114 (Thursday, April 13, 1995): B3, col 1.

Hart, Mickey, with K.M. Kostyal
2003 *Songcatchers: In Search of the World's Music.* Washington, D.C.: National Geographic.

Havelock, Eric A.
1963 *Preface to Plato.* Cambridge: Harvard University Press.
1986 *The Muse Learns to Write: Reflections on Orality and Literacy from Antiquity to the Present.* New Haven and London: Yale University Press.

Hay, James, Lawrence Grossberg, and Ellen Wartella
1996 "Introduction." In *The Audience and Its Landscape,* Eds. Hay, Grossberg, and Wartella, 1–5. Boulder, Colorado: Westview Press.

Heavens, Alan J.
1993 "One Neighborhood as Active as Its Mummers." *The Philadelphia Inquirer,* December 19, 1993.

Hebdige, Dick
[1979] 1993 *Subculture: The Meaning of Style.* London and New York: Routledge.

Heilbrun, Jacob
1996 "The News from Everywhere." *Lingua Franca* May/June 1996, 49–56.

Hirabayashi, Lane Ryo
1995 "Introduction: Why Read Nishimoto?" In *Inside an American Concentration Camp: Japanese American Resistance at Poston, Arizona,* by Richard S. Nishimoto, Ed. Lane Ryo Hirabayashi. Tucson: University of Arizona Press.
1999 *The Politics of Fieldwork: Research in an American Concentration Camp.* Tucson: University of Arizona Press.

Hisama, Ellie
1993 "Postcolonialism on the Make: The Music of John Mellencamp, David Bowie and John Zorn." *Popular Music* 12 (2): 91–104.

Hiss, Tony
1990 *The Experience of Place.* New York: Vintage Books.

Ho, Fred Wei-Han
1995 "'Jazz', Kreolization, and Revolutionary Music for the 21st Century." In *Sounding Off! Music as Subversion/Resistance/Revolution,* Eds. Ron Sakolsky and Fred Wei-Han Ho, Brooklyn: Autonomedia.

Hollman, Laurie
1992a "Before Parade, A Solemn Task." *The Philadelphia Inquirer,* December 30, 1992.
1992b "Two Worlds Join on Broad Street." *The Philadelphia Inquirer,* December 31, 1992.

Hom, Marlon K.
1987 *Songs of Gold Mountain: Cantonese Rhymes from San Francisco Chinatown.* Berkeley: University of California Press.

hooks, bell
1992a *Black Looks: Race and Representation.* Boston, South End Press.
1992b "The Oppositional Gaze." In *Black Looks: Race and Representation,* 115–31. Boston: South End Press.
1994 "Theory as Liberatory Practice." In *Teaching to Transgress: Education as the Practice of Freedom.* New York and London: Routledge.

hooks, bell and Cornel West
    1991 *Breaking Bread: Insurgent Black Intellectual Life.* Boston: South
    End Press.

Huang Shuyun
    1991 "Rich Cultural Life in Shenzhen SEZ." *Beijing Review*, 31–33,
    October 14–20, 1991.

Ivy, Marilyn
    1995 *Discourses of the Vanishing: Modernity, Phantasm, Japan.* Chi-
    cago and London: University of Chicago Press.

Jairazbhoy, Nazir A. and Sue Carole DeVale, Eds.
    1985 *Selected Reports in Ethnomusicology, Vol. VI: Asian Music in
    North America.* Los Angeles: Program in Ethnomusicology,
    Department of Music, UCLA.

James, Joy
    1997 *Transcending the Talented Tenth: Black Leaders and American
    Intellectuals.* New York and London: Routledge.

Jameson, Fredric
    1991 *Postmodernism or, the Cultural Logic of Late Capitalism.*
    Durham, NC: Duke University Press.

Jang, Jon
    1996 Letter to Isabel Yrigoyen, Villy Wong, and Mark Izu, c/o the San
    Francisco Jazz Festival; cc'd to Deborah Wong, 25 October 1996.
    1996 *Island: The Immigrant Suite* No. 2. The Kronos Quartet with
    Eva Tam. Unpublished recording.
    1997a Letter to Deborah Wong, 7 January.
    1997b E-mail note to Deborah Wong, 7 January.
    1997c *Island: The Immigrant Suite* No. 1. Jon Jang Octet. Compact
    disk with notes. Soul Note 121303–2.

Jang, Jon, James Newton, Wei Hwa Zhang, Genny Lim, and Francis
Wong
    1994 *Up From the Root: Asian American Music and Cultural Synthesis.*
    A symposium held on March 3, 1994 in San Francisco, California.
    San Francisco: Asian Improv aRts.

Jeffrey, Don
    1992 "I Was a Human Karaoke Hound." *Billboard* May 30, 1992, 104
    (22):K4.

Johnson, Carolyn Schiller
1995 "'Freaks of Imagination' and 'Brown Women Dancers': The Racialization of Foreign Dancers at Century's Turn in Chicago." Paper presented at the 40th Anniversary Meeting of the Society for Ethnomusicology, October 19–22, 1995, Los Angeles, California.

Jones, LeRoi
1967 "Jazz and the White Critic," in *Black Music*. New York: William Morrow & Co., Inc.

Jones, Steve
1990 "The Cassette Underground." *Popular Music and Society* 14 (1): 75–84.

[n.a.]
1992 "Karaoke Permit Rejected." *Los Angeles Times*, December 17, 1992.

Keil, Charles
1979 *Tiv Song: The Sociology of Art in a Classless Society*. Chicago and London: University of Chicago Press.
1984 "Music Mediated and Live in Japan." *Ethnomusicology* 28 (1):91–96.

Keil, Charles, Angeliki V. Keil, and Dick Blau
1992 *Polka Happiness*. Philadelphia: Temple University Press.

Kene, Thao
1959 "The 'Khene'-maker." In *Kingdom of Laos: The Land of the Million Elephants and the White Parasol*, Ed. René de Berval, 217–220. Saigon: France-Asie.

Kim, Elaine H.
1982 *Asian American Literature: An Introduction to the Writings and Their Social Context*. Philadelphia: Temple University Press.

Ko, John
1999 "Drumming Up a Storm." *Dialogue* (a publication of the Asian American Arts Alliance) (Fall 1999): 30–33.

Kodish, Debora
1993 "Philadelphia Folklore Project: *Lakhon Bassak* Project." Unpublished ms.

Kofsky, Frank
  1970 *Black Nationalism and the Revolution in Music.* New York: Pathfinder Press.

Kondo, Dorinne
  1995 "Bad Girls: Theater, Women of Color, and the Politics of Representation." In *Women Writing Culture,* Eds. Ruth Behar and Deborah A. Gordon, 49–64. Berkeley: University of California Press.
  1997 *About Face: Performing Race in Fashion and Theater.* New York and London: Routledge.

Kottak, Conrad Phillip
  1990 *Prime-Time Society: An Anthropological Analysis of Television and Culture.* Belmont, California: Wadsworth, Inc.

Koung, Leendavy and William Westerman
  1993 *Tipsongva: A Cambodian Folk Opera.* Program notes. Presented at the Painted Bride Art Center, Thursday, May 6th, 1993. Philadelphia: Philadelphia Folklore Project.

Kristof, Nicholas D.
  1996 "Rappers' Credo: No Sex, Please! We're Japanese." *The New York Times,* January 29, 1996.

Kumar, A.L.
  1984 "On Variation in Babads." *Bijdragen tot de Taal-, Land- en Volkenkunde* (BKI) 140: 223–47.

Laderman, Carol and Marina Roseman
  1996 "Introduction." In *The Performance of Healing,* Eds. Carol Laderman and Marina Roseman, 1–16. New York and London: Routledge.

Lai, Him Mark, Genny Lim, and Judy Yung
  1980 *Island: Poetry and History of Chinese Immigrants on Angel Island, 1910–1940.* Seattle: University of Washington Press.

Lakoff, George
  1987 *Women, Fire, and Dangerous Things: What Categories Reveal about the Mind.* Chicago: University of Chicago Press.

Lakoff, George, and Mark Johnson
  1980 *Metaphors We Live By.* Chicago: University of Chicago Press.

Lam, Joseph S.C.
1999 "Embracing 'Asian American Music' as an Heuristic Device."
Journal of Asian American Studies 2 (1): 29–60.

Lancefield, Robert
[Forthcoming] "Hearing Orientality in (White) America,
1900–1930: Music/Race, Voice/Body, Authenticity/Mimesis, Per-
formance/Media, Representation/Reception." Ph.D. dissertation
in process, Wesleyan University.

Lansing, J. Stephen
1983 "The Aesthetics of the Sounding of the Text." In *Symposium of
the Whole: A Range of Discourse toward an Ethnopoetics*, Eds. Jer-
ome Rothenberg and Diane Rothenberg, 241–257. Berkeley: University of California Press.

Lather, Patti
1991 *Getting Smart: Feminist Research and Pedagogy with/in the Postmodern*. New York and London: Routledge.
1992 "Post-Critical Pedagogies: A Feminist Reading." In *Feminisms
and Critical Pedagogy*, Eds. Carmen Luke and Jennifer Gore. New
York and London: Routledge.

Lee, Josephine
1997 *Performing Asian America: Race and Ethnicity on the Contemporary Stage*. Philadelphia: Temple University Press.

Lee, Robert
1999 *Orientals: Asian Americans in Popular Culture*. Philadelphia:
Temple University Press.

Lees, Gene
1995 *Cats of Any Color: Jazz, Black and White*. Oxford and New York:
Oxford University Press.

Leong, David
1998 "Interview with Kenny Endo." http://www.taiko.com/news/
inter_kennyendo_ 022098.html
1999 "Oedo Sukeroku Daiko FAQ Sheet." Rolling Thunder Resource
website. Version 1.01, http://www.taiko.com/history/
oedo_faq.html

Lewis, George E.
1996 "Improvised Music after 1950: Afrological and Eurological Perspectives." *Black Music Research Journal* 16 (1): 91–122.
(n.d.) "Voyager." Unpublished essay.

Leong, Russell
  1995 "Lived Theory (notes on the run)." *Amerasia Journal* 21 (1 & 2):
  v–x).

Lim, Genny
  1993 "Paper Angels." In *Unbroken Thread: An Anthology of Plays by
  Asian American Women,* Ed. Roberta Uno, 17–52. Amherst: University of Massachusetts Press.

Lim, Shirley Geok-lin and Amy Ling, Eds.
  1992 *Reading the Literatures of Asian America.* Philadelphia: Temple
  University Press.

[n.a.]
  1993 "Limits on Karaoke OKd." *Los Angeles Times,* January 14, 1993.

Ling, Amy, Ed.
  1999 *Yellow Light: The Flowering of Asian American Arts.* Philadelphia: Temple University Press.

Lipsitz, George
  1990 *Time Passages: Collective Memory and American Popular Culture.* Minneapolis: University of Minnesota Press.
  1994 *Dangerous Crossroads: Popular Music, Postmodernism and the
  Poetics of Place.* London and New York: Verso.
  1998 *The Possessive Investment in Whiteness: How White People Profit
  from Identity Politics.* Philadelphia: Temple University Press.
  2001 *American Studies in a Moment of Danger.* Minneapolis: University of Minnesota Press.

Lord, Albert
  1960 *The Singer of Tales.* New York: Atheneum.

Lornell, Kip and Anne K. Rasmussen, eds.
  1997 *Musics of Multicultural America: A Study of Twelve Musical
  Communities.* New York: Schirmer.

Lowe, Lisa
  1996 *Immigrant Acts: On Asian American Cultural Politics.* Durham
  and London: Duke University Press.

Lull, James and Wallis, Roger
  1992 "The Beat of West Vietnam." In *Popular Music and Communication,* 2nd ed., 207–236. Newbury Park, CA.

Lum, Casey Man Kong
1996 *In Search of a Voice: Karaoke and the Construction of Identity in Chinese America.* Mahwah, NJ: Lawrence Erlbaum Associates, Inc.

Lye, Colleen
1995 "American Naturalism and the Asiatic Body: Fín-de-siècle Encounters on the Pacific Rim." Paper presented at the University of Pennsylvania, October 23, 1995.

Macklin, William R.
1993 "In Wind as Stiff as Competition, Mummers Dazzle." *The Philadelphia Inquirer,* January 2, 1993.

Maira, Sunaina Marr
2002 *Desis in the House: Indian American Youth Culture in New York City.* Philadelphia: Temple University Press.

Malm, William
1959 *Japanese Music and Musical Instruments.* Tuttle.

Manalansan IV, Martin F.
2000a *Cultural Compass: Ethnographic Explorations of Asian America.* Philadelphia: Temple University Press.
2000b "Introduction/The Ethnography of Asian America: Notes toward a Thick Description." In *Cultural Compass: Ethnographic Explorations of Asian America,* 1–13. Philadelphia: Temple University Press.

Manuel, Peter
1993 *Cassette Culture: Popular Music and Technology in North India.* Chicago: University of Chicago Press.

Marcus, Russell
1970 *English–Lao, Lao–English Dictionary.* Rev. ed. Rutland, VT and Tokyo: Tuttle.

Marosi, Richard
2000 "Vietnam's Musical Invasion." *Los Angeles Times,* August 8, 2000, pp. A1 and A16.

Martin, Randy
1995 "Agency and History: The Demands of Dance Ethnography." In *Choreographing History,* Ed. Susan Leigh Foster, 105–115. Bloomington and Indianapolis: Indiana University Press.

Masaoka, Miya
1996 "*Koto No Tankyu* (Koto Explorations)." *Institute for the Study of American Music Newsletter* 25 (2): 8–9.

McClary, Susan
1994 "Constructions of Subjectivity in Schubert's Music." In *Queering the Pitch: the New Gay and Lesbian Musicology,* Eds. Philip Brett, Elizabeth Wood, and Gary C. Thomas, 205–33. New York and London: Routledge.

McClary, Susan and Robert Walser
1994 "Theorizing the Body in African American Music." *Black Music Research Journal* 14 (1): 75–84.

McCunn, Ruthanne Lum
1995 *Wooden Fish Songs.* New York: Dutton.

McDonogh, Gary
1993 "The Geography of Emptiness." In *The Cultural Meaning of Urban Space,* eds. Robert Rotenberg and Gary McDonogh, 3–15. Westport, Connecticut and London: Bergin & Garvey.

McGowan, Chris
1992a "Market Report: Can Karaoke Take Root in America?" *Billboard* May 30, 1992, 104(22):K1.
1992b "Karaoke's Cutting Edge: Laserdisc and CD + G: A Beefed-Up Video Component, Plus Instant Access, Offers Karaoke a Bright Future." *Billboard* May 30, 1992, 104(22):K1.

McLaren, Peter
1994 "White Terror and Oppositional Agency: Towards a Critical Multiculturalism." In *Multiculturalism: A Critical Reader,* Ed. David Theo Goldberg, 45–74. Oxford, UK and Cambridge, USA: Blackwell.

McLure, Steve
1992 "Japan, the Karaoke Capital." *Billboard* May 30, 1992, 104(22):K1.

Meltzer, David, Ed.
1993 *Reading Jazz.* San Francisco: Mercury House.

Miller, Terry E.
1977 "Kaen Playing and Mawlum Singing in Northeast Thailand." Ph.D. dissertation, Indiana University.

1979 "The Problems of Lao Discography." *Asian Music* 11 (1): 124–39.

1980 "Laos," *New Grove Dictionary of Music and Musicians,* Ed. Stanley Sadie. London and New York: Macmillan.

1984 Review of "Khamvong Insixiengmai, Thinking about the Old Village: Traditional Lao Music." *Asian Music* 15 (2): 159–61.

1985a "The Survival of Lao Traditional Music in America." *Selected Reports* 16: 99–109. UCLA: University of California, Institute of Ethnomusicology.

1985b *The Traditional Music of the Lao: Kaen Playing and Mawlum Singing in Northeast Thailand.* Contributions in Intercultural and Comparative Studies No. 13. Westport, CT: Greenwood Press.

Mitchell, W.J.T.
1995 "Postcolonial Culture, Postimperial Criticism." In *The Postcolonial Studies Reader,* Eds. Bill Ashcroft, Gareth Griffiths, and Helen Tiffin, 475–79. London and New York: Routledge.

Mitsui, Tôru and Shûhei Hosokawa, Eds.
1998 *Karaoke Around the World: Global Technology, Local Singing.* London and New York: Routledge.

Moerman, Michael
1988 *Talking Culture: Ethnography and Conversation Analysis.* Philadelphia: University of Pennsylvania Press.

Mohanty, Chandra Talpade
1995 "Under Western Eyes: Feminist Scholarship and Colonial Discourses." In *The Post-Colonial Studies Reader,* Eds. Bill Ashcroft, Gareth Griffiths, and Helen Tiffin. New York and London: Routledge. (Reprinted from *Boundary 2* 12 (3), 13 (1) (Spring/Fall), 1984.)

Monson, Ingrid
1995 "The Problem with White Hipness: Race, Gender, and Cultural Conceptions in Jazz Historical Discourse." *Journal of the American Musicological Society* 48 (3): 396–422.

Mowitt, John
1987 "The Sound of Music in the Era of its Electronic Reproducibility." In *Music and Society: The Politics of Composition, Performance, and Reception,* Eds. Richard Leppert and Susan McClary, 173–97.Cambridge: Cambridge University Press.

Moy, James S.
1993 *Marginal Sights: Staging the Chinese in America.* Iowa City: University of Iowa Press.

Nelson, Kristina
1986 *The Art of Reciting the Qu'ran.* Austin: University of Texas Press.

Nguyen, Phong Thuyet and Patricia Shehan Campbell
1990 *From Rice Paddies to Temple Yards: Traditional Music of Vietnam.* Danbury, CT: World Music Press.

Nishimoto, Richard S.
1995 *Inside an American Concentration Camp: Japanese American Resistance at Poston, Arizona.* Edited by Lane Ryo Hirabayashi. Tucson: University of Arizona Press.

Noll, William
1997 "Selecting Partners: Questions of Personal Choice and Problems of History in Fieldwork and Its Interpretation." In *Shadows in the Field: New Perspectives for Fieldwork in Ethnomusicology,* Eds. Gregory F. Barz and Timothy J. Cooley. New York and Oxford: Oxford University Press.

Norris, Christopher
1992 *Uncritical Theory: Postmodernism, Intellectuals, and the Gulf War.* Amherst: University of Massachusetts Press.

Noyes, Dorothy, Jan Greenberg, and Debora Kodish
1990 *Everything Has to Sparkle: The Art of Fancy Costume-Making.* 14-minute videotape. Philadelphia: Philadelphia Folklore Project.

Oelschlager, Max
1991 *The Idea of Wilderness.* New Haven: Yale University Press.

Okihiro, Gary Y.
1994 *Margins and Mainstreams: Asians in American History and Culture.* Seattle and London: University of Washington Press.

Oku, Shinobu
1998 "Karaoke and Middle-Aged and Older Women." In *Karaoke Around the World: Global Technology, Local Singing,* Eds. Tôru Mitsui and Shûhei Hosokawa, 55–80. London and New York: Routledge.

Olalquiaga, Celeste
1992 *Megalopolis: Contemporary Cultural Sensibilities.* Minneapolis and Oxford: University of Minnesota Press.

Oliver, Paul
  1984 *Songsters and Saints: Vocal Traditions on Race Records.* Cambridge, London, New York, etc.: Cambridge University Press.

Omi, Michael and Dana Takagi
  1995 "Thinking Theory in Asian American Studies." *Amerasia Journal* 21 (1 & 2): xi–xv.

Omi, Michael and Howard Winant
  1994 *Racial Formation in the United States: From the 1960s to the 1990s.* 2nd ed. New York: Routledge.

Ong, Aihwa
  1995 "Women Out of China: Traveling Tales and Traveling Theories in Postcolonial Feminism." In *Women Writing Culture,* Eds. Ruth Behar and Deborah A. Gordon, 350–72. Berkeley: University of California Press.

Ong, Walter J.
  1967 *The Presence of the Word: Some Prolegomena for Cultural and Religious History.* Minneapolis: University of Minnesota Press.
  1977 *Interfaces of the Word: Studies in the Evolution of Consciousness and Culture.* Ithaca and London: Cornell University Press.
  1982 *Orality and Literacy.* London and New York: Methuen.

Ortner, Sherry B.
  1995 "Resistance and the Problem of Ethnographic Refusal." *Comparative Studies in Society and History* 37 (1): 173–93.

Otake, Akiko and Shûhei Hosokawa
  1998 "Karaoke in East Asia: Modernization, Japanization, or Asianization?" In *Karaoke Around the World: Global Technology, Local Singing,* Eds. Tôru Mitsui and Shûhei Hosokawa, 178–201. London and New York: Routledge.

Pace, Richard
  1993 "First-time Televiewing in Amazonia: Television Acculturation in Gurupa, Brazil." *Ethnology* 32 (2): 187–205.

Palumbo-Liu, David
  1995 "Introduction." In *The Ethnic Canon: Histories, Institutions, and Interventions,* Ed. David Palumbo-Liu, 1–27. Minneapolis/London: University of Minnesota Press.
  1999 *Asian/American: Historical Crossings of a Racial Frontier.* Stanford: Stanford University Press.

Park, Dennis and Dina Shek
1996 "The Chinee Gal from Tokio: Racism and Exoticism in American Popular Songs (1900–1930)." Paper presented at the 13th Annual Meeting of the Association for Asian American Studies, Washington, D.C.

Pearlstone, Zena
1990 *Ethnic L.A.* Beverly Hills: Hillcrest Press.

Pemberton, John
1987 "Musical Politics in Central Java (or How Not to Listen to a Javanese Gamelan)." *Indonesia* 44: 17–30.

Pham Duy
1975 *Musics of Vietnam.* Ed. Dale R. Whiteside. Carbondale and Edwardsville: Southern Illinois University Press.
1995 *History in My Heart.* Ed. Nguyen Mong Thuong. Unpublished manuscript.

Phelan, Peggy
1998 "Introduction: The Ends of Performance." In *The Ends of Performance,* Eds. Peggy Phelan and Jill Lane, 1–19. New York and London: New York University Press.

Phelan, Peggy and Jill Lane, Eds.
1998 *The Ends of Performance.* New York and London: New York University Press.

Pitzer, Kurt
1995 "Court Jesters." *People Weekly* 43: 108–9, June 26, 1995.

Pollock, Della
1998 "Performing Writing." In *The Ends of Performance,* Eds. Peggy Phelan and Jill Lane, 73–103. New York and London: New York University Press.

Radano, Ronald
1993a *New Musical Figurations: Anthony Braxton's Cultural Critique.* Chicago and London: University of Chicago Press.
1993b "The Bounds of Black Musical Significance." Presented at the annual meeting of the Society for Ethnomusicology, Oxford, MS, October 29, 1993.
2000 "Black Noise/White Mastery." In *Decomposition: Post-disciplinary Performance,* 39–49. Bloomington: Indiana University Press.

Radhakrishnan, R.
  1996 *Diasporic Mediations: Between Home and Location.* Minneapolis and London: University of Minnesota Press.

Reyes, Adelaida
  1999a *Songs of the Caged, Songs of the Free: Music and the Vietnamese Refugee Experience.* Philadelphia: Temple University Press.
  1999b "From Urban Area to Refugee Camp: How One Thing Leads to Another." *Ethnomusicology* 43 (2): 201–20.

Reyes Schramm, Adelaida
  1989 "Music and Tradition: From Native to Adopted Land through the Refugee Experience." *Yearbook for Traditional Music* 21: 25–35.
  1991 "From Refugee to Immigrant: The Music of Vietnamese in the New York-New Jersey Metropolitan Area." In *New Perspectives on Vietnamese Music: Six Essays,* Ed. Phong T. Nguyen, 90–102. New Haven: Yale Center for International and Area Studies.

Rice, Timothy
  1997 "Toward a Mediation of Field Methods and Field Experience in Ethnomusicology." In *Shadows in the Field: New Perspectives for Fieldwork in Ethnomusicology,* Eds. Gregory F. Barz and Timothy J. Cooley. New York and Oxford: Oxford University Press.

Riddle, Ronald
  1983 *Flying Dragons, Flowing Streams: Music in the Life of San Francisco's Chinese.* Foreword by H.M. Lai. Westport, Conn.: Greenwood Press.

Roach, Joseph
  1993 "Carnival and the Law in New Orleans." *The Drama Review* 37 (3):42–75.

Rodgers, Susan
  1986 "Batak Tape Cassette Kinship: Constructing Kinship through the Indonesian National Mass Media." *American Ethnologist* 13 (1): 23–42.

The Rolling Thunder Taiko Resource
  http://www.taiko.com/rollingthunder.html

Rose, Tricia
  1994 *Black Noise: Rap Music and Black Culture in Contemporary America.* Hanover and London: Wesleyan University Press/The University Press of New England.

Roseman, Marina
  1991 *Healing Sounds from the Malaysian Rainforest: Temiar Music and Medicine.* Berkeley: University of California Press.

Said, Edward W.
  1978 *Orientalism.* New York: Pantheon.
  1994 *Representations of the Intellectual: The 1993 Reith Lectures.* New York: Pantheon Books.

Sam, Sam-Ang and Patricia Shehan Campbell
  1991 *Silent Temples, Songful Hearts: Traditional Music of Cambodia.* Danbury, CT: World Music Press.

San Francisco Taiko Dojo website
  http://www.taikodojo.org

Schafer, R. Murray
  1994 *The Soundscape: Our Sonic Environment and the Tuning of the World.* Rochester, Vermont: Destiny Books. (Originally *The Tuning of the World.* New York: Knopf, 1977.)

Schreiber, Norman
  1992 *The Ultimate Guide to Independent Record Labels and Artists: An A-to-Z Source of Great Music.* New York: Pharos Books.

Schechner, Richard
  1985 *Between Theater and Anthropology.* Philadelphia: University of Pennsylvania Press.
  1990 "Magnitudes of Performance." In *By Means of Performance: Intercultural Studies of Theatre and Ritual,* Eds. Richard Schechner and Willa Appel, 19–49.Cambridge: Cambridge University Press.

Schultz, April R.
  1994 *Ethnicity on Parade: Inventing the Norwegian American through Celebration.* Amherst: University of Massachusetts Press.

Seeger, Anthony
  1979 "What Can We Learn When They Sing? Local Genres of the Suya Indians of Central Brazil." *Ethnomusicology* 23 (3): 373–94.

n.a.
  1998 "Self-Study Report: Undergraduate Education in the Context of the Research University." Submitted in support of an application for reaffirmation of accreditation by the Western Association of

School and Colleges. University of California, Riverside, January 5, 1998.

Senelick, Laurence, Ed.
1992 *Gender in Performance: The Presentation of Difference in the Performing Arts.* Hanover and London: Tufts University Press and the University Press of New England.

Shah, Sonia
1994 "Presenting the Blue Goddess: Toward a National Pan-Asian Feminist Agenda." In *The State of Asian America: Activism and Resistance in the 1990s,* Ed. Karin Aguilar-San Juan, 147–58. Boston: South End Press.

Shaw, Donna
1993 "What a Train of Revelers to Behold!" *The Philadelphia Inquirer,* December 31, 1993.

Shimakawa, Karen
2002 *National Abjection: The Asian American Body Onstage.* Durham: Duke University Press.

Signell, Karl, producer. Commentary by William M. Anderson, Terence Michael Liu, and Anne Prescott.
1990 *Music of East Asia: Chinese, Korean, and Japanese Traditions in the United States.* (Series: Sounds of the World.) Graz: Stock & Stock. 3 cassettes.

Silverstein, Michael
1979 "Language Structure and Linguistic Ideology." In *The Elements: A Parasession on Linguistic Units and Levels,* Eds. Paul R. Clyne et al. 193–247. Chicago: Chicago Linguistic Society.

Slobin, Mark
1982 *Tenement Songs: The Popular Music of the Jewish Immigrants.* Urbana: University of Illinois Press.
1993 *Subcultural Sounds: Micromusics of the West.* Hanover, NH: Wesleyan University Press: University Press of New England.

Small, Christopher
1998 *Musicking: The Meanings of Performing and Listening.* Hanover and London: University Press of New England and Wesleyan University Press.

Smith, Arthur H.
1986 [1894] *Chinese Characteristics*. Singapore: Graham Brash (Pte) Ltd.

Smith, Suzanne E.
1999 *Dancing in the Street: Motown and the Cultural Politics of Detroit*. Cambridge: Harvard University Press.

Spivak, Gayatri Chakravorty
1988 "Can the Subaltern Speak?" In *Marxism and the Interpretation of Culture*, Eds. Cary Nelson and Lawrence Grossberg. Urbana and Chicago: University of Illinois Press.
1992 "Acting Bits/Identity Talk." *Critical Inquiry* 18 (Summer): 770–803.
1996 "How to Teach a 'Culturally Different' Book." In *The Spivak Reader*, Eds. Donna Landry and Gerald MacLean. New York and London: Routledge.

Spottswood, Richard K.
1990 *Ethnic Music on Records: A Discography of Ethnic Recordings Produced in the United States, 1893 to 1942*. With a foreword by James H. Billington. Urbana: University of Illinois Press.

Stone, Ruth
1982 *Let the Inside be Sweet: The Interpretation of Music Event among the Kpelle of Liberia*. Bloomington: Indiana University Press.

Sutton, R. Anderson
1985 "Commercial Cassette Recordings of Traditional Music in Java: Implications for Performers and Scholars." *The World of Music* 27 (3): 23–45.
1987 "Korean Music in Hawaii." *Asian Music* 29 (1): 99–120

Sweeney, Amin
1980 *Authors and Audiences in Traditional Malay Literature*. Monograph series no. 20. Berkeley: Center for South and Southeast Asia Studies, University of California.
1987 *A Full Hearing: Orality and Literacy in the Malay World*. Berkeley: University of California Press.

Sykes, Charles
1996 "Local Configurations of 'Soul': The Motown Sound and the Detroit African American Community." Presentation at the University of Pennsylvania, April 22, 1996.

Takagi, Dana Y.
1992 *The Retreat from Race: Asian-American Admissions and Racial Politics*. New Brunswick, NJ: Rutgers University Press.

Takaki, Ronald
    1989 *Strangers from a Different Shore: A History of Asian Americans.*
    New York: Penguin.

Tambiah, Stanley Jeyaraja
    1968 "Literacy in a Buddhist Village in Northeast Thailand," in Literacy in Traditional Societies, Ed. Jack Goody, 1968: 86–131, Cambridge: Cambridge University Press.
    1985 "A Thai Cult of Healing through Meditation," in *Culture, Thought, and Social Action: An Anthropological Perspective,* 87–122. Cambridge and London: Harvard University Press.

Taylor, Timothy
    1997 *Global Pop: Capitalism and Contemporary World Music.* New York and London: Routledge.

Tawa, Renee
    1992 "Karaoke: After 'Tiny Bubbles', It's All Japanese." *Los Angeles Times,* December 13, 1992, J1, J4.

Taylor, Diana and Juan Villagas, Eds.
    1994 *Negotiating Performance: Gender, Sexuality, and Theatricality in Latin/o America.* Durham and London: Duke University Press.

Tazuma, Larry J.
    1996 "Double Prejudice in Urban Radio." http://www.yolk.com/magazine/iss1/theo.html.

Tedlock, Dennis
    1977 "Toward an Oral Poetics." *New Literary History* 18: 507–19.
    1983 *The Spoken Word and the Work of Interpretation.* Philadelphia: University of Pennsylvania Press.

Tomlinson, Gary
    1992 "Cultural Dialogics and Jazz: A White Historian Signifies." In *Disciplining Music: Musicology and Its Canons,* Eds. Katherine Bergeron and Philip V. Bohlman, 64–94. Chicago and London: Chicago University Press.

Tran, Tini
    1998 "Local Link Gives Scattered Vietnamese a Meeting Place." *Los Angeles Times,* June 1, pp. A1, A16.

Tsou, Judy
    1996 "Images of Chinese in American Popular Sheet Music." Paper presented at the annual meeting of the Sonneck Society, Falls Church, VA.

Turner, Bryan S.
    1992 *Regulating Bodies: Essays in Medical Sociology.* London and New York: Routledge.

Turner, Victor
    1969. *The Ritual Process: Structure and Anti-Structure.* Ithaca: Cornell University Press.
    1974 *Dramas, Fields, and Metaphors: Symbolic Action in Human Society.* Ithaca: Cornell University Press.
    1982 *From Ritual to Theatre: The Human Seriousness of Play.* New York: PAJ Publications.
    1986 *The Anthropology of Performance.* Preface by Richard Schechner. New York: PAJ Publications.

Tusler, Mark
    1995 "The Los Angeles Matsuri Taiko: Performance Aesthetics, Teaching Methods, and Compositional Techniques." M.A. thesis, University of California, Santa Barbara.
    1996 "*Kata:* The Teaching and Development of Style in the Los Angeles Matsuri Taiko." In *The Body in Dance: Modes of Inquiry,* Conference Proceedings, Congress on Research in Dance. Department of Dance, University of Greensboro, North Carolina, 7–10 November 1996.
    1996 "'Rutsubo" (Taiko L.A.): Issues of Repertory, Performance Practices, and Ideologies." Unpublished paper presented at the annual meeting of the Society for Ethnomusicology, Toronto, ON.
    1999 "Taiko Drumming in California: Issues of Articulation and the Construction of Ethnic Identity." Unpublished paper presented at the Society for Ethnomusicology Southern California Chapter meeting, University of California, Riverside, 23–24 February 1999.

Uno, Roberta
    1993. Paper Angels: Genny Lim. In *Unbroken Thread: An Anthology of Plays by Asian American Women,* Ed. Roberta Uno, 11–15. Amherst: University of Massachusetts Press.

Vennman, Barbara
    1993 "Boundary Face-Off: New Orleans Civil Rights Law and Carnival Tradition." *The Drama Review* 37 (3):76–109.

Vernon, Paul
    1995 *Ethnic and Vernacular Music, 1898–1960: A Resource and Guide to Recordings.* Foreword by Benno Haupl. Westport, CT: Greenwood Press.

Visweswaran, Kamala
    1994 *Fictions of Feminist Ethnography.* Minneapolis: University of Minnesota Press.

Volkman, Toby Alice (Program Officer)
    1996 "Crossing Borders: Revitalizing Area Studies." Call for grant proposals issued by the Ford Foundation, December 20, 1996.

Wallis, Roger and Krister Malm
    1984 *Big Sounds from Small Peoples: The Music Industry in Small Countries.* London: Constable.

Walser, Robert
    1993 *Running with the Devil: Power, Gender, and Madness in Heavy Metal Music.* Hanover & London: Wesleyan University Press.
    1995 "Rhythm, Rhyme, and Rhetoric in the Music of Public Enemy." *Ethnomusicology* 39 (2): 193–217.

Wei, William
    1993 *The Asian American Movement.* Philadelphia: Temple University Press.

Welch, Charles E.
    1968 "The Philadelphia Mummers Parade: A Study in History, Folklore, and Popular Tradition." PhD. dissertation, University of Pennsylvania.
    1991 *Oh! Dem Golden Slippers: The Story of the Philadelphia Mummers.* Revised ed. Philadelphia: Book Street Press.

Weller, Ellen
    1998 "Use of Traditional Instruments in Improvised Music." Paper presented at the annual meeting of the Society for Ethnomusicology Southern California Chapter, UCLA, 28 February 1998.

West, Cornel
    1992 "The Postmodern Crisis of the Black Intellectuals." In *Cultural Studies,* Eds. Lawrence Grossberg, Cary Nelson, and Paula A. Treichler. New York and London: Routledge.

Westerman, William
1994a "'He Says You're Going to Play the Giant': Ethnographic Perspectives on a Cambodian Arts Class in Philadelphia." Working Papers #8. Philadelphia: Philadelphia Folklore Project.
1994b "Lakhon bassak: Historical and Ethnographic Background." Ms. in progress.

Whiteley, Sheila
1992 *The Space Between the Notes: Rock and the Counter-Culture.* London and New York: Routledge.

Wiegman, Robyn
1995 *American Anatomies: Theorizing Race and Gender.* Durham and London: Duke University Press.

Wilson, August
1981 *Ma Rainey's Black Bottom.* New York: Plume.

Witzleben, J. Lawrence
1997 "Whose Ethnomusicology? Western Ethnomusicology and the Study of Asian Music." *Ethnomusicology* 41 (2): 220–42.

Wong, Cynthia
1996a "'Asian for the Man!': Stereotypes, Identity and Self-Empowerment in Asian American Rap." Unpublished paper presented at the annual meeting of the Mid-Atlantic Chapter of the Society for Ethnomusicology, Peabody Conservatory, Baltimore, Maryland, March 22, 1996.
1996b "'We Define Ourselves!': The Negotiation of Power and Identity for Asian Americans in Hip-hop." Unpublished paper presented at the 13th annual meeting of the Association for Asian American Studies, Washington, DC, May 29–June 2.

Wong, Cynthia, with Fred Ho
1995 "The Musical Heritage of Asian Pacific Americans: A Selective Overview." Program notes for the 16th Asian/Pacific American Heritage Festival, New York, New York, May 6, 1995.

Wong, Deborah
1989/1990 "Thai Cassettes and Their Covers: Two Case Histories." *Asian Music* 21 (1): 78–104, Fall/Winter 1989–1990. [Reprinted in *Asian Popular Culture*, Ed. John Lent. Boulder, CO: Westview Press, 1995.]
1998 "Ethnomusicology and Critical Pedagogy as Cultural Work: Reflections on Teaching and Fieldwork." *College Music Symposium* 38: 80–100.

2001 *Sounding the Center: History and Aesthetics in Thai Buddhist Ritual.* Chicago: University of Chicago Press.

Wong, Sau-ling
1993 *Reading Asian American Literature: From Necessity to Extravagance.* Princeton: Princeton University Press.

Worth, Sol and John Adair
1972 *Through Navajo Eyes: An Exploration in Film Communication and Anthropology.* Bloomington: Indiana University Press.

Wurtzler, Steve
1994 "She Sang Live, But the Microphone was Turned Off: The Live, the Recorded, and the Subject of Representation." In *Sounded Theory, Sound Practice,* Ed. Rick Altman. New York: Routledge.

Yamada, Mitsuye
1983 "Invisibility is an Unnatural Disaster: Reflections of an Asian American Woman." In *This Bridge Called My Back: Writings by Radical Women of Color,* Eds. Cherríe Moraga and Gloria Anzaldúa, 35–40. 2nd ed. Latham, NY: Kitchen Table, Women of Color Press.

Yamamoto, Traise
1999 *Masking Selves, Making Subjects: Japanese American Women, Identity, and the Body.* Berkeley: University of California Press.

Yamauchi, Wakako
1993 "The Music Lessons: A Two-Act Play." In *Unbroken Thread: An Anthology of Plays by Asian American Women,* Ed. Roberta Uno, 59–104. Amherst: University of Massachusetts Press.

Yano, Christine R.
1985 "The Reintegration of Japanese Bon Dance in Hawaii after World War II." *Selected Reports in Ethnomusicology* 6: 151–62.

Yanow, Scott
1994 "Enthusiasm." *Jazziz* 11 (2): 28–33, ff.

Yoon, Paul Jong Chul
1998 "Negotiating Identity: Taiko in New York City." Paper presented at the annual meeting of the Mid-Atlantic Chapter of Society for Ethnomusicology, Williamsburg, Virginia, April 3, 1998, at the College of William and Mary.

1999 "Musical Spaces and Identity Politics: Negotiating an Asian American existence in New York City, the case of Soh Daiko." Paper presented at the 44th annual meeting of the Society for Ethnomusicology, Austin, TX, November 18–21.

2001 "'She's Really Become Japanese Now!': Taiko Drumming and Asian American Identifications." *American Music* 19 (4): 417–38.

Yoshida, George
1997 *Reminiscing in Swingtime: Japanese Americans in American Popular Music, 1925–1960.* San Francisco: National Japanese American Historical Society.

Zhang, Wei-hua
1993/1994 "Fred Wei-Han Ho: Case-Study of a Chinese-American Creative Musician." *Asian Music* 25 (1–2): 81–114.

1994 "The Musical Activities of the Chinese American Communities in the San Francisco Bay Area: A Social and Cultural Study." Ph.D. dissertation, University of California, Berkeley.

Zheng, Su de San
1992 "Taishan Muyu in America: An Unknown Treasure." *Music From China Newsletter* 2 (2), http://www.musicfromchina.org/newsletter/92-summer.htm.

1993 "Immigrant Music and Transnational Discourse: Chinese American Music Culture in New York City." Dissertation, Wesleyan University.

1994 "Making Music in Cultural Displacement: The Chinese American Odyssey." *Diaspora: A Journal of Transnational Studies* 3 (3): 273–288.

Zurbuchen, Mary Sabina
1987 *The Language of Balinese Shadow Theater.* Princeton: Princeton University Press.

Index